Drax of Drax Hall

'An important and timely book, in which Paul Lashmar uses the story of the Drax family's history as enslavers in Barbados as a microcosm of Britain's involvement in the transatlantic slave trade. What's so striking is the extent to which the current day wealth of the Drax family can be linked to their ancestors' enslavement of Africans beginning in 1627.'

—Laura Trevelyan, journalist and author of
A Very British Family: The Trevelyans and Their World

'A family story straight out of *Game of Thrones* – five centuries of exploitation, greed and horrific cruelty, and no regrets whatsoever. Old-school investigative reporting married with a fearless historian's eye for the truth produces this – shocking, fascinating, enraging. A brilliant book that anyone still trying to defend Britain's colonial history in the Caribbean will choke on.'

—Alex Renton, author of *Blood Legacy:*
Reckoning With a Family's Story of Slavery

'A timely retelling of the story of how one Englishman led the introduction of sugar and racial slavery to the Caribbean, as well as an eye-opening exploration of how the vast resulting profits were consolidated and enjoyed by generations of his descendants.'

—Matthew Parker, author of *The Sugar Barons:*
Family, Corruption, Empire and War

'Lashmar eloquently reminds us that history is never truly past. In this deeply-researched family history, we learn that the Draxes, an English family of wealth and privilege, were not only intimately tied to the origins of the Atlantic slave trade, but have lived unapologetically from its proceeds ever since. For anyone interested in a riveting account of history's unfinished business, this book is a must-read.'

—Jon Lee Anderson, *The New Yorker*

'The past is still with us. We must know and tell the truth about it if we are to flourish in the present and the future. Only then can the better angels of our nature fully emerge. Paul Lashmar's book is a powerful exercise in the truth-telling that is so necessary.'

—Alan Smith, First Church Estates Commissioner,
The Church Commissioners for England

Drax of Drax Hall

How One British Family Got Rich (and Stayed Rich) from Sugar and Slavery

Paul Lashmar

Foreword by David Olusoga

First published 2025 by Pluto Press
New Wing, Somerset House, Strand, London WC2R 1LA
and Pluto Press, Inc.
1930 Village Center Circle, 3-834, Las Vegas, NV 89134

www.plutobooks.com

Copyright © Paul Lashmar 2025

The right of Paul Lashmar to be identified as the author of this work has been
asserted in accordance with the Copyright, Designs and Patents Act 1988.

Every effort has been made to trace copyright holders and to obtain their
permission for the use of copyright material in this book. The publisher apologises
for any errors or omissions in this respect and would be grateful if notified of any
corrections that should be incorporated in future reprints or editions.

British Library Cataloguing in Publication Data
A catalogue record for this book is available from the British Library

ISBN 978 0 7453 5051 6   Hardback
ISBN 978 0 7453 5053 0   PDF
ISBN 978 0 7453 5052 3   EPUB

This book is printed on paper suitable for recycling and made from fully managed
and sustained forest sources. Logging, pulping and manufacturing processes are
expected to conform to the environmental standards of the country of origin.

Typeset by Stanford DTP Services, Northampton, England

Simultaneously printed in the United Kingdom and United States of America

To my family

Contents

List of Plates	ix
Foreword by David Olusoga	xi
Abbreviations	xiii
Prologue	xiv
Maps	xviii

Introduction	1

Part I Drax Hall, Barbados

1. James Drax Lands in Barbados	17
2. James and the Sugar Revolution	31
3. James Drax and Chattel Slavery	44

Part II The Erles of Charborough

4. An Estate Fit for an Erle	59
5. Walter the Puritan	76
6. Walter the Puritan and the English Civil War	94

Part III Barbados and the English Civil War

7. Sheath My Sword in James Drax's Bowels	115
8. Sir James, Slave Trader	127
9. Henry Drax and 'The Devil was in the Englishman'	141

Part IV Post-Restoration

10. Captain Thomas Erle and the Monmouth Rebellion	157
11. Colonel Thomas Erle – a Man of War	169
12. Henry and Betsy Drax	182

Part V The Grosvenor Years

13. Richard and Sarah Grosvenor, Royal Courtiers   201
14. Voices of the Enslaved   217
15. After Napoleon   235
16. Seeking Enclosure   248

Part VI The Wicked Squire

17. Captain Swing   263
18. The Squire Goes A-Hunting   276
19. Abolition and Compensation   288
20. John Drax, the Old Scoundrel   305

Part VII Four Barrels and a Smoking Gun

21. Commander Reginald Drax RN   325
22. Admiral Drax RN, Twice Retired   338
23. Richard Drax, 14 Years an MP   353

Part VIII Nemesis

24. In Conclusion   367

Archives	383
Family Trees	385
Ten Major Dorset Landowners 1883–2020	388
Acknowledgements	390
Index	392

List of Plates

1. Drax Hall house, Barbados, 2019.
2. Busts of Sir James Drax and his son Henry Drax in a former church in the City of London.
3. Nineteenth-century sketch of Drax Hall house and yard.
4. A quakerress and a tobacco planter in Barbados.
5. Sugar processing on a plantation, 1749.
6. Enslaved Africans.
7. Slave trafficking in Barbados, 1711.
8. Charborough House, the Folly Tower, lithograph circa 1840.
9. Charborough House, twenty-first century.
10. 'The Great Wall of Dorset', Charborough.
11. The Lion Gate and the Stag Gate on the Drax estate in Dorset.
12. The ruins of Ellerton Priory.
13. The effigy of Thomas Erle (1597) at St Mary's church, Morden, near Charborough.
14. Corfe Castle during the 1643 siege – the site of Walter Erle's defeat.
15. General Sir Thomas Erle MP (1650–1720).
16. The Battle of the Boyne, in which General Erle fought.
17. Elizabeth Countess of Berkeley, engraving by J. McArdell based on Sir Joshua Reynolds' portrait.
18. Countess Berkeley's daughter, Elizabeth, Margravine of Ansbach, attributed to Gainsborough, from *Connoisseur* magazine, March 1912.
19. Slaves with overseer. Line art by Everett of enslaved men working in sugar cane probably on a Caribbean plantation.
20. The eighteenth-century book known as The Instructions, co-authored by Edward Drax, Edwin Lascelles and others, at the Barbados Museum and Historical Society.

21. 'Barbarities in the West Indies', James Gillray, p. 125. Wright and Evans, No. 49. Reprinted, 'G.W.G.', 1830.
22. Mrs Frances Sarah Erle-Drax-Grosvenor (1769–1822).
23. Captain Richard Erle-Drax-Grosvenor (1762–1819) in his Dorset Ranger uniform at Charborough Park, 1795.
24. 'J.S.W.S.E. Drax Esq., Charborough Park', from *The Book of Sports, British and Foreign*, 1843.
25. Portrait of John Samuel Wanley Sawbridge Erle-Drax MP (1800–87) by Sir Francis Grant.
26. Admiral Reginald Aylmer Plunkett-Ernle-Erle-Drax by George Charles Beresford, 1 May 1918.
27. Jacob Rees-Mogg (right), then MP for North East Somerset, visits Boho Gelato's ice cream parlour, Weymouth, with Richard Drax, 18 August 2020.
28. Slavery Justice protest outside Charborough Estate, July 2021.

Foreword

David Olusoga

Chapters of a nation's past can, like chemical elements, be rendered inert; remaining dormant until exposed to an external pressure. The history of the pivotal role that England and then Britain played in the development of both chattel slavery in the Americas and the Trans-Atlantic slave trade is such a history. For much of the late nineteenth and early twentieth centuries slavery was a subject of little interest to successive generations of British historians. That vast, horrific and deeply consequential aspect of the national story became one of history's *terra incognita*.

It was not until the middle years of the twentieth century, as the British Empire stumbled towards its final decades, that the fossilised details of British slavery and the British slave trade were slowly excavated. Those first, tentative exhumations were often the labour of historians from North America and the Caribbean who were themselves descendants of the enslaved; figures like Eric Williams, the historian and politician from Trinidad and Tobago whose economic analysis of the abolition of the British slave trade and slavery remains influential 80 years after its first publication.

This book represents another step in that long process of historical salvage. Unusually, it is a work of both historical scholarship and investigative journalism. Its author, being both an academic and a journalist, has brought skills and perspectives from both professions to bear on his mission to write a first comprehensive history of a dynasty who are mentioned in almost every book on the early history of British slavery. A dynasty that until now have never been the focus of an exhaustive study.

Any proper exploration of the British Empire inevitably involves an encounter with the Drax family. Just as any history of that dynasty – as this book demonstrates – demands that they and their activities are seen within the wider context of British imperial history. The Drax family were key players – arguably *the* key players – in

xi

the origin story of British slavery. In the 1630s James Drax became the leading figure among a group of English planters on the island Barbados who pioneered the commercial production of sugar. The Barbados 'sugar revolution', as historian have come to call it, was one of the pivotal developments that afforded commercial viability to what was later to become the British Empire. Alongside the development of a tobacco cash-crop on land taken from indigenous peoples in Virginia and Maryland, and the later transformation of the East India Company from a joint stock company into a militarised quasi-sovereign entity, the emergence of a sugar economy on that small Caribbean island was one of the hinge moments of Empire.

In the 1640s and 1650s – as the pages of this book reveal – the Barbados sugar revolution spawned a new and terrible form of society – a slave society. Again, the Drax family were at the centre of the rapid transition from a system that relied upon white indentured labour to one based on African chattel slavery. The Drax Hall plantation, the first estate on which a crop of sugar was commercially grown and processed by any English planter, became one of the laboratories in which early English slavery was developed and finessed. Passed down within the Drax family for almost 400 years, Drax Hall has been described by the historian Sir Hilary Beckles, chair of the Caribbean Community Reparations Commission (CARICOM), as a 'killing field'.

This is a book about the economics of slavery in the seventeenth century, economics that James Drax helped pioneer and that were founded upon the ruthless commodification and lethal exploitation of enslaved Africans. But the story of the Drax dynasty is one that spans four centuries and around 14 generations. It takes us from James Drax in the 1630s to his descendant Richard Drax, the former MP for South Dorset, in the 2020s.

This book follows the money, tracing how wealth generated in the seventeenth century was passed down across those generations, but also expanded and solidified into land which in England brought with it power and influence. Finally, it is about not just the management of that wealth but also the concealment of its origins – right up to the twenty-first century.

Abbreviations

BDA	Barbados Department of Archives
BL	British Library
BMA	Barbados Museum Archives
CCCA	Churchill College Archive, Cambridge University
CJ	*House of Commons Journal*
CSG	Common Sense Group, UK Parliament
DEIC	Dutch East India Company
DHC	Dorset History Centre
EEIC	English East India Company
ERG	European Research Group, UK Parliament
IHA	The Institute of Historical Research
JBMHS	*The Journal of the Barbados Museum and Historical Society*
LMA	London Metropolitan Archives
NARA	National Archives and Records Administration, Washington, DC
RAC	Royal African Company
RUSIJ	*Royal United Services Institution Journal*
TNA	The National Archives, Kew, UK

Prologue

Drive into Dorset in the South of England along the shire's main A31 highway towards the county town of Dorchester and you roll past a formidable brick wall butted up tight to the highway that seems to go on forever. Several times the road and wall dog-legs and makes room for a towering Roman-style triumphal iron gate and stone entrance, crowned by an oversized lion or stag. This is the 'Great Wall of Dorset' built in the early 1840s with more than two million bricks and which circumscribes a private park. A second inner flank, a wood of mature beech and oak trees, provides a further screen, exuding an air of mystery about what might lie within.

What does lies deep inside is Charborough House, an elegant Commonwealth period mansion. It was built in the late 1650s for the Puritan Member of Parliament (MP) and English Civil War colonel Sir Walter Erle, from whom the current incumbent, Richard Grosvenor Plunkett-Ernle-Erle-Drax is a direct descendant. The earlier Tudor mansion had been burnt down during the war by Royalists as revenge against Sir Walter, who was on the side of Parliament.

Just before the restoration of Charborough House, another manor house was built on the Caribbean Island of Barbados, some 4000 miles from east Dorset, by slave labour. Drax Hall plantation house was constructed in the early 1650s for Sir James Drax, in the Jacobean style. It is now said to be the oldest intact European residential home in the Americas.[1]

Drax Hall plantation is also owned by Richard Grosvenor Plunkett-Ernle-Erle-Drax (who prefers to be known as Richard Drax). These two houses have been inextricably linked for nearly 400 years as wealth has been extracted from Drax Hall plantation in Barbados

---

1   There are three Jacobean manor houses surviving in the Americas. Barbados is also home to one of the others, St Nicholas Abbey, while the third is Bacon's Castle in Virginia, USA.

xiv

and sent for the aggrandisement of Charborough House and the Drax family in England.

The Plunkett-Ernle-Erle-Drax family are an exceptionally revealing example of one of the many landed gentry families who spread into the colonies and constructed slave plantations from the early seventeenth century. Their ancestor James Drax was among the settlers who landed on the uninhabited island of Barbados in 1627 and in a few short years turned the tropical island into the economic engine of Empire. Credited with inventing the British sugar industry, James Drax was able to do this by exploiting enslaved African people. Ennobled by both Oliver Cromwell and Charles II, Sir James Drax made his family far wealthier. The next generation of Draxes created the enormous Drax Hall plantation in Jamaica where they also worked enslaved people.

The Plunkett-Ernle-Erle-Drax family bloodlines were already experts in wealth extraction well before James Drax landed in West Indies. One of Richard Drax's direct line of descent ancestors – the Erle family from Devon – had acquired by marriage the Charborough Estate in Dorset by 1549 during the reign of Henry VIII. Each subsequent generation has sought to expand the family's riches. As this book reveals, there are some remarkable and controversial family characters: a servant in the courts of Henry VIII who was also an accomplished musician and composer; the two Warwickshire brothers, sons of a vicar by the name of Drax, who sailed across the Atlantic to seek their fortunes in the later 1620s. In the same period at Charborough there was Walter Erle, who was an MP and a colonel in the English Civil War. Two further generations along, there was General Thomas Erle, who, as the family legend has it, begat the 1688 Glorious Revolution by plotting in a Charborough icehouse with fellow conspirators to rid England of the popish James II and later fought in numerous battles including the Battle of the Boyne. When a member of aristocratic Grosvenors married into the family, he brought royal connections with George III. Then there was nineteenth-century squire John Sawbridge Erle-Drax MP who had a long life and a reputation as a sexual predator.

Britain outlawed slave trading in 1807, and ownership of enslaved people was outlawed in 1833. Over the next four years, about £20 million – a vast sum then – was paid to compensate several thousand enslavers, British people who had a stake in plantations in the colonies. *The Legacies of British Slavery* online database shows that the then incumbent of Charborough House for much of the nineteenth century, John Sawbridge-Erle-Drax, who married into the Drax family, received, on behalf of his wife, a considerable sum in compensation for freeing 189 enslaved Africans at Drax Hall.[2]

Eighteen generations of the family have owned Charborough. Thirteen of those generations have also owned a colonial plantation and for nine of those generations, owned and worked enslaved people. The Draxes are unique in that they are the only colonising family to still own a plantation in the West Indies. A plantation where, over 200 years, they worked thousands of enslaved people transported from Africa, most of whom died premature, often cruel, deaths.

In the third decade of the twenty-first century, Richard Drax has become iconic in the culture wars. A former BBC reporter and Conservative MP, he has been resistant to arguments about debts to the colonies and the descendants of enslaved people. In 2010, in the run up to the General Election, he was asked by the *Daily Mirror* newspaper about his historical obligations. He replied, 'I can't be held responsible for something that happened 300 or 400 years ago.' Richard Drax claimed the question was an attempt to smear him as a Conservative candidate: 'They are using the old class thing and that is not what this election is about, it's not what I stand for and I ignore it.' Certainly, after he was elected to Parliament, Richard Drax made it clear he was not interested in discussing slavery and reparations.

This is the story of the Plunkett-Ernle-Erle-Drax family. My narrative brings together all the family bloodlines contributing to Richard Drax's full four-barrelled name. I am not an expert or a historian of many of the aspects of the history of Britain and its Empire that are covered in this book, a duration of some 500 years.

---

2   www.ucl.ac.uk/lbs/project/details, last accessed 28 June 2024.

PROLOGUE

Some I have researched and written about before. Where I have not, I have drawn on those I thought were the best authorities. The book is selective, as I choose the key Drax family characters that I thought best represented the family ethos over the centuries. Their lives also helped answer some of the key questions this book has raised. Whenever possible, I tried to find the voices of the enslaved but there are only faint traces. Inevitably elite male voices dominate the archive material. I have tried to write a fair history and borne in mind that you cannot apply the liberal values of today to the past. However, there are some issues through time that can never be ignored or morally justified.

xvii

Maps

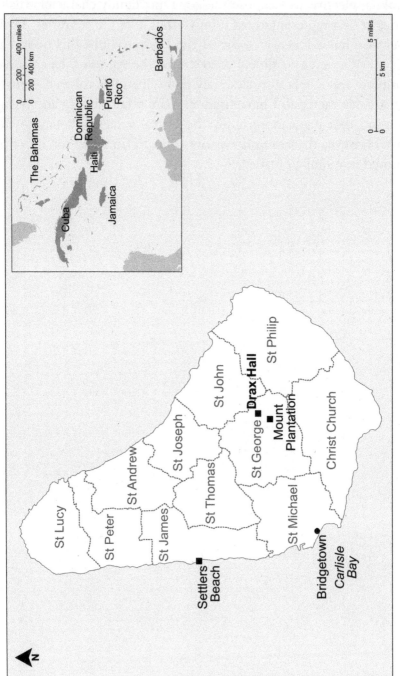

MAPS

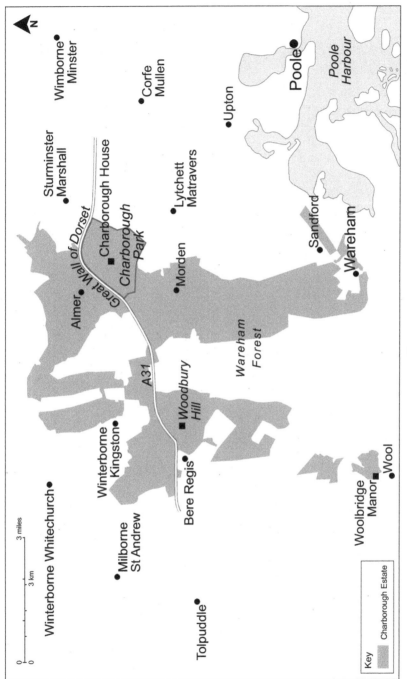

Dorset

Introduction

Not everything that is faced can be changed. But nothing can be changed until it is faced.

(James Baldwin)

I have lived in west Dorset in south-west England for many years. My interest in the Drax family began one day in June 2020, just after the Black Lives Matter (BLM) demonstration where the statue of the West Country merchant Edward Colston (1626–1721) had just been upended into Bristol Harbour because of Colston's involvement in slavery. I was driving home and listening to a BBC news item about the protests.[1] It just so happened I was driving along the side of the 'Great Wall of Dorset' that segregates Charborough Park from the A31 road. At the time I knew little of Richard Plunkett-Ernle-Erle-Drax except that he lived in the park, was a Dorset MP from the Conservative Party, and his ancestors had somehow been involved with slavery in centuries past.

As I drove alongside the wall, I wondered what an MP who has a historical legacy in slavery might be adding to the debate about the BLM protests. Once home, I spent a while with Google search and could only find one recent comment and that was in his regular column for the local newspaper, the *Dorset Echo*, with an attack on the protests: 'The desecration of the Cenotaph by rioters two weeks ago, on the actual D-Day anniversary, was beyond ironic.' He had relied on a media report that the letters BLM had been sprayed on the side of the Cenotaph. His agitation about defacing a memorial to the military dead was not surprising given he is an ex-Guards

---

1. Colston was a very successful merchant and became a major philanthropist in Bristol and into the twenty-first century many buildings, including the city's main concert venue and a school, were named after him. Increasingly, a recognition grew in this diverse city that his wealth had partly accrued from slavery and commemorating him was offensive to many of Bristol's population.

officer. However, it seems the original allegation was not accurate, and London's Metropolitan Police had swiftly confirmed the media report was wrong.[2] In his column, Mr Drax also expressed his concern about what he saw as the ethos of the BLM protests: 'A wave of intolerance has swept this country since the abhorrent killing of George Floyd in the US. To speak out against intolerance here is often condemned as racist in itself by those who would rewrite our history.'

Richard Drax has rarely commented on his own ancestors' history of owning hundreds of enslaved people over 200 years. As readers of the *Dorset Echo* knew, Richard Drax, as an MP, had been forthright on many other subjects in his columns, his blog and in the House of Commons. Richard Drax's popularity was bolstered by his views on immigration. Back in 2012, the *Dorset Echo* reported Richard Drax had issued a stark warning on immigration, insisting: 'I believe, as do many of my constituents, that this country is full.'[3]

As my research progressed, I realised Richard Drax, other than the brief skirmish with the *Daily Mirror*, had attracted little attention from the national media, except for some jokey pieces about him having a four-barrelled name. Although he had been an MP for a decade at the time, I could find no analysis of Richard Drax's political performance in the mainstream or regional media at all. Yet, he was an active part of a significant political shift in the Conservative Party to the right that had dominated the national agenda since the party had come into government in 2010. Later, I could see from his MP's expense declarations that Richard Drax was involved with the then secretive European Research Group (ERG), a faction of about 60 MPs who had lobbied for leaving the European Union

---

2. The Reuters-Thomson fact-check team also looked into the allegation and said it was not correct. Someone had sprayed the letters BLM on the wall of the Foreign Office, not the Cenotaph, and not on the day of the protests: www.reuters.com/article/uk-factcheck-cenotaph-idUSKBN23B36Q.

3. Mr Drax made his comments in support of a House of Commons motion calling for the UK population to be stabilised as close as possible to its then present level. Drax, who backed rigorous controls on immigration, said: 'I hope that we will have a firm and fair system so that the people who come into this country have visas and references and money in a bank account.'

INTRODUCTION

and had subsequently been central to the government's immigration policies.[4]

That Richard Drax seemed virtually unknown outside of his constituency intrigued me. At that time, in Parliament, he was low profile. A friend who was a long-standing Conservative MP did not know much about him. Parliamentary correspondents I spoke to knew little about him. True, he was not one of the big Tory players like Boris Johnson, Jacob Rees-Mogg, David Davis or Liz Truss. Looking at his voting record, it became clear he was an exemplar of a bloc of right-wing Conservative MPs. This relatively small group exerted power vastly more significant than their numbers, and no Tory Prime Minister could ignore them. The ERG had determined Tory Government policies since before Brexit, and its members right-wing radicals on a range of issues. Understand Richard Drax, I began to realise, and you can get some insight into what had happened to Britain since 2010. Richard Drax seemed worth understanding.

For months during Covid, while running a university department, I used any precious spare time to dig a bit further into his world. The more I researched, the more gripped I became. The first key question I sought to answer was, what does Richard Drax actually own and how much is he and his family worth? The House and Park are the jewels in the family's assets, their playground for riding, shooting, landscaping and the plain enjoyment of an abundance of beauty. The Park covers a mere 1500 well-ordered acres of the Charborough Estate. The family can be coy about the extent of their land and wealth. A then Conservative MP's wife from Devon who spent a weekend at the estate, recounted her failed attempt, over a sumptuous Charborough House dinner, to find out from Richard Drax how much land he and his family owned.[5] A Dorset

---

4. In a speech in Parliament in 2018 on the Agricultural Bill, Richard Drax said: 'Yes, I did vote for Brexit and yes, I am a turkey voting for Christmas because the subsidies that my farm receives will be considerably reduced, putting my business plan if not at risk, then certainly into review. I do not object to that: I voted to leave the EU because I believe that that is best for our country. I believe that this is a wonderful opportunity.' www.richarddrax. com/news/speech-new-opportunities-agriculture, last accessed 27 June 2024.
5. Sasha Swire, *Diary of an MP's Wife: Inside and Outside Power* (London: Little, Brown, 2020).

3

friend of mine recalled a dinner-party exchange he had witnessed some years earlier when Richard Drax's father, known as 'Wol', was still alive. One of the younger generation of the Drax family had been invited to dinner with family friends. One guest asked, 'How much land does your family own?' The young Drax answered he did not know, as Wol 'won't tell me'. 'Why won't he tell you?', asked the guest. 'Because then I cannot tell anyone who asks,' was the reply.

So how much land does Richard Drax and his family own? His then declaration to the Register of Members' Interest only stated he owned land worth more than £100,000 and had rental returns of more than £10,000 per annum. There was a London property worth over £100,000.[6] There were three limited companies he was the sole director of but as the accounts were filed under the 'Small and Medium Enterprises' exemptions they did not tell me much except that there was farming and rental.[7] He did say in the Register, 'Some income received directly, some received via family trusts either to me or to family members.'[8]

Previous estimates put the estate at 7000 acres, but it was likely that it was much larger.[9] A lot of research later, helped by author Guy Shrubsole,[10] I was able to confirm that Richard Drax and his family then owned at least 15,000 acres of farmland, heathland and woodland in south-east Dorset, mostly held through family trusts. Filings dated 2016, made to an obscure corner of the

---

6. This was later sold.

7. We also discovered that Mr Drax, the sole director of four Charborough companies, had failed to file correct accounts for eleven years: www.theguardian.com/world/2021/apr/04/wealthy-mp-with-slave-trade-links-failed-to-publish-accounts-for-four-of-his-firms, last accessed 28 July 2024.

8. The declaration also stated: 'Since 1 October 2014, accommodation at a property in Dorset has been provided to me with an annual value of £47,500 per annum. I received no other remuneration from this company. Hours: approx. 10 hrs per week. This arrangement ceased on 21 April 2021.' Can be seen at: https://publications.parliament.uk/pa/cm/cmregmem/200720/200720.pdf, last accessed 9 July 2024.

9. An example is from the *Daily Mail* of using 7000 acres: www.dailymail.co.uk/news/article-2427719/Fury-millionaire-Tory-MP-Richard-Drax-wants-huge-solar-farm-sprawling-estate.html, last accessed 27 June 2024.

10. Guy Shrubsole, *Who Owns England?* (London: William Collins, 2020). He estimated that the Charborough Estate had 13,870 acres in Dorset.

INTRODUCTION

County Council website, revealed there were many acres of land and at least 125 properties owned by Richard Drax and the Estate. There were several family trusts that held land, the one holding most of the land and properties was 'Richard Drax's 1987 Accumulation and Maintenance Settlement'.[11] Then I started looking in the Land Registry. However, it was of limited use, as the family have owned most of their land for more than 100 years, it precedes the requirement for registration upon sale. There were a few exceptions: one Land Registry record showed Richard Drax personally owned a prime beachside rental holiday home on Sandbanks in Poole Harbour, which is the second most expensive real estate area in the UK. At peak periods, renters are charged up to £6000 a week to rent the holiday home, which is worth around £5 million. I also discovered Richard Drax had inherited Copperthwaite moor high in the Yorkshire Dales, above the Drax family-owned 2000-acre farming estate at nearby Ellerton in Swaledale. Copperthwaite is on moorland popular for grouse shooting. Other family members own additional land on the Isle of Purbeck. It all amounts to a staggering amount of land: arable, woodland, heathland, irrigated by three key rivers, the Stour, Frome and Piddle all running into the Poole basin.

All in all, Charborough is a prime example of a landed gentry estate. Scraping data from the internet over several weeks, I could establish that one Charborough Estate entity, ACF (Drax Farm) Ltd, had received at least £7.5 million in the 20 years to 2019 in EU Common Agricultural Policy (CAP) subsidies for farming and land activities.[12] At the time of writing, the family estates have continued to benefit from the post-EU, UK government taper subsidies (£600k in 2022). How profitable was the Charborough Estate was not clear from the published accounts. He later said, though he is sole director, he does not take income from the farming companies.

---

11. These can be found at https://gi.dorsetcouncil.gov.uk/rightsofway/definitive map/landownerdeposits, and are LD/36, LD41-LD/44.

12. This historical EU information is hard to locate, and I am grateful to the website Farmsubsidy.org for saving the data. Sadly, the site is now defunct. I have the data scrape.

Richard Drax is head of an estate that employed a considerable number of people. A trim and fit man in his 60s, described by many who have met him as charming, Mr Drax advocates hunting, fishing and shooting, and the estate has significant business interests in both. The estate is considered to be one of the best shoots in Dorset and he rents property to a gundog training and kennels business. When I eventually calculated his family's property and land portfolio, I estimated that they are worth at least £150 million.

BARBADOS

What exactly was the Drax family historical connection to slavery? I quickly established the family were linked historically to the Drax Hall plantation in Barbados. Not just any plantation, but the same Drax Hall plantation in Barbados, created in the 1630s by Sir James Drax, that was the first plantation in the British Empire to produce sugar commercially. Drax Hall plantation was British colonialism's Sugar Plantation One. In Barbados in the 1970s, Dr Colin Hudson the innovative environmentalist and scientist, said of the planter, 'James Drax was possibly the most important man who ever lived in Barbados.' The word important implies the positive but Drax was also important in a very negative way. Sir James Drax was one of the first to employ the most inhumane form of slavery – chattel slavery – where not only were people enslaved for life but so were their children and their children's children in perpetuity.

Along my path of enquiry, to my surprise, several people had said the family owned the plantation until recently. Author Matthew Parker mentioned in his brilliant 2011 book on sugar and slavery that Richard Drax's father, Walter Henry Plunkett-Ernle-Erle-Drax, was said to be still the owner of the plantation and visited once a year. Furthermore, he sometimes took his oldest son Richard with him.[13] Walter had died in 2017, and his wife Pamela in 2019. So, who now owned the plantation? Walter and Pamela's wills were

---

13. Matthew Parker, *The Sugar Barons: Family, Corruption, Empire and War* (London: Hutchinson, 2011), p. 359.

INTRODUCTION

not much help as references to Barbados were vague.[14] There was no mention of Drax Hall in Richard Drax's 2020 Register of Members' Interests, so I thought it could not be him. I hypothesised the details of ownership disappeared into one of the family's many private trusts, or that it had been sold and was now controlled by an offshore entity where the new owners could not be traced (later, neither of these two hypotheses proved correct). I could make no progress, and my only hope was to get documented information from Barbados.

Two more Covid months went by. The Barbados equivalent of the British departments like the Land Registry that would have relevant information did not put their data online. Because of Covid, they were not responding to calls or emails. I needed someone in Barbados. Weeks later, I was lucky enough to connect to the former BBC TV investigative journalist Jonathan Smith, who spent much of every year in Barbados. I explained what I was trying to find out, and Jonathan offered to help. Over several months Jonathan persisted, visiting Barbados government departments. Mostly they were closed because of Covid. Sometimes they were just unhelpful, saying the material was boxed in an archive elsewhere. Then one day, 'Eureka', as Jonathan announced he had obtained documents from the Barbados business registry showing that Richard Drax had personally registered Drax Hall as a business some months earlier, in February 2020. The Barbados Land Tax Authority also confirmed he was paying the land tax on the plantation that they valued at nearly £5 million. The Authority even gave Jonathan a basic map of the Drax Hall and Drax Hope plantations.

So, in front-page articles for *The Observer* and the *Sunday Mirror*, we were able to detail how Richard Drax was then the wealthiest landowner in the House of Commons and controlled the British Empire's 'Sugar Plantation One' – Drax Hall and all it symbolised.[15] This estimate of Drax's wealth is relevant, as his constituency had some of the poorest residents in the United Kingdom in

---

14. Wills are publicly available in the UK.
15. Paul Lashmar and Jonathan Smith, 'Wealthy MP Urged to Pay Up for his Family's Slave Trade Past', *The Observer*, Sunday 13 December 2020, pp. 1, 2, 20–21.

7

the boroughs of Weymouth and Portland. Two years before South Dorset had been ranked 533rd among 533 parliamentary constituencies in England for social mobility – a marker of limited educational opportunity and diminishing life chances for young people.[16] Some 70 per cent of the population of the constituency live in Weymouth and Portland and they have become a 'coldspot' for social mobility. According to researchers, the area is 'an all-round poor performer … where residents experience low levels of quality jobs, low average wage and relatively costly housing'.[17]

It was Richard Drax's control over the former slave plantation that got the attention of other news media. Barbadian historian Sir Hilary Beckles, the chair of the Caribbean Community (CARICOM) Reparations Commission and Vice-chancellor of the University of the West Indies, told us: 'Today, when I drive through the Drax Hall land and its environs, I feel a keen sense of being in a massive killing field with unmarked cemeteries. Sugar and Black Death went hand in glove. Black life mattered only to make millionaires of English enslavers and the Drax family did it longer than any other elite family.'[18] One of the claims made by some critics of the Drax family was that all their wealth comes from the period of slavery. This book seeks to test this assertion.

From his parents' wills Richard Drax was to be the sole beneficiary of Drax Hall plantation. Asked before *The Observer* and the *Sunday Mirror* 2020 publication why he had not declared the plantation in the Register of Members' Interests, Richard Drax said that

---

16. The House of Commons Library measures social mobility for all parliamentary constituencies in England. In 2018, South Dorset ranked bottom among 533 constituencies. Demographically Weymouth and Portland dominates the constituency. See also G. Allen and L. Audickas, *Social Mobility Index by Constituency, England,* House of Commons Library (2018), p. 9; online at: https://commonslibrary.parliament.uk/research-briefings/cbp-8400.

17. Jenny Lennox-Wood and Phil Marfleet, '"Forgotten Towns" – Weymouth, Portland and the "Coastal Economy"', a report from the South Dorset Research Group 2022. Professor Phil Marfleet is also a lead figure in the 'Stand Against Racism, Dorset' group which has campaigned against Richard Drax's position on reparations.

18. The Caribbean Community (CARICOM) is a grouping of 20 countries: 15 Member States and five Associate Members.

INTRODUCTION

his parents' estates were still in probate and that when he filed documents in Barbados, it was as one of two executors. Later, he said he was told by the Registrar that he was not required to declare until probate was complete.[19] The media picked up *The Observer* story as there was a new interest in the critical history of the British Empire. If there was once a reluctance to discuss the shortcomings of the Empire, and especially Britain's deep engagement in slavery, that had now changed. That is also true of the peoples of the former colonies, who are now not so ready to dance and doff their caps to visiting British Royalty as they once were. They are asking questions.

A BATTLE FOR BRITAIN

Tensions in Britain, too, had escalated into a culture war. There is a persistent demand for a history of Britain that is not just a selective narrative of the Magna Carta, nurturing democracy, intrepid explorers, Britannia ruling the waves and fighting fascism. On the other side of the culture war are those who advocate the traditional history of the Empire, and like to emphasise British courage in battle, entrepreneurial spirit, the spread of Christian values, the industrial revolution and *noblesse oblige*. Those who promote this version of history see their critics as 'woke' troublemakers. Some 59 Conservative MPs and nine peers of the then informal 'Common Sense Group' complained that disagreement is not now tolerated through 'no-platforming' and the rise of the 'cancel culture'.[20] The

---

19. Richard Drax disclosed this information in his responses to a complaint to the Standards Commissioner in 2021 about his Register of Members' Interests disclosures. He was found not at fault for a number of the complaints. The Standards Commissioner admonished him for not declaring he had inherited a moor in Yorkshire and not keeping details of his London residence up to date. The Commissioner said, 'The Member accepted my decision, acknowledged his breaches of the Rules, and apologised for these breaches. The Member also agreed to add some additional wording to his Register entry to make a link between two other interests clearer.' That can be found at: www.parliament.uk/globalassets/documents/pcfs/rectifications/mr-richard-drax-mp-rectification.pdf, last accessed 14 July 2024. Richard Drax declared ownership of the plantation in his Register entry post probate in January 2022.
20. Richard Drax was not a member of the Common Sense Group.

Chairman of the Group, Sir John Hayes CBE, laid out the ideological battleground in his introduction to their 2021 manifesto: 'The battle of ideas has been drawn into sharp focus with the emergence of extreme cultural and political groups, Black Lives Matter, Extinction Rebellion, Kill the Bill et al. – subversives fuelled by ignorance and an arrogant determination to erase the past and dictate the future.' Reinforcing the sense of a war and echoing the tones of 1940, Hayes concluded, 'The business of politics is values – it's about place, purpose and pride. The Battle for Britain has begun, it must be won by those who, inspired by the people's will, stand for the common good in the national interest.'[21]

And so, woe betide those who challenge the shibboleths of British history. Professor Corinne Fowler co-edited the National Trust's report on country houses' numerous connections to slavery.[22] The report's publication received widespread media attention, with the right-wing media campaigning against Fowler and the National Trust. It seemed from their perch, the traditionalists believe that stately homes should only be viewed in terms of their architecture, lush interiors, the beauty of their surroundings, and the positive contributions to history of their ancestral owners. As a consequence of her perceived heresy, Professor Fowler has been the target of abuse from an army of trolls across social media.

In the Common Sense Group manifesto, Gareth Bacon MP proposed that the moral legitimacy of a 'woke' perspective is claimed by its adherents by placing a universally accepted idea at the centre of a web of otherwise unsavoury associated positions. The Group attacked the National Trust report as 'coloured by cultural Marxist dogma, colloquially as the "woke agenda"'. They concluded, 'A clique of powerful, privileged liberals must not be allowed to rewrite our history in their image.'[23]

---

21. *Common Sense: Conservative Thinking for a Post-Liberal Age* (May 2021), www.marcolonghi.org.uk/news/common-sense.

22. www.nationaltrust.org.uk/who-we-are/research/addressing-our-histories-of-colonialism-and-historic-slavery. Professor Fowler was also author of *Green Unpleasant Land: Creative Responses to Rural England's Colonial Connections* (Leeds: Peepal Treet Press, 2020).

23. www.telegraph.co.uk/opinion/2020/11/09/letterswill-police-break-armistice-day-ceremonies-wednesday/, last accessed 10 July 2024.

INTRODUCTION

THE ANCESTORS

From December 2020 we wrote sixteen news stories relating to Richard Drax and/or the legacy of slavery. Until recent years, no one seemed much interested in the Drax family. They just appeared to be another successful county landed gentry family elevated by the natural order of English society. But digging deep into their history while researching Richard Drax's affluence I began to see a historical narrative of power, wealth extraction and duty. The Drax ancestors have had wealth since at least the sixteenth century. In the Dorset History Centre, I found a copy of a privately published slim volume, *History of Charborough 1066–1956*, written by Richard's grandfather, which was fascinating, not least as its underlying message was that the elevation of the Plunkett-Ernle-Erle-Drax family was just the natural order of society. Too many things in British life are taken as the natural order when they are a human construct and far from natural. Order, or lack of it, is the result of power, power struggles, ideology and access to wealth and military resources. Down the years, the Plunkett-Ernle-Erle-Draxes seemed to have managed their dynasty well. The questions were staring me in the face. How had the Drax family quietly achieved their position of such status? What were the forces that had elevated the Drax family over the majority? How did they get that discreet eminence and how had they used it? Where had their wealth come from?

The story begins where the Plunkett-Ernle-Erle-Drax lineage first becomes apparent in the historical record. I start with the Erles who brought Charborough into the family. I hope this book provides some insight, through the history of the family into the development of Britain and its Empire.

If this book has a lot of focus on Dorset that is where the Drax family have lived for 500 years and own a fair chunk of the county. In that sense they are an example, if not entirely stereotypical, of the landed gentry.[24] The landed gentry are usually major figures in their county and that is their domain.

---

24. The eastern side of Dorset has a surprising number of landed gentry families that have held onto their estates for many hundreds of years.

What are my motives as author? As a journalist I believe that public figures should be transparent and accountable and much of my journalism has been in that vein. I saw the research as a fourth estate audit. I hope that 23 years as an academic has brought a more formal rigour to my research and analysis. I believe that we need to assess British society and Empire for what they really were and not retell romanticised myths. This belief has its roots in my childhood as a white working-class schoolboy in post-war east London. On the rare occasions slavery was mentioned, I was indoctrinated in the idea that Britannia was a progressive force, with the nineteenth-century Royal Navy intercepting slave ships and releasing African captives destined for enslavement.[25] Only much later I discovered the shocking extent of the British involvement in slavery in the sixteenth to nineteenth centuries. I felt the factual record should be set straight, so the current generation does not grow up as misled as mine.[26] It has taken me, as a child of the late British Empire, many years to fully understand that unreflexive history profoundly impacts on the world today with the failure to recognise the roots of discontent and the deeply embedded nature of racism.

My personal politics are mostly unlike Richard Drax's though there are a few positions I am congruent with, like supporting Ukraine. During his time as an MP, he also spoke from time to time on the freedom of the press in Parliament. My motivation for writing this book was my realisation that, in the same way that the story of Richard Drax tells us much about British politics in the twenty-first century, that an important strand of the history of the British Empire from the sixteenth century to the present day could be illuminated through this one family of landed gentry, the Draxes of Dorset and Barbados.

*   *   *

25. The debate about the motives and effects of the Royal Navy's West Africa Squadron rumbles on. The July 2024 edition of *History Today* magazine has a piece on exactly these questions by the author Mary Wills.
26. In the late 1990s, I was involved in a Channel 4 TV series on the subject. I was a development producer for *Britain's Slave Trade*.

INTRODUCTION

Addendum: two things arose when people became aware of my interest in the Drax family and knew the name. Firstly, they often believed that Ian Fleming used the surname Drax for Hugo Drax, the James Bond villain in *Moonraker* (1955), because the novelist did not like Admiral Drax, whom he knew in the Royal Navy. I do not believe that is correct. Admiral Drax and Commander Ian Fleming were friends, and there is no indication that he intended to cast the admiral as a villain by borrowing the Drax part of the admiral's surname. The other question that is asked is whether the Drax family owned the Drax power station. There is no connection except that the Drax family probably had roots in the Drax area of Yorkshire in the medieval period, the same area from which the power station takes its name.[27]

---

27. Chris Drakes runs a website based on his research over decades on the history of the Drax, Drakes and similar surnames: www.drakesfamily.org/.

PART I

Drax Hall, Barbados

1
James Drax Lands in Barbados

At the end of February 1627, the merchant sailing ship *William and John*, captained by Henry Powell, hove into a bay of a Caribbean island, to see a coast heavily wooded with dense and lush vegetation. The ship's crew and passengers had reached their destination, the island of Barbados.[1] The voyage from London would have taken at least five weeks and required no small feat of navigation skill, as a few degrees of error would have meant that the *William and John* would have continued to the coast of what is now Venezuela. But due to Powell's experienced navigation, they had arrived and identified a landing place on the western side of the island. Among the young men on board was James Drax who would be crucial to the development of Barbados from a densely forested island to the economic engine of the early British Empire. They were pioneers in exploring the West Indies, which they hoped would be a new world in which they could make their fortune. The story of the settlers reveals them as adventurers and entrepreneurs in a perilous environment. It is also a story that had a very negative element – slavery. The legacy of what happened in Barbados still reverberates down the centuries.

James Drax was the son of William Drax, the vicar of the village of Finham in the parish of Stoneleigh, Warwickshire. Just 18 years old, James had left his parents and siblings to join the voyage. We know little about the family. Some historians have suggested the Draxes were Anglo-Dutch, but this is very unlikely. The name Drax could be found in England after the Norman Conquest.[2] The Drax

---

1. By then, the Courteen Company or Association had merged with the English East India Company in the 1650s.
2. Chris Drakes stated on his website: 'The only publication that I have seen to date, which has a possibly correct origin is: *Dictionary of English & Welsh Surnames*, by Charles Wareing Bardsley, 1901, page 252 shows, "Drax", and its

17

coat of arms were originally awarded to Sir Edward Drax, knighted by the Black Prince in April 1367 at the Battle of Najera in modern-day northern Spain: hence the 'Prince of Wales' feathers.[3]

By 1627, English settling was already taking place in the Americas. The state and public persecution of Puritans, Separatists and Catholics motivated increasing numbers to migrate in the hope of freedom to practise their religion. Barbados was not the first island in the West Indies to be settled by the English. In 1620, a grant was received from King James I to colonise certain Caribbean islands, but with overall authority through James Hay, the Earl of Carlisle. Fifteen settlers arrived on the small island of St Christopher's, later better known as St Kitts – just 18 miles by eight miles – on 28 January 1623. They came to an agreement with the local Carib chief Tegremante to inhabit a section of the island.[4]

Some 360 miles south-east of St Kitts, the island of Barbados is located in the Lesser Antilles of the West Indies and is an almost triangular island. At 21 miles long and 14 miles wide at the maximum, it is about 167 square miles in area, which makes it slightly larger than the Isle of Wight. On the island's west side is the Caribbean Sea, and the Atlantic Ocean is to the east. Unlike some of the other islands, it is not volcanic and rose out of the sea relatively recently – less than one million years ago – by tectonic pressure. It is quite flat compared to other Caribbean islands, with the highest point at Mount Hillaby, which reaches 1115 feet above sea level. But mostly, it is an undulating landscape, with some hill ranges interspersed with deep gullies. It is more isolated than other islands, and St Vincent is the nearest, at 78 miles distance.

---

variation "Drakes", is a local name, meaning "of Drax", which is a valley near Selby, co. York.'

3. There was a John Drax, a naval logistician for the king who organised flotillas to carry English troops abroad. Over 1394–95, he assembled over 200 transport ships to freight Richard II's army to Ireland. He was one of several men who had organised Richard II's fleets in the 1390s who continued to be retained by Henry IV and Henry V.

4. David Brown, *Empire and Enterprise: Money, Power and the Adventurers for Irish Land during the British Civil Wars* (Manchester: Manchester University Press, 2020), p. 20.

If Barbados was unoccupied when the English settlers arrived, that had only intermittently been the case. Archaeological evidence suggests humans may have first settled or visited the island circa 1600 BCE. More permanent Amerindian settlement of Barbados dates to about the fourth to seventh centuries CE, by an ethnic group known as the Saladoid-Barrancoid. Settlements of Arawaks from South America appeared around 800 CE and again in the twelfth and thirteenth centuries. By the sixteenth century, an indigenous group (called Caribs by the Spanish) visited the island regularly. They were targets for the Spanish to capture as enslaved people and that probably explains why the island was empty at the time of the English settlers' disembarkation. Barbados was known to Europeans by the very end of the fifteenth century when Spanish navigators took possession, claiming it for the Crown of Castile. A map drawn by John Rotz for Henry VIII around 1542 showed Barbados. The Portuguese Empire claimed the island between 1532 and 1536 but abandoned it in 1620.

By the 1620s, Sir William Courteen and his brother Peter were maritime merchants and building a thriving business trading with the New World. In Protestant exile from Hapsburg-occupied Flanders, the Courteens operated a fleet out of the ports of London and Amsterdam. The possibilities for colonisation offered by the island were confirmed by John Powell, the captain of one of the Courteen brothers' own ships, *The Olive*.[5] On the way back to the port of London from resupplying a Dutch coastal colony off the mainland of South America, *The Olive* was forced to take shelter at Barbados due to bad weather, and the crew stayed on the island for a while. This would have been around 1624. Back in London, Powell reported to the Courteens of the 'goodness of the island'. Sir William decided forming a settlement on the island would be good business. With a view to profiting from this intelligence, in 1625 he petitioned for a Royal Patent of all unknown land in the south part of the world, which he called 'Terra Australis Incognita'. He prevailed on his friend and patron the 4th Earl of Pembroke[6] to

---

5. Some accounts say it was called *The Olive Blossom*.
6. The Earl of Pembroke was one of the wealthiest peers in the kingdom, with

DRAX OF DRAX HALL

persuade the king to grant them the islands of Trinidad, Tobago and Barbados to exploit.[7] Proceeding under the patronage of the earl, Courteen sent two ships captained by John Powell and his brother Henry. At some point outward bound, John Powell and his crew captured a Spanish ship and returned with their prize to England.[8] Henry Powell continued the voyage of the *William and John*. On board, besides the crew, were – and accounts differ – up to 80 settlers and ten indentured servants,[9] all with supplies of arms, ammunition and provisions.[10] The Barbados settlers will have likely landed on the fine white sand of a cove later named Settlers Beach.[11] By some accounts, Powell planted the Royal Standard to show the island was now an English possession.[12] The long voyage had had its moments of excitement. In some accounts, after leaving *The Olive, William and Mary* triumphed in a fight with a Portuguese ship, likely sailing between Africa and Brazil. As well as the

---

93 manors, four boroughs and estates scattered over ten counties from Middlesex to Yorkshire. Richard H. Tawney, 'The Rise of the Gentry, 1558–1640', *The Economic History Review*, Vol. 11, No. 1 (1941), p. 35.

7. From when Henry VII commissioned John and Sebastian Cabot to set up the King's Standard in the New World at the end of the fifteenth century and through to the Civil War, the kings of England assumed possession over lands newly found by their subjects, to the preclusion of the State itself. The plantations, or colonies, were the king's foreign dominions, his demesne lands in *partibus externis*, and not part of his kingdom in England. The proprietary colonies, like that of the Caribbee Islands, were erected into Provinces, within which the proprietor, as the king's deputy or governor, was invested with all the same royal powers which appertained to the king in his palace, both executive and legislative.

8. Unknown, *A Short History of Barbados: From Its First Discovery and Settlement to the End of the Year 1767* (London: Printed for J. Dodsley, in Pall-Mall, 1767), p. 4.

9. Indenture was a system devised by the Virginia Company – of which both the Earl of Carlisle and Oliver Cromwell were shareholders – in the early 1620s to provide labour for the colonies.

10. Accounts of the number of settlers vary from 50 to 80 including and in addition to indentured servants and enslaved Africans.

11. Four hundred years later, the Draxes retained an interest in Settlers Beach, owning shares in a hotel awaiting redevelopment on this idyllic white sand beach and bay.

12. Now known as Holetown.

loot, the crew are said to have taken ten or more enslaved Africans who were on board.

The English arrivals on Barbados disembarked, unloaded and began to build wooden huts. It was a dense forested environment and the settlers found it hard to get fresh water. According to a much-repeated legend, James Drax and his companions lived for a time in a cave, searching for provisions, hunting turtles and hogs and also clearing land for planting. Henry Powell and his ship went on to the South American mainland to visit a Dutch settlement there. He left his nephew, another John Powell, as governor in Barbados. Henry was visiting the Dutch colony on the Essequibo River in Guinea, which had been partly funded by the Courteens.[13] The governor there, Amos van Groenewegen, was a friend of Powell's as they had sailed together in the past in the Courteen fleet. Groenewegen was helpful, and he was able to trade for seeds and plants – Indian corn, cassava, sweet potatoes, plantains, bananas, tobacco, citrus fruits and melons, all of which would be able to grow on Barbados. Henry was able to return with 30 or so of the Arawak Indians to instruct the settlers in growing these crops. They were convinced by van Groenewegen and Powell to voyage to Barbados and teach the English how to grow the unfamiliar crops. In return, the Arawaks were promised land and that they would be able to return home after two years with £50 of metal implements such as axes, plus looking-glasses and beads.

Meanwhile, in May 1627, John Powell arrived at Barbados in the *Peter* with 80 more settlers.[14] Whatever Drax's intent was, it was a high-risk venture. To make a fortune out of a tropical island was playing against the odds. Life expectancy for colonists was short. Pirates, shipwreck, raids by Caribs and other Europeans, heat, weather, hard work and disease would take their toll on voyagers and settlers. Somehow James Drax, and his friends James Holdip and William Hilliard, avoided these pitfalls. The first years would have been incredibly tough. Drax is later said to have claimed that he had arrived with assets of no more than £300 and that he 'would

---

13. Trinity College, Dublin MSS G, 14, 15: Henry Powell's Examination.
14. Parker, *The Sugar Barons*, pp. 16–17.

not think of Home, meaning England, until he had turned that initial investment into a landed fortune worth £10,000 a year'.[15] How an 18-year-old had £300, a large sum at the time if his father was a vicar, is unanswered.

THE RIVAL ROYAL GRANT

Back in London, a serious problem arose for the settler expedition. James Hay, the 1st Earl of Carlisle, had been abroad on a diplomatic task when the Courteen ships had been commissioned and sailed. On his return to London, Carlisle interceded with King Charles I to say he had the grant for the 'Caribee Islands' from James I dating from before the king had died in 1625. One account written many years later recounted:

> When the Earl of Carlisle returned from his embassy, he was surprised to hear of the settlement that had been made upon an island that was within his prior grant and resolved to defeat it: to this end, he made an agreement with five or six of merchants of London for ten thousand acres in the nature of a lease to be settled under the direction of a person of their choosing. The choice fell upon Charles Wolverstone, who went to Barbados with sixty-four persons, to whom the ten thousand acres has been granted.[16]

The Earl of Carlisle was a flamboyant and decadent character and in deep debt, but he had come down from Scotland to London with James I and was viewed as loyal by the Stuarts – a quality possessed by few of their courtiers. He had been an important fixer for James I. After James' death, he had influence with his son.[17] The invest-

---

15. John Oldmixon, *The British Empire in America, containing the history of the discovery, settlement, progress and present state of all the British colonies on the continent and islands of America. With curious maps ... done from the newest surveys* (London: J. Nicholson, 1708), p. 11.

16. Unknown, *A Short History of Barbados*, p. 6.

17. Parker, *The Sugar Barons*, pp. 22–23.

ing merchants, including Yorkshireman Sir Marmaduke Roydon, a prominent City of London merchant and one of Carlisle's major creditors, fitted out a ship to sail to Barbados and assert the Earl of Carlisle's claim. Arriving on 5 July 1628, with 64 settlers on board led by Charles Wolverstone, they disembarked further south than had the Courteen settlers at a large anchorage thenceforth known as Carlisle Bay, and the settlement there became Bridgetown. Soon after his arrival, Wolverstone issued a proclamation which treated the Pembroke settlement as usurpation and summoned the first settler group to appear in Bridgetown where the Carlisle settlers had set up camp. They initially submitted to Carlisle's authority. But in February 1629, Henry Powell returned from the Dutch colony to the island with 100 armed men, enticed Wolverstone to a conference and then seized and shackled him. The Courteen contingent were back in charge.

Eventually the dithering of Charles I came to an end. 'Although most lawyers thought Courteen had the better claim, royal instructions were issued confirming Carlisle as the rightful proprietor. Carlisle had proved the more dextrous courtier to the fury of the Courteens, who had now sunk £10,000 into their venture.'[18] The Earl of Carlisle sent out Captain Henry Hawley to be deputy governor of Barbados, as an advance armed party to await Carlisle's appointed governor, Sir William Tufton, and more settlers. Arriving in June 1630, Henry Hawley was to prove to be more of a warlord than one to impose the rule of law in Barbados. He appointed a governing board from his entourage. Not long after arriving, he tricked the leaders of the Courteen faction onto his boat on the pretext of a peace conference. But he arrested them, and John Powell and his brother were shackled to the mast and eventually deported to the St Kitts colony.

When Carlisle's actual governor, Sir William Tufton, arrived, Barbados was suffering a severe drought; the food crops were not yet established and the island's feral pigs were being hunted out,

---

18.   Richard B. Sheridan, *Sugar and Slavery: An Economic History of the British West Indies, 1623–1775* (Baltimore, MD: Johns Hopkins University Press, 1974), p. 129.

which all caused a period called the 'Starving Time'. Tufton accused Hawley of retaining supplies for himself and his governing council while workers had nothing to eat. Hawley had Tufton arrested on a pretext, charged him with treason, and then had him executed by firing squad in May 1631. Having proved entirely ruthless, it was clear Governor Hawley would be the dominant figure in Barbados. Ever adaptable, James Drax and his friend William Hilliard defected to the Hawley camp. Hawley was to remain governor until 1640, running a corrupt regime that favoured his intimates.[19] Hawley reneged on the agreement with the Arawak Indians brought over from the Dutch settlement in 1628 by Henry Powell and enslaved them – they were only released many years later.

INDENTURED SERVANTS

Somehow, amid all this infighting, the settlers were starting up their plantations mainly along the coast. Ultimately, 771 grants to potential planters were made of 67,929 acres (not including the 10,000 acres granted to the Royden syndicate), an average of 88 acres.[20] Areas were cleared by the indentured servants and the few enslaved people on the island at that point. The system was wide open to exploitation of the servants. In Barbados, as in other colonies closer to the equator, servants from the British Isles were ill-suited to working in the heat, suffering from sunburn and heat exhaustion and thus more vulnerable to disease. When Captain John Fincham visited Barbados in 1632, he commented that the indentured workers were kept more like slaves than servants. Feelings between servants and their masters were often poor.[21] Parker wrote,

---

19.   Parker, *The Sugar Barons*, p. 26.

20.   Ibid.

21.   Indenture was a means for people to migrate and pay their passage by work on arrival. The servants tended to be poor, seeking to get away from the depressions and poor harvests in the British Isles in the 1620s and 1630s, but not always. Some were persecuted dissenters. Typically, they signed on for five years, but some for as much as nine years, in return for passage, food and accommodation and then were released at the end of the period to either settle in their own right or return home with a golden handshake payment of say £10. Records show many came from the south-west of England. Some left Dorset, a county where

'In 1634, an attempted rebellion was only foiled at the last minute by an informer. Two brothers considered ringleaders, the Westons, were seized, and one was executed as an example.'[22]

Resupply of the colony could be tricky as the ships had to find the relatively small and isolated island. Sir Henry Colt, who visited the island, compared the challenge of sighting Barbados as finding a sixpence thrown down on Newmarket Heath. Its isolation did provide some advantage in that it made it harder for Spanish or other potential raiders to find them. Sir Henry stopped over for a couple of weeks in July 1631 on his way to settle on St Kitts. Colt was very contemptuous of what he saw:

> For your soil is naught, nothing else but loose sand. Your ground which you esteem the best is but the leaves and dashes of your trees. Dig but half a foot deep and there will be found nothing else but Clay. Your water is thick and not of the best.[23]

He also found the planters less than industrious, 'all things carrying the face of a desolate and disorderly show to the beholder'. He wrote that in ten days, 'I never saw any man at work.' He went on to note: 'Slowth & Negligence must only cause this people to want.' Most of settlers were young men who were argumentative and often drunk, creating an environment that was 'ye quarrelsome conditions of your fiery spirits'. Instead, the settlers wasted their time and money in 'fighting and gambling'. Colt was captivated by the island itself, noting in his diary of all the places he had visited 'not any pleaseth me soe well'.[24] Colt's negative views of what he saw may have been accurate, but it cannot have applied to all the settlers. However, he liked the exotic fruits he saw there for the first time and what became known as the pineapple which he described

---

the pay for agricultural workers was notoriously low. Others came in numbers from East Anglia, Ireland and Scotland.

22. Parker, *The Sugar Barons*, p. 26.

23. Vincent Todd Harlow (ed.), *Colonising Expeditions to the West Indies and Guiana, 1623–1667* (London: Hakluyt Society, 1925), p. 91.

24. Ibid., p. 73.

as tasting 'unto a great white ripe strawberry'.[25] Colt recognised the potential and that the 'air and soil produceth with a marvellous swiftness'.[26] The ship he was sailing on to St Kitts, anchored in Carlisle Bay, he recorded, was having to deal with servants trying to get on board to stowaway and try to get home, or at least away from Barbados.

TOBACCO

Certainly, James Drax and others were making way with their planting. Initially, it was food stuff to supply the settlers and then their first crop of tobacco which they knew had grown well in the colonies of Virginia and Bermuda. From the beginning of settlement, the planters went about the task of producing tobacco, the most profitable American agricultural staple on the European market. They wished to compete with, and replace, tobacco from the Spanish colonies on the European market. In 1623, Virginia tobacco reaching England was worth one shilling and sixpence per pound, and in 1625 three shillings per pound. These prices were profitable enough to spark tobacco fever among the West Indies planters who, between 1624 and 1629, turned Barbados and St Kitts into tobacco economies. In 1628 these two economies exported some 100,000 lbs of tobacco to London where it was sold at a price of nine pence per pound.

Then suddenly there was another setback that nearly killed off the colony; the price of tobacco on the London market plummeted due to oversupply. What was bought was the better-quality tobacco from plantations in Virginia and Spanish colonies. In 1632, the Privy Council in London ordered the restriction of tobacco production in the Lesser Antilles. The order stated that the 'great abuse of tobacco ... is so notorious that the King has directed the planting of it to be limited in St. Christopher and Barbados ... until such time as more staple commodities may be raised there...'.[27] Many

25. Ibid., pp. 66–67.
26. Ibid., p. 91.
27. Privy Council to the Earl of Carlisle, January 1631, *CSPC* 1574–1660, f. 124.

tobacco growers in Barbados ignored this order, and by the end of the decade, their volume of tobacco exports was still rising while those of Virginia and St Kitts were falling. But it was clear that another more economic crop was needed. James Holdip told a visiting French priest, Anton Biet, that he and James Drax were among the first group of settlers.

> They lived by hunting, which was good enough, and from provisions which had been left them by the ship. They cleared a piece of land which they planted in tobacco, and this grew so well that they produced an abundance which obliged the head of the band to carry it to England in the first vessel they met. As tobacco was scarce enough, he made a lot of money from it, which gave him the means to bring forty or fifty men back with him. He himself found out that this Island's tobacco was not the best quality; that is why they wanted to see if cotton and ginger would be better.[28]

After noting the faltering of the tobacco crop to reap big rewards for the colonists, Colt wrote in his diary, 'But now the trade of Cottons fills them all with hope.'[29]

DRAX COMES OF AGE

Despite all these problems, James Drax, who must have been growing up very quickly, wrote home in 1630 in glowing terms, and persuaded his slightly older brother William and his sister Frances to come out to join him. James Drax was clearing a plantation which he called Drax Hall. He had such a good crop of tobacco in 1629 he could pay for 50 indentured servants the next year.[30] When his brother William arrived, he took on what would

---

28. Antoine Biet, *Voyage de la France équinoxiale en l'Isle de Cayenne, entrepris par les François en l'année MCDLII* (Paris, 1664), pp. 268–295; Jerome Handler (ed.), 'Father Antoine Biet's Visit to Barbados in 1654', *The Journal of the Barbados Museum and Historical Society*, vol. 33, no. 2 (1967), p. 69.
29. Harlow, *Colonising Expeditions*, p. 91.
30. Larry Gragg, *Englishmen Transplanted* (Oxford: Oxford University Press, 2003), p. 89.

become Drax Hope Plantation which lay next to Drax Hall Plantation. James probably took the view that blood was thicker than water and he could do with all the reliable support he could get in such a politically dangerous environment as the island. The gender of the population of Barbados was heavily skewed toward young men. Nevertheless, and probably because he was already standing out from the crowd for industry and assertiveness, sometime in the mid- to late 1630s, James Drax married Meliora Horton from a Somerset gentry family. She may have been his distant cousin, Parker suggested. 'It is known, however, that James and Meliora's first child, also named James, was born around 1639. He seems to have been a sickly child. A second son, Henry, was born two years later.'[31] Six more children were to follow. Around the same time as her brother, Frances married planter Christopher Codrington of the highly regarded old Gloucestershire family.

James Drax was becoming a leading figure on the island, and at this key time of developing the infrastructure, he was a Commissioner for Roads, which would have been a vital post, and a captain in the militia. Aside from the risks from external raiders, the indentured servants had already shown dissent internally. So, a militia had been formed, and planters were the officers. James was on the island's Council and Assembly. One of the earliest documents in Barbados is of the Council for Barbados signing an agreement, dated 19 July 1639, with an agent in England. It states that the proceeds of the shipment referred to were to be applied for the 'managing of certain affairs concerning the said Island'.

> The Parties of the first covenant: that before 25th July, there shall be shipped in and upon the good ship called the *Exchange of London* (whereof is Master of this present voyage Mr Richard Lucas) 48,000 lbs. of good tobacco 'for the management of certain affairs concerning the said Island'. The said John Deane covenants that before he shall go to any port, he shall land or cause to be landed at 'Waymaith [Weymouth in Dorset, England] or

---

31. Parker, *The Sugar Barons*, p. 30.

some other convenient port as wind and weather will permit' and deliver to Mr Edward Cranfield and Capt. Edward Shelley, Agent for the 'manageing of the cuntries affaires', Bills of Exchange to be charged upon Mr. John Lepourtree manager of London, of a hundred and four score pounds sterling (£180) within 5 days after sight and on arrival at 'Weymaith' pay and deliver to Shelley and Craunfield £20 sterling more and also allow them all such moneys as they may have occasion to use to the value of £1006. The said John Deane is to sell the tobacco (40,000 lbs.) for the payment of £200 aforesaid for the best advantage of the Inhabitants of the Island that he can. And in case the said tobacco shall not make ... penny per lb. 'clear of all charges' then the said Councell and Assembly.[32]

Also, the early records show that in November 1639, Captain James Drax bought from Captain Hawley 200 acres of land.[33] In June 1640, Samuel Andrewes, by Bill of Sale, sold a plantation containing 200 acres of land to Capt. James Drax, in consideration of 8,000 lbs of cotton to be him paid before the 'ensealing' of the same deed, provided that the said Captain James Drax 'hath delivered to him at the Indian Bridge by the said Samuel Andrewes 20,000 "foot" of sound cedar boards 10 foot long and 3 foot or upwards broad'.[34]

ENGLISH GENTLEMEN

So much of Drax, Codrington and other gentlemen's culture resembled the duties of English landed gentry at home, of engagement with administration and business. And part of that package of 'duties' was to be an officer in the militia. There were already apparent external and internal threats to the island and the ever-present danger of a Spanish, French or pirate raid. Parker said

---

32. George H. Hawtayne, 'The Record of Old Barbados', in James Rodway (ed.), *TiMEHRi, The Journal of The Royal Agricultural & Commercial Society of British Guiana*, vol. X (1896), p. 94.
33. Ibid., p. 98.
34. Ibid., p. 97.

of James Drax, 'From the paltry evidence that survives, we know he was physically tough, solidly built and a stickler for debts being paid on time, which was a rarity in the free-wheeling colonies.'[35]

By the mid-1630s, cotton production was increasing, and the planters were learning how to process it. It was very capital-intensive, requiring a gin mill and a market preparation process. James Drax, William Hilliard and James Holdip went into cotton cropping, and the latter became some of the biggest cotton growers on the island. The profit margin was quite small. Indigo – which could be processed into the rich blue dye – was also cultivated, and both products had a ready market in England. But by the beginning of the 1640s, these markets were saturated, and the price began to drop. Barbados was 'in a very low condition, in regard commodities (then there produced) were onely Tobaccoes and Cotton-wools, which (by reason great quantities transported from these to other places) was of very small value', and 'small hopes appeared of reading any fortunes there for the future for the Inhabitants'.[36]

A cash crop with a high-profit margin was needed, and it required a crop that was particularly suited to Barbados' soil and climate.

---

35. Parker, *The Sugar Barons*, p. 29.

36. Nicholas Foster, *A briefe relation of the late horrid rebellion acted in the island Barbadas, in the West-Indies. Wherein is contained their inhumane acts and actions, in fining an banishing the well-affected to the Parliament of England (both men and women) without the least cause given them so to doe: Disposessing all such as any way opposed these their mischievous actions* (London: Lowndes and Boydell, 1650), pp. 1–3.

2

James and the Sugar Revolution

Back in London, from the mid-seventeenth century, the elite were often to be found sitting in the elegant day rooms of their aristocratic town or country houses, offering their guests exciting new delights from across the known world. They had tea from China, served in porcelain cups and saucers also shipped from China and sweetened by sugar from the West Indies. Gradually, with the expansion of trade, empire and tastes, the status of sugar changed from an expensive rarity to a popular consumer commodity in Britain as in Continental Europe. Quickly the demand for sugar grew, and planters switched to mass production of this lucrative trade, and it became cheaper and accessible in the wider population. For many years, Barbados was the prime supplier.

The story of the successful introduction of sugar crops to Barbados has several variants. The distinguished historian Richard Sheridan said, 'there is good reason to believing' Captain Henry Powell brought sugar cane to the island from Suriname in 1627.[1] If Powell did, it was not initially taken seriously as a crop as it was not thought to be viable to crop, process or sell. Some sources said that James Drax's fellow first settler, James Holdip, was the first to grow sugar and made two limited attempts to grow cane commercially in 1639 and 1642, but it was unsuccessful.[2] But according to all sources, it was James Drax who was central to the founding story of the successful cultivation of sugar in Barbados. Requiring strenuous work under the hot tropical sun by the workforce to cultivate, sugar cane also required skill and organisation to bring forth a viable crop. James Drax led the way in making it a lucrative crop, but it was not an easy task.

---

1. Sheridan, *Sugar and Slavery*, p. 129.
2. Parker, *The Sugar Barons*, p. 13.

Richard Ligon's arrival in Barbados provided the most detailed account of the island. He found 'trees, such as I had never seen before ... many of them extreamly large and beautifull'.[3] At the time, Barbados was still so heavily forested that the scarcity of labour deterred potential planters from exploiting land in its interior. However, Drax's workers, including African and Carib enslaved people, cleared inland a plantation area on St George's Valley, near the 'Top of the Cliff', with the most fertile soil on the island. Here, it was said, away from the other plantations, Drax secretly experimented with growing sugar until he got it right. Some versions of the sugar foundation story say that, with Dutch help, James Drax had the expertise and equipment to produce a crop. Once cut, his workers used a three-roller mill and furnace coppers brought from Pernambuco to crush the canes, boil the juice, and eventually refine it into saleable sugar. The industrious James Drax's reputation in Barbados was sealed as a 'genious' (*sic*). The contemporary writer John Scott attributed the first plantings of sugar to James Holdip and James Drax:

> the sugar cane had been had from Brazile... and was first planted by one Colonell Holdip, who was the first that made sugar in Barbados, but it came to little untill the great industry and more thriveing genious of Sir James Drax engaged in that great worke who brough[t] Collonell Holdups essay, to soe great perfection...[4]

Drax Hall was in the interior on the border of St George's and St John's parishes. It is unlikely that sugar growing on such a small island could have been a secret for long. Other plantation owners started planting sugar cane. After poor annual harvests initially, Drax discovered that the crop should be cut after 15 months rather

---

3. Richard Ligon, *A True and Exact History of the Island of Barbados*, ed. David Smith, 5th edition, e-text, 2014 (1657), p. 119.

4. John Scott, *Some Observations on the Island Barbadoes* (1667) and transcribed by Jerome S. Handler and Lon Shelby, in 'A Seventeenth Century Commentary on Labor and Military Problems in Barbados', *Journal of the Barbados Museum and Historical Society*, vol. 34 (1973), 117–121.

than twelve for the best crop. After a period of experimentation, by 1644 he had planted, grown and milled sugar cane and sold refined sugar commercially. Drax Hall Plantation became Plantation One for the British sugar trade. After that the move to producing sugar was the obvious choice for planters. By 1645, Drax was taking three times the profit from land previously growing tobacco and other crops.[5] At this time land in Barbados was selling for about 10 shillings an acre. The success of the sugar crop would drive up the price of land.

THE SECRET

On arrival, Richard Ligon was told that sugar-making was new on the island and experimented with refining sugar, 'by new directions from Brasil, sometimes by strangers, and now and then by their own people'.[6] Through trial-and-error and consultation with the Dutch, Ligon reported that 'about the time I left the Island, which was in 1650 they were much better'd'. The planters, Ligon continued, had recently found the secret of refining sugar so it was pure white.[7]

As sugar became a major commodity, Drax and one of his partners, a pioneering settler from 1627, William Hilliard, also innovated with sugar as a form of reliable financial currency and were the first to pay for enslaved people and supplies with sugar. They thought efficient sugar production demanded that the workforce be closely managed and carefully coordinated. Sugar cane spoiled within a short time after being cut and had to be transported directly to the sugar mill for refining. Especially at harvest time cutting and processing became a 24/7 industrial operation requiring shifts. Working in the fields was always dangerous, involving sharp tools and the constant danger of bites from snakes, centipedes and other venomous creatures.

---

5. J.E. Buchanan, 'The Colleton Family and the Early History of South Carolina and Barbados, 1646–1775', PhD thesis, University of Edinburgh, 1989, p. 21.
6. Brazil was under Dutch control from 1630 to 1654.
7. Ligon, *A True and Exact History*, p. 85.

Crucial to quality sugar refining was the use of 'ingenios', the refining centre with their great mills and boiling vats. All this required investment, estimated at the time as around £14,000 for a three-year start-up for a sizeable plantation. Based on these initial successes, Drax and others expanded sugar operations rapidly by taking on a series of investors and business partners now seen as an early development of capitalism.[8] A notable investor was Dorset aristocrat Anthony Ashley Cooper, the 1st Earl of Shaftesbury, who funded Gerrard Hawtayne in his 205-acre sugar plantation.

A RUM BUSINESS

The production of a single hogshead[9] of muscovado sugar could yield as much as 100 gallons of molasses, and while some might be used for animal feed and yet more exported as a cheap alternative to sugar, most would be distilled by planters to make rum.[10] This provided them with an additional and extremely valuable export commodity and a useful product for the 'reward' of the enslaved workforce. So, every large plantation had a still house, in which was the still for combining molasses, inferior cane juice, and even the skimmed impurities from the boilers. It was by combining all of these ingredients 'that the greatt qvantaty of Rum is Made'. Once mixed in a large vat, these ingredients fermented for at least a week, after which the liquid was heated, vaporised in the still, and then condensed into rum. Making, storing and transporting the highly inflammable rum was dangerous work. Ligon recorded the gruesome death of 'an excellent' enslaved African who brought a candle too close to a barrel of rum in the still house.[11] Early on, planters were installing windmills – advanced technology that increased the output of muscovado – while the use of local clays in the refinement process increased the quality of muscovado produced in Bar-

---

8. Gragg, *Englishmen Transplanted*, pp. 136–137.

9. A hogshead is the size of a barrel used to hold sugar and other products. They measured 48 inches (1.22 m) long and 30 inches (76.20 cm) in diameter at the head.

10. Another by-product was treacle, which is similar to molasses.

11. Ligon, *A True and Exact History*, p. 93.

bados.[12] This all made sugar products more and more desirable on the European markets.

Ligon gave a detailed account of the various types of workers needed to run an *ingenio* and emphasised the importance of a 'Prime Overseer', observing that without such an employee, the planter alone will 'have too much to do'. This 'supreme overseer' was to be the intermediary between the planter and the 'subordinate overseers', receiving general instructions from the plantation owner and translating them into more specific directions further down the chain of command:

> The Prime Overseer may very well deserve Fifty pounds Per Annum, or the value in such Commodities as he likes, that are growing upon the Plantation; for he is a man that the master may allow sometimes to sit at his own Table, and therefore must be clad accordingly. The other five of the Overseers, are to be accounted in the ranke of Servants, whose freedome is not yet purchased, by their five years' service, according to the custome of the Iland...[13]

Ligon noted a group of enslaved African people residing on James Drax's plantation who were likely there because of their experience in sugar processing.

> Some of them, who have been bred up amongst the Portugalls, have some extraordinary qualities, which the others have not; as singing and fencing. I have seen some of these Portugall Negres, at Collonell James Draxes, play at Rapier and Dagger very skilfully, with their Stookados, their Imbrocados, and their Passes.[14]

THE REVOLUTION

Historian B.W. Higman described the sugar revolution as 'a concatenation of events located in the seventeenth-century Caribbean

---

12. https://whc.unesco.org/en/tentativelists/5942/.
13. Ligon, *A True and Exact History*, p. 172.
14. Ibid., p. 57.

with far-reaching ramifications for the Atlantic world' and said it consisted of six key elements: 'a shift from diversified agriculture to sugar monoculture, from production on small farms to large plantations, from free to slave labour, from sparse to dense settlement, from white to black populations, and from low to high value per capita output'. Like most of the revolutions of economic history, the sugar revolution concept has developed and diffused, tending to take on new elements and expanding claims made for its significance.[15]

Sugar came in various forms each with a different price, depending on purity. As the century progressed it was not just something available only to the privileged, albeit the less well-off might use lower purity. The multiple-refined white sugar remained the most expensive, but the poorer consumer could also buy ordinary brown sugar or dark viscous molasses, known as treacle. Recipe books from the period are filled with ideas for how to use the ingredient, from sprinkling on salad to a fine plum cake. Sugar was particularly useful as it kept fresh goods for longer, turning low-calorie perishable fruit into preserves and jams.

By 1637 the Drax brothers had created a third plantation called Mount next to Drax Hall. By 1643 the Drax brothers were growing sugar at Mount, Drax Hall and Drax Hope. Drax had at least 400 acres at Drax Hall by 1640 and was constantly buying and selling land, as were other leading planters.[16] In 1644 James Holdip sold 200 acres of Locust Hall plantation to Thomas Applewaite, a London cloth merchant. The deed stipulates that Holdip will provide to Applewaite 'so many sugar canes to plant upon his premises sold as shall be needful'. The land deal was also contingent on Applewaite receiving a batch of servants from an incoming English ship.[17] Edward Oistin,[18] Henry Hawley and James Drax

---

15. Barry W. Higman, 'The Sugar Revolution', *The Economic History Review*, vol. 53, no. 2 (May 2000), 213.

16. At some point, James bought his brother William out of his share of the plantations for £5000, a considerable sum at the time.

17. Deeds, RB 3/1, 536–8, Barbados Department of National Archives (BNA), and is also reprinted in Anon, 'Applewaite of Barbados, Pt. II', p. 11.

18. Oistin gave his name to the fishing village in the south-west corner of the island where today tourists and locals are attracted to the Friday-night fish fry for food, drink and music.

owned plantations of over 300 acres, which were then large by Barbadian standards; Captain Futter owned 1000 acres, and Hilliard over 700.[19] The average size of plantations was 80–100 acres. Sir Hilary Beckles, the Barbados historian of slavery, has said that even at an early stage of colonisation, capital was important in developing plantations and that is supported by the fact that 10,000 acres of the most fertile belonged to a London merchant syndicate.[20] By 1643 Barbados could be described as 'grown the most flourishing Island in all those American parts... [and] in all the world for the producing of sugar'.[21]

THE LIGON VISITATION

Those souls disembarking from sailing ships in Carlisle Bay arriving from British or African waters were met by a scene of organised chaos as they witnessed the loading and unloading of many vessels across Barbados' main harbour. It was a moment of emotional turmoil for those whose passage was complete, some having boarded voluntarily and others not. They found themselves in an exotic world where their futures were utterly uncertain. For the British emigres, if they arrived in summer, the heat alone would have been shocking. Many of those arriving were indentured servants. The British state also foisted a large number of deported vagrants and criminals to Barbados, all sentenced to provide involuntary labour for the plantations. On Ligon's ship was a group of servant women, 'the Major part of them, being taken from Bridewel [jail], and such like places of education'.[22] Private merchants also sold people to planters. At this time, to be 'Barbadosed' took on the meaning of the more modern term 'Shanghaied' as quite a few were

---

19. Hilliard was involved in at least 36 land deals on the island. See Deeds, Deeds Index and Counterdeeds Index, RB 3/43–44, BNA. On Hilliard as a council member, see 'Extracts from the Council Books of Barbados', 13 October 1641 to 2 May 1652.

20. Hilary Beckles, 'A Riotous and Unruly Lot', in S.A. Newman, *New World of Labor* (Philadelphia, PA: University of Pennsylvania Press, 1985), p. 22.

21. Parker, *The Sugar Barons*, pp. 12–14.

22. Ligon, *A True and Exact History*, p. 13.

kidnapped and put on ships. Children were stolen from their homes and shipped to the colony.

By his own account, Richard Ligon was over 60 on his arrival in Barbados and down on his luck. As David Chan Smith noted in his edited version of the Ligon book, Richard Ligon was a connoisseur of the good life of the gentleman and found beauty not only in places and people but in living itself:

> He was himself something of a 'bon vivant' schooled in the arts and the art of living well and was identified as a 'gentleman' in legal documents. For Ligon, the life of the gentleman had its own aesthetic, its own form of beauty and elegance and one which he describes when he comes to discuss the planters in Barbados. Foremost, the gentleman was defined by his separation from manual labour. The gentleman governed, judged, and exercised hospitality so that he might live a beautiful life. Through the gentleman's consumption and celebration of plenty, he marked himself as separate from the labouring classes under him and from whom he extracted his profits (in the case of planter society, the profit was from the sale of commodities rather than rents). Ligon aspired to this idealised lifestyle of the gentleman, celebrating the arts of the hunt and hospitality and taking pride in displaying his gourmand's knowledge of cooking. His writing describes how the privileged existence of the English gentleman was translated into the Barbadian context.[23]

Ligon took a liking to Drax and was the source of the famous quote that James Drax 'lived like a Prince', which was a positive in Ligon's view.[24] He admired the multi-course lengthy meals Drax provided for friends accompanied by quantities of strong liquor listed in detail over several pages. Ligon noted rarities found on Drax's table:

---

23. Richard Ligon, edited by David Chan Smith, *A True & Exact History of the Island of Barbados* (2004) p. xv, www.davidchansmith.net/_files/ugd/f295da_6be20a8c375345f9a9709c93affa13d7.pdf.

24. Another contemporary said that 'James Drax is the richest man in Barbados, if not the West Indies.'

Beef, we have very seldome any, that feeds upon the soyle of this place, except it be of Gods killing, (as they tearme it); for very few are kill'd there by mens hands; it were too ill husbandry, for they cost too dear, and they cannot be spared from their work, which they must advance by all the means they can. Such a Planter as Collonell James Drax (who lives like a Prince) may kill now and then one; but very few in the Iland did so when I was there.[25]

When Drax slaughtered a cow, it gave him a chance to create goodwill among his peers through a 'great Regalio, to which he invite[d] his fellow Planters'. Ligon's favourite places to dine were Colonel Modyford's coastal plantation and Drax Hall.

And for the Inland Plantation, I will make choyce of Colonel James Draxes, at whose Table I have found well drest, these following meates; for the first Course whereof there hath been two messes of meat and both equally good, and this feast is always when he kils a beef, which he feeds extreamely fat, giving him a dozen acres of Bonavist to go loose in, and due times of watering.[26]

And that was just one part of a feast. It has to be said that Sir Henry Colt was more impressed by the feast in his honour by planter Captain James Futter as the 'best' planter at the time. The feast included pigs, capons, turkey, chickens, maise, cassava and cabbages 'whose stemme or stalk was 200 feet long and you must cut them down with an ax [the young leaves of the cabbage palm]'.[27]

Historians of colonial seventeenth-century Barbados have noted that the island's planters engaged in excessive drinking. Richard Dunn commented how 'the chief planters in the English islands dined richly, drank copiously, and entertained lavishly... Dinner and after-dinner drinking lasted four or five hours.'[28] A contemporary

---

25. Ligon, *A True & Exact History*, p. 82.
26. Ibid., p. 82.
27. Harlow, *Colonising Expedition*, p. 76.
28. Richard S. Dunn, *Sugar and Slaves: The Rise of the Planter Class in the English West Indies, 1624–1713* (Chapel Hill, NC: University of North Carolina Press, 1972), p. 279.

diarist, Father Antoine Biet, noted that they indulged in quality, imported and locally made alcohol so that 'when they dine, no one is forced to drink, one drinks willingly... whatever one wants: wines from Spain, Madeira, the Canaries; French wines, and sweetened mauby'.[29]

Then, after one has dined:

A staff of African slaves and white servants cleared the table and set out a trencher full of pipes and another full of tobacco, along with a bowl full of brandy. They added sugar and eggs, set it on fire, and let it burn down. Next, the host took up a fine little silver cup, fill[ed] it with this liquor and [drank] to the health of whoever is in front of him. All present repeated this ceremony of communion and hospitality.

Such occasions were, according to Biet, merely a way to pass an afternoon for those elite island men.[30]

Contemporary historian Charles de Rochefort wrote that the Caribbean planters were men of 'Quality', because of their 'entertainments' and their well-dressed 'Tables'. De Rochefort said the planters of the Caribbean likewise attempted to 'outvye' each other for the grandest feast. Barbados' lack of local produce and isolation made the acquisition of food and European drinks an especially effective way to demonstrate individual wealth and quality. An eyewitness account by Henry Whistler of the *Venables* expedition[31] described the conditions on the island a year after Biet's 1654 visit:

---

29. Mauby is made from the bark of the mauby tree, boiled with cinnamon, orange peel, nutmeg and cloves, and sweetened to taste.

30. Biet, *Voyage de la France équinoxiale*. Fr. Antoine Biet, a French Jesuit priest and missionary, had been sent to Martinique and Guadeloupe. The French colony there had failed, and he was sailing with a group of displaced settlers who were on Barbados awaiting a passage to a European port. He kept a detailed account of his time on the island.

31. General Venables headed the Cromwell-supported Western Design, which is the name given for an English expedition against the Spanish West Indies during the 1654–60 Anglo-Spanish War. It was not a success.

The gentry here doth live far better than ours do in England... And they have that liberty of conscience which we so long in England have fought for, but they do abuse it... This Island is the dunghill whereupon England doth cast forth its rubbish. Rogues and whores and such like people who are generally brought here... A whore if handsome makes a wife for some rich planter... The Island of itself Is very delightful and pleasant... If the traveller does deny to stay to drink they take it very unkindly of him.[32]

PLANTATION WOMEN

There is little record of the role of plantation wives, but visitors' diaries give a few clues. Beit's description tells us that the planters viewed drinking in their social class as a male activity. Respectable Barbadian plantation women did not seem to have partaken in the more boisterous aspects of Barbadian drinking culture. They attended balls and other such occasions. Biet noted that plantation hospitality made it:

Not necessary for them to have taverns in the countryside, for when an English lady sees someone pass by, she freely asks if he needs anything. She invites him into the house, has him sit in a hammock... and she immediately brings some brandy or any other drink that is desired. She does this with such graciousness and with such good nature that one can ask for nothing more.[33]

Women's hospitality and generosity thus replaced the role of the tavern in English culture for island men. The twentieth-century historian couple, the Bridenbaughs, noted, 'As more women appeared in the colonies, household furnishings began to accumu-

---

32.   C.H. Firth (ed.), *Extracts from Henry Whistler's Journal of the West India Expedition. The Narrative of General Venables, with an Appendix of Papers Relating to the Expedition to the West Indies and the Conquest of Jamaica, 1654–1655* (London: Longmans, Green, 1900), pp. 145–147.
33.   Jerome Handler (ed.), 'Father Antoine Biet's Visit to Barbados in 1654', *The Journal of the Barbados Museum and Historical Society*, vol. 33, no. 2 (1967), 68.

late, and the old pioneer, masculine atmosphere dissipated in the better plantation houses.'[34] Father Biet was to write that, in her husband Major Byam's absence, his wife 'one of the most beautiful women I had ever seen', Dorothy Knollys, frequently hosted such admiring guests. According to Biet, who was clearly not above the delight of the opposite sex, said Knollys 'sighed deeply, saying that she would have hoped her husband had been on the Island, and that we would have seen much more to him'.[35]

Biet offered praise for island women but only for their service to the contentment of male guests. Biet defined gracious hostesses in these terms: 'She fills a pipe, lights it herself, and presents it when it is lit.' Women were ancillary in all accounts of Barbadian feasting culture. Their supporting roles confirmed their subordinate position within the household and island social structure. As elsewhere in Christendom, the hostess was judged according to 'feminine' qualities of 'beauty' and 'graciousness', whereas the same hospitality for a man spoke to his ability to provide and advanced his standing in society.[36] However admiringly writers like Biet looked upon island women, their actions ultimately spoke to the male host's generosity and worth in a largely unchallenged patriarchal world.

As scholars have noted of English culture at the time, the behaviour of all family members was seen as a reflection of the household head's masculine capability. As the later writer John Oldmixon confirmed, the 'fashionable and courtly' ladies of the island lent the male planters an 'Advantage of most of our [English] Country Gentlemen'. The graces of their wives, to outside male observers like this, largely affirmed the worth of the husband. Yet the gender segregation in Barbados seems to exceed that in English landed gentry social settings of the time.[37] Of all the merchants active in buying land and developing plantations in Barbados from the

---

34. Carl Bridenbaugh and Roberta Bridenbaugh, *No Peace Beyond the Line: The English in the Caribbean, 1624–1690* (New York: Oxford University Press, 1972), p. 135.

35. Biet, *Voyage de la France équinoxiale*, pp. 268–295.

36. Ibid., pp. 268–295.

37. John Oldmixon, *The British Empire in America, containing the history of the discovery, settlement, progress and present state of all the British colonies on the con-*

1640s to 1660s, only one was a woman. This was Beatrice Odiarne, who continued running the business after the death of her husband, Thomas.[38] Odiarne is a Huguenot name, and it is likely they were people who had moved to London as refugees and then onto the Caribbean. What she had been left by her husband was not a large tract of land.

The greatest problem for the planters, man or woman, was to get a workforce that could farm the difficult crop of sugar. Indentured servants from Britain were mostly not suited to the hard work in a hot climate and were only there because of their poverty back in Britain. Many were from the workhouses or prisoners of war. Hayes linked English destitution with transatlantic trafficking, which he referred to an 'an extreme version of a time-honoured hierarchy in England'.[39] James Drax was replacing his servants with what he saw as cheaper and better workers – enslaved people from Africa – who could survive longer in the harsh working environment of the integrated plantation.

---

tinent and islands of America. With curious maps ... done from the newest surveys (London: J. Nicholson, 1708), pp. 114 and 119.

38. Hilary Beckles, *The First Black Slave Society* (Kingston, Jamaica: University of West Indies, 2016), p. 17.

39. Nick Hayes, *The Book of Trespass* (London: Bloomsbury, 2020), p. 148.

3
James Drax and Chattel Slavery

How rich Barbados is, and how much worth
We well may see by Sugars, it brings forth
Of all the rest, the Richest Merchandize
And if by th' patern, we may judge ot'h' piece
How Rich it is in men, we well may see
By bringing forth brave Drax such men as thee.

(Richard Flecknoe, 'On the Riches o'th' Barbadoes',
from *Epigrams of all sorts*, 1670)

After a battle at sea, the crew of the *William and John* captured a Portuguese ship. On board the prize were the first enslaved people said to have been taken to Barbados for the English settlement, numbering around ten people. The *William and John* was on its voyage to take the Courteen settler party to the island early in the New Year of 1627. These captives were almost certainly from the west coast of Africa, where the Portuguese traded. Sources on slavery in Barbados are very scarce for this early period, and the enslavement of the original group of Africans is attested in two letters by the same person. Eighteen-year-old Henry Winthrop, who had arrived with the second colonising party of about '50 men', wrote to his uncle in August that, aside from English settlers, Barbados contained '50 slaves of Indyenes and blacks'.[1] Two months later, he notified his father that there were 'but 3 score of christyanes and fortye slaves of negeres and indyenes'.[2]

---

1. The 'Indyenes' may well have been the Arawak Indians that Henry Powell had brought back from the Dutch settlement to help with cultivation but were then enslaved by Governor Hawley. They were eventually released much later.
2. Henry Winthrop, Letter to Emmanuel Downing, 22 August 1627; Letter to John Winthrop, 15 October 1627. Winthrop Papers (vol. 1, 1645–9: 356–7, 361–2), Massachusetts Historical Society, Boston, MA.

The English had episodes of selling and using enslaved people before the settlement of Barbados. One of the best-known sea captains of the English Tudor period, Sir John Hawkins, was born into a wealthy maritime family in the port of Plymouth in the county of Devon. His father, William Hawkins, had sailed to the Americas in 1527 and traded in Guinea and Brazil and was also presented in the court of Henry VIII. By his mid-20s, John Hawkins was already making voyages to distant locations such as the Canary Islands. While mainly trading in textiles and sugar, there are reports of piracy by Hawkins. While several other Englishmen had already enslaved people from Africa by the mid-fifteenth century, Hawkins created what would be the English version of the triangular trade that took people enslaved in Africa to the New World.

Early in his career, in 1562, Hawkins led a voyage in which he kidnapped 300 Africans in what is now Sierra Leone and transported them to Spanish plantations in the Americas. There he traded them for hides, pearls and sugar. His missions were so money-spinning that he persuaded Queen Elizabeth I to underwrite his subsequent voyages and she ordered he should be given ships, supplies and guns in exchange for part of the profits. She also awarded him a coat of arms bearing a bound enslaved person. Initially English pirates made inroads into the slave trade by capturing other nations' slave ships and selling the African captives. In the earlier years of the seventeenth century, the Dutch were the leading maritime nation and slave-traders. The English swiftly sought to get into the maritime trade that the booming colonies opened up. The English triangular trade involved ships leaving London with goods to trade for enslaved people. Captives were then traded for sugar, tobacco and other commodities and they were taken to London or other European ports. It did not often involve the same ship going round the triangle as slave ship interior layouts were not suitable for carrying large loads of commodities. So different types of ships sailed the different routes. Those on board the *William and John* were not the first enslaved people taken to an English West Indian colony. In April and May 1626, merchants Maurice Thomson and

Thomas Combes sent three ships carrying 60 slaves to their 1000-acre tobacco plantation on St Kitts.[3]

David Brown, historian of seventeenth-century English maritime trading, noted the Atlantic slave trade had begun to have an impact on other areas of the English economy, which was orientated towards manufacturing cloth. English wool clothing quickly became important to the slave trade. One kidnapped African person on the Gold Coast 'could be purchased for approximately two bales of perpetuanos, a type of hard woollen cloth. The cost of manufacturing this quantity of cloth in England was less than ten pounds in 1659.'[4]

INHERENT DISCRIMINATION

One historian of slavery, Jerome Handler, showed from the records that Europeans automatically assumed that people with dark skins were slaves:

> In Barbados, they [enslaved Africans] were never sanctioned or made explicit in any law though they were implicitly present in the worldview of Anglo-Barbadians when Africans arrived with the first colonising party. In addition, African birth or descent, or 'race', was attached to slave status from the beginning of the colony, years before it was clearly implied in the island's slave laws.[5]

An early example of the slave trade to Barbados was the voyage of the English ship *Marie Bonadventure* which delivered 251 African captive to Barbados in July 1644. James Drax and William Hilliard purchased captive Africans. Drax paid by promising to ship to England 'soe much suger or other merchantable commodities as shall amount to the value of the said some of £726 sterling'.

---

3.   Robert Brenner, *Merchants and Revolution* (London: Verso, 2003), p. 127.
4.   Brown, *Empire and Enterprise*, p. 207.
5.   Jerome Handler, 'Custom and Law: The Status of Enslaved Africans in Seventeenth-century Barbados', *Slavery and Abolition*, Vol. 37, No. 2 (2016), 233–255.

Before long, more elements would be added to this trading system, but the global flow of goods, capital and profit became firmly established and was controlled by very few hands. The industrialisation of plantations as they grew from a cottage industry created ancillary work and jobs back in England. As early as 1653, a planter ordered iron castings from an Oxford foundry for his *ingenio* mill rollers. Tools were ordered on a large scale by planters. Some idea of the demand for metal manufacturers is given by the following order sent to England before the 1693 Barbados harvest: 50,000 nails, 600 hogshead and barrel hoops, ten brass fittings for the mill frame, twelve ladles, six skimmers, three sheets of lead, ten brass fittings for the mill frame, and a 70-gallon copper.[6] All these arrived and passed through the port of Bridgetown.

As historian Robin Blackburn pointed out, before the exploitation of the West Indies, all the English were known for was the export of woollen goods, but after the West Indies, not only were tobacco, rice, indigo, cotton and sugar exported but:

> the colonies imported nails, pots, buckles, implements and utensils of every description, together with a variety of textiles. The Navigation Acts not only channelled products to the metropolis but also ensured that the plantation colonies became significant customers for English goods. They permitted a multilateral pattern of trade between England, Africa, the plantation zone and the American colonies.[7]

Between 1550 and 1650, England underwent a profound commercial change and was transformed from a marginal island power on the north-west fringes of Europe, whose main overseas commercial activity was the export trade in woollen cloth, to a nation with an aggressive merchant community that ventured across the globe but particularly to the New World.[8] With demand outstripping

---

6.   Robin Blackburn, *The Making of New World Slavery: From the Baroque to the Modern, 1492–1800* (New York: Verso, 1997), p. 337.
7.   Ibid., pp. 267–268.
8.   Michael D. Bennett, 'Merchant Capital and the Origins of the Barbados Sugar Boom, 1627–1672', PhD thesis, University of Sheffield, 2019.

supply, the market price was high and planters in Barbados were growing rich. In the 20 months prior to 1650, the sugar produced had helped to raise the total value of Barbados crop to the vast sum of £3,097,800.[9]

THE CHATTEL SYSTEM

Into the 1630s West Indies planters relied on the indentured servants. To the entrepreneurial James Drax it was clear that their productivity was too low and that enslaved Africans could be worked harder and systematised to working long hours. As historian Professor Howard W. French noted, 'But it was in Barbados, and in particular on the Drax plantation, where the economic potential of this brutal system became most apparent.'[10] In 1641 James Drax purchased 22 enslaved people brought from Africa at the point where most planters still had none, or only a few, and were reliant on indentured servants. He purchased another 34 Africans two years later, and by the 1650s, up to 200 Africans were labouring and dying on his lands at any given time. This was a very large number for any kind of European enterprise in this era. In the earliest stages of the plantation economy white indentured labourers tended the fields alongside enslaved Black people. Most African captives at this early point came from the West African area known as Guinea. By 1644, the population of Barbados was estimated at 30,000, of which about 800 were of African descent, with the remainder mainly of English, Scottish or Irish descent. Early on, Drax bought a group of enslaved Africans, including a man named Moncky Nocco. He was to have a family that was to be the leading enslaved family of Drax Hall for several generations. He would become head of the first work gang

---

9. Carl Bridenbaugh and Roberta Bridenbaugh, *No Peace Beyond the Line: The English in the Caribbean, 1624–1690* (New York: Oxford University Press, 1972), p. 81.

10. Howard W. French, 'Chasing Slavery's Ghosts: The Drax Family Sugar Cane Legacy', *Mail and Guardian*, 21 January 2023, https://mg.co.za/africa/2023-01-21-chasing-slaverys-ghosts-the-drax-family-sugar-cane-legacy/, last accessed 11 June 2024.

of the plantation and is the only enslaved man in the early days of Drax Hall whose name is known.

DRAX AND THE INTEGRATED PLANTATION

James Drax continued to 'live like a Prince'. Around 1654, Drax is said to have invented the 'integrated plantation', which proposed an optimal ratio of two acres to every labourer. Plantations were divided up into 10-acre 'pieces', which allowed for staggering the crop. Drax restructured the operation of the plantation to maximise efficiency and created a model other planters copied. The visiting Jesuit priest Father Biet exclaimed how it 'was quite a sight to see 200 slaves working with sugar' at the Drax Hall plantation. Biet reported that one of Drax's overseers was a Frenchman named Monsieur Raince, who had previously worked at a sugar refinery in Rouen.[11] Integrated plantations needed economies of scale, so the dominant planters increased the size of their plantations, buying out smallholders. By 1657 plantation sizes had doubled, though only one or two ever exceeded 1000 acres. With the expansion of labour needed for intensified sugar production, the village where enslaved people lived was located further from the main house and nearer to the works at Drax Hall to maximise output in the fields and at the sugar processing works.

The demand for enslaved people was quickening. Professor French postulated that Drax must have calculated that it was cheaper to work enslaved Africans to their death and then replace them with newly imported Africans than look after them so they would live longer.

No one was spared, including pregnant women who were forced into the fields, often carrying atop their heads large vats of dung to fertilise the quickly depleted soils.

A consequence of this in-human bottom-line-dominated mindset was that the average life expectancy for Africans from

---

11. Ibid.

49

the moment of arrival in Barbados was as low as five years. This gradually became the template throughout the sugar-growing islands of the Caribbean.[12]

It was one of the Noell family of Barbados merchants who made, the now infamous, observation that it was possible to 'keepe three Blacks, who better and cheaper than one white man'. Drax took the view that his enslaved people were not just unpaid labour but could be used for amusement as though performing pets. James Drax would take Richard Ligon around the plantation. One Sunday, Drax took Ligon to see some of the 'amusements' that could be performed by his enslaved people. Ligon later described the scene:

> Excellent Swimmers and Divers they are, both men and women. Collonell Drax (who was not so strict an observer of Sundaies, as to deny himselfe lawfull recreations) would sometimes, to shew me sport, upon that day in the afternoon, send for one of the Muscovia Ducks and have her put into his largest Pond, and calling for some of his best swimming Negres, commanded them to swim and take this Duck; but forbad them to dive, for if they were not bar'd that play, they would rise up under the Duck, and take her as she swome, or meet her in her diving, and so the sport would have too quick an end. But that play being forbidden, the duck would make them good sport for they are stronger ducks, and better Divers by farre then ours: and in this chase, there was much of pleasure, to see the various swimmings of the Negroes; some the ordinarie wayes, upon their bellies, some on their backs, some by striking out their right legge and left arme, and then turning on the other side, and changing both their legge and arme, which is a stronger and swifter way of swimming, then any of the others: and while we were seeing this sport, and observing the diversities, of their swimmings, a Negro maid, who was not there at the beginning of the sport; and therefore heard nothing of the forbidding them to dive, put off her peticoate behind a bush, that was at one end of the Pond, and closely sunk down

---

12.   Biet, *Voyage de la France équinoxiale*, pp. 268–295.

into the water, and at one diving got to the Duck, pul'd her under water, & went back againe the same way she came to the bush, all at one dive. We all thought the Duck had div'd: and expected her appearance above water, but nothing could be seen, till the subtilty was discovered, by a Christian that saw her go in, and so the duck was taken from her. But the trick being so finely and so closely done, I begg'd that the Duck might be given her againe, which was granted, and the young girle much pleased.[13]

Henry Hawley was still the governor and considered by most on the island as a drunk and tyrant. Some academics have argued that he brought in the first ever informal slave code in Barbados in 1636' which laid down that enslaved black people brought to Barbados should be enslaved in perpetuity. However, some historians doubt it ever existed.[14] There is no actual physical record of the code. Equally, there is no evidence that Drax opposed the code's essence, and Drax already had more enslaved people on his plantations than any other planter.[15]

As the largest owner of enslaved people, James Drax would have influenced the rules as to how enslaved people were treated on the island. No one has located a copy of this 1636 code, and some historians do not believe a written code existed until one was published by the Barbados Assembly in 1661. James Drax was undoubtedly either the first or one of the first to impose chattel slavery on his captive people. As Richard Blome stated in 1678, describing chattel slavery: 'The Negro Slaves are never out of their Bondage and the

---

13. Ligon, *A True and Exact History*, pp. 52–53.
14. Reference to the 1636 slave code first appeared in a 1741 publication, *Some Memoirs of the First Settlement of the Island of Barbados*, and was said to stipulate that 'It was resolved that Negroes and Indians that came here to be sold, should serve for life, unless a contract existed to the contrary.' Jerome Handler discusses whether the code existed: 'An Early Edict on Slavery in English America: The Barbados Resolution of 1636 and the Island's Slave Laws', *Journal of the Barbados Museum and Historical Society*, vol. 65 (2019), 22–43.
15. Governor Hawley's tyranny ended with his arrest, and he was shipped back to London charged with corruption. He was replaced briefly by another English government appointment, who in turn was to be replaced after a year or so by Sir Philip Bell, an elderly and apparently wise man.

Children they get, are likewise perpetual slaves.' Mia Mottley, KC, Prime Minister of Barbados, has stated the imposition of chattel slavery was the beginning of racism.[16]

The belief system of these early settlers deemed that enslaving Africans was morally acceptable. As more enslaved people were brought to Barbados there is evidence that planters developed harsh working and living practices on their enslaved people from an early stage of colonisation. The white population grew to over 18,000 by the mid-1640s, including many indentured servants, both voluntary and coerced. During this period, 'Negro slaves' increased to around 6000, a number that rapidly rose as sugar production intensified. By the mid-1650s, the European population of approximately 25,000 exceeded the roughly 20,000 Africans. Between 1640 and 1660 alone, Barbados planters spent around £1 million purchasing enslaved Africans, perhaps twice the amount they spent on equipment, land, livestock, and everything else required for plantation agriculture.[17]

SLAVE LIFE

Richard Ligon described the brutal, repetitive lives of servants and enslaved people on the island. A bell rang them to 'work, at six a clock in the morning, with a severe Overseer to Command them'. Five hours later, they 'are set to dinner... a meagre affair of local roots and liquor made from sweet potatoes. At one a clock, they are rung out again to the field, there to work till six.' Living conditions, Ligon continued, were harsh:

> If it chance to rain, and wet them through, they have no shift, but must lie so all night. If they be not strong men, this ill lodging will put them into a sicknesse.

16.   Lecture at LSE, London, 6 December 2023, www.youtube.com/watch?v=Z-RCD5eoOzuI, accessed 11 June 2024.

17   Simon P. Newman (ed.), *A New World of Labor: The Development of Plantation Slavery in the British Atlantic* (Philadelphia, PA: University of Pennsylvania Press, 2013), p. 192.

They were housed in slave cabins. 'These Cabins are to be made of sticks, withys, and Plantine leaves, under some little shade that may keep the rain off; Their suppers being a few Potatoes for meat, and water or Mobbie for drink.'[18]

Other sources also indicate that life on the plantation was relentless. Sunday was a day of rest, but from Monday morning to the following Saturday afternoon, all hands on a plantation who laboured in the field were at work, daily, from sunrise to sunset. The enslaved Africans worked afield in gangs of 10 or 20, according to the ability of the overseers who supervised their work. It was so exhausting, back-breaking and dangerous that there was an attrition rate far higher than natural deaths. Probably most enslaved people were burnt out before they reached middle age. The enslaved were often dead by their fifth year in Barbados. Unlike many other slave systems, including some other European systems, enslaved people and their descendants were trapped in the system for life with only the remotest hope of emancipation. As time passed, avenues for enslaved people to achieve their freedom were closed off so that by the end of the seventeenth century even slaves who converted to Christianity could not be freed by their conversion.

The Code of 1661, which formed the basis of subsequent racially based laws throughout the English colonies of the Caribbean and mainland North America, was passed into law by the Barbados Assembly.[19] James Drax's close friend Colonel Modyford, as speaker of the Assembly, was deeply involved in drafting this piece of legislation entitled 'The Act for the better ordering and governing of Negroes'. This is the most infamous piece of legislation passed in the islands during the seventeenth century. Handler noted:

> The 1661 law repealed all former laws relating to enslaved people, but it incorporates some features of statutes enacted in the 1640s and early 1650s that were relevant to current issues and conditions. While most clauses in the 1661 law relating to public order and policing, a characteristic feature of most West Indian slave

18. Ligon, *A True and Exact History,* pp. 72–73.
19. A handwritten copy of the Code can be found in the BDA.

laws, enslaved people still required protection from 'the arbitrary rule and outrageous wills of every evil disposed person, and thus they should be protected *as we do many other goods and chattels*'.

Handler further points out that, although this Act does not define the status of 'slave', it is the first law which explicitly identifies slaves as chattel property. 'It bears emphasis that the language of this law does not suggest it is creating a new understanding of slave status but rather merely clarifying an already existing dimension of it.'[20]

The preamble of the Code assumes enslaved Africans are chattels, goods that can be moved from place to place, not human beings with rights. To justify this degradation, they were, as Edward Said would describe 400 years later, 'othered', reduced to a lesser racial – indeed subhuman – status.[21]

It was common at the time for the English to suggest that enslaved Africans were closer to monkeys than humans. The Code characterises them as 'a heathenish, brutish and an uncertain, dangerous kinde of people'. It was, in part, designed to protect the white population from the enslaved African population which was rapidly growing in number as the sugar industry expanded and the slave trade expanded to meet demand. Notably, it saw slaves as human, 'being created Men' but implied they were sub-human in that they had 'no knowledge of God'.

The Code divided plantations into a hierarchy of three, white owners, white servants and black slaves, all with different rights and obligations. Enslaved people had few rights, were constrained in just about every way and received much harsher punishments for infringing the laws. Masters had to provide their enslaved black people with one new outfit of clothes per year, but there were no

---

20.   Handler, 'Custom and Law', p. 233.

21.   Edward Said, *Orientalism*, 25th Anniversary Edition (New York: Vintage Books, 2003), p. 3. In his seminal book *Orientalism*, Edward Said proposed that the concept of the Orient was an assembly of mental maps and socio-cultural attributes constructed, represented and consolidated through the discourse of orientalism, that ultimately, served to define and consolidate Western identity, since 'European culture gained in strength and identity by setting itself off against the Orient as a sort of surrogate and even underground self'.

rules about their food or working conditions; masters could punish their slaves in any way they liked, and if the enslaved person died in the process, there was no penalty, though a heavy fine could be imposed for wantonly killing an enslaved person. The enslaved person had no recourse to a court of law. Indentured servants were better served by the Code, which had minimum food and clothing allowances, and they could appeal to the court if mistreated; the master could be tried for murder if the servant died at his hands. Brutal disciplinary practices compounded the misery. Ligon noted, 'If they complain, they are beaten by the Overseer; if they resist, their time is doubled.' Above all, Ligon's account highlights the extraordinary violence that planters in Barbados relied on to subjugate both servants and the enslaved. He professed that he had 'seen an Overseer beat a Servant with a cane about the head, till the blood has followed, for a fault that is not worth the speaking of; and yet he must have patience, or worse will follow'. A decade on, when writing his account of his visit, Ligon was still appalled at the excessive use of physical punishments, especially against whites, lamenting 'truly, I have seen such cruelty done to Servants, as I did not think one Christian could have done to another'.[22]

Such a dehumanised system needed enforcement. Enslaved people suffered harsh punishments for minor crimes, by whipping, branding or having their nose slit. Murder, rape, arson, assault or theft of anything worth above one shilling in value were capital crimes.[23] This system constituted a reign of terror for the African population (and those enslaved from other lands) of the West Indian islands. It was set up to control the working population, making the sugar industry and its vast profits possible. Some see the Slave Code of 1661 as the beginning of the institutional racism of white supremacist attitudes that were not seriously challenged until the late 1960s and have still not been dispelled. Fearful that they would have to treat their enslaved people better, they also removed the possibility of them being Christian. Though later, missionaries who

---

22. Ligon, *A True and Exact History*, p. 44.
23. TNA C.O. 30/2 Barbados laws 1645–1682.

wanted to convert the enslaved had some success in undermining these rules.

James Drax was not only a plantation owner, as we shall see, based on documents held in the archives, he was also engaged in human trafficking. The original British settlers, Drax, Holdip and Hilliard, were men of social standing in Barbados due to their plantations and the numerous public offices they held within the colonial council, assembly, militia and parish vestries. As in England, those with land controlled the levers of power. Braddick has written that elite English planters asserted a collective identity throughout the Atlantic by marking themselves through the purchase and display of the same luxury material goods. This 'material culture' and the comportment of oneself as a 'gentleman' were essential to social and political authority in the English Atlantic.[24] Meanwhile they accrued vast amounts of money. But wealth was to create envy and enemies. We will return to Barbados after revealing the dramatic events back in Britain that were impacting another key part of the family that would later merge with the Drax bloodline.

---

24. Michael J. Braddick, 'Civility and Authority', in David Armitage and Michael J. Braddick (eds), *The British Atlantic World, 1500–1800* (New York: Palgrave Macmillan, 2009), p. 115.

PART II

The Erles of Charborough

4

An Estate Fit for an Erle

Elegant and imposing, Charborough House nestles on a slight rise, screened from the outside world but with its own delightful panorama. Rebuilt, circa 1660, the mansion was created in the style of the most famous architect of the period, Inigo Jones.[1] In the centuries since it has been extended and restyled, most notably by the architect John Nash around 1810, with two rear extensions of the Victorian period.[2] It will forever be associated with the Plunkett-Ernle-Erle-Drax family who have resided at Charborough for five centuries. In *The Buildings of England*, the eminent architectural historian Sir Nikolaus Pevsner commented that Nash had homogenised the house by means of 'stucco, a new hipped roof and a central five-bay pediment carried on the north front on Ionic pilasters'.[3]

Imposing on the outside, the interior is said, by those privileged to be invited in, to be correspondingly impressive. Of the house's central feature, the staircase hall of circa 1718, Pevsner said, 'This represents high fashion of that moment, and is a room of first-rate quality.'[4] He also praised other decorative features of the house. The walls and ceilings were painted by the fashionable artist Sir James Thornhill, who was also responsible for the painted ceiling of the great hall of Greenwich Hospital and paintings in St Paul's Cathedral, London. A member of a family from nearby Wareham, Thornhill was the first artist ever to be knighted for his work, as the foremost decorative artist of his day, and to have him paint your interiors was a statement about your wealth and social standing.

---

1. The Drax family believe Inigo Jones may have designed it.
2. A very detailed description of the house, park and parish can be found at: www.british-history.ac.uk/rchme/dorset/vol2/pp160-173, accessed 11 June 2024.
3. Michael Hill, John Newman and Nikolaus Pevsner, *Dorset. The Buildings of England* (New Haven, CT and London: Yale University Press, 2018), pp. 190–191.
4. Ibid.

The high-quality art still hanging in the house includes numerous portraits of family ancestors.

Along the path is the private family chapel of St Mary, once the parish church of the long-lost village, but rebuilt in 1775 and then unsympathetically remodelled in the early Victorian period. Nearby are the estate's walled garden, a grove, a deer park, an icehouse, extensive outbuildings, stables, garages and offices. These all lie in the 1500-acre Charborough Park. Pevsner, who was not usually lavish with his praise, remarked, 'The landscaped Park is the most splendid in Dorset, the clumps and belts of trees majestically mature.' Within the park is the Highwood Garden, created by the present occupant's grandfather, Admiral Reginald Aylmer Ranfurly Plunkett-Ernle-Erle-Drax, which in his day contained a superb collection of rhododendrons and azaleas in a woodland setting.[5] There is a looming folly tower built in 1791 which is a significant landmark visible in the surrounding countryside. The great narrator of Dorset, Thomas Hardy, based his novel *Two on a Tower* on Charborough House, and as was his wont he renamed it for the fiction 'Welland House'.

Splendid as the park is, the family like their privacy and it is rarely open to the public.[6] The idea that the Drax family protect their privacy is nothing new. In *Hardy Country* (1905), Charles E. Harper noted the difference between Charborough Park and Hardy's fictional Welland House. 'Charborough is very closely guarded against intrusion, and none who cannot show a real reason for entering is allowed through the jealously closed and locked gates of the lodges.'

---

5. Charborough Park is four miles west-south-west of Wimborne Minster and one-mile south-west of Sturminster Marshall. The 1500-acre park includes some 12 acres of gardens. To the east and west, the park adjoins agricultural land, while to the south, it is bordered by a minor road leading south-east from the A31 road to Lychett Matravers, from which a further nineteenth-century brick wall separates it. There are extensive views to the north-west across the valley of the River Stour and west across the Winterborne valley from the high ground within the park: https://historicengland.org.uk/listing/the-list/list-entry/1000713?section=official-list-entry, last accessed 11 June 2024.
6. Then owned by Sarah Charlotte Elizabeth Ernle-Erle-Drax.

The residence of the fictional Lady Constantine was, by comparison, very readily accessible, and:

> as is occasionally the case with old-fashioned manors, possessed none of the exclusiveness found in some aristocratic settlements. The parishioners looked upon the Park Avenue as their natural thoroughfare, particularly for christenings, weddings, and funerals, which passed the squire's mansion, with due considerations as to the scenic effect of the same from the manor windows.[7]

The regime under Admiral Drax seemed to be more relaxed and in 1927, a few months before his death, Hardy asked to have another look at the folly tower. He was invited over for lunch and, despite a cold, walked with the family round the tower.[8] In the 2020s, as in 1905, Charborough Park is rarely open to the public. It hosts charity events and some school visits just a few days a year. It is a favourite location for dinners for Conservative Party supporters and shooting weekends. One well-known conservative writer told me Charborough is the best Dorset shoot, packed with pheasants. But 'Private. No admittance' signs at every entrance seek to deter the uninvited. The 'right to roam' campaigner Nick Hayes described in *The Book of Trespass*, which argues for public access to the huge swathes of private land in Britain, how he deliberately trespassed into Charborough Park with the intent of camping there for the night to make a symbolic point. He and a friend had wandered for several miles across the estate:

> Eventually, while making our way through planted pines, we were discovered by a gamekeeper. There's no way through here, he said, evidently expecting my friend and I to ignore the path on which all three of us were standing. Very politely, and in no uncertain terms, we were chucked off the land.[9]

---

7. Charles E. Harper, *Hardy Country* (London: Black, 1905), p. 173.
8. Ernle-Erle-Drax, *History of Charborough*, p. 99.
9. Nick Hayes, 'A Very English Theft: How the Countryside was Taken from the Public, Using Profits from Slavery', *Daily Telegraph*, 19 August 2020.

DRAX HALL

Just before Charborough House was rebuilt in Dorset, 4000 miles away, James Drax had erected a new house. Built of coral-stone, Drax Hall is a classic example of Jacobean manor house architecture, which was popular in England from when the two Drax brothers and a sister sailed from England in the 1620s. It has steep red gable roofs, coral-stone corner finials and casement gable windows. It could be more elegant, like nearby St Nicholas Abbey House. However, it boasts spectacular original carving on the grand three-storey staircase and the wide-arched doorway into the stair hall. Also, it has excellent stone carving and balustrades on the upper landing. Like Charborough, Drax Hall was built to demonstrate the position of its owners in the social system and to contain art and artefacts reflecting the owners' wealth and taste. Like Charborough, Drax Hall sat and still sits amid a working business, the sugar plantation that dates to the 1630s when the Drax brothers had it hacked out of the fertile forested St George's Valley. Today, at the top of the plantation's drive are two large oil cans with the sign 'Private no Admittance'.

These two houses, an ocean apart, lie at the heart of the Drax family's history and wealth. It is the story of one landed-gentry family's experience of the emergence the British Empire, the development of British society over half a millennium, and their interaction with the thousands of people who worked and slaved for them to create the family's wealth. Charborough is the epicentre of the Drax family story and is the chief, though veiled, indicator of the family's status. Drax Hall plantation was a lucrative colonial outpost from which its English proprietors derived considerable additional money. From the English and overseas income combined, the family has made Charborough House and Park an epitome of the British vision of what constitutes high culture and beauty, whether in architecture, representative or decorative art, or landscape.

The Draxes of Drax Hall in Barbados and Jamaica and Ellerton in Yorkshire became united with the Erles, the owners of Charborough House. The story of how the Erles came to possess and develop

Charborough is also significant. The current Plunkett-Ernle-Erle-Drax family traces the main trunk of the family tree back to the Erles of Somerset and Devon.

FROM THE BEGINNING

Twenty years after the Battle of Hastings, William the Conqueror commissioned the famous financial survey of the kingdom to record the land values on which taxation could be based. In 1087 the survey results were written up as what came to be known as the Domesday Book, a unique record of the state of post-Conquest England.[10] As Domesday records:

Rex tenet Cereberie – [the new Norman King] William, holds Charborough. The King has one manor, which is called Cereberie, which paid geld for 5 hides.[11] This manor is worth £9 per year, and when the man [Fulcred, a Norman Lord] received it, it was worth as much.[12]

The book notes it had 13 houses – occupied by five householders, four villagers, four smallholders and notably four slaves.[13] The Domesday Book entry for Charborough tells us that a watermill already existed at nearby Doddings.[14]

The history of Charborough from the eleventh century is recorded in detail in *The History of Dorset*, a voluminous and, for its time, a

---

10. Hundred: in the Domesday Book, within each fief, holdings are normally described in a regular geographical order, determined by the hundreds in which they were located. Hundreds were the primary administrative subdivisions of a county, with a significant role in financial, military, judicial, and political matters, centred upon the hundred court, which met monthly.

11. Geld: a tax paid to the crown by landholders under the Anglo-Saxon and Norman kings.

12. R.B. Pugh (ed.), 'The Domesday Survey of Dorset and the Dorset Geld Rolls', in *Victoria History of the County of Dorset*, vol. 3 (London: Oxford University Press, 1968), p. 66.

13. https://opendomesday.org/place/SY9297/charborough/.

14. South-east of the village of Bere Regis, Doddings Mill was on the Bere Stream, a tributary chalk river and later part of the Charborough Estate.

rigorous and methodical study by John Hutchins (1698–1773), a Dorsetshire clergyman and topographer.[15] Hutchins reported that Charborough was held by a succession of Norman knights and their descendants; the families involved over the next 400 years included de Paunton (by 1299), de Ivelton (by 1372), Morvyll (by 1397), Camel (by 1420) and the Wykes (c. 1450). Charborough was given over to sheep farming, on a feudal estate farmed by tenants, as was much of Dorset, with supportive arable farming.[16] King John had a hunting lodge in the nearby village of Bere Regis and visited the manor house there at least 16 times during his reign (1199–1216).[17]

In May 1348, the outbreak in England of the epidemic of the bubonic plague known as the Black Death, quite possibly brought in through the port of nearby Melcombe Regis (now part of Weymouth), caused significant disruption of the agricultural economy and consequent changes in land usage, wages and social structures. A plaque in Weymouth records that the plague arrived there, noting, 'It killed 30–50% of the country's total population.' Dorset was the first county in England to be ravaged. Dorset agricultural historian Barbara Kerr noted the impact of the plague, especially on the east Dorsetshire area:

The Black Death and the social unrest which succeeded it in the 15th Century accounted for the fall of many old families and the rise of new ones. The manor of West Morden passed to a servant of a man whose family had been manorial tenants, and a new star appeared in the firmament of East Morden: the Erles of Charbor-

---

15.   In the 1730s, John Hutchins, the vicar of the Dorset villages of Swyre and Melcombe Horsey and later rector of Holy Trinity, Wareham, began research for his *History of Dorset*. He spent nearly 40 years on the task. His wife Anne saved his work from destruction during the Great Fire of Wareham in 1762. Hutchins completed a draft before he died in 1773. The first edition was finally published a year later. It is worth pointing out that while an invaluable resource, it does contain inaccuracies. Updated by editors in the nineteenth century, it was written much closer in time to many of the events told. It still underpins the understanding of Dorset history.

16.   As far back as the Roman period, woollen clothing was exported from the local ports.

17.   www.bereregis.org/manor-bere-regis.htm, last accessed 10 July 2024.

ough.[18] The ascent of the Erles and many other rising families was favoured by the Tudors, who dreaded the over-mighty power of the old nobility even more than mediaeval monarchs had done.[19]

As we will see the Erles were to join with Draxes by marriage in the early eighteenth century. The Erles were of English rather than Norman origin and enlarged their landed estate significantly. They moved into Dorsetshire through shrewd exploitation of royal favour and a very good marriage. Henry VIII's schism from the pope and the Roman Catholic Church in 1534 created the Church of England in the spirit of Protestantism that crossed from the Continent. Some families were to benefit enormously from the turmoil, and one was the Erles.

WALTER ERLE THE MUSICIAN

Walter Erle I, whom I will call Walter the Musician, was the first Erle to rise to prominence and Charborough.[20] 'Nothing is known concerning Walter Earle', an early music expert declared in 1973 and, at the time, that was pretty well correct. All that was known was that someone of a similar name had written a pavane during the reign of Henry VIII.[21] A slow, stately dance, the pavane was popular in the sixteenth and seventeenth centuries, and 'Maister Earle's Pavane' was found in a sixteenth-century book of musical scores.[22] It would now seem that sometime around his twentieth

---

18. Erle gets a variety of spellings, including Earl, Erley and Earle. I will use Erle.
19. Barbara Kerr, *Bound to the Soil: A Social History of Dorset* (London: John Baker Publishing, 1975), p. 31.
20. The Erle, Drax, Ernle and other related families whom this book documents have, over the years, used a small range of Christian names such as Walter, Thomas, Edward, Richard, Henry, James, Sarah, Elizabeth, Jane, Caroline, etc., so I have taken the liberty of identifying them where necessary as I, II, III for clarity. This is not a formal suffix.
21. David Pinto, 'Walter Earle and his Successors', *The Consort*, vol. 49 (1993), pp. 13–16.
22. *The Complete Works of Anthony Holborne II Music for Cittern*, ed. Musakata Kanazawa (Cambridge, MA, 1973) featured no. 35, 'Maister Erles Pavane' for

year (circa 1535–40), due to the family's royal connections, Walter Erle was sent up from Devon to London and attached to a court of King Henry VIII. As he set off, this must have seemed an exciting adventure and an excellent opportunity to further himself. Walter would have been based at Hampton Court, which was Henry's preferred palace. He had taken it from the out-of-favour Cardinal Wolsey and refurbished this enormous, elegant complex with an opulence designed to reflect the home of the English king. This is where the young man from Devon would have spent much of his time as a royal servant, but also sometimes on the move, as the royal procession moved around the country.

Piecing together Walter Erle I's life in Henry's courts was a detective tale, with Professor Nicholas Sandon as the sleuth. Walter was born between the middle and end of the second decade of the sixteenth century. While researching his thesis on early music in the 1970s, the then doctoral student Sandon had come across variant forms of a surname, Erley and Erell, in the Peterhouse Henrician partbooks, a set of musical manuscripts dating from late in the reign of Henry VIII.[23] They contain the scores of 72 pieces of Latin Church music, including one called 'Ave vulnus lateris'. Sandon said of the piece, 'this votive antiphon in honour of one of the five wounds of Jesus is fluent and ambitious and shows an understanding of the vocal medium; it may have been sung by a small group of chamber singers rather than by a larger ecclesiastical choir'. Sandon deduced that this was the same person who composed 'Maister Earle's Pavane'. Curiosity about this myste-

---

cittern and bass viol: Anthony Holborne, *The Cittern Schoole* (1597) sig. Hv-H2. See also Cambridge, University Library MS Dd.4.23. ff. 2–3, 'Walter Earles Pavan'; and Giles Farnaby, 'Walter Earles Paven' for keyboard. *Musica Britannica* (MB) xxiv (London, 1965) no. 18, from Fitzwilliam Virginal Book, p.3 41. no [235].

23. Nicholas J. Sandon, 'The Henrician Partbooks belonging to Peterhouse, Cambridge (Cambridge University Library, Peterhouse Manuscripts, pp. 471–474): A Study, with Restorations of the Incomplete Compositions Contained in them'. Submitted by Nicholas John Sandon to the University of Exeter as a dissertation for the degree of Doctor of Philosophy in Music in the Faculty of Arts, February 1983.

rious composer led Sandon, then at the University of Exeter, to spend time poring through records of the Tudor period. He uncovered the first reference to a royal servant called Walter Erle in *The booke of Certayne of the Quenys Ordynary as yet to no place Appoynted*. This is the earliest surviving document he found in the archives which mentions Walter. It is a list from circa 1541 of 127 abovestairs members of a queen's existing household whose appointment to new positions is underway but incomplete. Erle is named as one of the 'three Pagis of the Chamber Ordynary'.[24]

Sandon said, 'This unusual document is a fair copy, not a draft, and it must have been compiled for a specific purpose by a well-informed administrator. Its title announces that it lists members of a queen's customary household whose appointment to new positions is envisaged but not completed.' He concluded the queen in question to be Catherine Howard, the fifth wife of Henry VIII who was later accused of adultery by her husband. Sandon stated, 'If this first record of Erle's presence at court establishes him as a page to Catherine Howard towards the end of 1541, it by no means proves that he was not at court in some capacity before this time.'[25] He noted David Pinto placed the list among records dating from early January 1540 and thus linked it with Anne:

> However, the membership of the higher ranks of the household named in the list shows such a strong Howard affinity that it is difficult to believe that the household is not Catherine's. Assuming that it was drawn up in full knowledge of current events, we can probably date it within the six weeks between 11th November 1541, when the Privy Council told Cranmer[26] of the King's decision about Catherine's immediate future, and 22nd December when a royal proclamation denied her the title of queen.[27]

---

24. Nicholas Sandon, *Edward Hedley Terrenum sitiens regnum. Walter Erle Ave vulnus lateris.* (Antico Edition RCM112, 2018), p. iii.
25. Ibid.
26. Cranmer was archbishop of Canterbury (1533–56) and a leader of the English Reformation who was responsible for establishing the basic structures of the Church of England.
27. Pinto, 'Walter Earle', pp. 13–16.

Though Walter seems to have left no personal written documents, there is archival evidence of Walter's relationship with music. A payment to him had been made in June 1542 for a pair of virginals in Hertford's household accounts drawn up by Edward's steward, including a 30 June 1542 payment of 40 shillings to 'Water Erley by my lady's comandement for a payre of virginalls', the lady in question being Anne Stanhope, Hertford's second wife. Sandon remarked that this reference, which appears not to have been noticed before is:

> significant for several reasons: it is the earliest dated reference to Erle in the orbit of the royal household; it is the earliest to link him with the Seymour family; it is – by several decades – the earliest to place him in a musical context and to associate him with a keyboard instrument; and it is the only known reference that spells his name in a manner identical with one of the Peterhouse spellings.[28]

Another clue to Erle's special position is that as a groom of the Privy Chamber, he is listed alongside several musicians when Queen Mary allocated their liveries, a hint of a dual role. But other grooms are not listed. It would seem that as well as being a royal servant, he was a musician of the Chamber.

Walter Erle kept a position at court after Catherine Howard's execution in February 1542 and, according to Sandon, was transferred to the household of Edward Seymour, Earl of Hertford, the eldest brother of Queen Jane Seymour, the third wife of Henry VIII.[29] Sandon deduced the politics of this move, 'I would see Erle's transfer to Edward Seymour's employment as being a way of keeping him at court until a suitable position within the royal household could be found; the King's marriage to Catherine Parr solved the problem.'[30] Erle returned to a royal household following the sixth and last marriage of Henry VIII to Catherine Parr on

---

28. Sandon, *Edward Hedley*, p. iv.
29. Jane died in 1537 after childbirth.
30. Sandon, *Edward Hedley*, p. iv.

AN ESTATE FIT FOR AN ERLE

12 July 1543 and became a Gentleman Waiter to that queen, as is evident from the final entry in a mid-1540s list of additions to the royal household's expenditure:

> Item, yt ye 2nd day of November in ye 35th yeare (i.e. of his reign, 1543), ye Kings pleasure was declared by ye mouth of Mr Herbert, yt Walter Earle shoud yearly have ye Wages of £10 in lieu of a Gent Wayter to ye Queens Grace.[31]

Here, three and a half months after the marriage of Henry VIII and Catherine Parr, Erle was allocated an annual salary as an attendant upon the queen. Catherine Parr outlived Henry by a year and eight months. Just three months after Henry's death, Catherine remarried to Thomas Seymour, 1st Baron Seymour of Sudeley, Lord High Admiral of England, the brother of Edward Seymour. As a long-time member of the court, Thomas Seymour already knew Walter Erle, whom he referred to in a letter to his wife as 'my old friend'.

DANGEROUS INTRIGUE

Edward Seymour was the 1st Duke of Somerset and the Lord Protector of England from 1547 until 1549, 'protecting' his nephew, King Edward VI, during his minority. In 1548 Edward Seymour's brother Thomas's 'imprudence and recklessness now became increasingly manifest', and Erle became caught up in his master's plans, which involved seizing control of his nephew, Edward VI. Thomas Seymour had offered the services of Walter the Musician to provide lessons on the virginal to Princess Mary, Edward's eldest sister. Shortly afterwards, at Thomas Seymour's request, Walter passed on a letter to Mary. What Walter probably did not know was the letter was an attempt to persuade Mary of Seymour's case to instigate a coup. The letter was later discovered by those investigating the plot and used as evidence against Thomas Seymour, for which he was executed. It must have been a nerve-racking period

---

31. Walter Erle (died 1581), Wikipedia, last accessed 11 June 2024.

for Walter. Luckily, his role in the conspiracy was deemed wholly innocent, and he suffered no penalty. However, he lost his patron and was absent from court circles for another two years.[32]

Further preferment followed when at Christmas 1550, Edward VI made Walter Erle a Groom of the Privy Chamber. Walter was a survivor in the mercurial world of the Tudor courts. As Sandon observed:

> When the King died on 6th July 1553 Erle could congratulate himself not merely on having survived the various crises of the reign but with having improved his position. An idea of his increasing affluence is given by the lay subsidy assessments made of him in November 1545 and April 1552: in the former year 22s at one shilling in the pound on income from land, and in the latter year 50s at one shilling in the pound on moveable goods.[33]

Erle had kept his membership of the Privy Chamber on the accession of Queen Mary, although the nature of his actual position is unclear. About a year later, Mary promoted him to the position of Gentleman.

Another early music historian to take an interest in Walter the Musician was Dr Andrew Ashbee BEM, and he noted that in 1556 Walter presented Queen Mary with a New Year's Gift, 'a booke covered with blacke vellet of the Comentary of Warre, in Englishe'.[34] At least in part, the key to Erle's rise was his musical ability and expertise in playing the virginal (a predecessor of the piano). Music and musicians were a prominent feature of life in Tudor palaces, particularly at the pleasure palace of Hampton Court. Dancing, masque and recitals were key entertainments that the king and his court enjoyed. On a winter evening in the household, Walter would have been requested to play to entertain with

---

32.   Sandon, *Edward Hedley*, p. vi.

33.   Ibid., p. vii.

34.   Andrew Ashbee, 'Groomed for Service: Musicians in the Privy Chamber at the English Court, c.1495–1558', *Early Music* (Oxford University Press), vol. 25, no. 2 (May 1997), 185–197.

the day's popular music. He was clearly accomplished, as evidenced by the rewards he was given. Further confirmation of Erle's musical activity is offered by a collection of vocal music copied in 1742 by John Immyns, founder of the Madrigal Society, where folio 1 recto is annotated, 'The following Seven from a Manuscript written in ye year 1551 and wch belonged to Walterus Erle one of the Gentlemen of ye Bedchamber to K. Henry ye 8th.'[35] Erle is now best known in early music circles for 'Ave vulnus lateri' from the Peterhouse College manuscripts.[36]

REWARDS AND MARRIAGE

On 2 November 1543 letters of patent were issued granting Walter Erle the offices of Bailiff and Hayward of the manor and hundred of Colyton, Devon, and of keeper of the park and mansion of Colcombe, just north-east of Colyton. These privileges had been confiscated in 1539 from the Marquis of Exeter on his attainder, with effect from the previous Michaelmas, with fees of 52s. per year as Bailiff and Hayward and 2d. per day as keeper of the park and mansion of Colcombe.[37] There were more benefits to come. Then the king's chief minister, Thomas Cromwell had seized land and treasures and destroyed or closed over 800 monasteries and other religious houses. Like many of his contemporaries at court, Erle used his privileged position to acquire, at presumably advantageous prices, former monastic lands following the dissolution of the monasteries. In September 1544, with two associates, his relative Thomas Strowde, and a James Paget, Walter raised the then enormous sum of £2875 12 shillings 3 pence to purchase, via the Court of Augmentations, sell-offs from various West

---

35. Sandon, *Edward Hedley*, pp. ix–x.
36. Sandon edited and revised the Peterhouse manuscript, and the Boston-based professional ensemble Blue Heron performed Erle's 'Ave vulnus lateris' live at First Church in Cambridge Congregational, on 3 February 2018: www.youtube.com/watch?v=Z53Kcv505Zg&t=176s, last accessed 11 June 2024.
37. Sandon, *Edward Hedley*, p. iv.

Country estates. They then re-sold at a profit, having received from the king the requisite licences.[38]

On 22 October 1549, the bells rang out at the then 300-year-old St Andrew's Church in Colyton, positioned near a fine Anglo-Saxon cross, as Walter Erle married Mary Wyke, the third of four daughters of another member of the Devon landed gentry, Richard Wyke of Bindon. Richard had died without sons around 1540, leaving four daughters, all co-heiresses. Mary's share of her inheritance included the manor of nearby Bindon and a half moiety of her father's larger estate at Charborough. With growing income from his position at court, Erle purchased the other moiety from Alice, Mary's elder sister, and made it his principal residence. The acquisition of Charborough was a significant step up for the Erle family. Sandon stated, 'His successful exploitation of his position, and his employers' evident appreciation of his services, are reflected in the numerous grants of property and other perquisites that he received over more than thirty years.' Erle had been given grants of other lands by the Crown in 1543, which Pinto said, 'started to make him a substantial local figure that he remained, residing chiefly at Charborough'.[39] Erle also received rewards from Princess Mary in 1544, 'perhaps for playing the virginals to her'.[40] In 1544 Thomas Seymour purchased several speculative acquisitions of former monastic lands from Walter Erle. Walter also had property deals with Edward Seymour, from whom he purchased a 21-year lease in Ottery St Mary, Devon, in 1548, including 'the Wardeyen's House' of the dissolved college.[41]

By then a Groom of the Privy Chamber to Edward VI, on 11 July 1552 he was granted the manor of Axmouth, Devon, that had fallen into Crown possession on the suppression of the Bridgettine Abbey of Syon, Middlesex.[42] In 1553 he was granted the reversion of the leaseholds of various ex-monastic properties in Devon,

38. Ibid., p. v.
39. Pinto, 'Walter Erle', p. 13.
40. Ashbee, 'Groomed for Service', p. 196.
41. Sandon, *Edward Hedley*, pp. iii–vi.
42. Pinto, 'Walter Erle', p. 13.

AN ESTATE FIT FOR AN ERLE

including part of Cistercian Dunkeswell Abbey.[43] The lease of the monastery Newnham Priory, in east Devon, also Cistercian, was prolonged to him by patent dated 18 December 1555. Erle did well during his years as a royal servant. The historians M.W. Helms and John P. Ferris judged, 'The Erles were not of much account in their native Devonshire before they moved to Charborough, which they had acquired by marriage, about the middle of the 16th century.'[44] Henry's sell-off of the Catholic Church lands maintained the dominance of landowners over the hierarchy of tenants and agricultural workers.

The time where Walter the Musician takes up residence at Charborough coincides, around 1549, with the period that the term 'landed gentry' began to be used. This emergent class encompassed those landowners who were not members of the nobility. The essential requirement was a country house and estate of some size. It was not exclusive, but, as it was informal, it required existing members of the gentry to accept any newcomer by dint of correct social manners, an understanding of the need to protect their collective interests and a willingness to assist in holding the offices of power in the county and military.

Now a wealthy gentleman, Walter made further acquisitions in the vicinity of Charborough, purchasing the manor and advowson of the vicarage East Morden 'with its appurtances in Morden, Litchet Matravers and Wareham, by the service of paying yearly 8s'. In ecclesiastical law an advowson was by right usually held by the Lord of the Manor to recommend a member of the Anglican clergy for a vacant parish, benefice, or to make such an appointment. He also held three parts of the manor of West Morden and acquired land in this area on 8 April 1564, from Philip Steynynges.[45]

---

43. Sandon, *Edward Hedley*, p. vii. The evocative ruins of Dunkeswell Abbey can still be visited.
44. www.historyofparliamentonline.org/volume/1660-1690/member/erle-sir-walter-1586-1665, last accessed 11 June 2024.
45. John Hutchins, *The history and antiquities of the county of Dorset* (London: W Bowyer and J. Nichols, 1774), p. 184.

END OF SERVICE

Following the death of Queen Mary in 1558 – she who had tried to reverse the Reformation much to the alarm of those who had speculated in monastic lands – Walter Erle, by then probably about 40 years of age, appears to have retired from court to concentrate on expanding and consolidating his holdings in Devon and Dorset. His name does not appear in the lists of active servants of the next monarch, Queen Elizabeth I (1558–1603), who reinforced the Reformation. However, he is still referred to as late as 1578 as 'of the Queen's privy chamber', perhaps an honorary title only. Walter requested from the queen the reversion of the parsonage of Morden; a warrant to grant the request, in consideration of his long service, was issued on 5 July; and on 18 November the grant itself was delivered, assigning to 'Walter Erle, of the Queen's privy chamber' the rectory and advowson of Morden, at a yearly rent of £12 3s. 4d., from Lady Day in that year.[46]

Sandon said of Erle:

> It appears, then, that whatever may have been the other qualities – gentle birth, influential connections, a pleasing countenance, an engaging manner, a quick wit – that helped to gain for Erle his admission to the Privy Chamber. This attribute kept him there and assured his success was his musical ability. He was lucky that Henry VIII and his daughters were so fond of music and so generous in their patronage of it. A significant part of Erle's contribution to the life of the royal household must have been musical, as a solo keyboard player, a participant in instrumental and vocal consorts, and a composer.[47]

Walter the Musician died a wealthy man and was buried on 8 November 1581 at Morden Church, near Charborough House. He would have been in his early 60s. He bequeathed to his wife Mary £20 in money, the income from the manor and parsonage of

---

46. Sandon, *Edward Hedley*, p. ix.
47. Sandon, 'The Henrician Partbooks', p. 87.

Axmouth, the income from 400 sheep, six bullocks, six cows and six calves, and the use of the house at Bindon and its contents during her life. The reversion of these properties and all his other assets and lands, including Charborough and the contents of his house, Walter left to his son Thomas Erle I, whom he required to pay the sum of £400 each to his two unmarried sisters Bridget and Mary, towards their marriage or maintenance.[48] To the parishes of Morden and Axmouth, he left 40 shillings each for the upkeep of the poor.

Born at Charborough, Thomas Earle I did not survive his father by many years, dying in 1597.[49] In Morden Church, under the east window of the chancel, is a monument of freestone, having, under a circular pediment, the figure of a gentleman in complete armour, suggesting a military man, kneeling on one knee, his hands uplifted. Behind him are two youths and a young lady in the dress of that age. On the wall, on two compartments, are two brass plates with the following inscriptions in Roman capitals:

HERE LYETH BURIED THE
BODEYE OF THOMAS EARLE,
THE SONE OF WALTAR EARLE,
WHOE DEPARTED FROM THIS
LYFF THE 16th DAYE OF
MARCHE, IN THE YEARE OF OUR LORD GOD 1597.

Born in 1586, Thomas Erle I's oldest son, Walter, was ten when his father died. His brother was Christopher Erle. As the eldest, Walter II inherited over 11,000 acres, of which around two-thirds lay around Charborough House. He became a ward of the Crown, and his wardship was eventually sold to Sir Carew Raleigh in 1605. On succession, Walter Erle II was to prove very different from his grandfather and to lead a life far more dramatic in the turbulent first half of the seventeenth century.

---

48. There was a third daughter, Honor, but it is not known what became of her.
49. A snapshot of the already extensive wealth of the Erle family is provided by Hutchins quoting Thomas Erle (II)'s estate at the time of this death. Hutchins, *The history and antiquities of the county of Dorset*, p. 498.

5

Walter the Puritan

The talented royal servant Walter the Musician steered a pragmatic course through the religious turmoil of the sixteenth century, in all probability beginning as a conventional Roman Catholic, accommodating himself to successive changes of official religious policy, and dying at least nominally an Anglican. His son Thomas's spiritual inclination is unknown, except that he was buried at Morden Church after his early death. It can be assumed he was at least outwardly an Anglican. Thomas I's sons, Walter II and Christopher (1590–1634) were to adopt a more identifiable and distinctive religious ideology. They appear to have been brought up as conventional Anglicans, but in their teens, they took up a more austere version of the Protestant faith that came to be known as Puritanism. How and where this change of heart occurred is uncertain, but it seems likely that their time at Oxford University was influential as it was a hotbed of Puritan zeal.[1]

While teenagers, Walter and Christopher Erle were sent up from Charborough to Oxford at an age that would now be considered very young but was not unusual in the seventeenth century.[2] Walter matriculated at Queen's, a college which was noted for being 'godly', in January 1602 at the age of 15. Often the next stop for graduates

---

1. The word Puritan first appeared in the 1570s as an adjective describing the characteristics of Protestants whose religious beliefs diverged from Catholicism more radically than the contemporary doctrines of the Church of England. J.T. Cliffe described the typical Puritan as 'a zealous Calvinist who placed a very high value on piety and holiness (to the extent that he might be considered "precise") and who preferred a simple form of religious worship with the emphasis on godly preaching': John T. Cliffe, *The Puritan Gentry: The Great Puritan Families of Early Stuart England* (London: Routledge & Kegan Paul, 1984), p. 2.

2. Universities were then more like sixth-form colleges than the modern university. Many aristocratic students treated them more like finishing schools than places for serious study and did not even bother to graduate.

was 'sowing wild oats' on the streets of London, but it is unlikely that the now Puritan Walter would have taken this path. In 1604 he became a student of the Inner Temple, one of the London Inns of Court where aspiring barristers were, and still are, trained. However, he did not complete his studies. His younger brother Christopher went up to Christ Church, Oxford, in June 1608, entered the Middle Temple (another Inn of Court) in 1609 and was called to the bar there in 1617.[3]

The pattern had been set for the Erles. The aristocrats and gentry networks controlled nearly all the levers of county power as Lords, MPs, Lord Lieutenants, Sheriffs, town governors, patrons, magistrates, militia officers and philanthropists. They had near total control over their tenants and peasants through land and farm rents, employment, wages, religious expression, education and homes.

After inheriting the Charborough Estate, Walter Erle II was to live a long and eventful life. He was an MP for over 48 years whose influence was felt far outside his native Dorset. He was an early holder of what the twentieth-century sociologist Max Weber called the Protestant work ethic and was able to become wealthy with his later interests in London. Indeed, he was to become a proto-capitalist. Much more is known about Walter than most of his relatives because he actively participated in some of the more dramatic moments of the first half of the seventeenth century. Many of his activities and speeches entered the historical record, with twenty-one speeches in the 1660 'Convention' Parliament surviving in transcription. As an MP he was also an active member of some 58 Commons committees over the years. Towards the end of his parliamentary career, he was Father of the House.

Having come of age, Walter the Puritan first concentrated on improving his inherited estates. He acquired the manor of Langton Matravers in the south of Purbeck in 1609.[4] However, his legally

---

3. He went on to hold many civic posts in Dorset, including serving as MP for Weymouth and Melcombe Regis in 1621, Lyme Regis in 1623, Poole in 1626, and Lyme Regis again in 1628.

4. The Register of the Parish of Morden contains the following entry of burial: '1611. William Lamberte, Earles man, buried xiii January.' William Lambert was

dubious efforts to evict a sitting tenant at Axmouth were 'much misliked', and he was chastened by Lord Ellesmere, the Lord Chancellor, for his 'hard conscience' and also condemned by Chancery that same year. He made his home at Charborough House but frequently visited Dorchester, a two-hour or thereabouts hard horse ride away to the west.

Walter's political career started in Dorchester and developed from his and his brother's religious views. Dorchester is built on the once prosperous Roman town of Durnovia. Following Henry VIII's reformation, Dorchester had little tolerance for Catholicism. At the time the town was developing a taste for the austere sect of Presbyterianism. In the early seventeenth century, it was small by modern standards, with around 2000 inhabitants, and confined within its defensive walls, three churches and mostly wooden shops and houses. Wealth came from sheep, with an estimated 500,000 farmed across the downlands of the county, and the export of woollen goods.

A notable feature of the time was a close relationship between many of the Puritan gentry and their religious preceptors or 'godly divines'. 'The latter appear in various roles: authors, schoolmasters, university dons, chaplains, parish clergy and lecturers. The Puritan squire, for his part, had the key role of patron', Cliffe explained.[5] Walter and Christopher Erle found their godly divine in the Reverend John White. Born of a respected Hampshire family, White had been elected a fellow of New College in 1595, and it was there that he was won over to the ideals of the emergent Puritan theology. At the age of 31, he was appointed rector of Holy Trinity Church, Dorchester, one of the town's three churches. He arrived on 11 November 1605, just a week after Guy Fawkes and his fellow Catholic conspirators had tried to blow up the Houses of Parliament. David Underdown, a historian of seventeenth-century Dorchester, wrote that 'White intended to make Dorchester a

---

party to a Recovery of Lands at Langton, purchased by Walter Erle, and was a man of substance, as he left legacies to the poor of the two parishes. He may have been an agent or steward to the Erle family.

5.   Cliffe, *Puritan Gentry*, p. 2.

reformed, godly community, a "city on a hill", a new Jerusalem."[6] His evangelical sermons were to substantially influence Dorchester's burgesses, triggering a crackdown on 'drunkards, fornicators and Sabbath breakers'. Two of White's closest supporters were Walter and Christopher Erle. The Erles had become an influential family in the county, and their star continued to rise.

FIRE FROM HEAVEN

On 6 August 1613, Dorchester experienced a disaster when a great fire cut a swathe through the town. The inferno wiped out two-thirds of the town, destroying 300 homes and costing the local economy around £200,000. Many inhabitants came to believe it was a 'fire from heaven': a stark message from God for townsfolk to mend their ways. For John White, the fire signalled the need for spiritual improvement, and he knew he was the preacher to bring that change. Over the next 20 years, a time of increasing political and religious turmoil all over Europe, Dorchester became the most religiously radical town in the kingdom, deeply sympathetic to the Protestant cause in the unfolding Thirty Years' War (1618–48), the climactic and decisive episode in the century-long contest between traditional and radical believers for hegemony in continental Europe.

For those decades, the Puritans succeeded in establishing Dorchester education and social care systems that would not be widely replicated until after 1945. Dorchester was said to be the most charitable town for its size in England.[7] It was one of the few places that emulated to some degree the social services that pre-Reformation religious orders had sought to provide. According to contemporary accounts, despite his Puritan values, the Reverend White was a reasonable man, not an immoderate zealot.

In 1614 at the age of 28, Walter, already a freeman of the town, was elected the MP for the harbour town of Poole.[8] He was to be

---

6. David Underdown, *Fire from Heaven* (London: Fontana, 1993), p. ix.
7. Ibid., p. 128.
8. Poole was then an important port in what we now know to be the second-largest natural harbour in the world.

the first of the Erle surname to enter Parliament, although some relatives had already done so. At this time, and indeed up until 1832, being elected to a parliament entailed charming, coercing or bribing the tiny number of people who had the right to vote: adult male owners of freehold property. 1616 was an important year for Walter. Firstly, in May, he was knighted by King James I. Whether he received the accolade on merit or paid for the privilege (which was common at the time to top-up the royal coffers) has yet to be discovered. Three days later, he married Ann, daughter and heir of Francis Dymock.[9] With her dowry, Sir Walter acquired the manors of Eckington and Pipe in the West Midlands.[10] Walter and Ann's marriage was to last 37 years. Walter's election increased the risk of his hardening religious views bringing him into conflict with the Crown. He was far from alone in this. The beginning of the Thirty Years' War in 1618 brought added tensions. Fear that the war would destabilise England led James I to attempt a rapprochement with Spain, much to the disgust of the militant anti-Spanish party, which had among its leaders Sir Walter Raleigh of Sherborne Castle in north Dorset. In 1618 the Spanish ambassador to James I was instrumental in prevailing upon the king, and indeed the leading aristocrat of Dorset was executed on a trumped-up charge of treason. The most consistent opponents of the king's Spanish policy were the Protestant clergy, who saw in the appeasement of Spain a glimmering danger of Catholic resurgence in England.

Puritan preachers strove unceasingly to undermine the negotiations with Spain.[11] When Parliament met in 1621, Sir Walter Erle had been re-elected for Poole. The power of the Puritan lobby was increasing but was not uncontested by the king. Erle was becoming increasingly prominent, delivering at least 29 speeches and being nominated to sit on eleven committees in this period. Religion was central to his political activity. Meanwhile, rumours of Popish plots circulated widely. On 5 April 1624, Dorchester's William Whiteway wrote in his diary that 'Two men were found Landed at Lullworth,

---

9. *Regs. St. Botolph, Bishopsgate, London*, ed. A.W.C. Hallen, i. 54.
10. 1 Car. I (1625).
11. www.britannica.com/event/Thirty-Years-War, last accessed 11 June 2024.

a Spaniard and an Englishman with many letters to divers Papists, they were apprehended by Sir George Trenchard, and Sir Edward Lawrence, restrained and then dispatched to London.'[12] James I was growing more unpopular. Historian Laurence Stone explained, 'respect for the King had been reduced by his association with a sexually depraved court, a pro-Spanish foreign policy, and a popish queen; respect for the baronetage had been sapped by the admission of men who were not even regarded as gentlemen, respect for the knighthood by the indiscriminate mass creations of James and Buckingham.'[13]

THE NEW WORLD

Small as it was, Dorchester was to play an important part in the colonisation of what we now call the United States. English exploration and settlement of the Americas began during Elizabeth's reign but made little initial progress. It was partly economic in motivation, the aim being to find sources of wealth outside Europe to avoid trading and competing with countries loyal to the papacy. However, the prospect of finding land overseas for the settlement of Englishmen who found religious conformity with the State repugnant was already in people's minds. While Puritan zealotry, evangelism and sobriety may have been welcome or tolerable to many in Dorchester, it was not always well received elsewhere. In many areas of England where they were fewer in number, they were persecuted, beaten in the street, refused employment and generally repressed. As early as 1607, some Puritans went into self-exile in Holland. A new phase of religious emigration began when the *Mayflower* carrying the Pilgrim Fathers landed at Cape Cod on Christmas Day 1620. John White recognised the religious and commercial potential that settlement in New England offered and, with his usual energy, promoted it.

---

12. William Whiteway, *William Whiteway of Dorchester: His Diary 1618 to 1635* (Dorchester: Dorset Record Society, 1991), p. 61.
13. Laurence Stone, *The Crisis of the Aristocracy, 1558–1641* (London: Clarendon, 1965), p. 749.

Named after Elizabeth I's maidenhood, the Virginia Company was an English trading company given royal approval on 10 April 1606 with the object of colonising the eastern coast of America; the area around the landing place was itself named Virginia. Sir Walter Erle and Christopher Erle acquired shares in the Virginia Company on 11 May 1620.[14] Moreover, Sir Walter attended meetings of the company, including one on 21 May 1621. A year later, he was appointed to the Council of Virginia, the government-led body which officially oversaw American colonial ventures. Assisted by the Erles, John White sought ways to help Puritans suffering religious repression and decided that the best option was to set up trading settlements in the Americas. The first few years of this enterprise were problematic. A group of Dorchester merchants obtained a fishing licence from the Council for New England on 20 February 1622, entitling them to search for a site for a colony. The council granted the necessary patent to Sir Walter Erle. The new company purchased a ship – the *Fellowship of* 40 tons with three guns – that set out for New England in the summer of 1623. Walter Erle II and John White met in Dorchester to agree on the organisation of the venture, which they envisaged would have a religious agenda. For this purpose, they formed a company of 125 associates, including 20 preachers. Two local civic leaders, Edward Clarke and Anne Erle's brother Thomas Pelham, invested in the Dorchester Company. Diarist William Whiteway joined in March 1623 and became one of the twelve members elected to serve under Governor Sir Walter Erle on the New England Committee. On 15 December 1623, Whiteway wrote in his diary:

> Sir Walter Erle, Governour of the New England plantacion, came hither to advise with the rest of the planters about the ordering of businesse. A share is £5 a year to be paid yearly for 5 yeares, and then shalbe made a distribution of the profits. I have subscribed to be one Share.[15]

---

14. Sir Walter acquired five shares.
15. Whiteway, *Diary*, p. 56.

WALTER THE PURITAN

Altogether, the company's initial fund came to more than £3000. Dorset historian Maureen Weinstock wrote of the third venture of the Dorchester Co.: the few cargoes to the New World which appear in the port books (i.e. of Weymouth):

> In January 1625, Sir Walter Erle and Company sent out in the *Fellowship* 8 hundredweights of meal, 40 quarts of malt for the provision of the Christians planted in New England. On 27th February he sent more meal, malt and 6 cattle in the *Amity*.

> On 23rd January 1625, the *Fellowship* left for New England and landed cargo again in Weymouth on 11th September; the *Amity* sailed on 27th February and was back on 31st August. The *Fellowship* from Virginia carrying 300 beaver and other skins for William Darby (a Dorchester merchant) and the *Amity* with 7 hundredweight of dried fish, 8 tons of trayne oil, 141 fox skins, 14 racoon, 25 martin, 5 otter, 8 beaver, and 1 muskrat skin for Richard Bushrod (another Dorchester merchant).[16]

Three other laden ships had arrived from Virginia with *Fellowship*. However, the *Fellowship*'s voyage had not been a great success as it had arrived too late in the season for productive fishing and left 14 men and provisions to occupy a site at Cape Ann, Massachusetts, which they called Gloucester. Optimistically, in March 1626, Sir Walter and his brother-in-law Sir Richard Strode obtained the Privy Council's permission to export cattle to America. However, by the following year, the company's capital of £3000 was exhausted, and the plantation was abandoned. These circumstances may explain Erle's decision to sell his Warwickshire estates in April 1626 to Sir Walter Devereux.[17] The Dorchester Company's main achievement was establishing the colony at Cape Ann in 1623; this was subsequently taken over in 1639 by Maurice Thomson and John

---

16. Maureen Weinstock, *Studies in Dorset History* (London: Longmans, 1953), p. 40.
17. www.historyofparliamentonline.org/volume/1604-1629/member/earle-walter-1586-1665, last accessed 13 June 2024.

83

Winthrop II, who will again appear in this story. What it did do was to give Sir Walter Erle connections with the transatlantic trade that would benefit him greatly in later years.

After stabilising from its shaky start, the Virginia Company did not do well either. After a massacre of settlers by the indigenous population, the company was wound up by James I in 1624, and Virginia was designated a royal colony. Out of the Dorchester Company, the Massachusetts Bay Company emerged, successfully fostering New England's settlement with increasing voyages. John White continued to play an active role well into the 1630s. In 1634 William Whiteway was able to enter in his diary: 'Mr Neuburgh of Marshwood Vale and many others set sail from Weymouth towards New England: and 27 of the same Mr John Humphreys and his wife the Lady Susan Fiennes, set sail likewise for the same place. This summer, there went over to that plantation at least twenty sail of ships and in them 2,000 planters.'[18]

THE ROYAL SUCCESSION

After his father's death, Charles I had come to the throne in March 1625. Soon afterwards, in an effort to placate the Puritans, an Act was passed that prohibited bear baiting, bull baiting, interludes, common plays and other 'unlawful' forms of recreation on the Lord's Day.[19] Though viewed as a move in the right direction, it did not satisfy the Puritans, who had, by this time, an ever-growing list of criticisms of government policy. In May 1625, Charles was married by proxy to the 15-year-old French princess Henrietta Maria in front of the doors of Notre Dame de Paris. Many members of the Commons opposed his marriage to a Roman Catholic, fearing it would undermine the official establishment of the reformed Church of England. Charles told Parliament that he would not relax religious restrictions but then promised to do precisely that in a secret marriage treaty with his brother-in-law, Louis XIII of France. Sir Walter Erle rapidly became a most vigorous critic of the king, whom

18.   Whiteway, *Diary*, p. 143.
19.   Cliffe, *Puritan Gentry*, p. 42.

he considered equivocal on popery and receptive to Arminianism[20] and presiding over an immoral court. He was emerging as a leading figure among the Parliamentary Puritans.

In May 1625, Sir Walter was appointed a deputy lieutenant of the county, replacing Sir John Strangways. Sir Walter was undertaking the roles expected of a member of a large landowning family in the county and using the powers that his rank brought with it. He had been appointed a magistrate in 1615 and exercised his powers vigorously. As a Justice of the Peace, he sat at the Quarter Sessions, which rotated between Beaminster, Blandford Forum, Sherborne, Shaftesbury and Dorchester. He was therefore involved in handing out typical sentences of the day. For example, in January 1626, he presided over the court at Blandford Forum from the 10th to 12th where, on being convicted, Bartholomew Forde, Anthony Dunford, English Tucker, John Martin and Simon Cornish were all branded. William Wyatt, Robert Johnson and Ethelred Johnson were whipped and then released whilst Thomas Symonds was stocked at Blandford for four hours and then released.[21]

Ownership of manors and estates often required proprietors to provide for the spiritual welfare of the inhabitants by choosing, supporting and maintaining the incumbent (providing a 'living') of each parish church. Sir Walter and other puritan landowners would therefore attempt to provide suitably minded ministers to the livings at their disposal. In Cliffe's words, 'Puritan Ministers were often treated like close family friends: they acted as executors and trustees and might even play a part in marriages negotiations; they might be asked to advise on, and make arrangements for, the education of the children; and they sometimes received handsome

---

20. Arminianism: By claiming that the death and atonement of Jesus made possible the salvation of all who would receive him, the Dutch theologian Jacobus Arminius (1560–1609) contradicted John Calvin's belief that God not only chooses some people to be saved but also creates some who will be damned, which was a central tenet of Puritanism. It was seen by Puritans as a serious, almost heretical, position.

21. https://freepages.rootsweb.com/~fordingtondorset/genealogy/Files/SirWalterErle.html, last accessed 13 June 2024.

gifts under the wills of their patrons.'[22] Erle did his best to place Puritan preachers in each of the livings of which he was patron.

ROYAL 'LOAN' SHARK

On 2 February 1626, King Charles I was crowned but without his wife, who refused to attend a Protestant ceremony. Later that year, the Commons, having failed to pass a bill granting the king a financial subsidy, left the Crown virtually bankrupt. Charles, therefore, demanded a general loan from leading figures in the counties, a form of fundraising known as ship money, utilising a long redundant medieval law aimed at coastal communities. It was deeply unpopular. The Earl of Suffolk and Sir Robert Nanton, master of the Court of Wards, were sent down to Dorset to demand monies from those selected in the county. William Whiteway's diary for the 13 January 1627 recorded that:

> All men in this County subscribed except Sir John Strangeways, Sir Walter Earle, Mr Tregonwell,[23] and Mr William Savidge attorny. For refusing, these men were bound to answer it at the Council table, from whence three former were sent prisoners to the fleet[24] and the last unto the new prison in Clarkenwell.[25]

Sir Walter was to be held in Fleet prison for a year. The king did not want to try the refusers so much as punish them. Sir Walter demanded a trial in the Court of King's Bench, the most senior criminal court in the land. The refusers' chief lawyer, Mr Ley, defended them so effectively, invoking their right to *habeas corpus*, that the court decided that they should be set at liberty. However, the king's attorney requested time to consult with the king, and Sir Walter was not released until 11 January 1628, when he was the

---

22. Cliffe, *Puritan Gentry*, p. 136.
23. The landed-gentry Tregonwell family lived to the north of Charborough and reappear episodically in this book.
24. The Fleet Prison.
25. Whiteway, *Diary*, p. 87.

last of the refusers to be freed.[26] He was soon once again representing the interests of Dorset in a complaint about the cost of billeting troops and the problems caused by demobilised soldiers:

> In my County, under the colour of placing a soldier, there came 20 in a troop to take sheep. They disturn markets and fair, rob men on the highway, ravish women, breaking in the night and enforcing men to ransom themselves, killing men that have assisted constables that have come to keep the peace.[27]

Erle also continued his opposition to prerogative taxation, and in 1636, in another exaction of ship money, Charles demanded tax across the whole nation. Sir Walter again refused to pay, as did other leading local Puritans, including William Strode and John Browne, and in 1637 the defaulters had their goods seized by the sheriff of Dorsetshire. A list drawn up by the sheriff, Sir Thomas Trenchard, in April 1636 of those who had not paid, shows that Sir Walter Erle owed £3 6s 8d for lands in Morden, £5 3s 0d for lands in Combe Almer and £4 11s 0d for lands in Charborough.

After the king dissolved Parliament in 1626, the next parliamentary session did not begin until 20 January 1629. When it did commence, the House of Commons resolved that their concerns over religion, particularly the perceived dangers of popery and Arminianism, should take precedence over all other business. In what was said to be an emotional speech, Sir Walter Erle said that he feared that popery and Arminianism working together would help bring in a tyranny heavily influenced by Spain. He made a passionate personal declaration:

> that which for an undoubted truth I have from the Church of England heretofore received, that will I stand to and forgo my estate, my liberty, yea my life itself rather than forgo it. As for passing of bills, settling reveries and the like with settling Religion,

---

26. Ibid., p. 92.
27. Samuel R. Gardiner, *History of England from the Accession of James I to the Outbreak of the Civil War* (London: Longmans, 1884, 10 vols, Vol. vi), p. 254.

I must confess I have no heart to it. Take away my Religion, you take away my life and not only mine the life of the whole State and kingdom.[28]

In a debate, the House made it clear that the majority wanted Arminianism stopped in its tracks, before it had a chance to burgeon into a revival of popery. The king, who was concerned about the growing vociferousness, ambition and strength of the Puritans, refused and dissolved Parliament. The two sides were on course for a catastrophic collision.

In 1629, tensions between the king and Parliament further escalated. As a prominent critic of King Charles, the Puritan Sir Walter Erle, perhaps sensing it was a good time to keep his head down, travelled to the war-torn Low Countries to get some experience in military campaigning. There, England was supporting the United Provinces, which sought to vanquish the Spanish who controlled swathes of northern Europe. Sir Walter joined Baron Horace Vere, one of the 'fighting Veres', who was commander of English forces in the combined Anglo-Scottish-United Provinces army at the siege of 's-Hertogenbosch.[29] The well-fortified town was one of the chief Spanish military bastions in Brabant. The siege had been set by the Dutch Prince Frederic Henry in April 1629. After months of heavy fighting, the Spanish surrendered the town in September.[30]

Sir Walter was to make much of his military experience, claiming later that he was a 'sword man rather than a gown man'.[31] A friend of the Erle family and leading Dorset aristocrat, Sir Anthony Ashley

---

28. Cliffe, *Puritan Gentry*, p. 155.

29. The Vere family produced several hugely effective commanders in that period.

30. Some English officers who were afterwards distinguished soldiers in the English Civil War served under Vere. Among them were Thomas Fairfax and Philip Skippon, the future organisers of Oliver Cromwell's New Model Army; Jacob Astley and Thomas Glenham, the future royalist generals; Sir John Borlase; and Henry Hexham, the historian of the Dutch wars.

31. Mary F. Keeler, *Long Parliament, 1640–1641: A Biographical Study of Its Members* (Philadelphia, PA: The American Philosophical Society, 1954), p. 166.

Cooper, commented on the impact of Sir Walter's military experience on the park at Charborough:

> Sir Walter had been a Low Country soldier, valued himself upon the sieges and service he had been in; his garden was cut into redoubts and works representing these places, his house hung with the maps of those sieges and fights [that] had been most famous in those parts.[32]

Back at Charborough, Erle resumed the duties expected of the landed gentry. During the 1630s, Sir Walter consolidated his links with the leaders of the opposition to Charles's regime. Walter was a close ally of the influential William Fiennes, 1st Viscount Saye and Sele and had been involved with the attempted impeachment of Lord Buckingham back in 1626. The Puritans suspected Buckingham of being a secret Catholic. The Duke of Buckingham was the Stuarts' closest political ally and immensely powerful but had made serious political and military mistakes. He was targeted by parliamentarians as a way of getting at Charles. To save him, Charles dissolved Parliament in June. Buckingham's case was then tried before the Royal Court of Star Chamber where the charges were dismissed. He was murdered in 1628.[33]

A historian of the seventeenth century, D.H. Pennington, observed that the Erles, like the great majority of the gentlemen chosen for Parliament in October 1640, came from a small and closely-knit landed community of their native county. Sir Walter's principal estate at Charborough was within five miles of the borough of Wareham, where he held some property, and was a little further from Poole, where he was MP. His son, Thomas, was member for Wareham; his brother, Christopher, had formerly sat for Poole and

---

32. William D. Christie, *Memoirs, Letters and Speeches, of Anthony Ashley Cooper* (London: John Murray, 1859), p. x.
33. As an ardent anti-papist, Sir Walter later targeted Edward Sackville, the fourth Earl of Dorset and Henrietta Maria's Lord Chamberlain. In 1641 Sir Walter Erie opposed the re-enfranchisement of the town of Seaford in Sussex on the grounds that 'the lord of the town [Sackville] [was] a papist'. Whether Sackville was a Catholic is still open to debate as he managed his religion discreetly.

Lyme Regis. The Erles were related by marriage to the Trenchards, one of whom, John, was secured as the other member for Wareham. John's sister was married to Sir John Strangways, member for Weymouth, and father of one of the members for Bridport; his sons-in-law, John Bingham and William Sydenham, were later members of the Long Parliament for Shaftesbury and Weymouth respectively. Almost every county had a similar network of relationships among its members. But, of course, they did not stop at county boundaries. Pennington continued:

> Thomas Erle's wife was Susanna Fiennes, daughter of Viscount Saye and Sele, and through the widespread connections of the Fiennes family, the Erles were related to Hampden, Cromwell, St. John, Holles, and many parliamentary families in the eastern counties.[34]

Some notable Dorset names are repeated over the centuries as friends and allies of the Erles and, in some cases, as their rivals or enemies.[35]

THE LONG PARLIAMENT

From 1629 to 1640, Charles I tried to rule as an absolute monarch, refusing to call Parliament and unilaterally imposing taxes that were widely viewed as oppressive and illegal. Charles's need for more money finally forced him to recall Parliament, and it reconvened on 3 November 1640. It was to become the longest Parliament in English history. Not only was the reputation of the king for running the country plummeting, but so was that of the aristocracy. As educated landed gentry, men like Sir Walter Erle felt they could better represent the nation's interests. Historian Laurence Stone has written that MPs had convinced themselves that the House of Commons was by its very nature an infinitely more substantial

---

34. Donald H. Pennington, 'A Day in the Long Parliament', *History Today*, vol. 3, no. 10 (October 1953), 682.
35. Walter Erle's brother was to die at the age of 44 in 1634.

body than the House of Lords. Since Tudor times, there had been a massive transfer of manors – the basic landowner format.[36] In a sample of some 3300 manors in ten counties, out of 730 held by the Crown and the peerage in 1561, some 430 had left them (if new creations are ignored) by 1640, while the gentry had acquired an additional 400 manors and 'that the share of the gentry had risen from two-thirds when the period began, to four-fifths at the end of it'.[37] However, it was at a cost for the rest of the population, who were hard-pressed.

Charles's main aim in reconvening Parliament in 1640 was to get funds for the Scottish War. The Covenanters opposed his imposition of The Book of Common Prayer on Scotland, and other religious impositions, so war was the outcome. However, the new Parliament's first act was to arrest Charles's chief adviser, Thomas Wentworth, Earl of Strafford. Another Charles supporter, the diminutive Archbishop Laud, soon followed him into captivity. On hearing the news, back in Dorchester, where Laud was viewed as almost Catholic, the bells of Holy Trinity rang out 'for the happy success of the Parliament'.[38] Instigated by Parliament, Strafford's trial began in March 1641, and its real purpose was a power play to neutralise King Charles.[39]

The primary accusation against Strafford was that of subverting the law, alongside more detailed charges rested on his administration in Ireland and the north. He conducted his defence with great skill, and it looked at one point as though he might be acquitted. Two Dorset MPs were to take important parts in the trial. Among the eleven impeachment managers were Walter Erle and George Digby of the aristocratic family from Sherborne in Dorset. Sir Walter's task was to accuse the king's minister of planning to bring over an army from Ireland to conquer England. His attempt

---

36. A manor is a unit of English rural territorial organisation usually consisting of an estate under a lord enjoying a variety of rights over land and tenants, including the right to hold court. Often there was a manor house.

37. Tawney, 'The Rise of the Gentry', 35.

38. Hutchins, *History of Dorset*, vol. ii, p. 402.

39. Laud was beheaded on Tower Hill on 10 January 1645.

to prove the allegation failed for lack of witnesses upon which he 'was very blank and out of countenance'. Digby, who was hedging his bets, 'in a very witty and rhetorical speech took off Sir Walter', and the queen, who was present, asked who Digby was ridiculing. When she was told his name was Sir Walter Erle, she commented 'that water dog did bark but not bite, but the rest did bark close'.[40]

With the case failing, the leader of the Commons, John Pym, introduced a bill of attainder. Although King Charles had promised to protect the Earl of Strafford's life, Whitehall was surrounded by a large dangerous crowd who wanted the earl executed. Believing that if he were not executed, it would place Charles in an impossible political position, Strafford released the king from his promise. Strafford went to the scaffold.

The king believed that Puritans, including five of his most prominent critics in the House – John Pym, John Hampden, Denzil Holles, Arthur Haselrig and William Strode, plus the peer Viscount Mandeville – had encouraged the Scots to invade England and that they were intent on turning the people against him.[41] Rumours reached the court that the Puritan clique also planned to impeach the queen for alleged involvement in Catholic plots. Charles attempted to arrest the five MPs on 4 January 1642. Charles entered the House of Commons with the Duke of Roxburgh at his side and backed up with a troop of soldiers. The MP for Bridport (in Dorset), Roger Hill, described in anger the hundred-armed men as 'desperate soldier, captains, and commanders, of papists, ill-affected persons, being me of no rank or quality, divers of them being traitors in France, Frenchmen fled hither, panders and rogues'. He was convinced that the band had come 'to fall upon the House of Commons and to cut all their throats'.[42] Fortunately for the five MPs, they had been forewarned and had slipped out of the House and the king's band left empty-handed. Parliament was united in its fury at the king's audacity in raiding the House.

---

40. Hutchins, *History of Dorset*, vol. ii, p. 498.
41. These MPs were all friends and allies of Walter Erle.
42. Adrian Tinniswood, *The Verneys: A True Story of Love, War and Madness in Seventeenth Century England* (London: Vintage, 2008), p. 159.

Meanwhile, Parliament had voted for the lay subsidy to pay for the Scottish War. According to historian Tim Goodwin, it was much evaded:

> The commissioners, who in Dorset included Sir Walter Erle, his neighbour Thomas Tregonwell and his son Thomas Erle, often let off their friends. Oliver Lawrence and Thomas Thornhurst of Alfpuddle [near Charborough], were taxed on lands worth £2 a year, which was a ludicrous figure, almost certainly less than a hundredth of the true value.[43]

Ultimately the House of Commons refused to approve new taxes unless Charles agreed to restrictions on his powers. The king refused, and the Civil War broke out in 1642.

---

43. Tim Goodwin, *Dorset in the Civil War* (Tiverton: Dorset Press, 1996), p. 26.

6

Walter the Puritan and the English Civil War

Fuelled by his aversion to the Stuarts and Catholics, Sir Walter Erle was one of the leading Parliamentarians who resisted compromise with the king and forced the way to what would be a bloody war. When the Civil War finally broke out in 1642, it did so ad hoc across the country, ignited by different burning grievances. There is no single date it started, although the 15 July, when the Earl of Essex was appointed Captain General of Parliament's forces, or the 22 August when the king raised his standard at Nottingham, are clearly significant landmarks.[1] The English Civil War is often conceived in simple binaries as Roundheads versus Cavaliers, as men in floppy hats versus those in lobster pot helmets, the People's Parliament versus the absolutist king, Puritans versus High Church Protestants, English Anglicans versus Scottish Calvinists, English Anglicans versus Irish Catholics, and that is just some. All are partially true, but a complex mix of all these and more was at work. Religion, emancipation, the price of food and ownership of land were all in this heady mix. The fight for the commons, including against enclosures, was also an important part of the English Revolution.

Tim Goodwin, a historian of the Civil War in Dorset, wrote that it was not one of the most important counties. It had no great cities, no great manufacturing base, and its population was about 2 per cent of the country. Yet, he noted:

It provides an almost perfect microcosm of much of the nation, a complex mosaic of rural, urban and maritime life. Arable and

---

1. Ann Hughes, *The Causes of the English Civil War* (Basingstoke: Palgrave, 1998), pp. 168–169.

pastoral agriculture dominated the county, as it did the whole of England. However, there were also medium-sized inland towns like Sherborne and Dorchester with their small-scale industries and the important ports of Poole, Weymouth and Lyme, which had regular links with the continent, the New World and even further afield.[2]

No great battles were fought in the county, but it was the scene of many more minor battles, constant skirmishes, and notable sieges.

It was, with so many fights to be had, the perfect location for Sir Walter to make his mark as a military leader. As the senior Parliamentarian in Dorset and potential military leader, Sir Walter Erle had surveyed the state of the county's defences in May 1641. It was not impressive. He found an assortment of small cannons in the towns, five in Dorchester, seven in Lyme, 22 in Weymouth and four in Poole. Many towns, like Dorchester and Wareham, still retained part of their medieval walls. By the start of the Civil War the leaders of Dorset included several other Puritans, notably John Browne of Frampton and Sir Thomas Trenchard of Wolfeton.[3] The strong bonds of the Puritan gentry, although not a majority, stopped Dorset from following the greater part of the South-west into the Royalist camp. Mobilised in the late summer of 1642, Erle took his Dorset-trained band and marched north with fife and drum to join the young Earl of Bedford and Denzil Holles in their siege of Sherborne Castle. This was the first Civil War engagement in Dorset, starting on 2 September 1642 and which turned into a fiasco, with the Parliamentarians rebuffed by a smaller force from the town. Back in Dorchester, Sir Walter raised his own troop of horse, but it took the field under another's command.[4]

---

2. Goodwin, *Dorset in the Civil War*, p. 1.

3. Of the 700 gentry families in England with estates worth over £1000, 172 families supported Parliament, and of those, at least 128 were Puritans (Cliffe, *Puritan Gentry*, p. 45).

4. https://historyofparliament.com/2020/06/30/the-horticultural-heroism-of-sir-walter-erle/#:~:text=Of%20the%20seventeenth%20, last accessed 13 June 2024.

George Leddoze, a merchant of Dorchester, had been taken into custody and was examined by two of the town's Justices of the Peace. Leddoze declared that he had been taken as a spy by the Royalists and interrogated at Sherborne Lodge by Lord Poulett, Sir Ralph Hopton, Sir John Stawell and Sir Henry Berkeley. When asked whether he was for king or Parliament, he replied 'for both'. Lord Poulett had said that all Parliamentarians for the militia were proclaimed traitors and crop-eared rogues, and that Erle was the wickedest rogue of them all and one of the Devil's limbs. The other gentlemen, reported Leddoze, said the same, that the king would assist with a great army, and that had it not been for Erle and such rogues, these tumults would not have arisen. Hopton further declared that God was plainly with them (the Royalists) in protecting so small a number; that their company shot but once, killed two and maimed 15 more, that those who took up arms for Parliament were bloodsucking robbers.[5]

Erle's preparations for war had reached the ears of the king, and in December 1642, Charles issued a declaration offering a free pardon to all rebels in Dorset 'except Denzil Holles esquire, and Sir Walter Erle, knight, against whom we shall proceed according to the rules of the law, as against traitors and stirrers of sedition against us'.[6] Sir Walter returned to Westminster in January 1643. During the negotiations over the Treaty of Oxford – trying to find an accommodation with the king to avoid war – he allied himself with the more hawkish elements who opposed a lenient peace with the king.

ERLE'S MILITARY METTLE

Given his role in the siege of Sherborne had been minor, this was 'sword man' Sir Walter's first chance to show his mettle in the field of battle when, in June 1643, it was decided that the imposing Corfe Castle, the 'guardian to the Isle of Purbeck', needed to be dealt with. By then, it was the only major royalist strongpoint in Dorset that

---

5. Arthur R. Bayley, *The Great Civil War in Dorset, 1642–1660* (Taunton: Barnicott and Pearce, The Wessex Press, 1910), p. 46.
6. Goodwin, *Dorset in the Civil War*, p. 42.

still needed to be captured. The castle was 'so ancient as without date, yet all her walls and towers, are all in very good repair... The walls round about her are very strong and large.'[7] Sir John Bankes had bought the castle in 1636 from the Hatton family. As Charles's Attorney General, Bankes, 'a grave and learned man', was with the king in the north when a Parliamentary force of 500 to 600 soldiers headed to Corfe.[8] Sir Walter Erle was the commanding officer, and his deputy was Sir John Trenchard. In the absence of her husband, Lady Bankes, a staunch royalist and by all accounts a powerful personality, sealed herself in the castle with her four daughters, a handful of her family retainers and some Corfe villagers.

Comfortably, Sir Walter had set up his siege headquarters at Wareham, two miles from the castle, as he thought the town of Corfe was too vulnerable from sniping and possible sallies by the royalist garrison and embarked on a variety of eccentric stratagems to take the castle.[9] His first attempt involved two medieval siege engines, the 'sow' and the 'boar', which were quickly discovered not to be bulletproof. In desperation, the next attack led by Sir Walter involved ladders to scale the walls. It also failed. A contemporary account says that the royalists jeered that Sir Walter had lost his nerve: 'he put on a bear's skin, and to the eternal honour of this knight's valour be it recorded, for fear of musket shot... he was seen to creep on all fours on the sides of the hill to keep himself out of danger'. This version was from a royalist newspaper, *Mercurius Rusticus*.[10]

Nonetheless, the idea that Sir Walter suffered some collapse pervaded and was inevitably seen as cowardice and damaged his reputation. Worse was to follow for Dorset's Roundheads. After

---

7.   Leopold G. Wickham Legg, 'Survey of the Western Counties', 1635, pp. 69–70.

8.   Even today, the ruins of Corfe Castle are imposing on the top of a steep hill.

9.   https://thehistoryofparliament.wordpress.com/2020/06/30/the-horticultural-heroism-of-sir-walter-erle/, last accessed 13 June 2024.

10.   Bruno Ryves was a convinced Laudian and a Royalist when war broke out, joining the Royalist army. His main claim to fame was his civil war journalism, for he was the sole author of the periodical *Mercurius rusticus* ('The Rustic Mercury'). The paper was not known for its impartiality.

one of the king's armies took Bristol on 26 July 1643, they then quickly overran Dorset, capturing Dorchester without a fight on 2 August. Royalist commander the Earl of Carnarvon, having with him a considerable body of horse and dragoons, arrived in Purbeck, whereupon Sir Walter Erle raised his siege on 4 August 1643 so precipitately that he left his tents standing, together with his ammunition and artillery, all of which fell into the hands of Lady Bankes' household. The siege had cost the Parliament forces 100 dead and Erle rushed to Poole harbour, whence he took a ship for Southampton and eventually turned up in London.

The Royalist press had a field day, and Sir Edward Hyde (later Earl of Clarendon) observed wryly that Erle had made 'more haste to convey himself to London than generals use to do who have care and charge of others'. Dr Patrick Little concluded that, according to contemporary records, the failed Corfe Castle siege damaged Sir Walter's reputation as a commander. 'An armchair soldier was not the ideal local commander for a strategically important county, and Erle's career as a military commander was brief and inglorious, marked by indecision and poor planning.'

Dr Little suggested the evidence is less than compelling on Sir Walter's self-claimed soldiering before the Civil War. 'In reality, Erle's military experience was slight: he had indeed joined Lord Vere in the Low Countries in 1629, but only for a few months as an observer; he had subsequently been a deputy lieutenant in Dorset and may have had dealings with the local militia in the 1630s.'[11] At this point in his career, Little noted, Erle was becoming better known as an MP for his 'inexhaustible appetite for humdrum committee work and something of an obsession with the minutiae of parliamentary procedure'. For his next appointments, organising military logistics and creating wealth off the back of it, Sir Walter was much better suited.

Not long after arriving in London, Sir Walter was appointed the Lieutenant-General of Ordnance, a job that played to his administrative strengths. At one point, he demonstrated an unsuspected

---

11. https://thehistoryofparliament.wordpress.com/2020/06/30/the-horticultural-heroism-of-sir-walter-erle/.

skill when he managed to decipher some intercepted but coded Royalist letters that had been captured at Dartmouth, and 'he had the thanks of the House for it'.[12] His new role gave him control over the provision of artillery and weapons for the parliamentarian forces. He was to be closely involved in provisioning the highly disciplined Puritan-manned New Model Army. These were soldiers who were said to go to war with a copy of Calvin's Geneva Bible in their back pockets. This was support he later regretted, when the NMA became powerful radicals.

Dorset had been taken by Royalist troops. Arriving later, Prince Rupert and his Royalist forces, in keeping with their reputation for indiscipline, and despite promises to the contrary, plundered Dorchester. They raided John White's house where 'they seized upon a great number of books, manuscripts of divinity, evidence, writings and other goods of great value which they sold off'.[13] Wisely, White followed Erle to London, where he was granted the sequestered parish of Lambeth and remained there for the next three years.[14] Meanwhile, Sir Walter had business to enact for Parliament and himself, as an MP and 'Adventurer'. He was to become a vital link between Parliament and London's merchant adventurers who were central to England's colonisation and trade.[15]

Before the Civil War had started, Parliament had manoeuvred the king into appointing Robert Rich, the Earl of Warwick, instead of Charles's own nominee, for the key post of Lord High Admiral.

---

12. Goodwin, *Dorset in the Civil War*, p. 118.

13. Frances Rose-Troup, *John White: The Patriarch of Dorchester* (New York: G.P. Putnam, 1930), p. 312. Later, John White was able to buy some of the books back.

14. John White's modest house is still standing in Dorchester, situated behind the Dorset County Museum. There is a plaque on its wall describing the robbery by Prince Rupert's troops.

15. I use the term 'merchant adventurers' as a generic term to cover those merchants who were also pioneering entrepreneurs who set up international trade. Adventurers tends to mean prepared to invest in new projects. However, the Merchant Adventurers were the Fellowship of Merchant Adventurers, England's cloth exporting monopoly during the early modern period, and not the merchants who were adventurers in other things without a title. There was a company of adventurers into new lands, and the fen drainage adventurers, and many more in the same and later periods.

The earl was popular with seamen and a good choice to take control of the navy for Parliament. As Edward Hyde later complained, 'This loss of the whole navy was of unspeakable ill consequence to the king's affairs.' Because Parliament held London, the nation's economic and centre, it was able to raise very large loans, and collect customs revenue and taxes. Thomas Hobbes observed in his famous tome *Behemoth*, 'But for the city the Parliament never could have made the war.'[16] The Earl of Warwick had been involved in early settlement and the first slave-trading in the American colonies.[17] He was close to the merchant adventurers. Once the Civil War started, London's merchant adventurers, some of whom had effectively been pirates and often were still privateers, realised doing business with the Parliamentary side was likely to be more lucrative and less difficult than capturing Spanish, Dutch and Portuguese galleons. Most participants in this early lucrative Atlantic trade had English Puritan or Dutch Calvinist affiliations, religious ties they shared with the peers who backed these enterprises.

Alongside their interests in the Atlantic these merchant adventurers also attempted to make money out of Irish conquests. Historian David Brown described how in the 1640s they 'through a series of shrewd and timely investments, principally in Ireland, gradually assumed control of supplying the English parliamentary war effort'. Brown continued, 'Their financial innovations played a key role in parliament's ultimate victory over the king and helped drive the subsequent conquests of both Ireland and Scotland.'[18] These 20 or so merchants offered to help if the rewards were high in the long term and showed shrewd flexibility in their dealing to help Parliament: this was a shared-ownership speculation in the conquest of Ireland.

16. Edward Earl of Clarendon, *The History of the Rebellion and Civil Wars in England* (Oxford: The Clarendon Press, 1888), p. 202.

17. In August 1619, one of the privateers sponsored by the Robert Rich, the *White Lion*, arrived at Point Comfort, Virginia with 20 enslaved people from Ndongo (in present-day Angola). The Africans were sold to Governor George Yeardley of the Colony of Virginia. The *White Lion* and the *Treasurer* had captured the African people from the Portuguese slave ship *São João Bautista* which was bound for Veracruz.

18. Brown, *Empire and Enterprise*, preface.

Brown noted that the gentry, merchants and modest artisans who invested in this endeavour intended that their money would finance a private army to crush the Irish rebellion that had broken out in October 1641. Then, having raised £250,000 to conquer Ireland in 1642 they, 'sent it instead to fight for Parliament in England'.[19] Sir Walter Erle was to be a key middleman between the merchants and Parliament.

The Adventurers elected a committee to represent their interests which met in secret at Grocers' Hall in London between 1642 and 1660. With their heavily armed ships, trade experience and political connections, they achieved control over England's external trade, dictating key policies for Ireland and the colonies and financing Parliament's war against Charles I. Parliament formed The Committee for Irish Affairs to negotiate with the Adventurers. It is not known exactly which MPs attended the inaugural meeting on 8 January 1642, but as an indication, 14 MPs were nominated to a subsequent parliamentary group on 19 February 1642 as the 'Commissioners for the Speeding and Dispatching of the Businesses for Ireland'. These MPs, dealing actively with the emergency in Ireland, included Walter Erle the Puritan, Oliver Cromwell and Denzil Holles. 'In addition to the London MPs who had direct connections with the Atlantic merchant community, the Committee for Irish Affairs was further dominated by men with colonial Atlantic connections', observed Brown, and he identified Sir Walter Erle as one.[20]

On 7 February 1642, Parliament approved the raising of a 20,000-strong Scottish army as a privately underwritten military operation, financed with a 'Brotherly Assistance' loan. This loan was managed from Warwick House, home and centre of operations of the Earl of Warwick and the headquarters of the Adventurers clique. The proposal was that the Adventurers' funders would be rewarded by dividing up a huge chunk of Irish lands taken from the Catholic landowners. The terms of Brotherly Assistance enabled the Warwick House entrepreneurs to seek money from outside

19. Ibid., Chapter 3.
20. Ibid., p. 56.

their circle. A significant tranche of this money, £50,000, was raised and sent to the Scottish army in November 1641. A receiver for Brotherly Assistance, Walter Erle was one of the MPs who lent money, some £500 in his case. 'The merchants who framed early drafts of the Adventure significantly undervalued Irish land to make their investment as profitable as possible.'[21] The Adventurers did have trouble getting the lands they were promised, and it took time after the war to resolve. Walter's son, Thomas Erle MP, also became involved and was on a committee of inquiry when money for one loan was under-collected and shown to have been diverted into the pockets of several of the collectors.[22]

THE GUNPOWDER POT

Sir Walter Erle was not just involved in the merchant adventurers' dealings for Ireland, but also the Adventurers' entry into the saltpetre trade as the Civil War ground on. Saltpetre was a vital competent for making gunpowder and was not found in nature in many places and not at all in the British Isles. Where it did occur, saltpetre crusted on the surfaces of walls and rocks, and in caves, and formed in some soil systems in Spain, Italy, Egypt, Iran and India. It could be manufactured by letting some kinds of organic substance decay. Human excrement and urine were the main source for those who could not obtain natural saltpetre. Obtaining high-quality natural saltpetre in quantity cemented the relationship between the Parliamentarian army and one company of the Adventurers who were able to control the Asia trade, and deprive the Royalist army of such supplies. Indian saltpetre was of the highest quality, with more explosive power than other varieties, increasing the range of cannons and matchlock guns that used it. An Adventurer sponsored a colonisation and trading expedition to Nosy Be, north of Madagascar, in 1645, which, while a failure in colonisation, was successful in obtaining large quantities of spice and saltpetre.

21. Ibid., p. 71.
22. Ibid., p. 130.

Once the Adventurer William Pennoyer[23] shipped the saltpetre to England, the job of organising the making of quality gunpowder for the army was with the Committee for Powder Match and Bullet, comprising of the Adventurers Sir Walter Erle, Samuel Vassall,[24] Sir Robert Pye, John Rolle, Alexander Bence and Thomas Pury.[25] The Adventurers' underwriting of the cost of Cromwell's army and facilitation of the production of copious amounts of gunpowder gave Parliament a distinct edge. Cromwell's victory at Naseby in June 1645 was decisive in that it removed any possibility of a Royalist victory. Brown explained the Adventurer's strategy:

> From this point on, their interests were aggressively promoted by the leaders of the New Model Army, leaving them less exposed to the shifting political sands of Westminster. In return, the Adventurers provided the New Model Army with the financial means to prosecute their military campaigns. Their control of finance also enabled the Adventurers to keep a tight grip on military supplies.[26]

The Adventurers' leader Maurice Thomson's next move was the accumulation of shares in the East India Company proper.[27] In order to obtain permission to set out on its voyage in 1645, the English East India Company (EEIC) agreed to pay a fine to support Parliament's army in Ireland.[28]

---

23. William Pennoyer was a member of the Levant Company, another exploratory and entrepreneurial venture. He had been in partnership with Maurice Thomson as a privateer in the 1630s.

24. Samuel Vassall was Maurice Thomson's key trading partner in Virginia and the West Indies and was also an investor in the Massachusetts Bay Company.

25. TNA SP28/350/3, f. 3.

26. Brown, *Empire and Enterprise*, p. 145.

27. Maurice Thomson started his business career as a Virginia tobacco planter in the 1620s, was also a privateer in the Caribbean with William Pennoyer in the 1630s (see above, note 23), and was a major private sector financial facilitator for Parliament. He rose to become governor of the English East India Company in 1657, the apex of England's merchant hierarchy. As Brown, *Empire and Enterprise* noted, Maurice Thomson is rarely found directly in parliamentary or other official records, but he was never more than one step removed from central political figures and decisions.

28. The English East India Company was a private corporation formed in

Royalists despaired of the advantage that the merchants' funding of Parliament's armies brought. Brown noted: 'Despite Cromwell's impressive military credentials, (the Royalist Duke of) Ormond later described the Adventurers' war chest as the more formidable adversary.'[29] As Brown showed, the EEIC was controlled by the Adventurers by then, even if they only owned the ships and cargo of general voyages and not the actual company shares. The shares had little value if the ship-owners could charge what they liked and owned the cargoes in any case. Brown detailed how the EEIC ships exported bullion to Asia and exchanged it for several valuable commodities, including saltpetre. During that time, while amassing enormous wealth and power, the Adventurers laid the fiscal foundations for England's empire.

A PAUSE

Puritans both, Sir Walter and his son Thomas Erle II would retain a political profile even after the first part of the war finished. During 1645, they remained personally on good terms with the statesman Viscount Saye and Sele, whose daughter was married to Thomas. The Viscount was seen as one of Parliament's hawks. But then Sir Walter drifted away from his leadership and started to side with the less hawkish Presbyterians. The main reason for this seems to have been his alarm over the increase in power of the radical sectarians, especially in the New Model Army. Sir Walter now took an interest in Presbyterian schemes for reform of the Church rather than the more radical New Model Army proposals. He voted with Denzil Holles and his allies, who increasingly saw Oliver Cromwell and the radicalism he stimulated in such sects as the Levellers and Diggers as more of a threat than the monarchy. Sir Walter co-operated with the Scots commissioners over the peace negotiations of 1646 and 1647, supporting a Presbyterian church settlement and

---

December 1600 to establish a British presence in the lucrative Indian spice trade, which until then had been monopolised by Spain and Portugal.

29.　James Butler, the Duke of Ormonde, led the Royalist forces which fought against the Cromwellian conquest of Ireland.

acting as one of the four MPs chosen to present Lord Newcastle's propositions for peace to Charles.[30] He also backed Holles' efforts to disband the New Model Army in 1647, activities that threatened to have him impeached, but he avoided that fate, probably because of his links with Viscount Saye and Sele.[31]

Sir Walter ventured back to Dorset once the Parliamentarian army had soundly defeated the king's armies in the South-west. While he had been in London, the Royalists had burnt down his home, Charborough House. It appears that it was revenge for Parliamentarian forces' destruction of the manor house of John Turberville in January 1644. However, the leaders of the Parliamentary party in Dorset were said to have done well for themselves, at least according to royalist publications at the time. Sir Walter was said in one to be 'worth £1000 per annum in time of peace, but in time of war worth £5000 per annum'. His son Thomas Erle II was said to be 'a great committee man [who] punisheth his and his father's enemies, and rewards himself and his friends'.[32] The accounts no longer exist, but it is likely that Sir Walter and his son's close connections as MPs on war committees, while linked to the Adventurers, had made money during the war, and that may explain their ability to rebuild Charborough House and other property lost during the fighting. While he was mostly in London during the war, Thomas kept the home fires burning as a member of Dorset's Standing Committee, a small group of leading figures who effectively ran the county for Parliament.[33]

---

30. The Newcastle Propositions were drawn up by the Westminster Parliament as a basis for a treaty with King Charles I in July 1646 after the defeat of the Royalists in the First Civil War. The king had surrendered to Parliament's Scottish allies rather than to Parliament itself and was held in semi-captivity at Newcastle.
31. Richard Cust, 'Erle, Sir Walter (1586–1665)', *Oxford Dictionary of National Biography*, 2004 https://doi.org/10.1093/ref:odnb/37399, last accessed 15 June 2024.
32. George Bankes, *The Story of Corfe Castle* (London: John Murray, 1853), pp. 231–232.
33. Thomas Erle often reappears in the minutes and notes of the Standing Committee. The Dorset papers are one of the few sets of County Standing Committee notes to have survived to the present day. They can be found in the Dorset History Centre.

Brown believed that the Civil War gave Sir Walter opportunities to profit:

> Given the number of financial committees, Sir Walter insinuated himself onto, he was doing rather well out of the war. Committees such as Sequestrations and Bishop's Land were great sources of opportunity for those with the cash to scoop up these assets on the cheap. His early involvement in Virginia and New England strongly suggests that he was of an entrepreneurial bent. His involvement in opposition to the Forced loan, 1626–7, implies that he was not short of cash even at this earlier stage. These earlier colonial and political experiences place him in the tight circle of peers and merchants who instigated the Adventure for Irish land. I haven't found any link between Erle and Ireland prior to 1642, but the speculation offered a potentially great return, and many of his co-investors were people he had been dealing with in earlier colonial ventures for decades.[34]

After the defeats that destroyed his armies, in 1646 Charles put himself into the hands of the Scottish Presbyterian army besieging Newark and he was taken northwards to Newcastle upon Tyne. After nine months of fraught negotiations, the Scots finally arrived at a settlement with the English Parliament. In return for a payment of £100,000, and the promise of more money in due course, the Scots left Newcastle and moved back over the border. Before they left, they had handed Charles over to the parliamentary commissioners in January 1647. He was held under arrest.

REGICIDE

The second part of the Civil War took place between February and August 1648 in England and Wales. The Royalist rebels were crushed. Historian of the Civil War Ann Hughes believed that many men who went to war against the king in 1642 had limited

---

34. Brown, correspondence with the author, 1 August 2022.

objectives, fought reluctantly and were horrified at the political and religious radicalism they had unleashed:

> It is worth remembering that the parliamentarians of 1642 had done much to unleash popular radicalism. They promoted the war against the King as a godly war in which all true Christians should join, and they had, as the representatives of the people, appealed to the people without defining too closely what they meant.[35]

With Charles held by Parliament, on 6 December 1648, the radical, Colonel Thomas Pride and troops from his regiment, stood outside the entrance to St Stephen's Chapel and, as the House of Commons convened that morning, arrested 45 Members and excluded a further 186 whom the army thought unlikely to support its intention of putting the king on trial. Sir Walter was one of those arrested and held long enough to prevent them interfering in the trial. Pride's Purge left a 'Rump' of just 200 Members. Among these, a determined clique unilaterally forced through an 'Act' on 6 January 1649, establishing a court to try Charles I for high treason. Regardless of the widespread opposition to the trial, a guilty verdict was pushed through. The death warrant was signed by only 57 of the 159 commissioners of the high court originally established by the Rump. On 30 January 1649, King Charles I was beheaded outside the Banqueting House on Whitehall.

The English Civil War was the bloodiest in British history per head of population, causing casualties on a scale – some 200,000 dead – that would not otherwise be seen until the First World War. The destruction of property and the economy was on a similar scale. Protector Oliver Cromwell died in 1658. Sir Walter Erle sat in his successor's Parliament, that of Oliver's son Richard, but by this stage, Erle was getting a reputation for being a parliamentary bore – one observer noting that he 'took a liberty to stand up twenty times a day'.[36] Sir Walter was re-elected as the Member for

---

35. Hughes, *Cause of the English Civil War*, pp. 172–173.
36. J.P. Ferris and P. Little, HoP, *Commons, 1604–29, 1640–60*.

Dorset in the 1659 election. In the heated debates in that Parliament, the robust language created tensions. Sir Walter was something of a disruptive force. A speech by Colonel William West was interrupted by Sir Walter Erle on the grounds that it was confused, whereupon Edmund Ludlow complained that: 'if every man should answer to what part of his speech is excepted against, when would your debate end?'

The Long Parliament was dissolved in March 1660. With the Restoration, the Convention Parliament was held. Elected as a 'free parliament', with no oath of allegiance to the Commonwealth or the monarchy, it was predominantly Royalist in its membership. It assembled for the first time on 25 April 1660. Sir Walter, as MP for Dorset, was on the benches. As Father of the House, he argued vigorously for a moderate religious settlement and warned of the dangers of the Militia Bill, as well as sitting on many committees.[37]

BACK IN DORSET

After Corfe Castle had been finally taken, it was partly demolished so that it could serve no further military use. At the end of the war, some stone and timber were carted off by the Erles, including a large oak beam, from the badly damaged Castle for the rebuilding of Charborough House. This was more than just a symbolic gesture of victory. After the Restoration, in August 1661, Sir Ralph Bankes, son of the late Sir John and the formidable Lady Bankes, wrote to Sir Walter demanding the return of the oak beam and other salvage. Sir Walter's reply was dismissive: 'As for the things themselves, the quantity and value of them, certainly they are nothing near as considerable as I perceive you apprehend them to be – five or six loads of timbers and stone being in points of value no such great matter.'[38] Following further acrimonious correspondence, compensation was paid, but the timber remained at Charborough,

37. Walter Erle, *Oxford Dictionary of National Biography*. The Militia Bill was a running dispute between Charles II and Parliament about who would have control over the militia.
38. Bankes, *The Story of Corfe Castle*, p. 258.

where its residents can still see the disputed beam. It is said that the two families did not speak to each other for 300 years. Though Walter had been deprived of his rental incomes for several years, his refreshed finances to rebuild Charborough House on such a scale will have come from his dealings with the Adventurers.

The republican government in the 1650s continued raising revenue by selling off royal forests and supporting the drainage and enclosure of the fens. It passed laws that eliminated all remaining feudal restrictions and charges on landowners but made no changes to the tenures of farmers and cottagers. There is no evidence that Sir Walter opposed this. Historian Christopher Hill highlighted the vested interests that remained despite the ethos of the Civil War. Since the king was one of the largest and most hated enclosers, many anti-enclosure protesters expected Parliament to support their case after the Civil War, but again they were to be disillusioned. Almost all MPs were substantial landowners (like Sir Walter Erle). 'Thus landlords secured their own estates in absolute ownership and ensured that copyholders remained evictable.'[39]

Power had shifted from the aristocracy to the landed gentry. As Tawney noted, 'if, in 1600, it could be said that the more prosperous gentry had the incomes of an Earl, and in 1628 that the House of Commons could buy the House of Lords three times over', the argument advanced in some quarters in 1659 that – since the nobility, who once held two-thirds of the land and now held less than one-twelfth – the day for a House of Lords was passed, was perhaps not surprising.[40] The Erles of Charborough had benefitted from the rise of the gentry at the aristocracy's expense, and from the Civil War more generally.

POST-WAR DORSET

At the age of 74, Sir Walter retired in 1661 from public life. He remained an active Justice of the Peace till the year of his death. It

---

39. Christopher Hill, *Puritanism and Revolution: Studies in Interpretation of the English Revolution of the 17th Century* (London: Schocken Books, 1968), p. 191.
40. Tawney, 'The Rise of the Gentry', p. 37.

was said that even when he was too ill to hold a pen, the force of his personality enabled him to dictate a will complicated in both its testamentary and personal provisions. He was buried at Charborough on 1 September 1665. Sir Walter had visceral anti-papist and hierarchical views. To Sir Walter, his core was his religion but that was pragmatically tempered, and he carefully reinforced his position and control over the lower orders. It was religion that had encouraged him to seek the removal of power from the king and ultimately to regime change. He may have regretted the course of events he had helped to set off. Walter was not an archetypal 'Puritan' in lifestyle, having extravagant gardening tastes. Patrick Little wrote:

> Of the seventeenth century MPs and peers who created gardens to adorn their country estates, perhaps the most unlikely was Sir Walter Erle. Sir Walter, who represented Dorset constituencies 11 times between 1614 and 1660, was a puritanical figure with an inexhaustible appetite for humdrum committee work and something of an obsession with the minutiae of parliamentary procedure. Yet Sir Walter saw himself not as a pompous politician but as a dashing soldier.[41]

Sir Walter's only son, Thomas (II), born in 1621, had married Susanna, the fourth daughter of William Fiennes of Broughton Hall in Oxfordshire. Thomas Erle was chosen as a commissioner on the trial of the king in 1649 but did not take part. But Thomas pre-deceased his parents, dying on 1 June 1650. Thomas II had two sons and two daughters. His eldest son seems to have died early in adulthood, though he had married into the Trenchard family of Wolfeton, near Dorchester. His second son, Thomas III, was born in 1650 the year of his father's death. His mother married again, to Robert Hawley, and this saw him moving into a Cavalier household. His Puritan grandfather Walter (II) was not happy with this arrangement. Grandfather was resolved to relocate him and com-

---

41.   https://thehistoryofparliament.wordpress.com/2020/06/30/the-horticultural-heroism-of-sir-walter-erle/#:~:text=Of%20the%20seventeenth%20century%20MPs,unlikely%20was%20Sir%20Walter%20Erle.

mitted his education to sound Puritan trustees. Following in the footsteps of his father and grandfather, Thomas Erle III was sent to Trinity College, Oxford, where he matriculated, leaving on 12 July 1667, aged 17. He succeeded to the ownership of his grandfather's estate in 1650. Later he was to prove to be a vigorous anti-papist, warrior and leader.

PART III

Barbados and the English Civil War

7

Sheath My Sword in James Drax's Bowels

Far away as it may have been, the English Civil War had repercussions in the Caribbean and severe ones for the Drax family. The Parliamentarians on Barbados were an influential body, counting as they did among their number James Drax, his brother William, Captain Thomas Middleton, Captain Reynold Alleyne and Constant Silvester. Under the canny leadership of Governor Bell, Barbados had sought to remain discreetly neutral, and for a while, Bell was successful. The colonists sent reassuring responses to both Parliament and the king's ministers. This approach reflected the freedom of being 4000 miles away from London. While religion and politics dominated in the British Isles, with the inhabitants of Barbados the pursuit of wealth seemed to be the driving motive. The surviving original settlers were finally beginning to rake in great financial returns and took a pragmatic and tolerant approach to running the island. The early settlers did not discourage Jews, Quakers and Catholics from settling if they brought economic benefits.

Adventurer merchants who were doing well out of the English Civil War were able to expand into the slave trade. Leading Adventurers Maurice Thomson, Pennoyer, Samuel Vassall[1] and the Noells, as well as James Drax, built up a dominant position in the carrying trade for enslaved Africans and Caribbean sugar.[2] Enslaved people were typically sold for sugar, which could then be resold for even greater profits anywhere in Europe. In June 1650, the English East India Company (EEIC) merged with the Maurice Thomson-con-

---

1. Samuel Vassall was a ship-owner, trading partner in Virginia and the West Indies, as well as an investor in the Massachusetts Bay Company.
2. John C. Appleby, 'English Settlement During War and Peace', in Robert L. Paquette and Sidney L. Engerman (eds), *The Lesser Antilles in the Age of European Expansion* (Gainesville, FL: University Press of Florida, 1996), pp. 86–104.

115

DRAX OF DRAX HALL

trolled Courteen Association and the new company was given the monopoly of trade with East Asia.

As he left no memoir, it is not clear why James Drax supported Parliament. He was not of the Puritan mindset. Ligon said Drax, 'who was not so strict an observer of Sundays, as to deny himself lawful recreations'.[3] He may have been influenced by his father to moderate Anglicanism. The best guess is that Charles II's overriding of the Earl of Pembroke/Courteen charter with reassigning the grant of Barbados to the Earl of Carlisle and all the consequential grief had marked Charles as untrustworthy to Drax. Unlike the Virginia colony, the inhabitants of Barbados did not have the number of Puritan and Separatists dissenters that would bring them into tension with Royalists and Catholics. However, as the war continued, a number of displaced landed gentry washed up in Barbados, who, in the following years, bolstered by their sense of the natural order by education and entitlement, would reach for leading roles in the island's governance. For both sides, back at home the Civil War was causing financial ruin for many landed-gentry families. They encouraged male members – often those who were not the oldest son – to go out into the world to make their fortune. As Beckles noted of the emigres to Barbados, 'Remaking old fortunes drove the ambitions of most of the men of means who arrived there in large numbers. This circumstance unlocked and liberated unaccountable entrepreneurial aggression; market thinking, and actions transcended pedagogies of social restraint and respect for traditions of human relations.'[4]

Attempts to prevent the English Civil War from spreading to Barbados were hindered by these migrations. Philip Bell did well while the ascendancy of Royalists and Parliamentarians back in England were in a state of flux for most of the war. The most dangerous of all new arrivals to the stability of Barbados was the Royalist landed gentry. This immigrant group were described by Dunn as 'able and aggressive men'. One such family were the Colle-

---

3. Karen O. Kupperman (ed.), *A True and Exact History of the Island of Barbados* (Cambridge, MA: Hackett Publication, 2011), p. 104.
4. Beckles, *The First Black Slave Society*, p. 238.

tons who were to become one of Barbados' leading planter families by the end of the century. The family's Caribbean history originates with John Colleton, the second son of a former Sheriff of Exeter. John was a Royalist and very active at the beginning of the Civil War, serving as a captain of foot soldiers.

Another was Thomas Modyford, who was a son of the mayor of Exeter, and had fought on the Royalist side in the early stages of the war. He was taken prisoner at Exeter after the royalist garrison surrendered in April 1646. He took with him to Barbados his employee Richard Ligon, who had also been taken prisoner. As with all Royalists captured by Parliament, Modyford and Ligon were liable to pay fines and penalties for resistance. Modyford had sold up his estate and came with £1000 to buy a plantation and another £6000 to maintain it for the next three years. Their ship sailed to Barbados via the Cape Verde Islands, where they purchased enslaved Africans, traded in exchange for wide-brimmed hats. On arrival in Barbados, Modyford had negotiated the purchase of half of a 500-acre plantation from William Hilliard – who was keen to return to England – with its 96 enslaved Africans and 200 acres already in sugar. Modyford was determined to make his fortune, declaring that he would not return to England until he had made £100,000 from sugar. Then there were the Walronds, ardent Royalists. Humphrey Walrond of Ilminster, Somerset, was the inheritor of a landed estate, fought for the king and was taken prisoner. He was given up as a hostage when Bridgwater surrendered to the Parliamentarian army of General Fairfax on 23 July 1645, and he was lodged as a prisoner in the Gatehouse, London. His petition to be allowed to pay a fine, dated 28 October 1645, was granted. Walrond had reached Barbados by 1649. His brother Edward, a lawyer, also settled there.

The Walronds saw the possibility of turning Barbados into a Royalist centre of resistance. Their first step was to orchestrate the dismissal as the island's treasurer, Colonel Guy Molesworth, and put in his place Major William Byam, a Royalist nominee of their own. The Walronds thereupon collected an armed force and marched on Bridgetown, which was by now the capital and contained the island administrative offices. The governor was warned, but after arresting Humphrey Walrond, he released him and conceded to most of their demands.

Tension grew between the two sides, and a pamphlet war broke out. The Royalists ones were notably threatening, and the threat was primarily aimed at James Drax.

> Friends, take my advice, There is in hand a most damnable designe, the Authors are Independents, their ayme is wholly to Casheere the Gentry and Loyall, and to change for our Peace Warre and for our Unity Division, Colonel Drax, that devout Zealot (of the deeds of the Devil, and the cause of that seven headed Dragon at Westminster) is the Agent: Now that the Workman may have his hire, I could wish that there were more Covenanters besides myself, for (truly I cannot conceal it) I have vowed to impeach him and to prosecute him, but not in point of Law, for then I know he would subdue me (but at the Point of Sword): Let me desire such as tender Religion, the Loyal, the safety of the Island, and being of our present Government, they before-armed against the pretence of Liberty, for thereby is meant Slavery and Tyranny. But I halfe repent this motion of the Pen, purposing with all expedition to Action. My ayme is at Drax, Middleton, and the rest.
>
> Vivat Rex.

One hot-headed Royalist declared his intention towards Drax, 'I shall thinke my best rest but disquiet until I have sheathed my sword in his Bowells.' When Governor Bell found that the Royalists were not only distributing 'scandalous papers' and spreading rumours and reports in many parts of the island, but were also openly arming, he issued a declaration. However, no paper proclamation by Governor Bell was now going to stop the Royalists, who had determined to possess the island for the Royal cause.[5]

James Drax, supported by Governor Bell, tried to contain the Royalists by armed force but discovered he could muster only 100

---

5. The Royalists on Barbados coordinated with other islands and the Virginia colony, where the governor offered Charles Stuart a home and base to regroup to retake England.

SHEATH MY SWORD IN JAMES DRAX'S BOWELS

men and was heavily outnumbered. Led by the Walrond family, the Royalists arrested James Drax and over 90 others, including Captain Nicholas Foster, who was later to write an account of the confrontation or 'Rebellion' as he described it.[6] The Roundhead contingent was put under house arrest at Drax Hall, with 18 musketeers guarding them. 'The next morning, they were again brought before the Assembly and condemned to fines in sugar in the manner hereinunder stated, namely: – Lieut. Col. James Draxe to pay 80,000 lbs of Sugar. Captain Thomas Middleton, Lieut. Thomas Rous, Lieut. John Johnson Constant Silvester, Captain John Hockeridge and Thomas Pearse, J Captain Reynold Alleyne, Thomas Mathews were all fined less.'[7]

A new governor, Francis Lord Willoughby, arrived in Barbados in 1650, having obtained a lease of the proprietorship of the island from the second Earl of Carlisle on 29 April of that year. Had not Willoughby intervened, the Walrond contingent would likely have had Drax and other Parliamentarians executed. It is not hard to believe that the Royalist sympathies of some planters did not include seeing the potential of their own economic benefit by the seizure of the plantations of the Draxes and other Parliamentarians. Drax and his family left the island for England. Willoughby sequestered the property of James Drax and other Parliamentarians in 1651.[8] As English supply and trading ships arriving at Barbados became less frequent, the colonists redirected their trade mostly to the Dutch. At the time, it was Amsterdam, not London, which was the trading capital of Europe.

SEND IN THE FLEET

The response of the English Commonwealth, now firmly in power after the execution of Charles I, was the reconquest of the colonies.

---

6. William Drax seems to have been off the island at this time, possibly in London.

7. Nicholas D. Davis, *The Cavaliers & Roundheads of Barbados, 1650–1652: with some account of the early history of Barbados* (Georgetown, British Guiana: Argosy Press, 1887), p. 165.

8. Perfect Account of the Daily Intelligence from the Armies, December 31, 1651–January 7, 1652.

Distant Barbados had become a weak link in the Parliamentary financial system forcing the English state, for the first time, to intervene directly in colonial affairs. They despatched several fleets: the main fleet, under the command of Admiral George Ayscue and Edward Thomson, was assigned to retake Barbados and the second fleet, under Robert Denis and Edward Courtis, sailed to Virginia to suppress the Royalist uprising there. The attacks were coordinated with two further squadrons already in place in other theatres. The third squadron was the main Parliamentary navy under General Robert Blake. Blake's task was to contain Prince Rupert's resurgent Royalist fleet off the coasts of West Africa and to prevent the prince from interfering with the Caribbean mission. The fourth squadron, privately owned but synchronised with the state, was a slave-trading expedition sent by the Adventurers to the Gambia.

The news arrived in Bridgetown, brought by a Dutch merchant ship, that the Royalists on the island had been proclaimed rebels by an Act of Parliament and a fleet was on its way. The reports stimulated the Royalists into a fervour, and they acclaimed they were ready to fight and stand by one another to the last man. Ayscue and his fleet of seven ships eventually arrived in December 1651. The first thing Ayscue was aware of was that Carlisle Bay was full of Dutch ships. The Royalists had been diverting sugar to Amsterdam, and some of the profits were making their way to Charles Stuart in exile to support the Royalist cause. Ayscue immediately seized 14 Dutch ships.

James Drax was said to be on the Ayscue recapture mission. The story goes that Ayscue, with Drax's behind-the-scenes help, eventually defeated the Royalists after several serious skirmishes, but only because of the timely defection of some island military including a militia regiment under the command of Thomas Modyford. Ayscue took possession of the island in January 1652. Colonel Walrond was one of the nine senior Royalists banished by an Act of the Assembly. Byam was another. Byam, Biet opined, had been banished for wanting to 'uphold the authority of his King against the unjust usurpation of my lord Cromwell... [and]

his plantations... [were] plundered and ruined'.[9] They were told not to return until 25 March 1653. The Ayscue expedition was paid for by the amount of refined sugar seized on the island, some 530,000 lbs.

In another move to assert its authority over the colonial empire, the English Parliament had passed the first of the Navigation Acts. Cromwell and his Parliament needed money for the Treasury and were well aware that Barbados was creating enormous wealth, but a lot of that was ending up in Holland rather than England. The Act restrained planters from selling their sugar and other products to non-English merchants or to be carried by non-English ships. From that time onward, the sugar trade would be monopolised by English traders, with the product taken to England and then transhipped to Europe. The Act was clearly in England's interest rather than the colonies and asserted the principle that the colonies existed for England's benefit. The colonists deeply resented the Act and believed that they could obtain better prices by auctioning their sugar to a wide variety of European merchants, rather than passing it through middlemen in London. Resistance to the Navigation Act through smuggling and attempts to have the acts repealed occurred throughout the century.

After his return to Barbados, James Drax reasserted himself on the island with brio. It is not hard to imagine him cantering along the dusty roads between Drax Hall and Bridgetown and then visiting fellow island leaders on their plantations. As Civil War tensions had not totally subsided, he, likely as not, would ride with a bodyguard or two in case any Royalist still felt the need to deliver the promised disembowelling. Always with an eye to efficiency, he inspected plantation lands to ensure the overseers had maintained them in his absence. Not long after his return, he ordered the building of the new Drax Hall house. He was a man on a roll and had clearly made a host of contacts while in London around the Adventurers merchant circle and was now an influential man there and in

---

9.   Biet, *Voyage de la France équinoxiale*, pp. 268–295. This was William Byam, an ardent Royalist who fled after Ayscue's victory to Suriname, where he later became governor.

DRAX OF DRAX HALL

Barbados. Drax had been away from the island for about two years but reintegrated into the island in a short time.

Matthew Parker wrote that Drax was ever the adaptable:

It might also have been helpful that Drax himself seems to have borne no grudges from that bitterly divisive time or held less firm political views than his Royalist detractors had alleged back in the days of the pamphlet war. And now he was happy to work with the new authorities.[10]

Regardless of the Cavalier versus Roundhead disputes, the industrious James Drax's reputation in Barbados was sealed as he was a 'genious'.

A COMPLICATION

There is a complication to this generally received chronology of Drax's return. According to most histories, James Drax was in England and returned to the island in December 1651 when he arrived with the Ayscue fleet. However, in the London Metropolitan Archive are the original handwritten records of two depositions for the Mayor's Court of Depositions. The Mayor's Court was a major way of resolving legal disputes about trade to and from the City of London. The 24 July 1651 deposition by John Ladd of London, a mariner aged 28, confirmed that he was the Master of the *Samuel*. He stated that the *Samuel* was anchored in Carlisle Bay off Bridgetown in April 1651, when sugar loaded by the merchant Robert Arundell was taken off by Lieutenant Colonel Drax and put on board a Dutch ship. A linked October 1651 deposition, made at the request of a merchant Nicholas Enos of London, and sworn by Bartholomew Howard of Ratcliffe, Middlesex, mariner, master mate of the *Samuel* of London, aged 45, and William Tucker of Shadwell, Middlesex, boatswain, aged 23, also stated that sugar loaded on the ship in Barbados was taken off by Lieutenant Colonel Drax (MCD3).[11]

---

10. Parker, *The Sugar Barons*, p. 107.

11. Patrick McGrath (ed.), *Vol XIX Merchants and Merchandise in Seventeenth*

SHEATH MY SWORD IN JAMES DRAX'S BOWELS

What the depositions suggest is that Drax came aboard and ordered the sugar cargo (or at least part of the cargo) diverted to a Dutch ship. The depositions were requested by Nicholas Enos, a joiner in London who had married Anne Drax (sister of James and William) and became involved in Drax's business interests. The depositions clearly imply that James Drax was on the island in April 1651. We do not know what happened in the actual court case the depositions were recorded for, because those records were destroyed during the 1940 Blitz on London. It is either Drax's interests suing Arundell or, more likely, vice versa. It provides some useful links. It connects Bartholomew Howard with Drax, which is significant as other contemporary records show Howard was working with the Guinea Company, which was heavily involved in the triangular trade. Many cases in the Mayor's Court were merchants to ship owners trying to get reimbursement for the loss of cargo or ships. It is possible that Drax owned or leased the *Samuel*.

The London merchant supremo Maurice Thomson and leading Barbados merchant John Wood had been awarded the Guinea Company patent by the English Council of State to exploit trade along the west coast of Africa, including trading in enslaved people. If the explanation that the case involving Drax moving sugar from the *Samuel* to a Dutch ship is one of mistaken dates, and if he did redirect the sugar to a Dutch ship after 1651, he would have been breaking the recently imposed Navigation Act.[12] That is not totally surprising, as Drax had become a law unto himself and was by then one of the biggest plantation owners with at least 700 acres and 200 enslaved people. He and a couple of his close associates were getting hard to handle. In August 1653, Governor Daniel Searle dropped Drax from the island's Council and relieved him of his rank as colonel of the militia and did the same to Colonel Modyford and

---

Century Bristol (Bristol Record Society's Publications, 1955), p. 243. Original to be found in MCD3 at London Metropolitan Archives. Robert Arundell was a merchant in Barbados, active in the 1650s.

12. Another explanation is that 'Lieutenant Colonel Drax' is one of his brothers who may have been on the island at the time. Certainly, John Drax was an officer in the militia.

accused them of being 'unsatisfied spirits'. Parker suggested, 'Maybe they had been too blatant in their illegal trading, even for the corrupt Searle, or had become too serious a threat to his authority.' Neither took it lightly: from January 1654, both Drax and Modyford were organising petitions to Cromwell to be allowed to be reinstated to their former militia and political positions on the island.[13]

Most of the new wave of British migrants came from the consequences of the Civil War back home. Oliver Cromwell discovered he could sell his Royalist captives and made a handsome profit for his Treasury. And after Cromwell's victories at Worcester, Drogheda, and Dunbar in 1649–51, Irish and Scots prisoners were forced to migrate to Barbados and other West Indies colonies. A letter in the Erle papers from Oliver Cromwell discusses the logistics of moving Scottish prisoners of war to England.[14] In many cases, they would have then been escorted onto transports to Barbados. The impact of all these new migrants on the islands was opposed by many of the existing settlers. According to a planters' petition, some 12,000 prisoners of war alone were sent to Barbados between 1649 and 1655. Some took their families with them, only to find themselves separated at their destination.

Despite the influx of migrants, the planters had trouble getting the workforce they needed. Indentured servants or prisoners of war proved poor workers. In Barbados, labourers endured a daily routine of exhausting manual work, such as 'grinding at the mills, attending the fornaces, or digging in this scorching island', regardless of their class or age. In early 1659 several petitions listing the grievances of servants were sent from the British ports. In Barbados, the situation with indentured servants deteriorated. Historian Jerome Handler explained:

In Barbados's early history, white indentured servants, particularly the Irish, often resisted the harsh conditions under which they lived. On at least two occasions, in late 1633 or early 1634

---

13. Parker, *The Sugar Barons*, p. 72.
14. This letter can be found at CCCA GBR/0014/ERLE 5/1.

SHEATH MY SWORD IN JAMES DRAX'S BOWELS

and the late 1640s, they planned revolts that were aborted before the plans could be put into effect.[15]

The hostility of Irish servants toward their masters was also manifest in the apparent involvement of some in later slave plots or alleged plots, as well as reflected in various precautions that planters took against the possibility of revolt, both by servants and the enslaved. Many lived on plantations with a handful of white overseers. There was the militia, but requests were sent back to England by the Assembly to provide a force of regular soldiers to protect the island from rebellion within and invasion from without. Ligon reported that living close to a disaffected workforce did make the planters nervous and described that plantation houses were built with gutters which carried rainwater into cisterns that were:

> within the limits of their houses, many of which are built in manner of fortifications, and have lines, bulwarks, and bastions to defend themselves in case there should be any uproar or commotion... either by the Christian servants, or Negro slaves.[16]

Even so, desperate planters would pay well for indentured servants. A letter, now held in the Bristol Record Office, demonstrated this point. The Record Office explained: 'Among the surviving records, we have a letter from a man in the West Indies begging his sister to make a great effort to find an indentured servant for him since servants could be sold at a high profit.'[17]

While there was plenty of evidence of the harsh treatment of these indentured servants, there was always the danger of them

---

15. Jerome Handler, 'Slave Revolts and Conspiracies in Seventeenth-Century Barbados', *New West Indian Guide*, vol. 56, nos 1/2 (1982), 5–42, p. 7.

16. Ligon, *A True and Exact History*, p. 70.

17. B.R.O. Depositions 1654–1657, 7th July 1657. The business of transporting servants to the plantations was considerable. There is a good deal of information about this in the Bristol archives, and a few extracts have been included in Douglas (1955) from the volumes called 'Servants to Foreign Plantations', which were published as *The Bristol Registers of Servants to Foreign Plantations, 1654–1686*, edited by P.W. Coldham (Bristol: Clearfield Co, 1988) (Ref. Bk/438). There are also some references to this trade in The Deposition Books.

taking legal action if they made it back to England. The planters gradually turned to the slavery of non-British people, mostly from Africa but also some indigenous people from the region. This was about to explode into a huge international trade in human trafficking, and what the historian Sir Hilary Beckles has described as the 'The First Black Slave Society'.[18]

---

18. Beckles, *The First Black Slave Society.*

8
Sir James, Slave Trader

The successful production of 'white gold' catapulted Barbados from a minor colony to a critical component in the burgeoning triangular trade. By 1645, the Dutch West India Company was disintegrating, and this created a vacuum the Merchant Adventurers were happy to fill, both to service the English Caribbean sugar plantations and to gain access to the main slave markets in Brazil and Spanish America. A primary source of profit for the Dutch had been the supply of enslaved people to Spanish and Portuguese colonies, a trade that Thomson, Wilson and separately the Noells (who were also close to James Drax) moved into. The African gold trade was also of importance and this, with the profits in American silver from the sugar and slave trades, enabled the completion of the Adventurers' Atlantic trade loop. It was this highly complex and integrated supply chain. The resulting duties had provided Cromwell with the cash he needed for the invasion of Ireland.[1]

In March 1653, Drax was engaged in the triangular trade with at least two ships. He bought 'One great storehouse lyeing and being in the Bridgetown', from Robert Hooper and Martin Bentley, both neighbours and sugar merchants. The 'One great storehouse' is described as 'commonly knowne and called Vandesteere house', suggesting it had been built for a Dutch trader. Hooper and Bentley also sold Drax 'one New store house which was built on the said land by the said Robert Hooper and Martin Bentley'.[2] Access to the slave trade was at the centre of this exchange, with Drax releasing his share of two slave voyages to 'the Coaste of Africa and thence

---

1. Brown, *Empire and Enterprise*, p. 168.
2. In 1654, for instance (the same year that Drax is believed to have invented the integrated plantation), the merchant Robert Hooper possessed a 200-acre plantation with a workforce of 101 unfree labourers (35 servants, 66 enslaved Africans), satisfying the optimal ratio of two acres to every one labourer.

bound hither' in exchange for urban property. Drax's two vessels were the 'good ship the *Samuell*' now captained by Samuel Cooke, and the pinnace *Hope*, mastered by William Goodladd. Drax sold Hooper and Bentley one-eighth of the ships' slaves and one-fifth of the cargo and profit. The ships had set out from England and picked up a cargo of enslaved people. The cost was £454 sterling or '54,490lbs weight of good muscovado sugar', and part of the arrangement was that Drax could select from the cargo 'two male and two female' from each vessel once they arrived in Barbados.[3]

The Slave Voyages database records the voyages by the *Samuel* and the *Hope* in 1654:

Samuel, Capt Samuel Cooke
Owners: James Drax, James Hooper, Robert Bentley and (probably) Martin Bentley
Voyage: London – Africa – Barbados
No. of slaves embarked: 314
No. of slaves disembarked: 242
Hope, Capt William Goodlad
Owners: James Drax, Robert Hooper, Martin Bentley
Voyage: London – Africa – Barbados
No. of slaves embarked: 314
No. of slaves disembarked: 242

Ian Friel, an expert on early shipping, told me that the *Samuel* would almost certainly have been a three-masted ship, with square sails carried on the fore and mainmasts and a triangular lateen sail on the mizzenmast towards the stern, and the *Hope* a smaller ship:

The fact that the database records the same slave numbers for each ship almost certainly means that this was the total of the slaves carried by both vessels. The horrendous death rate in transit – 23% – was not unusual on early slave voyages.[4]

---

3. The documents can be found at BDA RB3/629/630.
4. I. Friel, correspondence with the author, 24 January 2022.

Father Biet wrote a description of Bridgetown in 1654, and its harbour, noting the island capital's wealth. Biet counted 300–400 buildings in the island capital, and observed the majority were inns, stores and warehouses, filled with the island's goods for import or export. Biet, however, found the concentration of taverns and inns in Bridgetown a source of violent public disorder that the priest felt complemented the brutality he witnessed on the island's sugar plantations.[5] At this time, at least a hundred ships a year were visiting the port, many bringing indentured servants, prisoners and enslaved people to Barbados to work on the plantations. The harbour would be alive with boats and launches plying to and from the large wooden sailing ships anchored in the bay. The enslaved Africans were unloaded, as were the fine imports for the planters, the food staples and wood from New England, while the commodities of cotton, sugar and tobacco were on the harbour side waiting to the transported to the ships, bound for Europe.

DRAX RETURNS TO ENGLAND

Sometime late in 1653, James Drax lost his wife, Meliora. Like many of the women in this story, we know little of Meliora as there is no contemporary written record about her. Parker said of Meliora, 'Certainly, she must have been tough. In the space of 14 years, she had produced eight children who survived infancy, quite an achievement at the time.'[6]

Meliora was in London at the time of her death, and it is not known where the children were, but they probably did not return with James with Ayscue's fleet. James junior was aged about 15, Henry about 12, and John 11, but most likely, they were at school in England, and there is evidence that a fourth son Samuel matriculated from St John's, Oxford, in 1661. During the time Biet was in Barbados, James Drax decided to leave for London in 1654:

While we were in this Island, this Colonel Drax embarked on a trip to England. We saw the esteem in which he was held, for the

---

5. Handler, 'Father Antoine Biet's Visit to Barbados', p. 66.
6. Parker, *The Sugar Barons*, p. 78.

day of his departure he came to visit the Governor who entertained him and many others. Then, after dinner, he was accompanied to the place where the ship was to embark by more than two hundred of the Island's most important people, all well mounted and marching two by two in a column headed by the Governor and Colonel Drax As he arrived at the embarkation place, the ship fired a volley of all its cannons, and, having been put in the launch to go out to the vessel, all the persons accompanying him fired their pistols. Then, having seen him go up into the vessel, they turned back so as to escort the Governor, marching in the same order in which they had come.[7]

James Drax would have been reunited with his children on his return to England. Soon after, he found a new wife, Margaret Bamfield, from a landed-gentry family in Somerset. She was younger than him, and the marriage involved considerable financial arrangements to her benefit. Whether Drax intended to leave Barbados permanently is unknown, but that was what occurred. If he returned, it was not recorded. He became a major representative of Barbados' interests in London, leaving the running of the plantations to his Barbadian contacts. Later when James the younger was older, he went to Barbados to run the plantations and lasted only a short time before returning to London. There are indications that James junior suffered from ill health throughout his short life.

While a lot of money could be made from the colonies, it was a financially risky business. In 1656, a violent rainstorm hit Barbados, devastating many plantations by destroying crops, animals, buildings and killing people. When the news reached London, the merchants petitioned Parliament on 18 November for a licence to restock their plantations. The state records note:

Petition of Martin Noell, Wm. Chamberlain, Col. Draxe, Col. Hooper, Peter Leere, Capt. Manyford, and Mr. Batsen, merchants, planters, and traders to Barbadoes, to the Lord Protector

---

7. Biet, *Voyage de la France équinoxiale*, pp. 268–295.

and Council. Have received intelligence that by reason of extraordinary rains, lately fallen in the island, almost all their horses, neat cattle, negroes, and other servants, are destroyed, and their works must lie still unless speedily supplied. Pray for licence to transport thither 600 horses and 600 neat cattle.

It was endorsed. This was just one of many such petitions.[8]

In England, James Drax continued to thrive. In December 1657, he was called in for a meeting by the Lord Protector, Oliver Cromwell, and was knighted. Cromwell knew the work he had done for Parliament in Barbados and saw him as a driver of the West Indies economic boom. In September 1659, merchants and planters who traded to Barbados gathered for a meeting at the Cardinal's Cap, a tavern in London situated at the meeting point of Cornhill and Lombard Street. These increasingly powerful men with political connections within Westminster and business interests in the English Caribbean included Martin Noell, Thomas Povey and James Drax. The purpose of their meeting was to interview a new candidate for the position of governor of Barbados. Vincent Gookin, an MP and colonial bureaucrat, was in advanced talks with the Council of State to secure his appointment to the office. Although the details of their conversation are now lost, the merchants ended their meeting impressed with Gookin's qualifications and gave him their 'full approbation'. Two things were to scupper the scheme: Gookin dying, and the Restoration. Nevertheless, Michael Bennett observed: 'The meeting convened at the Cardinal's Cap in 1659 suggests that London merchants did not just purchase plantations and establish trade routes to Barbados, but also sought to exert political influence over the colony in the era of the sugar boom.'[9]

After Oliver Cromwell died in 1658, his son Richard took over as Protector, but the Protectorate soon disintegrated, and Charles

---

8. www.british-history.ac.uk/cal-state-papers/colonial/america-west-indies/vol1/pp450-452.
9. Bennett, 'Merchant Capital and the Origins of the Barbados Sugar Boom', p. 209.

II took the Crown when the monarchy was restored in 1660. Sir James Drax, as with many other former Parliamentarians such as Sir Walter Erle, had to find ways to come to an accommodation with the Royalist government. There were suggestions that Charles would allow Barbados to accede to Spain, but he was aware of the value of the island and, according to Matthew Parker, came to an agreement with the planters. The State recognised the land purchases of the previous 30 years, proprietary dues ended, and Barbados sugar was given protected status:

> In return, Charles would receive customs revenue from the island at 4.5% of the value of all exports, and he insisted that the colonists buy manufactured goods only from England. Everything had to be transported in English or English colonial ships, and tropical produce such as sugar could only be carried to England or another English colony, even if it was subsequently re-exported to the Continent.[10]

The Navigation Act would stand. The old regime was resumed, though without the monarchical absolutism which meant less Royal power.

Under King Charles II, Sir Francis Willoughby was sent back to Barbados as governor for the second time. After Willoughby's arrival, Colonel Modyford was tried for treason over his change of sides to Admiral Ayscue back in 1651. He brought family influence to bear and was found not guilty. That Sir James Drax survived the Restoration score-settling and kept his position was undoubtedly because of his central role as a key node in a network of Caribbean trade. Drax, as one of England's more successful West Indies merchants, was appointed to Whitehall's Committee of Trade and Plantations.[11] Whether Sir James Drax and the Puritan Civil War entrepreneur Sir Walter Erle met, they inhabited some of the same mercantile circles in the same period. Both were effectively

10. Parker, *The Sugar Barons*, p. 117.
11. Calendar of State Papers, Colonial Series, Vol. II, 4 (item no. 12).

landed gentry, but Sir James was more the *nouveau riche*, and sugar money spoke.

CITY WHEELER DEALER

Over the following years, James Drax continued to extend his business connections in London and Amsterdam while remotely managing his plantation in Barbados. On 7 July 1660, the governor of the English East India Company (EEIC) announced that James Drax had been elected to one of their committees: other familiar names elected that day include Sir William Thomson, Maurice Thomson, Thomas Kendall, Peter Middleton and Christopher Willoughby. Thirteen prominent investors in Barbados occupied seats on the EEIC court of directors between 1650 and 1670; James Drax was one. The expansion of the colony's own resident merchant community in response to the consumer demand created by the sugar boom meant that the island had become a regional centre for transnational trade in the Caribbean by the 1660s funded by merchant capital.

Despite his growing shire land portfolio, Sir James Drax now remained London based. His local church was St John of Zachary, where the West India merchant Martin Noell was also a congregant, a quarter mile from St Paul's Cathedral. It was burnt down in the Great Fire of London in 1666 and was not rebuilt, but busts of Sir James and Henry Drax were rescued and taken to the nearby church of St Anne and Agnes where they are to the present day. Sir James gave money to the preachers and the poor of the parish and at least one of his sisters was married there. More tragically, three of his infants with Margaret are buried there. One child, Jacob, born in 1658, did survive though nothing is known about him. Sir James probably owned lands in Hackney, which may explain why his eldest son was known as James Drax of Hackney.[12] On 18 February 1661, Sir James Drax and a group of leading West India merchants were granted an audience with Charles II and Drax's knighthood

---

12. Parker, *The Sugar Barons*, p. 116.

was raised to a baronetcy. In the summer of 1661, Sir James became ill and died. He was about 52 years old. The funeral was at the Noell family-owned Camden House in Chislehurst, Kent, and he was buried at St John of Zachary. Four shillings was paid for the 'ring of ye Great Bell for Sir James Drax'.[13] Not a man to harbour grudges, he left money to his wife's brother, Warwick Bamfield, an extreme Royalist.[14]

SIR JAMES' EPITAPH

So, what to make of Sir James?

Sir James was undoubtedly an adventurer, an entrepreneur, an innovator, physically robust, had Protestant views, was a possible proto-democrat, an early influential capitalist and a networker. He was not entirely pragmatic and must have been intelligent. He undertook a high-risk business opportunity and succeeded. In contrast, many others in similar pursuits died in shipwrecks, of disease, or natural disasters, from being killed or captured by pirates or other rival European forces. Other colonists went bankrupt through crop failures or lack of money. He was lucky to have survived nearly three decades in the Caribbean, which few did.[15] In Barbados, after his return from exile, he was greatly admired by white society. Of Drax, historians Carl and Roberta Bridenbaugh said Barbadians 'could scarcely have failed to be dazzled by the high social position that sugar wealth assured the master of a great plantation. He was served, obeyed, and respected by everyone, not merely his retainers'. What his indentured servants or then his enslaved workers thought of him, we do not know. The Bridenbaughs list dignity, taste, good manners, *noblesse oblige*, a certain imperiousness as the contributions of leading planters of the late 1640s brought to the Caribbean:[16] much the same attributes as the British landed gentry sought to

---

13. Records of two City Parishes, p. 391.
14. Parker, *The Sugar Barons*, p. 107.
15. Between 1647 and 1650, an epidemic ran through Barbados, killing at least 8000 white inhabitants and uncounted enslaved people. It was probably the bubonic plague.
16. Bridenbaughs, *No Peace Beyond the Line*, p. 137.

affect. Exploitation, cruelty and greed were not listed. He created an enormous amount of wealth for himself ('he lived like a prince'), his family, the elite of the Caribbean, the City and the British Empire. We don't know how much, because there are no detailed accounts of the Drax Hall plantation of the seventeenth century in the public domain. Drax represents a dramatic and dynamic shift to capitalism from feudalism. In his book *Sweetness and Power*, Sydney Mintz asserted that 'most students of capitalism (though not all) believe that capitalism became a governing economic form in the late 18th century and not before'. Mintz pointed to the presence of industrial factories embedded in the fields of early Caribbean sugar estates, which challenged 'the opinion of most authorities'.[17] All this needed investment, and the City of London merchants put money in. By 1701 the English exporters shipped goods worth £542,000 to the American colonies and Africa, representing about an eighth of total domestic exports. Sir James would be today a free marketeer. He did not like the Navigation Acts, a product of the Mercantilist mindset, despite their positive impact on British capitalism, because they imposed a monopoly which could then enforce on him a high price when he bought enslaved people. He sought to evade the Act by buying by a back route at lower prices. Free trade versus protectionism has been a contentious issue over the centuries. There is no indication that he thought a hierarchical society with plantation owners and the merchants at the top, overseers at the next level, indentured servants at the next and enslaved people at the bottom was anything but the 'natural order' in Barbados. The Normans did a good job of making the English think in terms of hierarchies. There was an enforced 'natural order' of race and religion within the British settlers, which was in the first level English and Welsh Protestants, the second Scottish Protestants and then at the bottom Irish Catholics. A Virginia Puritan colonist in 1630 summed it up as a 'divine order':

God almightie in his most holy and wise providence hath soe disposed of the Condicion of mankind, as in all times some

---

17. Sydney W. Mintz, *Sweetness and Power: The Place of Sugar in Modern History* (New York: Viking Penguin, 1985), p. 55.

must be rich, some poore, some highe and eminent in power and dignitie; others mean and in subjeccion.[18]

The profound issue with Sir James Drax was not his status but that his innovations included slavery; indeed, he and his associates industrialised slavery. There is an argument today that you cannot judge people by modern liberal standards or by the concept of human rights. There is also the contention that life, then, tended to be brutal, short and often violent, and so attitudes to other humans were different. People died violently all the time, as in the English Civil War, the Anglo-Dutch War, the War of Jenkins Ear and so on. But James Drax excelled at a brutal trade and established chattel slavery. This book collates the evidence that Drax was not just an enslaver; he also shipped and traded in the enslaved. There are subsidiary arguments that other European nations did it, that Africans themselves did it, Arabic traders did it and that white people were taken captive and enslaved, especially by the Barbary States. It is complex. But at the fundamental moral level, slavery is and was reprehensible. Sir James Drax helped create an industry that displaced up to twelve million West Africans and other ethnicities over more than two centuries, disrupted vast areas of Africa, and further brutalised any who had contact with it. He led in turning Barbados into a slave society. We do have accounts of general treatment of enslaved people in Barbados, which will be covered in a later chapter. Ligon was appalled by some of what he saw in how overseers treated servants and enslaved people, as were Biet and other contemporary visitors. It is not known whether the visitors were at Drax Hall at the time of their observations.

With the death of Sir James, the eight children of Sir James Drax were variously in England and Barbados. Sir James' second wife Margaret was still in Barbados. As seen by her marriage arrangements with Sir James, Margaret was an astute financial manager,

---

18. John Winthrop, 'A Modelle of Christian Charity', in Edmund S. Morgan (ed.), *The Founding of Massachusetts: Historians and the Sources* (Indianapolis: Indianapolis Press, 1964), p. 190.

and archive documents show that she invested in the Hudson Bay Company. She went on to marry a Colleton and have a new family. On his death, Sir James' son (James II) inherited his baronetcy and married a wealthy heiress, but in March 1663, he died (the cause is not recorded) aged 24. This may well have come as a shock to his brother, the second son, Henry. The Drax family history has it that he may have been living on a newly acquired property in Lincolnshire with about 1760 acres of farmland. He would later make other purchases in England, including a townhouse in London's Bloomsbury Square. It is likely Henry was in Barbados at the time of his older brother's death. He returned and was in England from early 1664 to mid-1666. In February 1665, 24-year-old Henry Drax, married 20-year-old Frances Tufton, the daughter of the Earl of Thanet. The marriage indicated that the Drax family was on the rise socially. Not long before the Great Fire of London, Henry and Frances went to Barbados to look after the plantations. By June 1667, he was on the Barbados Council.

JAMAICA

Sir James Drax's nephew, William II, was to benefit from one other of his uncle's enterprises, which in time opened up the possibility of a plantation in Jamaica. Back in 1655 a Parliamentary flotilla – part of Cromwell's Western Design initiative to expand English colonisation – had failed to capture the island of Hispaniola from the Spanish after weeks of skirmishes. The financing of this fleet, according to some sources, came in part from James Drax and partners. Instead, the English force took off and captured Jamaica from the Spanish. On the coast, the English built the settlement of Port Royal, a base of operations where piracy flourished. Conditions in Jamaica were disorganised, and a number of British governors came and went. Some African enslaved people took advantage of the political turmoil and escaped to the island's interior mountains, forming independent communities. They became known as the Maroons and were insistent that they were not prepared to return to slavery. That created a formidable force capable of fighting a guerrilla war.

In 1664, Colonel Thomas Modyford, now forgiven for his treason and knighted, was sent as governor to Jamaica to sort matters out and with a remit to develop Jamaica. He took his not inconsiderable household with more than 1000 enslaved workers. Jamaica was a much larger and more difficult island to run. It featured mountains and plenty of places for rebels to hide out. But it had tremendous potential for plantations. Modyford had the king's permission to allot settlers one million acres of land. His inner circle of wealthy sugar magnates was to be allocated thousands of acres. As part of the deal, settlers in Jamaica were given a grace period before they had to pay the 4.5 per cent duty to the king. Dunn noted:

> During his seven years in office in office Modyford issues 1800 land patents totalling upwards of 300,000 acres – triple the acreage of Barbados. The finest farmland in the Parish of St Andrews, St Catherine, St John and Clarendon on the south coast was laid out, much of it in large allotments.[19]

A number of small plantations were operating in St Ann's, known as The Garden Parish because of its rich soil.[20] Although the Spanish had engaged in some cultivation of sugar in Jamaica, their production was limited and only for local consumption. By the 1660s, sugar production proved so profitable there that once English control of Jamaica had been consolidated, Governor Modyford wasted no time in establishing sugar production on an industrial scale. Given the closeness of the two families, it is likely that Governor Modyford was in discussion with the Drax family about the opportunities offered by Jamaica, especially by planters who had learnt

---

19. Dunn, *Sugar and Slaves*, p. 154.

20. St Ann's is a historical location because Christopher Columbus, the Italian explorer working for Spanish monarchs, had found his ships rotting out from underneath him and was forced to run them aground at St Ann's Bay. The Spaniards set up a fortified camp on the shore and sent several of their crew, accompanied by Arawak paddlers, in a dugout canoe to Hispaniola in order to organise a rescue expedition. It was a year before Columbus and his men were rescued.

the plantation trade in Barbados. In 1669, Sir James Drax's nephew, William, sailed to Jamaica from Barbados. He likely bought out the smaller plantations or was given government land grants from Modyford, and he cleared extra ground to found the Drax Hall plantation, which lies on the north coast just to the east of St Ann's Bay. To the west of Drax Hall was the plantation Cardiff Hall which had been created by Blagrave, who had been a regicide of Charles I. For William Drax II, the reasons for emigration from Barbados to Jamaica would have been compelling. Barbados was getting overcrowded and as a 1675 report boasted, a sugar works with 60 enslaved people in Jamaica could make more profit than one with 1000 'in any of the [other] Caribee Islands, by reason the soil is new'. In 1668, the Governor of Barbados complained that the island 'renders not by two-thirds of its former production by the acre; the land is almost worm out'. Bajan planters kept increasingly large flocks of animals to provide dung that could revitalise the soil.

According to their history, the Drax family believe that the founder of the Drax Hall Estate in Jamaica was Charles Drax, who was said to have been part of the Parliamentarian expedition in the 1650s to expel Spaniards. But this does not seem to have been the case. Charles was William's son and took over the plantation around the time of his father death in 1691. The public records in Jamaica do not indicate when the Drax Hall great house was constructed. Ultimately, the Jamaican plantation was to be 4000 acres stretching from the fertile coastal plain to the mountainous highlands of St Ann's parish. It was considered a large and successful plantation and had a workforce of some 320 enslaved Africans producing a sugar crop. The slave village site at Drax Hall was located south and east on a rise of the eighteenth-century great house.[21]

---

21. Charles Drax was member of Assembly for St Ann in 1702, St David in 1707, St Mary in 1708, St George in 1710 and St James in 1719. Charles Drax of St Ann, Esquire. Estate probated in Jamaica in 1723. Slave-ownership at probate: 307 of whom 167 were listed as male and 140 as female. 120 were listed as boys, girls or children. Total value of estate at probate: £8765.43 Jamaican currency of which £6424 currency was the value of enslaved people. Source: UCL Slavery database.

Meanwhile the number and size of plantations in Jamaica expanded as did the number of enslaved people forced to work on the island. For planters who were absent, business was done in London at the Jamaica Coffee House, in St Michael's Alley, Cornhill, whose foundation dates probably from the last decade of the seventeenth century. Here the masters of ships engaged in the Jamaica and Guinea trade called to collect letters and were to be seen by merchants or others at stated hours. To this coffee house letters were addressed to the agents and probably to other merchants and planters from their correspondents in Jamaica.[22]

The wider Drax family would own an estate in Jamaica for a few decades, and it was gradually sold out of the family by 1770. Although the Jamaican plantations poured money into the broader Drax family coffers, these were not the Draxes who were to become the Plunkett-Ernle-Erle-Drax branch. For that branch, we need to return to Henry Drax I and Barbados.

---

22.   Lilian Penson, 'The London West India Interest in the Eighteenth Century', *The English Historical Review*, vol. XXXVI, no. CXLIII (July 1921), 376.

9

Henry Drax and 'The Devil was in the Englishman'

On the island of Barbados, the drawbacks of Sir James Drax's integrated plantation system were beginning to reveal themselves. Once the contracts of indentured servants had expired, they were accorded the status of freeman in Barbados and could purchase land and unfree labourers of their own.[1] Some had bought small plots with the ambition to expand. However, as the island transformed into large sugar plantations worked by enslaved Africans that were deemed more commercially viable, these English smallholders were being bought out.[2] This consolidation meant that smallholders and aspirant indentured servants who had completed their time had no opportunity to expand, so they trickled out of the island. This reduced the number of white freemen on the island. The new integrated form of sugar plantation required a large force of enslaved labour carefully coordinated by overseers.

Sir James Drax's younger brother, John, was running part of the family's Barbados shipping business, living a little way from Drax Hall and Bridgetown in St Michael's parish. He was actively involved in the plantation, civic life of the Island and was a colonel in the island militia. But John Drax was increasingly concerned with the security of white people on the island. He was on the Barbados Assembly and co-signed a letter with Ferdinando Gorges and seven others in July 1669 to a Mr Nicholas in London.[3] 'That

---

1. By contrast, enslaved Africans living in Barbados were afforded no such liberty. They were subject to greater control and more brutal punishments.
2. It was reminiscent of the enclosures that were taking place back in England, with 'improving' landowners displacing smallholders.
3. The Gorges were a prominent landed gentry family in south-west England and owned great chunks of land, including in Dorset, where their holdings included Shipton Gorge and Bradpole.

141

they may send the arms and ammunition, &c., which his Majesty has given to Barbados by the first ships, Mr. John Champante will wait on him for the order.' John Drax wanted to make sure that munitions were sent so that any rebellion could be put down. The letter also implies preparation for a slave-trading voyage, which would also pick up the arms.[4] In a later letter to the Assembly in 1670, John Drax expressed alarm at the rising rate of white emigration from Barbados. He warned that this undermined the island's white population and made them increasingly vulnerable to the 'First Attempt', a euphemism for violent rebellion by the enslaved. His proposal was the creation of a manufacturing base on the island to replace costly imports and to 'find Imployment for many of your poor [who] would continue not [to] goe off because they know not how to subsist in Barbados'.

The historian Lilian Penson noted that there were two principal differences between the society of the islands of the West Indies and that of the southern colonies of North America. In the West Indies there was greater disproportion between the enslaved Africans and the white populations, and amongst the proprietors of the plantations, absenteeism was far more rife. 'These differences made the protection given by the mother country essential to the islands, as preventing not only foreign aggression, but also rebellion at home.'[5]

John Drax was also troubled that the enslaved labour force was developing an artisan class capable of jobs like blacksmithing and cooperage. In John Drax's view, to protect against the displacement of white artisans – many of whom were former white indentured servants – the proposed jobs must be exclusive 'in this trade nor in any other [may] there be any Negroes employed except Artificers belonging to the sugar work'. The Barbados legislators blamed skilled slave labour and land consolidation for displacing the aspirations of poor working whites. As enslaved African men became

---

4.   1 p. [Col. Papers, Vol. XXIII., No. 26.], www.british-history.ac.uk/cal-state-papers/colonial/america-west-indies/vol5/pp581-600. Col. John Drax to Barbados Assembly, 14th December 1670, CO31/2: 15, TNA, last accessed 1 July 2024.

5.   Penson, 'London West India Interest', p. 373.

HENRY DRAX AND 'THE DEVIL WAS IN THE ENGLISHMAN'

artisans, they acquired some mobility. At the time, more and more African blacksmiths, dockworkers, coopers and haberdashers moved about the island, in and out of Bridgetown, making money for their owners and making connections for themselves. Efforts to curb white reliance on African artisans were unsuccessful not least because of the considerable economic gains for whites that owned them. In retaliation against owners who allowed this, the Assembly proposed taxes on 'every Negro where there is no sugar works'. In his letter, John Drax's proposals allowed for African artisans at sugar works only so long as their owners did not contribute to the problem of slave mobility by hiring them out.[6] However, John Drax was not able to follow through his proposal as within the year John Drax succumbed to ill health and died.[7]

Sir James' second son, Henry Drax, was now in charge of Drax Hall and Drax Hope. He was very much in the mould of his father, and his plantations were economically successful. He sat on the Council of Barbados which voted to retain the 1661 Slave Code. He too was soon a colonel in the militia. Like his father he was accused of breaking the commercial law by disembarking captives from Africa in isolated parts of the island to avoid registration and taxed. Among his alleged offences, he was accused of under-reporting the weight of ships' cargoes that were being sent to Britain. He was summonsed by the Lords of Treasury in London to explain why the actual weights of cargoes did not match the paperwork.[8] Henry Drax's first wife died, and he remarried in 1671, again into an aristocratic family, to Dorothy, daughter of Lord Lovelace. Eight years later, Henry Drax decided to return to London, not least to face the Lords of Treasury. He had been in the tropical climate of Barbados for some 20 years. He perpetrated one final Act that would reverberate not only in Barbados but also across the Caribbean through the slave states in the Americas and even, in its sentiments, through to the modern world.

---

6. Col. John Drax to Barbados Assembly, 14th December 1670, Co31/2: 15, PRO. 10.

7. John Drax died in 1671 and his will is available: PROB 11/338 Eure 1-54.

8. Journal of Lords and Plantations, *The Calendar of State Papers, Colonial, North America and the West Indies 1574–1739*, vol. 10, 10 June 1680.

THE DEVIL WAS IN THE ENGLISHMAN

Written circa 1679, 'Instructions on the Management of a Seventeenth-Century Barbadian Sugar Plantation' is a manual of how to run a sugar plantation.[9] It was almost certainly written by or for Henry Drax to make sure his manager Richard Harwood ran the plantation effectively in his absence.[10] The 'Instructions' are based on Henry Drax and his father's experience focusing on the means necessary to achieve the 'finall productt of all our Endewors'.[11] The full document is the most informative as to the practices on a seventeenth-century plantation. It was widely copied over the next hundred years and used across British colonies, but no copies were thought to survive until a version was found misfiled at the Bodleian Library, Oxford. This infamous guide details how to use slave labour to maximise profit, which demonstrated his actuarial obsession with his slaves' births, deaths, idleness, sickness, labour and yields. In the document, the writer lists enslaved people as chattels alongside animals and properties.

Further, Harwood was only to concern himself with running the plantation, and 'The Instructions' told him firmly that he should never be away from his workplace.[12] The distiller was to be paid by achieved production, and that person had to distil 14,000 gallons of rum from a season's crop. If he did not, he was to be regarded

---

9. Henry Drax, 'Instructions which I would have observed by Mr Richard Harwood in the Mannagment of My plantation acording to the Articles of Agreement
betwene us which are heare unto Annexed', 1679. Rawlinson MSS A348, fol. iov, Bodleian Library, University of Oxford.

10. Harwood was the son of John Harwood who had been a royalist soldier captured at the Battle of Newbury in 1643 and transported to Barbados.

11. The historian Peter Thompson made a detailed study of 'Instructions' including the Rawlinson version: Peter Thompson, 'Henry Drax's Instructions on the Management of a Seventeenth-Century Barbadian Sugar Plantation', *The William and Mary Quarterly*, 3rd ser, vol. 66, no. 3 (2009), 578.

12. The 'Instructions' consist of 24 handwritten pages. It is unsigned, undated, and is in two hands and is almost certainly a copy or variant of an earlier original. Copies of the 'Instructions' were apparently preserved in Barbados for a considerable period, and subsequent generations of planters.

HENRY DRAX AND 'THE DEVIL WAS IN THE ENGLISHMAN'

as failing in his contract and paid nothing. The distiller was at all times liable for the distillery's contents and had to sleep with the key to its lock in his pocket. The curer, whose judgement as to when dried sugar cones could be knocked out was vital to production quality, should eat at Harwood's table but only so that Harwood could better keep an eye on him to make him fearful of neglecting his duties. Harwood was instructed on how to buy enslaved people of quality for the plantation to make up for any losses:

> I suppose to supply the places of those that shall be deseased or Dy you will wantt a yearly Recrute of 10 or 15[. O]r itt may be if by Any Contagious distemper theire Happen a greatt mortality[,] which I beseech the great god of marcy to defend you from[,] twenty or mor[,] which if I doe not furnich you with from England I would have you buy with the adwice and Assistance of My Cozn Ltt. Colonel John Codrington on of my Attorneys heare. [L]ett all that you buy be Choyce Young Negros Who will be fitt for plant Service.[13]

Drax's preference was to buy 'Cormante or gold Coast Negros', who had 'always Stood and proved best in this plantation[,] theirefor you will doe welle to buy of that Nation than any other'.[14]

'Instructions' does make a number of minor concessions to the Drax Hall and Drax Hope workforces. The first order to Harwood was that he maintained a plentiful table to support his 'family' of white and black plantation workers. Drax specified the acreage and crops to be set aside for feeding his slaves (though he also accepted that his slaves might still steal to satisfy hunger). Drax told Harwood to provide for himself and any Drax that was eating with him:

> as also for the plenty relief of all sutch Either Whites or Blacks that shall take Sick in the family that you keepe A plenty full table[.] For furnishing of which I doe allow you the proceede

---

13. Drax, 'Instructions', 1679.
14. Thompson, 'Henry Drax's Instructions', p. 585.

DRAX OF DRAX HALL

or produce of all Sheeps hogs Turekeys Dung hill fouls Ducks pigons and Rabbets.[15]

He required Harwood to employ a doctor and cautioned him against abuse of the slave workforce. He warned Harwood that '[Y]ou most Never punish Either to Sattisfy your own anger passion', described the 'End' of punishment as the reclamation of the 'Mallyfactor', and hinted that he had hired Harwood precisely because he could control his 'passion'. 'Instructions' stated that the organisation of the enslaved into gangs was the best method 'to prevent idleness and make the Negroes do their work properly'. At Drax Hall, the enslaved were divided in five or six gangs according to their sex, age and strength ranging from the 'ablest and best' reserved for 'holing and the stronger work', through to 'the more ordinary Negroes in a gang for dunging', down to the children's gang, which could be tasked to weeding. In 'Instructions', Henry Drax deemed the sugar-boiling house 'the place where your cheife skill will be required … wherefore your greatest Care Immaginable must be there used & the most of your time must be there Spent'.

Henry Drax had all but eliminated indentured servants from the workforce and increased the number of enslaved people to 327 persons. In the 'Instructions' he is assuming an annual mortality rate of 3 to 5 per cent. Drax also told Harwood that, if he had his way, he would employ no unskilled white labourers:

> I shall Not leave you many white Servants[,] the ffewer the better were itt No Incumbantt duty on all to keepe the Number the Act of Militia reqwirs for the Countreys Service[,] which Number [I] Shall Endevor to Send you Imediatly after my Ariwall In England of Which there shall be as Many tradesmen as I Can posibly procure.[16]

Like most plantation owners, Henry Drax saw himself as a godly person and responsible for the spiritual wellbeing of his 'family',

---

15. Drax, 'Instructions', 1679.
16. Ibid.

though dependent on race. In 'Instructions', Henry Drax insisted that 'Every Sonday all the family of Whites be Called in to heare Morning prayer acording as its Established by the Church of England.' At least some of his instructions extended the concept of family to include black workers:

[I] wold have you Continue Kind to Moncky Nocco who has bene ane Exelentt Slawe and will I hope Continue Soe in the place he is of head owerseer. [L]ett his allowance upon Incoradgment be as greatt as they have[,] being that is to say[,] besyds his own dyett in the hous[,] tenn pounds offish or flesh allowd him to dispose of as he shall think fitt to his mother wifes and family besyds other Clothes[,] a new Sarge Suit Every year and A Hatt.[17]

Drax singled out several other enslaved people, along with key white workers, for special allowances and Harwood's 'Countenance'. By the 1670s, the Drax family had enslaved three generations of Moncky Nocco's family on the Drax Hall plantation. Within the family and the black community on the plantation, his mother, as an elder woman, a parent, and a grandparent, undoubtedly occupied an honoured and influential position. Drax instructed the overseer to distribute extra rations to Nocco, who portioned them out to his family, in reward for his good service. However, it reflects the respect that was sometimes shown by the English landed gentry to a particular servant due to their length or effectiveness of a service. This could be a butler or a nanny kept on long after their age allowed for productivity but allowed sentimentality and provided an example to newer staff of the benefits of loyalty.

Historian Dr Peter Thompson concluded of Henry Drax:

For Drax, the ends justified the means in labour relations. On the evidence of the 'Instructions', he therefore treated his labourers, free white and especially enslaved black, as an alienated commod-

---

17. Ibid.

ity in the manner that was the norm across the island. That this alienation was grounded in Barbadian agronomy and shaped by the production cycle as well as by racial prejudice helped ensure its permanence.[18]

In 1676, one anonymous enslaved African remarked, 'The Devil was in the Englishman' alluding to Henry Drax. 'The devil was in the Englishman that he makes everything work; he makes the Negro work, he makes the horse work, the ass work, the wood work, the water work and the wind work.'[19]

THE CONSEQUENCE OF REBELLION

Why did enslaved people not rebel? At points they intended to. Barbados was not an easy place to organise a slave rebellion. It did not have mountains, like some other islands, where rebels could hide out or seek refuge, and the forest cover was rapidly being cut down. Barbados is relatively flat and small, enabling regular soldiers and militia to move quickly. Firearms were hard to acquire. But in June 1675, a rebellion had been planned for three years. Centred in Speightstown, a network of enslaved Africans on plantations prepared themselves. According to a later account by the island's Governor Atkins, a domestic enslaved person overheard an 18-year-old Coromantee enslaved person discussing plans for such a rebellion.[20] She informed her 'masters', and the authorities acted quickly and arrested many suspected enslaved Africans.

Henry Drax was among those who hunted down those involved in the plot. More than 100 were cross-examined in court, and 17 were found guilty immediately. Six were burned alive, and 11 beheaded, their bodies were dragged through the street of Spei-

---

18. Thompson, 'Henry Drax's Instructions', p. 578.
19. Anonymous, *Great Newes from the Barbadoes* (London: L. Curtis, 1676), pp. 6–7.
20. A Coromantee was a slave from the Gold Coast, as it was known then, or modern-day Ghana. They were prized over the enslaved from other areas and discussed, as one commentator noted, in the same way as a horse owner might refer to an Arabian horse.

ghtstown and then burned. A further 25 were later executed, and five hanged themselves in jail. The owners of the executed enslaved people were compensated. The militia was strengthened, and enslaved people were banned from using musical instruments in case they used them to signal from one plantation to another or whip up rebellion. In 1683 another plot was discovered, and yet another in 1692. There is no record of the enslaved at Drax Hall being involved.

How were the enslaved treated who were deemed to have rebelled or done something wrong? Sir Hans Sloane, the Anglo-Irish physician, naturalist and collector, visited the West Indies, including Barbados.[21] He dispassionately described the punishments meted out to enslaved people and how enslaved people were tortured and executed in the 1680s:

> The punishments for crimes of slaves, are usually for rebellions burning them, by nailing them down with the ground on crooked sticks on every limb... then applying the fire by degrees from the feet and hands, burning them gradually up to the head, whereby their pains are extravagant. For crimes of a lesser nature Gelding or chopping off half of the foot with an ax. These punishments are suffered by them with great constancy. For running away they put iron rings of great weight on their ankles... For negligence they are usually whipt by the overseers with hard wood switches, till they are all bloody... After they are whip't till they are raw, some put on their skins pepper and salt to make them smart... these punishments are sometimes merited by the blacks, who are a very perverse generation of people and although they appear harsh yet are scarce equal to their crimes.[22]

---

21. Sloane collected 71,000 artefacts on his journeys which he bequeathed and provided for the foundation of the British Museum, the British Library and the Natural History Museum.

22. Mimi Goodall, 'Consumption of Sugar in the British Atlantic World 1650–1720', PhD thesis, Brasenose College, University of Oxford, 2022, p. 60.

DRAX OF DRAX HALL

The Drax family had acquired considerable wealth from their plantations. The first woman subscriber, in June 1670, to the Hudson Bay company was Margaret, the second wife of Sir James Drax.[23] Living at Drax Hall she was a close neighbour of the Colletons, another West Country family who were dominant in the plantation business in the Americas. The Drax family became linked by marriage to the Colletons. Life in Barbados at the end of the 1670s was going through a particularly bad patch, with disease rampant on the island claiming many lives. The leading figures were still doing well. Drax and the Colleton families acted as agents for Barbados' planters and merchants, were widely trusted, and even acted for non-conformists such as the Huguenots. However, Governor Atkins felt they were too powerful and were a challenge to him. The king was annoyed that Atkins had passed laws without royal assent. Atkins said his position was impossible: 'You will please consider me as the King's Governor here; and that you are pleased to put the opinion of merchants or people that are concerned in this Island (Colleton and Drax) in balance with me Is something hard to bear.'[24]

Again, the 4000-mile distance from London resulted in leading figures ignoring English law when it suited them and when the financial benefits outstripped the risk. Like his father, Henry Drax bought from 'Interlopers', non-Royal African Company (RAC) ships violating English law, as did other leading West Country planters, including his relative Christopher Codrington[25] and

---

23. E. Rich (ed.), *Minutes of the Hudson's Bay Company 1671–1674*, 2 vols (Toronto: The Publications of the Champlain Society, 1942), I, pp. xxi, aaw, 218–222.
24. J.E. Buchanan, 'The Colleton Family and the Early History of South Carolina and Barbados, 1646–1775', PhD thesis, University of Edinburgh, 1989, p. 162.
25. Christopher Codrington arrived in Barbados in 1640 and married the daughter of James Drax. He acquired more estates in Barbados and Antigua, as well as the entire island of Barbuda. He was later named Captain General of the Leeward Islands. His son, also Christopher, retired to his estates in Barbados. The estates passed to his first cousin, William Codrington, who disinherited his own son and his wealth passed to his nephew Christopher Bethell Codrington, who in the eighteenth century substantially extended and renovated Dodington Park near Bristol.

John Hallet.[26] A contemporary letter from the RAC's factors on Barbados, Edward Stede and Stephen Gascoigne, on 23 December 1678 to headquarters explained how Christopher Codrington and Henry Drax were buying enslaved people from unauthorised trading ships rather than the RAC's ships as required by law. They told the company that troops were sent to intercept the ship, but it had gone before they arrived at the landing point. Stede and Gascoigne complained that they were told that 'his Brother Collo. Drax and. Collo. Sharpe bought all the cheife negroes out of the Interloper which as report goes were sold also at very low rates which if true wee presume is done upon a designe of prejudice to the Company'. The three men were also organising slave-trading voyages.[27]

DISSENT

The harsh treatment of enslaved people was not universally accepted. Even in the seventeenth century, a hundred years or more before the abolitionists waged a concerted campaign, some visitors to the West Indies were appalled. Father Anton Biet had been upset about the treatment of enslaved people on some plantations he visited. But it did not mean he rejected slavery outright. Aphra Behn, the pioneering woman author and playwright, wrote *Oroonoko or The Royal Slave*, published in 1688, which is regarded as one of the first abolitionist and humanitarian novels published in the English language. One famous sentence is: 'But Caesar told him there was no faith in the white men, or the gods they adored; who instructed them in principles so false that honest men could not live amongst them; though no people professed so much, none performed so little.'

Leaving behind his 'Instructions', Henry Drax returned to England and his name appears in a list of persons who left Barbados bound for London in 1679: '2nd April. Drax, Henry Esq. On the ship *Thomas Honor* for London. Lowther, Christopher a servant belonging to Col. Henry Drax in a ship *Honor* (Captain

26. Blackburn, *The Making of New World Slavery*, p. 255.
27. Ibid.

Tho. Warren) bound for London'.[28] Author Richard Dunn noted the seventeenth-century Caribbean colonist built a truly impressive sugar-producing system, especially when one considers the tradition-bound character of English farming at this time:

> The sugar planter utilised agricultural techniques radically different from those they knew at home and learnt how to manipulate men, beasts and machines on a far larger scale than their cousins in Virginia or Massachusetts.... In the pre-industrial world of the seventeenth century, the Caribbean sugar planter was a large-scale entrepreneur. He was a combination farmer-manufacturer.[29]

Estimates suggest there were 50,000 enslaved people living in Barbados by 1700, even though merchants had transported approximately 212,000 captive Africans to the island since the founding of the colony. As Bennett noted, this was 'a sobering testament to how the Barbadian plantation system required a steady supply of labour to replace those who perished from rigorous work regimes and the tropical disease environment'.[30] As the trade developed, sugar came in various forms, each with a different price, and as the century progressed it was not something available only to the privileged. The multiple refined white sugar remained the most expensive, but the poorer consumer could also buy ordinary brown sugar or dark viscous molasses, known as treacle. Recipe books from the period are filled with ideas for how to use the ingredient, from sprinkling on salad to a fine plum cake. Sugar was particularly useful as it kept fresh goods for longer, turning low-calorie perishable fruit into high calorie preserves and jams.[31] Some 170,000 hundredweight of sugar were imported from plantations through London from 1663 to 1666 of which brown sugar made up 70 per cent and white sugar 30 per

---

28. *Journal of Barbados Museum and Historical Society*, vol. I.
29. Dunn, *Sugar and Slaves*, pp. 188–189.
30. Bennett, 'Merchant Capital', p. 164.
31. www.history.ox.ac.uk/article/how-england-became-the-sweetshop-of-europe#:~:text=Sugar%20first%20came%20to%20England,in%20Brazil%20during%20othe%201500s, last accessed 1 July 2024.

cent. The vast majority of these imports were from Barbados. The value of this sugar was approximately £270,000. The figure for all of England from 1699 to 1701 was 488,650 hundredweight of which brown sugar made up over 88 per cent, molasses nearly 8 per cent and white sugar was nearly 4 per cent.[32] Demand was still increasing.

If Henry Drax's decision to return to London was motivated by health reasons, it did not pay off as he died three years later in 1682, aged 41, at his townhouse on Bloomsbury Square, London. By the time he died, his English estates were producing as much revenue as Drax Hall. In a letter from Mrs Sarah Fountaine (youngest daughter of Sir Thomas Chicheley, Master of the Ordnance to Charles II) to her brother-in-law, Richard Legh of Lyme, written on 26 September 1682 (Legh manuscript at Lyme), she said,

> My Dear Cozen Drax is dead buryed this day. He has left my neghbour Shatterdon's oldest son 6 thousand a year at least to be managed to he comes att age by trustees for him: and in the meanetime a hundred a year to breed him he has left everybody that is related to him good Legaasays and his wife extreme well; though the particulars I will know when my negbour return to London.[33]

Unlike his father, Henry did put aside £2000 for the benefit of the island (albeit the planters) to which he owed his wealth: to establish a free school or college at Bridgetown. But the money was never used for the purposes it was intended for and was 'borrowed' by local government and disappeared.[34]

On Henry's death the plantations passed to his sister Elizabeth Drax's son, Thomas Shetterden, for whom there is some evidence that he spent some time in Barbados. The gruelling work of the enslaved people at Drax Hall plantation produced at least £6000 a year for Thomas and perhaps some lesser sums going to other family members, which was a goodly sum of annual income for a

---

32. Goodall, 'Consumption of Sugar', p. 60.
33. *Notes and Queries*, 28 November 1921, p. 436.
34. https://househistree.com/people/henry-drax, last accessed 1 July 2024.

gentleman. Having changed his name to Drax to inherit, he married Elizabeth Ernle of Wiltshire, which would be the catalyst for the merger of the Drax, Ernle and Erle families. When Thomas Shetterden Drax died in 1702, his eldest son, Henry Drax (henceforth Henry Drax II), became the new owner of Drax Hall and Drax Hope. His mother took care of his affairs until he came of age. He would take the family into new royal circles.

PART IV

Post-Restoration

10
Captain Thomas Erle and the Monmouth Rebellion

In 1685, an adventurous 23-year-old woman made the first of her many tours around England that would be recounted in her popular book, *The Journeys of Celia Fiennes*. From that year until 1703, Celia made increasingly long journeys, riding side-saddle and noting what she saw. It was then very unusual for a young woman to travel for pleasure. For a start, the roads could be dangerous, not least from highwaymen. She was not quite solo. Celia was generally accompanied by one or two family servants. She was reputedly the first woman to visit every county in England. The surviving portrait supports her reputation as a determinedly independent woman. Celia stated her reasons for travel in her introduction: 'both ladies, much more gentlemen' should 'spend some of their time in journeys to visit their native land and be curious to inform themselves... of the pleasant prospects, good buildings, different produces and manufacturers of each place'.[1] Celia had been born at Newton Toney near Salisbury, the home of her father Colonel Nathaniel Fiennes, second son of William 8th Baron and grandson of the First Viscount Saye and Sele, both of whom had been for Parliament during the Civil War.

This first tour went as far south-west in England as Lyme Regis, Dorset. On her way back via Dorchester, she entered Charborough country where she noted: 'We pass over Woodbery [Woodbury] Hill eminent for a great Faire that is kept thee of all things.'[2] Moving

---

1. Celia Fiennes, *The Journeys of Celia Fiennes* (London: Cresset Press, 1947), p. 1.
2. Once an Iron Age Fort, the hill was the site of the biggest fair in England, a Glastonbury Festival of its time – five days long at peak – from the beginning of the thirteenth century through to 1951. It is east of the village of Bere Regis and part of the Charborough Estate.

eastwards, Celia continues to Charborough House just over a mile down the main highway and describes what she sees:

> The road passed Cherbery [Charborough], the foot of the hill; on the stop stands the pretty seat of Mr Earles my relation. The house is a new built house on the brow of hill when you have a large prospect of 20-mile, round, you may see Shaftesbury then 16 miles off; there is a good wood behind the house, good garden walled'd with plenty of fruit, good fish and decoy ponnds.[3]

Celia was visiting Thomas Erle (III), the son of her aunt Susanna Erle (née Fiennes).[4] Thomas had inherited Charborough from his grandfather as a teenager in 1665. Celia provided a rich description of the then interior of Charborough House:

> There is a very good hall at the entrance that leads you to a large parlour and drawing room on the right hand that opens to the gardens, a very good little parlour with servants room, and another parlour for smoakeing, all well wainscoated and painted, and the offices convenient; the chamber are good and lofty and sizeable good furniture in the best 2 Chambers, in an angle the staires leads up halfe way into the middle of the house and so divides in four parts and runnes to each angle a cross visto wayes through the house.[5]

Thomas had been to Middle Temple to study law and married Elizabeth, daughter of Sir William Wyndham of Orchard Wyndham in Somerset, at Charborough in 1675.[6]

---

3. Fiennes, *The Journeys of Celia Fiennes*, pp. 14–15.
4. Susanna had been married to Thomas Erle II who died in middle age.
5. Her journey in south Dorset has been immortalised more recently in a song 'What Celia Sees' by the Ridgeriders, which refers to her visit to Woodbury Hill.
6. Thomas's marriage was a social step up for the family. Her father was the MP for Somerset and also the Sheriff of Somerset. According to the Drax family history of Charborough, Elizabeth Wyndham brought to the family royal blood, for she was descended from the Plantagenet King Edward I (1272–1307) and his father Henry II (1206–1272).

CAPTAIN THOMAS ERLE AND THE MONMOUTH REBELLION

Having visited, Celia Fiennes then carried on through Blandford and to her home near Stonehenge. Celia's visit coincided with a time that would see a dramatic change in the life of her cousin Thomas, who was to become one of the most prominent of all the Plunkett-Ernle-Erle-Drax ancestors. Thomas had ensured that the Charborough Estate was being run well enough to allow him time to engage in public life. He hired Joseph Dolling of Corfe Castle, who was part of a large and well-regarded Purbeck family, to be the estate manager.

Thomas Erle undertook the roles expected of a senior member of the county gentry and had been made Deputy Lieutenant of Dorset in 1674 at the age of 24 years. At this point, his life seemed centred around Dorset, but that was about to change. His legal training saw good use around the county, where he was appointed a Justice of the Peace in 1678. He had, though, met disapproval from the higher authorities for refusing to prosecute religious dissenters and for a period, he was taken off the bench. These judicial tensions existed across the country, and it was not unusual. The Erle family's partial control over the borough of Wareham bought him his seat in Parliament, and he was elected twice in 1679 and was to be an MP for much of his life. However, like a number of others of the Whiggish persuasion, he bent in the wind during the 'Tory reaction' of the early 1680s.

On Erle's entry into the first Exclusion Parliament, Ashley Cooper (by then Lord Shaftesbury), a leader of the Whig faction, marked his friend as 'doubtful' in the coming vote to exclude from the throne of Charles II's heir, his brother, James, Duke of York. At the beginning of the decade, it had become widely known the Duke of York had undergone conversion to the Roman Catholic faith, and the predominantly Protestant public was aghast. The potential for a future Catholic king was the core issue in a political crisis that haunted the English government for much of the rest of Charles II's reign. As it happens, Thomas Erle did vote for the exclusion of the duke, but that vote failed, and the king dissolved the Parliament. His re-election in Wareham without opposition or expense in 1681 suggests that his handful of voters were satisfied with his position on exclusion. *The History of Parliament* said the sitting Members for Wareham were 'chosen, without expense' in their absence, the magistrates thriftily treating the electors with beer and biscuit.[7]

Ashley-Cooper had fought for King Charles I during the Civil War, and then defected to Parliament. However, at the Restoration, he was pardoned by King Charles II and had become an influential politician. A supporter and patron of the philosopher John Locke and a defender of civil liberties, he had also acquired a joint share in a sugar plantation in Barbados and a share in the slave ship *The Rose*. Support for his Exclusion Bill is seen as a marker in the division of MPs into Tories and Whigs, where there are clear enough consistent differences to see them as two political tendencies that would eventually become political parties. Thomas Erle can be marked as a Whig.

The events of 1685 triggered a major change of career for Thomas Erle, who would rise to be an important military figure. He was to prove to be a vigorous anti-papist, warrior and leader. He was also crucial to the family mergers that would eventually lead to the four-barrelled name and the incorporation into the family of the wealth generated by the Barbados slave-worked plantations.

One of the key issues, especially in the South-west, was the right to be a religious dissenter to which Thomas was sympathetic. He was inactive in the Oxford Parliament, but much engaged in Dorset not least as an officer in the militia.[8] In the region, the boroughs of Bridgewater, Wells and Poole all lost their charters by refusing to impose high Anglican theology on congregations. Such was their level of obstinacy, the authorities believed these towns were preparing to restart the Civil War. On 3 July 1683, militia Captain Erle, then at home at Charborough, was ordered by the Lord Lieutenant, the Earl of Bristol, to go with Richard Fownes MP, a captain of horse in the militia, to search Poole for arms.[9] King Charles II had

---

7.   www.historyofparliamentonline.org/volume/1660-1690/constituencies/wareham, last accessed 17 June 2024.

8.   www.historyofparliamentonline.org/volume/1660-1690/member/erle-thomas-1650-1720, last accessed 17 June 2024.

9.   The letter can be found in the Erle Archive at Churchill College Archive,

issued orders for militia commanders to ensure they had 'volunteers who offer assistance formed in troops apart and trained; the officers to be numerous; disaffected persons watched and not allowed to assemble, and their arms seized'.[10]

THE DUKE OF MONMOUTH

On 6 February 1685, Charles II died. Although he had eleven children by his mistresses, he had no legitimate child to succeed him. Thus, he was succeeded by his brother, the Duke of York, James II. Thomas Erle with his Puritan roots and sympathy with dissenters was a little more active in James II's Parliament, being named to the committees to relieve the Earl of Cleveland's creditors and suppress pedlars. But, as a militia officer, he had to put those committees aside with the news of the Duke of Monmouth's landing at Lyme Regis on the far western side of Dorset. James Scott, 1st Duke of Monmouth, was the eldest illegitimate son of Charles II and had been banished in 1682, suspected of planning a coup. He stayed at the court of William of Orange in Holland for some time, and William warned him not to act against James II on the new king's accession. Having left William's court, Monmouth announced his claim to the throne and plotted a coup to overthrow his uncle. Monmouth landed at Lyme Regis on 11 June 1685 with a number of supporters. Over the next days, his growing army of English dissenters, nonconformists, mostly farm workers from the South-west, sided with him and they fought a series of skirmishes with county militias and regular soldiers.

As an officer of the Red Regiment of the Dorset militia, Thomas Erle was ordered to assemble the East 'Blandford' company under his command and head to Bridport in the west of the county to intercept any of Monmouth's rebels. He did not hesitate; despite any reservations he might have had about King James. The militia arrived in time for a fight. Under the overall command of Thomas Strangways, the militia placed themselves on the east side of

---

Cambridge, GBR/0014/ERLE 2/4.
10. CSPD, 1660, p. 150.

Bridport and barricaded the bridge. Some 40 cavalry and 400 foot soldiers of Monmouth's army, under the command of Lord Grey and Nathaniel Wade, came into Bridport from the west, where they encountered the militia. Sporadic fighting occurred in the town, with some casualties including a militia officer called Edward Coker. As Monmouth's men moved along the town's East Street, the rebels found the east bridge barricaded and well-defended by musketeers, perhaps performing the eight or six-rank firings advocated by contemporary drill books. As militia historian Chris Scott noted:

> Whoever set the deployment also placed men in the buildings lining the street as it approached the barricade. This was a skilfully managed plan of defence which obliged the attackers to advance into a constricted place where they would be subjected to close-range crossfire. This they duly did in some disorder, due in no small part to the way the road narrows as it approaches the bridge.[11]

With Lt Colonel Samuel Venner, Monmouth's third in command, wounded, Nathaniel Wade led the attack, followed by Grey's Horse. Their musketeers gave the barricade a volley which shook the militia defenders, but their 'officers had with much adoe prevailed upon theyre souldiers to stand', maintain their line, and return fire. Grey pushed the rebel cavalry through its foot soldiers and tried to advance upon the barricade but another volley from the militiamen killed two infantrymen and caused them to shrink backwards. Some fled, upon which the mounted force broke and bolted back to Lyme. The Dorset Militia marched out of Bridport on 18 June ordered to shadow the rebel force in on the Dorset–Somerset borders.

---

11.   Christopher L. Scott, 'The Military Effectiveness of the West Country Militia at the Time of the Monmouth Rebellion', PhD thesis, Cranfield University, 2013, p. 269. Scott ran a civil war re-enactment group and was moved to take a doctorate after realising that accounts of the negative performance of the militia during the Monmouth Rebellion were not accurate as they had been impacted by various historians' and writers' own agendas. His thesis addresses the question 'Was the militia in the second half of the seventeenth century an effective military body?'

Over the next week, various skirmishes continued, and Monmouth's army began to realise that the tide was turning against them. The coordinated Scottish rebellion failed. The rebellion was to end with the defeat of Monmouth's army at the Battle of Sedgemoor on 6 July 1685, delivered by forces led by Louis de Duras, 2nd Earl of Feversham and John Churchill.[12] Now touching 35 years of age, Captain Thomas Erle and his friend Thomas Chafin took part in the battle as volunteers, but there are no recorded details. Erle had presumably with the agreement of his commander, Strangways, left the militia patrolling the Dorset and Somerset border.

Monmouth fled the field of battle but was cornered on 8 July while heading towards the south coast ports to escape the country. The Sussex Militia had been active in securing the port of Poole in Dorset and patrolling Hampshire. The militia arrested Monmouth and escorted him to London. With Monmouth now locked up, Parliament passed an Act of Attainder on 13 June, sentencing Monmouth to death as a traitor without the need for a trial.

Militia units had rounded up many of those from the South-west who had joined the Monmouth rebellion. The subsequent Bloody Assizes of Judge Jeffreys in Dorchester tried Monmouth's supporters; some 320 people were condemned to death and approximately 800 were sentenced to be transported to the West Indies for ten years' hard labour. One example was the Dorset man Azariah Pinney who had been taken prisoner at Sedgemoor. He was sentenced to be hung, drawn and quartered at Bridport but given a reprieve on payment of £65. Instead, he was handed over to Jerome Nipho for shipment to the West Indies. Nipho was the Queen's Secretary and one of a number of people close to James that were given previously condemned men as slaves, a valuable gift.[13] Released from

---

12. John Churchill was the eldest-surviving son of Sir Winston Churchill (1620–1688) of Glanvilles Wootton, Dorset, and Elizabeth Drake, whose family came from Ash, in Devon. He would become one of the greatest generals in British history with his succession of victories against Louis XIV, especially at Blenheim in the age of Queen Anne. He became the first Duke of Marlborough. Sir Winston, was a Royalist and, after the Restoration, was MP for Weymouth from 1661 and Lyme from 1665.

13. Rodney Legg, 'Bettiscombe', *Dorset Life,* June 2009.

his period of enslavement, Pinney later became a successful businessman, owning enslaved people, and his son became Chief Justice of Nevis.[14] Court favourites of the king allotted these rebels in batches of 100, intending to sell them to the West India merchants at a price of £15 per head. Many were sent to Barbados and Barbadian planters were pleased to have the free labour, and the enslaved prisoners were quickly put to work in the mills, boiler houses, and sugar cane fields about the island.

PLACEMEN

James II took advantage of the rebellion to exert greater control over the military, inserting Catholic officers into the army to ensure he had loyalists in command. Scott observed:

> This desire for personal control was fuelled by his and his Tory government's wariness of a militia influenced by the Whig Party, coupled with a memory that his father had lost his crown through having too small a military force to crush his parliamentarian opponents in early 1642. These fears manifested in a desire to diminish the status and role of the militia, Parliament's potential military instrument, and to replace it with an enlarged royal army loyal to his person. This was a bold and controversial move as no previous monarch had sought to dispense with the local defence force.[15]

While there is no record of his state of mind, Thomas Erle was likely conflicted, supporting a king who intended to allow greater freedom for Catholics and, consequently, less room for Protestants. As a borderline Whig, he had taken part in suppressing a West Country rebellion driven by people who wanted more freedom to

---

14. John Pretor Pinney disposed of their plantations and returned to England in 1783. The Pinneys were a famous family connected with slavery as merchants working out of Bristol, owning Bettiscombe Manor, north of Bridport, Dorset. An Azariah Pinney was MP for Bridport from 1747 to 1761.

15. Scott, 'The Military Effectiveness', p. 77.

dissent. However, Erle had made an impression as a military officer who showed courage in battle and had clear leadership and organisational qualities. After Sedgemoor, John Churchill presented Thomas Erle to King James, but it was an 'unpropitious time for those who had voted for the *Exclusion Bill* in 1679, as he had done, and he received a predictably chilly reception'.[16] Even so, he was already a significant and powerful figure in the county and was now entering the national stage.

Captain Erle had recovered the Erle name as warriors from the embarrassment of his grandfather's alleged loss of nerve at Corfe Castle. Buoyed by his military success and growing county and national reputation, he began plotting to get rid of James II. This of course, made him a traitor, but he was to be on the right side of events. Early on, he recognised that William of Orange was a potential replacement for James II. What recommended William was that he was born outside of the Stuart dynasty (though he had married into it) and was a hard-line Protestant. In May 1687, James II ordered the militias of Cornwall, Devon and Dorset not to muster until further notice: 'The King would have you take care the militia within your Lieutenancies of Devon, and Cornwall will not be mustered until you receive his direction.'[17] The missive went to the Earl of Bristol concerning the Dorset Militia.[18] James was suspicious about the loyalty of the militia even after the Monmouth Rebellion. He was right. Thomas Erle already had plans for Dorset's military to assist in regime change.

THOMAS ERLE'S PART IN JAMES II'S DOWNFALL

William Henry, Prince of Orange, was born in The Hague in 1650, the same year as Thomas Erle. The prince engaged with English politics through his family connections. In November 1670, at age 20, he had travelled to England to urge Charles II to pay back at least a part of the 2.8 million guilder debt the House of Stuart owed

---

16. *Oxford Dictionary of National Biography*, entry on Erle.
17. CSPD, 1686–87, p. 437.
18. CSPD, 1686–87, p. 437.

the House of Orange. Short of money, as ever, Charles was unable to pay, but William Henry agreed to reduce the amount owed to 1.8 million guilders in the hope of getting at least some repayment. Charles found his nephew William Henry to be a dedicated Calvinist and patriotic Dutchman. William Henry found that his personal behaviour differed from his English Stuart uncles, Charles and James, who were more interested in drinking, gambling and sexual promiscuity.

A year after the defeat of the Duke of Monmouth, and now a militia major, Erle is said to have convened a group of conspirators from the surrounding area, who met in the icehouse in the Grove at Charborough Park to plan to overthrow 'the tyrant race of Stuarts'. Erle had been sacked from his offices earlier in 1688 for his negative response to the king's questions concerning the repeal of the Test Acts. He had decided that while the Duke of Monmouth was not worthy of taking the English Crown, the Prince of Orange could be imposed on the Stuarts as a 'Protector' and bring them to heel. This meeting is said by the family to have led to the 'Invitation to William', signed by the 'Immortal Seven', and it resulted in the Glorious Revolution. Whether that is true is discussed later.

Certainly, the 'Immortal Seven' conducted the secret correspondence with William of Orange from April 1687. The seven men felt that Protestant dominance was threatened by what they saw as an increasingly arbitrary and authoritarian monarch. The letter informed William, Prince of Orange, that if he were to land in England with a small army, the signatories and their allies would rise and support him. They told him they were pleased to hear that His Highness was 'willing to help us'. The greatest supporter for the Prince of Orange to usurp James II was William's wife, Mary, whose dislike of Catholicism and her stepmother was so strong she was prepared to be estranged from her father. William agreed, but not with the intent of taking the throne so much as changing the politics to support Protestantism. Over a few months, William built and assembled an armada to transport, not the small army suggested by the immortal seven, but a substantial Dutch and mixed force, with a band of exiled English supporters. Briskly they sailed into Torbay, on the south-west coast of England, with a favourable easterly wind – seen as a sign from God, as the prevailing wind is usually south-westerly. Debarkation started at the fishing port of Brixham, some 200 miles from London, on the night of 12–13 November 1688.

After some consolidation, the prince began moving east in easy stages, with aristocrats and landed gentry joining him often with their military units. According to Narcissus Luttrell, who was from Devon and the contemporary chronicler of Parliament, Major Thomas Erle had raised a troop in Dorset to join the prince.[19] Assisted by Erle, Colonel Sir William Portman persuaded his subordinates in the Dorset Militia, John Digby, the Earl of Bristol and Thomas Strangways, a veteran of the Battle of Bridport, to raise the county forces for the prince. The Dorset regiment had secured Dorset for the Prince of Orange by the end of November. So complete was the opposition of the western gentry to James that Royalist Secretary Middleton complained from Salisbury on 23 November that: 'It is not to be admired that we have little intelligence, since none of the gentry of this or adjacent counties come near the Court…'[20]

Next, many of those who were expected to support the king defected to the Prince of Orange. The most significant was John Churchill (later the Duke of Marlborough), the head of James II's army (who was friendly with Thomas Erle). The defection of Churchill, whom James had raised from a pageboy and relied on implicitly through all the vicissitudes of the last nine years, was a body blow to James. 'Oh, if my enemies only, had cursed me,' James is said to have cried, 'I could have borne it.' On 19 November, King James joined his main army of 19,000 troops at Salisbury, but it was evident his army was hesitant to fight and the loyalty of his com-

---

19.   Nicholas Luttrell, *Brief Historical Relation of State Affairs from September 1678 to April 1714* (Cambridge: Cambridge University Press, 1857 and 2011), p. 482.
20.   P.J. Norrey, 'The Relationship between Central and Local Government in Dorset, Somerset and Wiltshire, 1660–1688', PhD thesis, Bristol University, 1988, p. 431.

DRAX OF DRAX HALL

manders doubtful. On 20 November, reconnaissance dragoons led by Irish Catholic officer Patrick Sarsfield clashed with scouts from William's army at Wincanton. There was also a minor skirmish at Reading on 9 December, also featuring Sarsfield.

Slowly the prince's army progressed towards London, passing Stonehenge on the way. The Prince of Orange had brought with him a printing press, and he used it as he overnighted to print declarations designed to win the hearts and minds of the English population. By the 23rd, confidence was sufficient that the South and South-west were held for the prince that the Earl of Bristol ordered Thomas Erle to dismiss the Dorset regiment he had raised. As the Orange army moved closer to London, they found that resistance had melted away and they had won an almost a bloodless victory. James left London in haste, realising he had little support.

James' departure – seen as an abdication by the Prince of Orange's followers – significantly shifted the balance of power in favour of William, who took control of the provisional government on 28 December. Having no desire to make James a martyr, William had let him escape. James was received by his cousin and ally, Louis XIV of France, who was a sworn enemy of the Prince of Orange. Louis provided James with a palace and a pension. Archbishop Sancroft and other Stuart loyalists wanted to preserve the line of succession. However, they recognised keeping James on the throne was no longer possible, and they preferred Mary either be appointed his regent or sole monarch. However, it became clear the only sensible solution was to give the Crown to William and his wife, so they became joint monarchs. In his correspondence Colonel Erle makes it clear that he was delighted with the new monarchs and was happy to continue to serve.

11

Colonel Thomas Erle – a Man of War

After several months in France, the deposed James II had left for Ireland and from March 1689 raised an army, including many Irish Catholics, to regain the crowns of the three Kingdoms. James' allies controlled much of Ireland and the Irish Parliament. James also had the backing of his French cousin, Louis XIV, who did not want to see a hostile monarch on the throne of England. Louis sent 6,000 French troops to Ireland to support the Irish Jacobites to provide a total force of some 23,500. As a Stadtholder of the Netherlands, William assembled 36,000 Dutch and allied troops from the continent as well as England and Scotland.

Thomas Erle's military career had been consolidated by the leading part he had played in suppressing the Monmouth Rebellion and supporting the Glorious Revolution in Dorset. He was given command as a colonel of a foot regiment that he raised that became the 2nd Battalion of the Luttrell's Regiment.[1] A military confrontation was inevitable. Like many other English regiments, Colonel Erle's was ordered to Ireland on 29 April 1690. He was to see serious action at the head of his regiment in the battles of the Boyne, Aughrim and the siege of Limerick.[2] The Battle of the Boyne took place across the River Boyne close to the town of Drogheda on 1 July 1690. Erle and his regiment were heavily engaged in the battle and William's army won. Most of James' army were raw recruits while William had large numbers of professional soldiers and also more modern muskets. James left Ireland after

---

1. Colonel Francis Luttrell formed the regiment in 1688 from independent companies raised in Devon.
2. William's success at the Battle of the Boyne is a critical moment in the history of Ireland from the Protestant and Unionist perspectives even to this day. The Prince of Orange is known to them as 'King Billy', and the Orange Order is a Protestant cultural tribute to the Dutch king.

the defeat and never returned, but his supporters battled on. Erle went on with the English Army to the siege of Limerick, a city in western Ireland besieged twice in 1689–1691. On the first occasion, in August to September 1690, its Jacobite defenders retreated to the city after their defeat at the Boyne. With his mixed army of Dutch, Danish, German, English and Huguenot troops, William III tried to take Limerick, but his army was repelled and had to retire into their winter quarters.

Colonel Erle was to take a prominent role in the Battle of Aughrim that took place nearly a year after the Boyne. It was again fought between the predominantly Irish Jacobite army and the forces of William III on 12 July 1691, under General Ginkell in County Galway. The battle was one of the bloodiest ever fought in the British Isles: 5,000–7,000 soldiers were killed.[3] The Jacobite defeat at Aughrim meant the effective end of James' cause in Ireland, although the city of Limerick held out until the autumn of 1691. The eighteenth-century historian John Hutchins provided a detailed account of Thomas Erle's part in the battle of Aughrim. The battle was fought partly in a bog, so was difficult and the Protestant army came under heavy fire:

> But the Irish had so well ordered the matter that they had an easy passage for their horse among all these hedges and ditches, which, yet being observed by the valiant Colonel Erle, he encouraged his men, telling them, 'there was no way to come off but to be brave'. However, the hedges being both flanked and fronted and exposed to the entire enemy's fire from the neighbouring hedges, they were forced from their ground, and to retreat again to the bog with considerable loss. And among others, the brave Colonel's Erle and Herbert being taken prisoners, the former, after being twice taken and re-taken, at last, got clear of the enemy, but the other (as was reported) was 'barbarously murdered' by the Irish when they saw he was likely to be rescued. Eventually, the battle was restored, and the English won a complete victory.[4]

3.   https://heritage.galwaycommunityheritage.org/content/category/places/battle-of-aughrim-visitor-centre, last accessed 1 July 2024.
4.   Hutchins, *History of Dorset*, vii, p. 499.

Erle was severely wounded in the battle but later recovered and was rewarded with offer of an Irish estate.[5] The war in Ireland lasted three years and was bloody and destructive. What followed was the appropriation of lands and property of the Catholic gentry and merchants and their exclusion from any form of suffrage or representation, a sore that lasts to the present day. With the subjugation of Ireland achieved for the moment, Erle returned to Charborough and Parliament.

In 1692, Erle, now a general, transferred from Ireland to Holland and commanded his men at the Battle of Steenkerk, which went badly, and his half-brother Francis Hawley was killed in action. The English army was now being engaged to help the Dutch fight against their Spanish and French enemies. On his visits home, General Erle's rare contributions to Parliamentary debate mainly related to the armed forces. In the 1692–1693 session, Erle made a speech in the House of Common for the first time in a full debate, against the motion to employ only English officers in the army:

> No man is of less sufficiency to speak than myself. I have had the honour to serve in three or four Parliaments and have not troubled you. I was a colonel of foot in the engagement at Steenkerk, where the ground was mistaken, and so we were forced to retreat. As to the question, no man is more pleased than I for English officers to command the English army; but I do not think that three- or four-years' service can make a general. I wish we had men fit; but before you have them, pray do not rid yourselves of all foreign generals. I hope when you come to the question you will not part with all the foreign generals before you can have some of your own to come into their places.

Erle was made a brigadier-general on 22 March 1693 while on active service and left his sick bed – suffering severe gout possibly as a result of his affection for red wine – at Mechlin to head his brigade at the Battle of Landen. He was again wounded. He needed

---

5.   In 1690, the 19th Regiment supplied detachments for Ireland and Jamaica, incurring heavy losses from disease, including Luttrell, whom Thomas Erle replaced.

time for recuperation and was given a home-based post, but these were not to be his last battles.

THE ENGLISH EAST INDIA COMPANY

The earliest known engagement with profiting from the slave trade of the Erle line of Charborough ancestors came at the end of the seventeenth century. Convalescing, Thomas Erle had time to attend to domestic issues, and he was quite clearly wealthy enough for substantial investments. At the end of the year, his name appears as a subscriber of £2333.6.8 to the General Joint Stock for East India under the charter of 11 November 1693.[6] There was no trade that the EEIC would not participate in. As early as the 1620s, the EEIC had begun using slave labour and transporting enslaved people to its bases in South-east Asia and India, as well as to the island of St Helena. Although some of those enslaved by the company came from Indonesia and West Africa, the majority came from East Africa – from Mozambique or especially from Madagascar – and were primarily transported to the company's holdings in India and Indonesia. The EEIC's archives were established when the East India Company first engaged in the slave trade. 'The East India Company launched its first extensive enslaving expedition in 1684 when Robert Knox, the captain of *Tonquin Merchant*, received instructions to purchase 250 slaves in Madagascar and deliver them to St Helena [in the South Atlantic].'[7] And in the long term the Erle family made a profit.

On recovery from his wounds General Thomas Erle returned to his military career with a series of important posts. Erle's main concern then was on his military career, pay and promotion. When one of his regiments was ordered to disband in March 1699, Erle

---

6. DNB Thomas Erle and All Souls College MS. 152D EF 45B.
7. Richard B. Allen, *European Slave Trading in the Indian Ocean, 1500–1850* (Athens, OH: Ohio University Press, 2015), p. 37; see also: E/3/90, f. 180, London to St. Helena, 5 April 1684; E/3/90, ff. 182–183, Instructions to Captain Robert Knox of the Tonqueen Merchant, 4 April 1684; Royle, *Company's Island*, p. 86; Allen, *European Slave Trading*, p. 37.

remained loyal to William III and said he was 'willing to lay down' his men, though it must have been a blow. Treasury documents for payments in 1698[8]/1699[9] show that listed in Erle's remaining regiment are several Dorset associates. Joseph Dolling, presumably the same person as his estate manager, is there, as is a Lt Colonel Robert Freke. Also listed is Henry Trenchard from the family seat of Wolfeton, Henry Hawley and Robert Strangways.

Erle had changed his view that there should be no standing army but only militia units – a popularly held view in England in the seventeenth century. What had most likely concerned him and others was the potential for a Catholic monarch with a Catholic-led standing army to threaten the 'liberties' of all Protestant citizens. On 8 January 1698, he spoke in Parliament against a reduction of the military establishment, explaining 'the defenceless condition they would be in without some troops to make a stand'.[10] He led a bill to naturalise the foreign-born children of armed forces personnel. For the 1698 general election, Erle, who held mainly Whig views, appears to have entered into an agreement with his political rival George Pitt who owned property and several advowsons in the borough and who primarily was a Tory, to share the parliamentary representation of Wareham and not challenge each other's interests.

Picture in your mind General Thomas Erle mounted on his horse making his way from Charborough eastwards on the main south coast road. A small man then aged 50 in 1700, he would have been dressed in his army uniform, cloaked if the weather was poor, with his tricorn hat and knee-high leather boots. He would have been armed with a sword and firearms, as the highway could be dangerous. As he made his way through the New Forest, his destination, Portsmouth, on the south coast of England and the major Royal Navy base, was a day's horse ride east from Charborough

8. www.british-history.ac.uk/cal-treasury-books/vol13/pp272-287, last accessed 19 June 2024.
9. www.british-history.ac.uk/commons-jrnl/vol12/pp561-583, last accessed 19 June 2024.
10. By 1699 he would vote in favour of a standing army, presumably to maintain Protestant hegemony.

Park. On arrival on any given day, Portsmouth docks would be full of first-, second- and third-rate warships of the line, some undergoing repairs and refurbishment.

General Erle's only surviving child who made it into adulthood was Frances. She had married Sir Edward Ernle in 1693, who added to the Erle family estate the properties that Ernle owned at Maddington and Etchilhampton. Sir Edward Ernle came from a landed family that had been elected for Devizes since the early part of the sixteenth century.[11] With Sir Edward's help, Thomas Erle had bought the lord of the manor of Bishops Canning in Wiltshire for £3500, further expanding the Charborough Estate's holdings.[12] Bishops Canning had been the home of the Ernles for many generations before the move to Maddington. Another election at the end of 1701 had General Erle take his seat at Wareham. At the end of the year, he received a significant posting when he was appointed commander-in-chief of the land forces in Ireland under the lord lieutenancy of the Earl of Rochester. Rochester had written on 5 December 1701, telling Erle: 'I think I cannot appoint a fitter man'. Rochester had written 'there's no man here but himself to whom the care of the army can be committed'.[13] He was added to the Irish Privy Council and was one of the three Lord Justices during Rochester's absence in England. He set sail for Ireland in April 1702.

LAST YEARS OF SERVICE

Thomas Erle's next promotion – to lieutenant-general – did not come through until 11 February 1703. However, Erle was then shown a further mark of favour when he was given the command of a newly raised regiment of dragoons in June 1704. In April of the following year, Erle left Ireland to take up a new appointment as lieutenant general of the Ordnance. His correspondence shows

---

11. Sir Edward was the son of Sir Walter Ernle, who was lineal descendant of Walter, Lord Hungerford, who was beheaded in reign of Henry VIII.

12. The deed can be found at CCCA GBR/0014/ERLE 2/20.

13. The letter can be found in the Erle archive at Churchill College, Cambridge GBR/0014/ERLE 2/53.

that General Erle was now an important figure around Whitehall. On 1 May 1705 he received a note inviting to attend her majesty in her drawing room the following Thursday.[14] A three-quarters portrait of General Erle at this time showed a round-faced man with a serious disposition. It is the portrait of a military man, and he is posed in fully body metal armour with a large white wig. He has his sword sheathed and his walking stick in his hand. In the background, there is a battle scene.

Thomas Erle had a reputation as a rake, a distinguished historian of the period has suggested. Professor Harry Dickinson compiled the correspondence between General Erle and his then friend Henry St John, from 1705 to 1707 the Secretary for War, and noted that they both shared a 'common interest in wine and women'. While correspondence is mainly about the progress and politics of the military campaigns that Erle is engaged in, in one letter St John, a well-known libertine, writes in terms of one rake speaking to another, of sleeping with his London mistress. 'I got to Town last night early, writ my Letters, lay with my Mistress, and after nine hours continued to sleep, find myself in perfect health, so that I discover with great joy in yr humble servant a Constitution fit for one that is Secretary to so many Rakes.'[15] Thomas Erle's mind occasionally turned to his Charborough home, and he had left behind the 'Memorandum What Should be done this winter at Charborough', dated 1705. This included instructions as to lop the three rows of trees in the Elm Court; plant five or six good young elms on the Down and to sow turnip seed in the Pigeon Close plantations.[16]

At the end of the Parliamentary session of 1706, Erle received an order to go as second-in-command under Earl Rivers – Richard Savage – in a diversionary assault on the French coast. After the descent had been delayed by contrary winds and then cancelled, Erle

---

14.   CCCA GBR/0014/ERLE 2/32.

15.   H.T. Dickinson, 'The Correspondence of Henry St. John and Thomas Erle, 1705–8', *Journal of the Society for Army Historical Research*, vol. 48, no. 196 (Winter 1970), 205–224.

16.   CCCA GBR/0014/ERLE 4/6.

stayed with his troops, who were sent to join Lord Galway's army in Spain which was engaged in the War of the Spanish Succession. He remained there during the winter of 1706/1707, sending Marlborough melancholy accounts of the military position in January 1707, and also revealing he was feeling unappreciated, to which the duke replied that the queen was pleased with Erle. On 25 April 1707, General Erle and his troops took part in the Battle of Almanza to the south-west of Santander. The result was a decisive Bourbon victory that reclaimed most of eastern Spain for Philip V of Spain. Of Lord Galway's multinational army, the Portuguese flank fought hard but then broke and fled, leaving the English centre exposed. 'Lieutenant-General Erle commanded the centre and in spite of a desperate resistance was ultimately overcome by immensely superior numbers. Erle was wounded in this battle and lost a large number of his officers and men killed or wounded.'[17] Some accounts suggest Erle lost his right hand during the battle.

Estimates vary, but Galway's army lost as many as 7000 killed and a large number taken prisoner. The battle is considered to be one of the costliest fought by the British Army in the period.[14] General Erle escaped the battlefield along with most of the cavalry and remained in Spain until the end of September, increasingly dissatisfied and in poor health. Arriving back in England, he headed to Parliament to defend Galway in the Commons on 24 February 1708, during the debate on the deficiency of English troops at Almanza. He gave this public display of loyalty, despite private misgivings about the generalship of the campaign. While he was still at Charborough, he was informed that he was to be commander-in-chief of a risky descent on the French coast. The expedition was late in starting, and the original plan of landing at Saint Valery to capture Abbeville was abandoned. After one false start, the force eventually landed at Ostend. Winston Churchill, in *Marlborough, His Life and Times*, praised Erle for other operations in the campaign:

---

17.   John W. Fortescue, *The History of the British Army. Vol 1* (London: Macmillan, 1899), pp. 485–487.

General Erle, whom Marlborough had reinforced at Ostend till he perhaps had 7000 British infantry and a large number of vehicles and horses, in spite of his gout behaved with zeal and skill. He succeeded in draining a large part of the inundation between Nieuport and Ostend. He occupied Leffinghe, and there built a bridge over the canal.[18]

Back at Charborough, Thomas's wife Elizabeth was not well. Sir Edward and Frances Ernle moved back to Charborough for a time to look after her. Frances Ernle movingly wrote to her father on 17 September explaining his wife had collapsed and was in poor health.[19] Elizabeth died in 1710 and was buried in the chapel at Charborough.

Thomas Erle had fought in England, Ireland, Flanders and Spain, risen to the rank of general, and was commander of Irish and English land forces during Queen Anne's reign. While there is no doubt of Thomas Erle's courage in the face of battle, his papers also reveal the day-to-day discussions of running a military campaign. A master of the logistics and the financing of King William's and the Duke of Marlborough's military operations, Erle's post-Revolution career belongs at the heart of the new fiscal-military state. His political persuasion as a Whig led to problems and both he and Marlborough were stood down from their posts in 1712 because of their political loyalties. It is curious that while rising to high military rank, he was never knighted or given an aristocratic title. There are some indications that his 'love of the bottle' may have been an issue and a likely cause of gout that rendered him unwell and ultimately needing to retire. In Parliament, he was usually dutiful, though often an absent member. He rarely spoke. Meanwhile, the first of the House of Hanover monarchs of England, King George I, was crowned in 1714, and he distrusted the Tories, who he believed opposed his right to succeed to the throne.

---

18. Winston S. Churchill, *W.S. Marlborough; His Life and Times. Volume 2* (London: George G. Harrap, 1934), p. 446.

19. The letter can be found in the at Churchill College Archive, Cambridge GBR/0014/ERLE 2/40.

In his last years, General Erle, now in retirement and rankled by lack of appreciation, turned back to his paternal estate. The generational objective of expanding the Charborough Estate meant the family had been early into enclosures, often a controversial process. Before the enclosures, there was much common land in Morden parish. General Thomas Erle was involved in enclosures in Morden with West, East and Meadow fields in 1695. The Erles were the lords of the manor of great swathes of land and therefore the nominal landowner, even where the commoners had rights of 'commons' use of the land. Usually, enclosure was agreed with the tenant farmers, as it was in Morden. The commoners, however, will have lost access to their communal land.[20] Despite his frequent complaints about being 'straghtened', he poured money into improvements to Charborough Estate. He also has enough money to invest in the English East India Company and to turn down offers of Irish lands. In the house itself, General Erle oversaw the insertion of the grand staircase hall in Charborough and in 1718 commissioned the famous artist Sir James Thornhill to paint the walls and ceilings around it in classic Baroque styling. These are considered to be Charborough's finest features and with Thornhill at the height of his powers would have cost a small fortune.

If General Erle was sounding depleted in energy and wealth, new blood and money were about to join the Erle line. The Erle papers in Churchill College reveal a correspondence between Sir Edward and General Erle. In June 1719, a letter was sent by the general to Sir Edward Ernle at his Maddington home about granddaughter Betsy.[21] The correspondence said it was clearly time she married and that friends were asking why she had not tied the knot. The general already knew the pressing suitor, who was Sir Edward's nephew and a member of the Drax family which was related to Ernles through marriage. There had been resistance at first from Betsy's father, Sir Edward Ernle, and her maternal grandfather, General Thomas Erle. Although Henry Drax of Pope's Common, Hertfordshire and

---

20. John Chapman and Sylvia Seeliger, *Enclosure, Environment and Landscape in Southern England* (Stroud: Tempus Publishing, 2001), p. 49.
21. CCCA GBR/0014/ERLE 2/20.

the Ellerton Estate in Yorkshire had been schooled at Eton College and matriculated from Magdalen College, Cambridge in 1710, the letters suggest that Sir Edward and the general were not enthusiastic.[22] The general's words, however, are measured and quite liberal for the time, indicating that love was important in a relationship.

The general's correspondence also implies he was rich in land and property but short of ready cash. Other correspondence suggests his wife's father, also a member of the landed gentry, had died in a poor financial state.[23] Henry Drax however had an income from the Barbados plantations of some £6000 a year plus income from the Drax English estates. Among the pre-nuptial correspondence, Henry wrote to General Erle, essentially asking him to intercede favourably with Sir Edward. Henry's hand is neat, clear, and well-expressed with appropriate decorum and respect for his elders.[24] General Erle started to school young Henry on the ways of Dorset landed gentry, to show leadership and control of the decision-making processes for the country and county. After the ailing general decided to vacate his seat at Wareham, Henry Drax was returned as a Whig at a by-election there in 1718. Henry dutifully maintained the family's hard-line position towards Catholics and was probably tougher on dissenters than General Erle. On 23 December 1719, Henry Drax then 26 years of age, and his first cousin, 22-year-old Elizabeth 'Betsy' Ernle, married in a grand ceremony bringing together the Erle and Drax dynasties through the connections of the Ernle family.

MARRIAGE AND DUTIES

How did Henry balance his Barbados and English interests? Other absent landlords had learnt to their cost that being too absent left

---

22.   How and when the Ellerton estate was acquired by the Draxes is unclear. Chris Drakes of the family website says it was acquired by the Drax family when Ellerton Priory was dissolved by Henry VIII. Others suggest it was acquired by Sir James Drax from his sugar wealth. My view after discussing with Chris Drakes is that Gabriel Drax bought the estates shortly after dissolution and what Sir James bought was the lordship of the manor. See: www.drakesfamily.org/id50.htm, last accessed 1 July 2024.

23.   CCCA GBR/0014/ERLE 2/20.

24.   CCCA: GBR/0014/ERLE 6/1.

you open to fraud. As with his father before him, Henry was to spend time in Barbados, but mainly resided in England. An absence in Barbados may explain why his father-in-law took the Wareham seat for some years after 1722, as Henry and Betsy may well have been at Drax Hall. Certainly, running a plantation 4000 miles away had its problems. In the Churchill College archives, there is a letter to Henry from an unnamed London factor for the Drax Hall plantation written around 1720.[25] The letter is badly written and hard to read, and possibly a draft. The factor stated that a Mr Chester who was responsible for buying, selling and shipping the plantation's slaves, animal supplies and exporting the plantation's sugar was either incompetent or defrauding the Draxes.[26] The factor had been attempting to reconcile several years of the plantation accounts with those accounts kept in London for Henry Drax.[27] His efforts had failed. Most significantly, further into the text, the letter gets into the detail of the purchase of enslaved people and then horses, both treated as property. The factor is complaining about the lack of detail and implying that the accounts hide fraud.[28] This letter indicates that Drax Hall plantation needed at least 30 new enslaved people a year to maintain its numbers suggesting a mortality rate that may have been higher than 10 per cent per year.

25. CCCA GBR/0014/ERLE 6/3.

26. It is likely this is Mr Chester who was the agent for the Royal African Company in the West Indies and had also been an agent to the governor. Chester had a long and controversial time on the colony.

27. Looking after Drax Hall's interests was Madam Elizabeth Colleton of the famous Barbados family and the wife of John Colleton. She was the sister of Sir Edward Ernle, MP, widow of Thomas (Shetterden) Drax and was Henry Drax II's mother. She had remarried into the Colleton family but was responsible for the Drax Trust. Henry Drax II was the older half-brother of James Edward Colleton from his mother's second marriage. James was born circa 1709 in Barbados. Eventually, he left Barbados and returned to the family's ancestral home in south-west England. Like Henry, he was an absentee plantation owner. In a list of inhabitants of St Peter parish, Barbados, circa 1780, Colleton was listed as owning 82 enslaved people. It is possible that this was the same person as listed for St John, Barbados, in 1774, where the name is given as James Edward Colletons of Cliff Plantation and where the number of enslaved owned was 205.

28. CCCA GBR/0014/ERLE 6/3.

The Drax Hall plantations were not the only source of overseas income for the Erle and the Draxes, either based in full or part on enslavement, there were also investments. Sir Walter Erle is said to have had an interest with the Adventurers in the mid-seventeenth century and General Thomas Erle had invested in the EEIC.[29] In 1720, when he was in his 71st year, General Erle's fragile body finally gave out and he was buried in the family vault at the Charborough chapel alongside his late wife. Frances Ernle died in 1728 and Sir Edward in 1729 at Maddington. Charborough was to shift from being home to a military leader to a succession of politicians for 100 years.

---

29. These were to pay out for his descendants.

12
Henry and Betsy Drax

Newly wed, Henry and Betsy Drax initially lived at the Drax Estate at Ellerton in Swaledale, Yorkshire, as records show that some of their six children were born and baptised there in the 1720s. The first was Thomas (IV) on 23 September 1721, who was given the new hyphenated surname Erle-Drax – a mark of the merger of these influential families.[1] Ellerton was remote in the Swaledale valley, the river ran through and could be very beautiful in the summer but bleak and cold in winter. The nearest major town was Richmond, seven miles away, where local gentry would socialise. As the Member of Parliament for distant Wareham, Henry Drax, a Whig, carried status from his wealth and connections.

Henry was one of the MPs who were given shares in 1720 by the South Sea Company.[2] In his case, these were scandals of eighteenth-century Britain, as the country became gripped by what become known as the South Sea Bubble. It also appears that General Erle invested in the South Sea Company before his death. The House of Lords passed the South Sea Bill, which allowed the company a monopoly in trade with South America, in return for a loan of £7 million to finance the war against France. The company underwrote the British National Debt, which stood at £30 million, on a promise of 5 per cent interest from the government. Shares immediately rose to ten times their stated value, speculation was rampant and all sorts of companies, some ridiculous, some fraudulent or just optimistic, were launched.

Then the bubble burst. Stock values plummeted and people all over the country lost all their money. Porters and ladies' maids who

---

1.   The surname Ernle was not incorporated and only appeared in the surname again in the early twentieth century.

2.   One of the South Sea Bubble directors who orchestrated the corruption was Jacob Sawbridge, who appears again in a later chapter.

had bought their own carriages became destitute almost overnight. There was a wave of suicides. The Postmaster General took poison and his son, who was the Secretary of State, avoided the scandal by contracting smallpox and dying. The South Sea Company directors were arrested – this impacted on the Sawbridges, another and later strand of the Drax family – and their estates forfeited. Some 462 members of the House of Commons including Henry Drax, and 112 peers, had interests in the South Sea Company. Despite the bubble bursting, the company continued and began to make some return on its commercial activities. Henry lost only the value of the shares and any profit he had hoped for, but it was damaging to be associated with scandal, and the gift of shares looked perilously like bribery.[3]

The wealth from slave-based activity was spreading across the country in many different income streams. Beneficiaries did not have to be directly involved in slavery themselves. Between 1715 and 1739, slave trading constituted the main legal commercial activity of the South Sea Company. Like King George I, the Hanoverian, George II was a governor and shareholder of the South Sea Company.

---

3.   A later and protracted dispute between distant Drax family members for a share of the profits of General Erle's South Sea investments ended up in the case in the Court of Chancery entitled 'In the Case of Draper *v.* Drax', culminating in 1744. The case files shine some light on the family and its internal politics. They refer to a sum of £3132.9.0, the return on investments in South Sea Annuities, which was to be divided between Thomas Drax and four others. The last part of the document runs as follows: 'In consequence of it being impossible now to work out the Accounts it has been arranged that one-fifth of the entire fund should be paid to the parties entitled to Thomas Drax's Estate in discharge of his claim on the Fund and that the remaining four-fifths should be divided among those now representing the next of kin of Thomas and Elizabeth Shetterden and an order of the Court has lately been made to that effect.' Researching the Drax family in The National Archives, it becomes clear that like many other families engaged in slavery-based businesses, legal cases proliferated, whether concerning the plantation, disputed wills, slavery voyages or investments. Often these cases set one side of the family against another. It is hard not to conclude that greed was the motivator. The Draper v. Drax case also demonstrates how it was not just the plantation owners and slave traders who made money off the backs of the enslaved.

DEATH OF THE TURBERVILLES

In 1729, after the death of her parents, Betsy inherited Charborough and the other Ernle and Erle holdings, and her husband Henry, who was already wealthy, was to share in the inheritance for the period of his life. They moved their English base to Dorset where they merged into the county's landed gentry. Through the eighteenth century, the Drax family used their sugar-enhanced wealth to build extensively in the wider Charborough Estate agricultural buildings, such as modern mills and barns, as well as many cottages for the swelling number of farm workers and craftsmen they needed to run the estate.[4] While occasionally benign, the family were generally rich enough to benefit from the misfortunes of their neighbours, a classic case being that of the Turbervilles.

Today, the real-life Turberville evokes its use in the fictional context of Thomas Hardy's novel *Tess of the D'Urbervilles*.[5] The Turbervilles were a landed-gentry family in east Dorset who are said to have descended from Sir Payne de Turberville, who came from France at the time of the Norman conquest of 1066 through from the thirteenth to the early eighteenth centuries, and who held land around Bere Regis. During the Civil War and Commonwealth, the Catholic Turbervilles were Royalists, and John Turberville fought for the king. Their lands included what had been King John's hunting lodge at Bere Regis and the attractive if small manor house nearby at Wool.[6] After the Civil War, John Turberville was

---

4.   Many of the buildings still on the estate date to this century, although, as will be recounted, many workers' houses were allowed to decline, and some were demolished from the nineteenth century onwards.

5.   Hardy called Bere Regis 'Kingsbere' in his novels.

6.   The Wool manor house is at Woolbridge, a farm on the north side of the river, near the bridge, adjoining to Wool, whence it derived its name. It anciently belonged to the Abbey of Bindon and subsequently it came to the Turbervilles: www.opcdorset.org/EastStoke/EastStoke-Hutchins.htm, last accessed 1 July 2024. The manor house is where Charles Harper notes that Hardy set a tragic moment in the Tess of the D'Urbeville's story. 'The air of bodeful tragedy that naturally enwraps the place… as the scene of Tess's confession to her husband. It was here the newly married pair were to have spent their honeymoon' (Harper, *Hardy Country*, p. 124).

HENRY AND BETSY DRAX

fined £700 for being part of the Royalist army. The original Bere Regis manor house had been burnt down during the war. The historian Hutchins later noticed that the rear portion of the manor house was dated 1648, as Turberville, like Sir Walter Erle, rebuilt.

In the early eighteenth century, the Turberville male line died out. Sir John Tuberville's niece, Mary, married Major William Duckett in 1721. Mary gave birth to twins Frances and Elizabeth, who were never known to have lived apart. In the churchwardens' accounts, the rates of parochial duties customarily received from the lord of the manor are, after 1704, attributed to 'The Widow & Coheirs of Esq Turberville'. Mary sold the manor to Squire Henry Drax in 1733, but he allowed the family to remain in the house.[7] The largest of the Turberville farms, Roke, immediately north of Bere Regis, which had once been a separate manor, was taken over by the Draxes. Next, in 1755, Henry Drax bought the manor of Winterton Muston to the east of the estate from the Tubervilles, completing the transfer of lands from one family to another. The Turberville line became extinct in east Dorset.[8]

Meanwhile, Henry Drax II was trying to run the Drax plantations in Barbados from England. One draft letter of 1731 shows him writing to a Mr Walker whom he ascribed as a friend and is clearly working with a Mr Walcott and a Mr Jones managing the plantation. These three names are all from plantation-owning families and it is likely the three were acting as Henry Drax's agents. Finally, Henry said he had heard that coffee-growing was being trialled in the West Indies and asked Mr Walker to experiment with coffee as a crop.[9]

---

7.   Later the twins were moved to London, probably on the death of their mother. They died within a day of each other, aged 77, at Pursers Cross, Fulham, and were interred together at Putney on the same day in February 1780. I thank the local historian of Bere Regis, John Pitfield, for this information: https://bereregis. org/turberville-family.htm.

8.   The local story is that Mary's twins were vulnerable, and Henry Drax bought out the Turberville estate after the mother died (possibly as late as 1749) for a pittance. It was Henry who moved the young women to London, who then lived in very basic conditions.

9.   This letter is in the CCCA GBR/0014/ERLE 6.

185

FREDERICK, PRINCE OF WALES

Henry Drax and the family visited London frequently. From 1733 he rented an impressive house in Park Place, Hanover Square, built shortly after the ascension of George I and named in honour of the new king.[10] The parish was fashionable with wealthy absentee plantation owners for many years. Henry Drax's wealth and London connections resulted in him making contact with the royal family. When Henry and Betsy had a son born in March 1736, he was named Frederick in honour of the prince, who become one of the child's godfathers. Henry was to benefit from Prince Frederick's patronage with salaried appointments including the stewardship of the Prince of Wales' Dorset manors in 1737.

Born on 31 January 1707 in Hanover, Frederick was the eldest son of George II. His parents left for London at the time of death of his grandfather George I, and Frederick did not see his parents for 14 years. In 1728, Frederick was finally brought to Britain, was created Prince of Wales on 8 January 1729, and was fourth in line to the crown. His mother and father, Queen Caroline and George II did not like their son. Queen Caroline is reported as saying 'Our first-born is the greatest ass, the greatest liar, the greatest canaille and the greatest beast in the world, and we heartily wish he was out of it.' 'My God', she said, 'popularity always makes me sick, but Fretz's popularity makes me vomit.'

With his large debts, the Prince of Wales relied for an income on his wealthy friend and Whig politician George Bubb Dodington. Although his lifestyle was decadent, he associated with a number of talented men, notably George Lyttleton, William Pitt the Elder and to a lesser extent George Carteret. He built the vast Eastbury House at Tarrant Gunville in Dorset, a huge folly mansion begun by the previous generation. Eastbury was just a few miles north of Charborough. In further patronage, Henry was made secretary to the prince. The spiky diarist Horace Walpole, in his correspondence suggested the appointment was something of a joke, claiming Henry could not even write his name.[11]

10. LMA BRA/432/0---7.
11. Walpole's diaries, with their many references to the Drax family, can be

Henry Drax's friendship with Frederick had its benefits but also its costs. Frederick arranged a goodly time before that he would visit Charborough for a few days at the end of August 1741. As a result, Henry had a whole wing added to the house for the prince's visits and comfort. This included 'The Long Room', a peculiar shaped room with a circular centre with two long wings which was built for cockfighting to entertain the prince. Frederick's entourage toured the area during his stay and his visit to Poole is recorded in *The Englishman's Journal*, Saturday 12 September 1741 (No. 239). Extract from a letter from Poole:[12]

On Wednesday last his Royal Highness the Prince of Wales came into this Part of the Country: He was row'd from Litch-et-Bay to Brownsey by Aaron Durell, Christopher Spurrier, Martin Fiander, and Joseph Millar, all Masters of Vessels, in a Boat belonging to one of them, which they cover'd, as well as time would permit, with red Cloth: The Surveyor of his Majesty's Customs perform'd the Office of Cockswain. As his Royal Highness came down the River he was saluted by the Thunder of 21 Guns, planted at Ham for that purpose. One hundred and seventeen Vessles, of different Denominations, spread the Channel and accompany'd him to the Bar. When his Royal Highness landed at Brownsey he walked upon the publick Platform for about half an hour, then retir'd into a Room in the Castle, which was fitted up for his Reception. Several of our Gentry of both Sexes were introduced to his Presence by Henry Drax, Esq., and he was pleased to accept their Compliment in the most polite and obliging Manner.[13]

---

found here: https://walpole.library.yale.edu/, last accessed 12 July 2024.

12. 12th September 1741 (No. 239).

13. Poole, like so much of Dorset, had benefitted from the plantations and slave trade but more as a support to provisions to the island, especially barrels of fish. Poole men had been fishing in Newfoundland waters for many years when they responded to the new markets. The port's trade with Newfoundland provided exports of salt, nets, cloth and provisions. From Newfoundland, fish were transported to the West Indies or to the Mediterranean.

THOMAS ERLE-DRAX

Henry and Betsy's first son, Thomas Erle-Drax, graduated from Oxford in 1740. His family exerted its local influence on voters, and he was elected as MP for Corfe Castle in 1744 and held the seat there for three years.[14] Like his father he was a supporter of the Prince of Wales and his political faction. The journey to Parliament and back could be hazardous even for an MP. As one newspaper reported in 1746, Thomas, riding along Popham Lane near Stockbridge, presumably on his way to Dorset from Westminster, was robbed by a highwayman of 20 guineas and a gold watch. The highwayman was pursued, arrested and held in Winchester Gaol. On another occasion, in the early evening of 20 February 1748, the Exeter Waggon was robbed at Turnham Green, to the west side of London. The items taken included a box 'containing Writings, and Title Deeds of Lands in Wareham' belonging to Henry Drax and the Charborough Estate. The robbers were two men on foot and three on horseback. An advert in the *London Gazette* said his majesty would pardon anyone involved if they made 'for better discovering and bringing to Justice the persons concerned in the said robbery'. In addition, Henry Drax Esq. offered a reward of £50 on the conviction of the offenders. Anyone wanting to claim the reward could apply at his London house in Pall Mall.[15]

At the general election of the summer of 1747, Thomas had stood for Wareham with his father, Henry Drax, and they were elected. The *London Evening Post* reported:

We hear from Wareham in Dorsetshire, that before Henry Drax and his Son, took Leave of their Friends in that Town, their Steward paid all the Innkeepers Bills; and the Wednesday following Mr. Drax gave them a grand Entertainment at his Seat at Charborough, where dined at one Table 140, and in the Evening

---

14. www.historyofparliamentonline.org/volume/1754-1790/member/drax-thomas-erle-1721-89.
15. *London Gazette*, 5 March 1748–8 March 1748.

this Entertainment was concluded with a Ball: They all wore Orange-colour'd Ribands.[16]

This was a thank you for the successful election, but it was premature. Both the Draxes were unseated on the petition of their opponent John Pitt (in a dispute over the franchise), the committee declared their election void and that their opponents Pitt and Hodgkinson had been duly elected. There was a double return, on which diarist and Whig politician Horace Walpole reported to Sir Horace Mann on 26 January 1748: 'The House is now sitting on the Wareham election, espousing George Pitt's uncle, one of the most active Jacobites, but of the coalition and in place, against Drax, a great favourite of the Prince.'[17] The next year in November, *The General Advertiser* noted that Henry Drax Esq., the secretary to his Royal Highness the Prince of Wales had arrived at his house in Pall Mall 'for the Winter Season'.[18] The life of the eighteenth-century squire suited Henry allowing him to divide his time between the bucolic charms of Charborough and the social high life centred round the prince in London.

DEAD FRED

Frederick, the Prince of Wales, died at his home, Leicester House in London, on 31 March 1751, at the age of 44. He was buried at Westminster Abbey. A popular epigram to The Prince of Wales ran:

Here lies poor Fred who was alive and is dead,
Had it been his father I had much rather,
Had it been his sister nobody would have missed her,
Had it been his brother, still better than another,
Had it been the whole generation, so much better for the nation,
But since it is Fred who was alive and is dead,
There is no more to be said!

---

16. *London Evening Post*, 11 August 1747–13 August 1747.
17. Horace was the youngest son of Prime Minister, Sir Robert Walpole.
18. *General Advertiser*, 18 November 1749.

The death must have been a huge blow to Henry Drax II's aspirations. As the politician Horace Walpole noted in his diary, Henry Drax had been promised a barony on Frederick's accession. Henry Drax's last election was in 1754 for Wareham. Thomas and his father had stood at Wareham again against the Pitts of Encombe.[19] After the election of April 1754 had been declared void, a compromise was arranged by which Thomas Erle-Drax withdrew, and his father Henry was elected. In the elections of December 1754 each family returned one Member. The next year, Henry Drax died at Charborough leaving behind three sons and five daughters and his body was interred in the family vault.

As the eldest son, Thomas, now 37, succeeded and had three inheritances, those of the Drax, the Ernle and the Erle, making him a very wealthy man. This included the plantations in the West Indies. A few months later, Thomas married Mary St John, a daughter of John St John, Baron St John of Bletso. Thomas, like his father, showed no interest in following the traditions of the Drax and Erles to become militia officers. Meanwhile, a rival's strategy to control the rotten borough of Wareham was in its early stages. According to a survey in the Calcraft papers at Rempstone in 1753, there were about 500 tenements at Wareham, of which more than a hundred belonged to the Draxes and above 50 to the Pitts.

In that period a new figure appeared on the Wareham political scene. Sir John Calcraft acquired the sprawling eleven-square-mile estate and manor of Rempstone in Purbeck, to the south of Charborough. He had made his money by arranging contracts for the army. A liberal, Sir John was an MP known as Honest John and was said to be the *eminence grise* behind the anonymous satirical writer Crafterio. Some years after his purchase of Rempstone, Calcraft started a campaign of buying out smaller homeowners in Wareham so he could get a parliamentary seat. Sir John would eventually succeed in his plan. But in 1761 Thomas Erle-Drax was returned to Wareham without a contest and received Henry Pelham's whip through his friend Robert Nugent, who had married his sister,

---

19. The Encombe Estate was based round Encombe House on the southern coast of the Isle of Purbeck. The current house was built by John Pitt in 1735.

Elizabeth. Nugent had been a follower of the Prince of Wales and attached himself to Henry Pelham's faction after the prince's death.

On 21 June 1764, Nugent wrote to Lord Grenville that he had tried to get Thomas an Irish peerage: 'As I see in the public papers that some Irish peers have been now created, I must beg leave to put you in mind of Mr. Drax's wishes upon this subject. He does not know that I ever mentioned them to you.' Grenville replied on 24 June: 'I understood from you that Mr. Drax wished this, but was far from being very eager about it, which made me avoid entering upon the subject unless I had thought it very likely to.'[20] When Lord Rockingham took office, Drax followed Lord Nugent into opposition and voted against the repeal of the Stamp Act.[21] Thomas supported the interests of the West Indies planters, so it is unclear why he supported the maintenance of the Stamp Act.[22] Neither is it hard to imagine that keeping the cider tax went down well in his constituency or estate, but then they were unlikely to have been voters.[23]

Money was pouring into Charborough from Barbados as demand for sugar outstripped supply. In a 1759 pamphlet, Joseph Massie complained about sugar price fixing: 'Sugars are now consigned by the Sugar-Planters, to a Sett of Men whom they have made Servants, and are not sold to the People of Great Britain until the same will fetch such excessive high Prices, as Avarice, or Exorbitance suggest to the said Planters to fix thereon.'[24] Benefitting

---

20. www.historyofparliamentonline.org/volume/1754-1790/member/drax-thomas-erle-1721-89, last accessed 15 July 2024.

21. Lord Rockingham was a Whig grandee and served as Prime Minister of Great Britain between 1765 and 1766, and again in 1782.

22. The Act imposed a direct tax on the British colonies in America and required that many printed materials in the colonies be produced on stamped paper produced in London, carrying an embossed revenue stamp. Printed materials included legal documents, magazines, playing cards, newspapers, and many other types of paper used throughout the colonies, and it had to be paid in British currency, not in colonial paper money. The purpose of the tax was to pay for British military troops stationed in the American colonies after the French and Indian Wars. Political opposition was expressed in a number of colonies, including Barbados and Antigua, and by absentee landowners living in Britain.

23. DRAX, Thomas Erle (?1721-89), of Charborough, Dorset | History of Parliament Online, last accessed 19 June 2024.

24. Sheridan, *Sugar and Slavery*, p. 257.

from his wealth, like his father Squire Henry, Thomas Erle-Drax was very much the Dorset country gentleman and a social character among the county set performing the duties of gentry. As was expected, some philanthropy was bestowed, and the Erle-Draxes became connected to London's Foundling Hospital, perhaps the most important English charity of the eighteenth century. The Foundling Hospital had an additional wing built in 1752 by public subscription. The new hospital was described as 'the most imposing single monument erected by eighteenth-century benevolence'. Over four years, Parliament provided funds that meant every child brought to the hospital had to be accepted. Almost 15,000 were admitted, and the hospital could not keep up with the number of branch hospitals that had to be built.

In 1758, Thomas and his brother Edward were elected hospital governors, presumably after donating a considerable sum. Over the years, a disproportionately large number of the governors were from Dorset, and other familiar names include Churchill, Clavell, Damer, Gundry, Pitt, Pleydell and Trenchard. There were many diversions in the social rounds of town and county. The author of *The Decline and Fall of the Roman Empire*, Edward Gibbon, visited Blandford in 1760 as a 23-year-old Hampshire Militia captain. He noted, 'Our stay at Blandford was very agreeable, and the weather was fine. The gentlemen of the county showed us great hospitality, particularly Messrs Portman, Pleydell, Bower, Sturt, Brain, Jennings, Drax and Trenchard, but partly through their fault, and partly thro' ours, their hospitality was often debauch.'[25]

Thomas Erle-Drax took his role as head of the Charborough Estate seriously and sought to improve his lands. He bought and then substantially renovated and expanded Cranbourne Lodge, a gem in the Cranbourne Chase.[26] The substantial Abbot's Court Farm was purchased in 1765 from the Tregonwell family. Abbot's Court was to become an important farm in the estate structure. Although Thomas increased the size of the estate and undertook

---

25. From *Dorset Life* magazine, November 2019, but sadly the magazine has now closed.
26. It was later sold to Lewis Tregonwell.

renovations to the house, he did sell some land. Thomas Erle-Drax sold his interest at Wareham to Calcraft, and this included the rights to be lord of the manor, the freehold of 52 associated houses, ten cottages, two shops, numerous cellars, gardens, pieces of land and meadow.[27] In the March 1768 election, Thomas did not stand, and Calcraft had the choice of both Members, and Wareham was henceforth a Calcraft pocket borough, never again contested in this period.[28] Why Erle-Drax had sold the Manor of Wareham is not clear, it may be because the Great Fire of Wareham of 1762 had left the town devastated. The records show that wealthy Calcraft had lent Thomas Erle-Drax some £5000 earlier in the year of the sale.[29]

Thomas enjoyed fox-hunting on the Drax estate.[30] The owner of another Dorset estate at Iwerne Stapleton, Peter Beckford, nephew of the Jamaican plantation owner William (and by then owner of Drax Hall plantation on Jamaica) would stay over at Charborough when hunting.[31] If well organised and financially supported, the life of the squire in the mid-eighteenth century was a round of pleasure at home and business was conducted in London with like-minded men feathering their own interests. The landed gentry had a range of limited duties usually around hospitality. Some, just a few women, though, sought a more exciting life, intellectual stimulation and travel.

---

27. The indenture of his sale of the manor and borough of Wareham for £10,000 is dated 16 August 1768.

28. www.historyofparliamentonline.org/volume/1754-1790/constituencies/wareham.

29. Despite the rivalry, a Calcraft was married to one of Thomas's younger sisters.

30. Thomas Erle-Drax had the cartographer Isaac Taylor survey the estate between 1773 and 1777 and draw up maps and terriers of the estate. This was a massive task, as the estate was already some 12,000 acres; there are some 20 very large maps in the Dorset History Centre marking the adjoining lands with the names of neighbouring owners such as the Churchills, Trenchards and Tregonwells. The maps in Dorset History Centre are quality copies and the originals are held in the Drax Family archive. They allowed the twentieth-century agricultural historian Barbara Kerr to demonstrate how the Erle-Draxes consolidated fields into larger farms doing away with life-holders wherever possible.

31. Gwen Yarker, *Georgian Faces* (Dorchester: DHNAS, 2010), p. 17. Later, Elizabeth would become Lady of the Bedchamber to Queen Charlotte.

THE SCANDALOUS DRAX WOMEN

Two of the most extraordinary women ancestors of the Drax family were Henry and Betsy Drax's daughter, Elizabeth Drax, and her daughter, also called Elizabeth. They were very different personalities and both became mired in scandal, which is why more is known about them than other women of the family. Their stories are a diversion from the Charborough thread, but nonetheless well worth telling. Born around 1720, Elizabeth the elder became a Lady of the Bedchamber to the Princess of Wales in 1745, undoubtedly because of her father's connection with Frederick. It was a prestigious sinecure that she would hold for nearly 30 years, and she was paid a handsome £400 a year. This Elizabeth would create a family linkage between the landed gentry of the Draxes and the aristocracy of the Berkeleys, considered one of the most distinguished families in the kingdom. The Berkeleys were of Saxon and Norman descent and with an ancestral seat at Berkeley Castle in Gloucestershire. Elizabeth the elder married the 3rd Earl of Berkeley's son, Augustus, an officer in the Guards.[32]

Before he married, Augustus had a notorious affair with the married Frances, Lady Vane, whom the 21-year-old Augustus had met in Paris. To get over the affair, Augustus Berkeley rejoined his Guards regiment and returned to his duties.[33] Augustus' friends advised him to make a match with Elizabeth Drax. She married Augustus, now Lt Col. Berkeley at St James Church, Westminster, in 1744. Again, Augustus had picked for a partner a woman who was not monogamous. The diarist and political figure of the period, Horace Walpole, knew her well and darkly confided that Elizabeth Berkeley's sins were not just her numerous love affairs, but there was something far worse, which he never specified. 'There is nothing so black of which she is not capable. Her gallantries are white specks about her.' As the biographer Julia Gasper commented, 'Whether she was selling state secrets to a foreign power

---

32. Augustus succeeded his father as earl in 1736.
33. In 1745 he fought in the Battle of Culloden, where the highlanders of Bonnie Prince Charlie suffered massive casualties.

HENRY AND BETSY DRAX

or just cheating at cards, we are left to guess.'[34] Elizabeth the elder had children with Augustus, who died in 1755. She was noted in London for her Tuesday night soirees which were attended by the elite and fashionable. She later married the prominent politician Robert Nugent MP, and then had two more daughters. A three-quarter-length portrait of her painted by Sir Joshua Reynolds in 1759 shows a fair-haired woman with a demure expression, strong nose and full lips dressed much in silk, all set in an outdoor location.

The younger Elizabeth Berkeley was the last of Augustus and Elizabeth's daughters and had been born in 1750. In Elizabeth the younger's remarkably candid and insightful 1828 memoirs, she remembered her mother as 'having no love for children' and palmed her and her sister Georgia off on a Swiss governess.[35] Elizabeth the younger had a more remarkable life than even her mother. She was to be a well-travelled woman of intellect and talent and was not prepared to bow to the decorum of the time. She had scandals, lovers and husbands, and was to be a great writer of plays, poems and stories, spending much of her life in Europe at various courts. Just 17 in 1767, she married Mr William Craven, who was near twice her age and who later became the sixth Earl of Craven. She did not want to get married and did not take to William Craven who was by all accounts a plain and dull man. But he persisted and her mother cajoled her into the marriage. William and Elizabeth had seven children together, but the marriage was not a success. As she grew older Elizabeth started to take control of her life. Both Elizabeth and her husband had affairs, including Elizabeth's liaison with the French ambassador, the Count of Guines, in 1773, which even made it into the pages of the *Morning Chronicle*.[36]

Despite Horace Walpole's dislike of her mother, Elizabeth the younger was friendly with Horace and corresponded with him and

---

34. Julia Gasper, *Elizabeth Craven: Writer, Feminist and European* (London: Vernon Press, 2018), p. 3.

35. Elizabeth Berkeley (née Drax) died on 29 June 1792, aged 72 and was buried at Berkeley Castle.

36. Allegedly, her affair took place at Craven Cottage, which she owned. That is now the site of the Fulham Football Club ground, which is named after the cottage.

visited his home at Strawberry Hill, a remarkable house near the Thames built in a neo-Castle fairy tale style. His Strawberry Hill Press published some of her early work. During this period, she wrote a satire on German snobbery and several plays.[37] Walpole stated his admiration of Lady Craven and wrote poetry to her.[38] He sent the Reverend William Mason an ecstatic review of her comedy, *The Miniature Picture*, performed at Drury Lane in May 1780:

> She went to it herself the second night in form, sat in the middle of the front row of the state box, much dressed with a profusion of white bugles and plumes, to receive the public homage due to her sex and loveliness... It was amazing to see so young a woman entirely possess herself; but there is such an integrity and frankness in her consciousness of her own beauty and talents, that she speaks of them with a naïveté as if she had no property in them, but only wore them as gifts of the gods.

Lord Craven was apparently not happy about Walpole's fondness for Elizabeth. According to a section in her 1828 memoir, Craven took up with a 'lower class' woman. Elizabeth complained, 'He was weak enough to form a connection with a worthless and abandoned woman who he met at an inn.' In 1783, he and Elizabeth separated, and begrudgingly he agreed to pay her a small settlement of £1500 a year. A half-length portrait of Elizabeth painted at about this time by Ozias Humphry shows a handsome woman with inquisitive full eyes, a Romanesque nose, a strong jaw and a dress and scarf in the French style. She resembles her mother. Another, more flattering full-length portrait by Sir Thomas Beach in 1777 shows her with a harp and music stand with flowing clothing in the classical style.

---

37. Columnist Horace Walpole, it may be recalled, did not like the early feminist Mary Wollstonecraft or her writings and described her as 'a hyena in petticoats'.

38. Walpole's diaries, https://walpole.library.yale.edu/, last accessed 12 July 2024.

With her youngest son Richard Keppel accompanying her, Elizabeth Craven went to live in France. In Paris, she came to the attention of the queen of France who found her engaging company. In 1785 Elizabeth became romantically involved with a nephew of the famous Admiral Henry Vernon, who was also called Henry. A man of the sea, Henry had signed up with the Spanish navy for adventure and in battle proved himself a hero. The couple travelled extensively in Europe, including France, Italy, Austria, Poland, Bulgaria, Russia, Greece and Turkey. Whilst on her travels, she wrote to Christian Frederick Charles Alexander, the Margrave of Brandenburg-Ansbach-Bayreuth, whom she had met in France. The margrave was part of the Prussian royal family with a wife back at home. In 1787, Elizabeth visited the Margrave of Ansbach and successfully displaced his mistress in his affections. Together they travelled to Berlin to arrange the sale of the margrave's principality to the king of Prussia for a very handsome sum. *Journey through Crimea to Constantinople* was published in 1789. Subsequently, she visited Ansbach and set up home with the margrave. She wrote what were known as petit plays in French for the court theatre, *La Folle du Jour* and *Abdoul et Nourjad*. The margrave's ailing wife died in early 1791, as did Lord Craven that September. In October 1791, Elizabeth married the margrave in Lisbon. She took to using the title Margravine of Ansbach though it was never conferred.

The following year the margrave settled in England, where the more moralistic members of society avoided the couple, but they befriended musicians and actors, and the more rakish of the Regency set. George III disapproved of her marriage, viewing it as unequal as the margrave was a member of the Prussian royal family and Elizabeth was merely the daughter of an earl. In 1785, Walpole wrote of Lady Craven to Sir Horace Mann:

She has, I fear, been *infinitamente* indiscreet, but what is that to you or me? She is very pretty, has parts, and is good-natured to the greatest degree; has not a grain of malice or mischief, almost always the associates, in women, of tender hearts, and never has been an enemy but to herself.[39]

Julia Gasper has suggested that Craven's literary works are overlooked. 'If they were read more widely, she would surely be recognised as one of the most significant early feminist writers in English belonging to the generation of Mary Wollstonecraft.'[40] In her treatise on marriage, *Letters from a Peeress of England to her Eldest Son*, written in 1784, Elizabeth advised him how a husband should treat a wife and made it clear she deplored the laws of marriage as they then existed in England. At the outset, she protested that 'Marriage is the source of all misery of that part of humankind which most deserves to be happy. I mean the softer sex, whose education and nature makes it bear I patient and dumb regret the arbitrary power an English husband has over his wife.' She wrote:

> So do not imagine, because the law has put your wife intirely in your power, that it is just or right she should be so. I have heard men boast of that power, as if was constituted by their merit. Trace that power to its source, and you will find it proceed from the natural propensity Englishmen ever had for tyranny. It was men who made the laws, and those give man an unlimited power over his wife.[41]

After the margrave's death, Elizabeth Craven moved to Italy where she passed her time sailing, gardening and writing her memoirs.[42] Back at Charborough the resident Draxes were enjoying a period of high social elevation through their contacts with George III and his family.

---

39. *Dictionary of National Biography* (1891).
40. Gasper, *Elizabeth Craven: Writer, Feminist and European*, p. xviii.
41. Elizabeth Craven, *Letters from a Peeress of England to her Eldest Son* (London: Debrett, 1784), p. 3.
42. She died in 1828 at Craven Villa in Posillipo and was buried in the English Cemetery at Naples.

PART V

The Grosvenor Years

13
Richard and Sarah Grosvenor, Royal Courtiers

The current twenty-first-century resident of Charborough House, Richard Drax's second name is Grosvenor, and it sits before his full quadruple-barrelled name. This is a tribute to the merging of the Grosvenor aristocratic family with the Erle-Draxes in the late eighteenth century. A marriage was to bring further wealth, an entrée into King George III and his circles, but it then saw an extraordinary series of personal tragedies.

EDWARD ERLE-DRAX

The last head of the family with just the double-barrelled Erle-Drax surname was the second son of Henry Drax. Edward took an interest in managing the Drax Hall plantation in Barbados; it seems likely he took that responsibility off his older brother's shoulders during his life. The sugar trade was volatile. The trade routes were disrupted when England lost her mainland American colonies after 1776 and with it the control of the cotton-growing slave economy that supplied some cotton to the British mills of the early Industrial Revolution. The American colonies had been big purchasers of cotton goods from Britain. However, the sugar monoculture of Barbados remained intact. The West Indies are in a sessional hurricane zone and in October 1780 a tremendous hurricane swept through Barbados. St Michael's Cathedral in Bridgetown was in its path and its impressive spire, with its clock and bells, collapsed into the church crushing the tomb of a member of the Lascelles family. Edward Ellcock, the churchwarden of St George's, reported that it had done some £6000 worth of damage to Drax Hall plantation, effectively wiping out a year or more of income – such were the vagaries of plantation ownership. It is more than likely some of the enslaved people in their flimsy homes would have died or been injured.[1] Edward Erle-Drax may have sailed to Barbados at this point to oversee the reconstruction of the plantation. A stint at Drax Hall would explain his knowledge of the management of slave-worked sugar plantations.

As his ancestor Henry Drax I had done over a century earlier, Edward Erle-Drax was a co-author in 1786 of another notorious manual on running a slave plantation: 'Instructions for the Management of a Plantation in Barbadoes and for the Treatment of Negroes.' The title page includes: 'The following Instructions are offered to the consideration of proprietors and managers of plantations in Barbadoes.' Although multiple authors are listed for the 64-page book, the first-person singular is used throughout, and it is believed the main author was Edward Erle-Drax, keeping up the Drax family long-standing reputation as leading exploiters of enslaved people. Absent or present, Edward Erle-Drax continued to manage as the landlord of the Drax Estates in Barbados.[2]

In the introduction is printed in bold capital letters: 'THE INCREASE IS THE ONLY TEST OF THE CARE WITH WHICH THEY ARE TREATED.' The pamphlet calls for an organised system of encouragement of childbearing by enslaved women within the wider context of a 'better treatment' policy. It emphasises the need to implement a series of prenatal policies to assist pregnant women in the delivery of healthy babies. The 'Instructions' were written for the management of a plantation of 260 acres of land, of which 160 were cane land. The author argued the case that the 'Negroes' be treated with 'humanity' especially if the owners wanted to get the most of their involuntary workforce. It is written as a guide to good practice rather than as a description of actual workings (pp. 21–31). The patronising tone of racism

---

1. BDA Queree/Hughes papers.
2. Another listed author, Phillip Gibbes was a member of the Barbadian Society for the Improvement of Plantership, and the 1789 autobiography of the former enslaved African Olaudah Equiano contained a description of him as 'the most worthy and humane gentleman'.

is reflected in item 16: 'The Blacks are commonly addicted to Thieving; if it be for their Belly, it is the more excusable, but I hope none of mine will ever have Occasion to be Thieves for Want; but if at any Time they are taken stealing Sugar, Mollasses, or Rum, they must be severely handled.' Edward's comments in 'Instructions' is the clearest indicator of family views on their enslaved people since Henry Drax wrote his earlier manual on slaves. Not much had changed. Edward viewed his enslaved people as sub-human.

Edward Drax also recommended that a manager be paid a salary of no more than £100 per year. Unlike Henry Drax's seventeenth-century manual, these 'Instructions' were sown with benign and pious comments towards the enslaved with one eye towards the growing power of the emergent British abolition campaign lead by Quaker Thomas Clarkson and MP William Wilberforce.

Following his brother's death, Edward's time as the head of the English and Barbados estates was short, as he died a little more than a year later. Wealth was pouring into the family coffers. He managed one last project as he built the famous folly tower at Charborough, which lay a short distance from the house and provided a panoramic view of the estate. In Charborough House, there were and still may be, portraits of Edward and Mary Drax and their infant daughter hung in the dining room over the east door. It is possible that this is by the famous (and expensive) artist of the time, George Romney. It was another signal of the family's increasing wealth and status. The Erle-Draxes were about to take a further step up in royal society through the female line. Edward Erle-Drax was anti-abolition and anti-papist. His much longer-lived wife, Mary (née Churchill), was to become a prolific correspondent with many of the leading women and men of the day and accompanied the new head of the family and his wife to many of the social events with the royal family.

GROSVENOR MEETS ERLE-DRAX

In August 1778, *The Times* reported a forthcoming wedding. 'Miss Drax, daughter of Major Drax, stands forward as one of the most elegant and accomplished young Ladies of the present day: for she, in a great measure, owes this to the good sense of her mother's system of education: Mr. Grosvenor is the happy man who is about to bear away this prize, the weight of which will be full one hundred and fifty thousand pounds.'[3]

The wedding took place at Charborough the next March when Edward and Mary Erle-Drax's daughter, 19-year-old Sarah Frances, married 26-year-old Richard Grosvenor, then the Member of Parliament for West Looe in Cornwall, one of the boroughs controlled by his powerful aristocratic family. Like other incomer husbands, in marriage he was required to take the family name Erle-Drax before his own to have the benefit of Charborough, Drax Hall and the family's other estates in Lincolnshire and Yorkshire.[4] He held land in Somerset. Marrying into the Grosvenor family, even the second tier, was a step up for the Erle-Draxes in society.[5] The Grosvenor family ancestry could be traced back to when Gilbert le Grosvenor came to England with William the Conqueror.[6]

Richard and Sarah Frances' son, Richard Edward, arrived on Christmas Day in the year of their marriage. By late 1791, now the head of the Erle-Drax family, Richard was already an active part of the landed gentry with all its duties and benefits. There was a rigid extended Grosvenor family hierarchy, and Richard Erle-Drax-

---

3. *The Times*, 21 August 1787.
4. Often they were known by the reduced surname Drax-Grosvenor.
5. Richard was the eldest son of Thomas Grosvenor of Swell Court, Fivehead, Somerset and Deborah Skynner of Walthamstow, Essex. His father, Thomas, in turn, was the second son of Baron Grosvenor.
6. In the 600 years that followed, the family grew its landholdings, finances and status, establishing a home in Eaton, Cheshire, in the early 1440s; investing in coal, stone and lead mines in the 1580s in Denbighshire and Flintshire; and seeing its finances drained in the 1640s when supporting the king during the English Civil War. In 1677, lands to the west of the City of London came into the family following the marriage of Sir Thomas Grosvenor to Mary Davies, daughter of a scrivener. Mary was heiress to the manor of Ebury, acquired by her great-grandfather, Hugh Audley, a clerk of the Court of Wards and Liveries. The centuries that followed saw Grosvenor develop those lands. The Grosvenor family are the wealthiest aristocratic family in the UK in modern times under the Duke of Westminster. They own swathes of London, including Grosvenor Square in Mayfair.

Grosvenor had had to vacate his government seat for East Looe when his cousin, Lord Belgrave, came of age in 1788. But Richard's father, Thomas Grosvenor, told the Prime Minister, William Pitt the Younger, that 'it is not pleasant to him, neither is it to me, that a young man of his great expectations should cease to be one of the Senate', and had solicited a peerage for his son.[7] Richard's father pointed out that this would enable Lord Belgrave to step into his own seat for Chester and so allow his son to remain in the House.[8] In support of his claim, Thomas Grosvenor asserted that his son's recent marriage to the Drax heiress, whose inheritance included property in Barbados, meant that 'between the two families an estate of between 12 and 13 thousand pounds per annum will devolve upon the young people'.[9] Richard Erle-Drax-Grosvenor was without a seat until September 1794, when his relation Assheton Curzon returned him for the vacancy at Clitheroe created by his own elevation to the peerage. As part of the recurrent theme, Richard asked Pitt for a peerage but met with a flat refusal.[10]

THE YEOMANRY

In the spring of 1794, with tensions with France mounting, the 1st Lord Milton of Milton Abbey,[11] Joseph Damer, raised the Dorset

---

7.   ERLE DRAX GROSVENOR, Richard (1762-1819), of Charborough Park, nr. Blandford Forum, Dorset and Swell Court, Som. | History of Parliament Online, last accessed July 2024. Pitt had a lot on his mind at this time, not least having lost the colony of North America and signed in that year The Triple Alliance with Prussia and Holland to restrict French expansion.

8.   The Grosvenor family sat for Chester without a break from 1715 until 1874 and, during that time, held both seats for 42 years.

9.   The expression 'great expectations' could not be a clearer reference to the 'natural order' of English society. When Edward Erle-Drax died in 1791, his will said his estate was worth £9000 a year as it passed to his daughter Sarah Frances Erle-Drax Grosvenor.

10.   ERLE DRAX GROSVENOR, Richard (1762-1819), of Charborough Park, nr. Blandford Forum, Dorset and Swell Court, Som. | History of Parliament Online, last accessed 1 July 2024.

11.   Milton Abbey is eight miles north-west of Charborough Park.

Volunteer Rangers, a militia light cavalry regiment. Contemporary registers show that Richard Erle-Drax-Grosvenor signed up at the start, as did his nearby gentry neighbour and relative through marriage, George Churchill. James Frampton of Moreton to the west was also another troop commander. The main reason for the formation of new militias was to counter a much-feared French invasion. There was still resistance, as there had been in General Thomas Erle's time, to having a large standing army, but the perceived threat of Revolutionary France and invasion overcame such concerns for liberty; the regular army needed many more troops if it was to cover the threatened coastlines.[12]

The militia units were selective about who could join. There was political unrest in the country and concern that the lower orders may revolt like the French and dispense with the monarchy. Over the course of a week in June 1778, following a petition to repeal the 1778 Catholic Relief Act,[13] London experienced nightly 'tumults' as rioters attacked foreign embassies, politicians' homes and prisons and attempted to attack the Bank of England. The riots were finally quashed when King George III sent in 10,000 troops and empowered them to fire on the crowds. The last thing the king wanted to do was provide potential rebels with military training and equipment through the militias, so recruits were screened. Forming the new militias in 1794, the government did their best to make sure they were 'to consist of none but known respectable Housekeepers, or persons who can bring at least two such Householders to answer for their good behaviour'. Dorset militia officers had to have 'a residence and income from land to the amount of fifty pounds a year within the county'. Initially, there were half a dozen troops of cavalry covering the coastal strip to approximately eight miles inland, each commanded by a captain. As the threat of invasion

---

12. Resistance to a standing army was eroded by necessity, not least to muster a large army to fight in the Scots in the 1740s and then in North America during the War of Independence from 1775. It had become clear that a large standing army was a requisite for the Empire.

13. Although the Act did not grant freedom of worship, it allowed Catholics to join the army and purchase land if they took an oath of allegiance.

intensified, fresh troops were raised, to protect inland areas.[14] There is a fine portrait of Richard in his Dorset Rangers uniform painted in 1795.

BONEY BY MOONLIGHT

To anyone living on the Dorset coast, the threat of Napoleon's arrival was terrifyingly real. In her 1909 book of reminiscences, Mrs Jane Panton relates a Purbeck, Dorset-based story told to her in her younger days:

> I have spoken to an old lady who saw Napoleon land in Lulworth Cove, and the account she gave me of the event is one I never forgot, and which I may as well reproduce here; as it will illustrate how real was the reason for the terror that the mere name of Bonaparte inspired, in the early days of the nineteenth century.

The lady, born in 1784, had learnt French working for her father, a china merchant at Sèvres. Later, she married a yeoman farmer in Dorset and as they farmed next to the sea, he, like so many other locals, was also a smuggler. Late one evening, he had not returned from his smuggling activities and his wife became worried that he was so late and set out over the hills to look for her missing spouse. Panton wrote that as the wife reached Lulworth Cove a long-boat came rowing swiftly and silently into the moonlit space, and she had just time to lie flat down behind some rocks when the boat's keel grated on the shore, and two men disembarked, while the sailors kept the boat afloat so as to be ready to push off once more in a moment should they be disturbed.

> Description had made her familiar with the appearance of Napoleon; to her horror she recognised him; and by listening to his conversation, she discovered that he was discussing with one of his officers whether it were possible to land his soldiers on that

---

14. David Clammer, *The Muster Roll of The Dorset Volunteer Rangers, 1799* (Dorchester: PDNHAS, 2013), pp. 56–61.

particular portion of the coast. They had a map, over which they pored for a few minutes, which naturally enough appeared to her hours; finally, Napoleon shrugged his shoulders, folded the map, and, ejaculating 'Impossible!' went back to the boat, and he and his officer were rowed quickly out of the Cove into the open sea.

Panton said she had her story, 'from the lips of the woman who saw it, who lived to be about a hundred and four'.[15]

THE JOURNAL OF MARY FRAMPTON

It is hard to get a sense of the women of the Erle-Drax family's daily life or their personalities. If they wrote diaries or personal accounts, they have not survived or made their way into the public domain. However, it is possible to get a sense of the lives of women from Dorset's landed gentry because Mary Frampton, a close friend of Sarah Frances Grosvenor Erle-Drax, wrote a diary between 1779 and 1846 that was edited into a journal by her ancestor Elizabeth Mundy and published in 1885. The book includes letters written by her mother, Phillis Frampton, and correspondence by the two women. They document the day-to-day existence of women of their class, discussion of their families, the goings-on in London and national and international politics, especially about Napoleon Bonaparte.

Phillis' maiden name was Byam, and she was the daughter of an heiress of Samuel Byam, Esq. of Antigua (deceased 1761). Major Byam on Barbados was encountered in the chapter on Barbados during the Civil War. In the intervening years, the Byams had become one of the most prominent plantation families in the West Indies, especially in Antigua, and owned many enslaved people. Phillis' father did not make a success of his business, so Phillis and her family moved to sell their Antigua estate in 1768.[16] Phillis'

15. Jane E. Panton, *Fresh Leaves and Pastures* (New York: Brentano's, 1909), pp. 206–208.
16. Vere Langford Oliver, *History of Antigua* (London: Mitchell and Hughes, 1895), Vol 1, pp. 107–108.

1. Drax Hall house, Barbados, 2019. (Jonathan Smith)

2. Busts of Sir James Drax and his son Henry Drax in a former church in the City of London. (Chris Drakes)

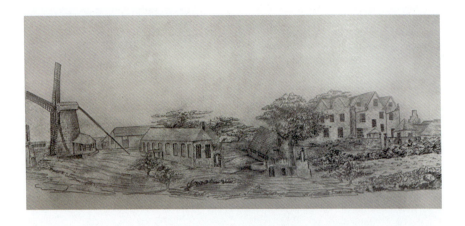

3. Nineteenth-century sketch of Drax Hall house and yard.
(Wikimedia Commons)

4. A quakerress and a tobacco planter in Barbados.
(Wikimedia Commons)

5. Sugar processing on a plantation, 1749. (Wikimedia Commons)

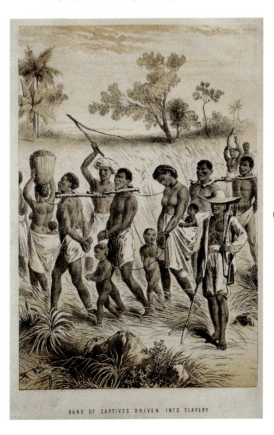

6. Enslaved Africans. (Wikimedia Commons)

7. Slave Trafficking in Barbados 1711. (Wikimedia Commons)

8. Charborough House, the Folly Tower, lithograph circa 1840.

9. Charborough House, twenty-first century. (Wikimedia Commons)

10. 'The Great Wall of Dorset', Charborough. (Wikimedia Commons/John Palmer/Creative Commons Attribution-ShareAlike 2.0 license)

11. The Lion Gate and the Stag Gate on the Drax estate in Dorset. (Chris Drakes)

12. The ruins of Ellerton Priory. (Matthew Hatton/Wikimedia Commons, licensed for reuse under the Creative Commons Attribution-ShareAlike 2.0 license)

13. The effigy of Thomas Erle (1597) at St Mary's church, Morden, near Charborough. (Mike Searle, licensed for reuse under the Creative Commons Attribution-ShareAlike 2.0 license)

14. Corfe Castle during the 1643 siege – the site of Walter Erle's defeat. (Wikimedia Commons)

15. General Sir Thomas Erle MP (1650–1720). (Author copyright)

16. The Battle of the Boyne, in which General Erle fought. (Wikimedia Commons)

17. Elizabeth Countess of Berkeley, engraving by J. McArdell based on Sir Joshua Reynolds' portrait. (Author copyright)

18. Countess Berkeley's daughter, Elizabeth, Margravine of Ansbach, attributed to Gainsborough, from Connoisseur magazine, March 1912.

19. Slaves with overseer. Line art by Everett of enslaved men working in sugar cane probably on a Caribbean plantation. (Edmund Olliver, *Cassell's History of the United States*, 1874–77, vol. 2. American School, Public domain, via Wikimedia Commons)

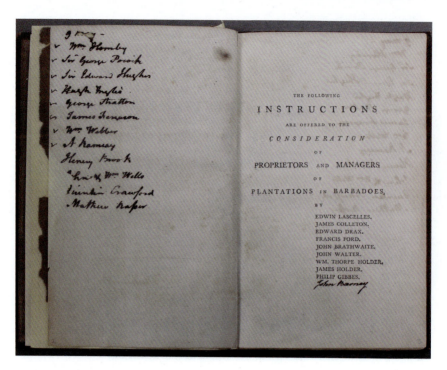

20. The eighteenth-century book known as The Instructions, co-authored by Edward Drax, Edwin Lascelles and others, at the Barbados Museum and Historical Society. (Barbados Museum and Historical Society)

21. 'Barbarities in the West Indies', James Gillray, p. 125. Wright and Evans, No. 49. Reprinted, 'G.W.G.', 1830. (Wikimedia Commons)

22. Mrs Frances Sarah Erle-Drax-Grosvenor (1769–1822). (By kind permission of a private collector)

23. Captain Richard Erle-Drax-Grosvenor (1762–1819) in his Dorset Ranger uniform at Charborough Park, 1795 (probably an etching of a portrait by Hoppner or Romney).

24. 'J.S.W.S.E. Drax Esq., Charborough Park', from *The Book of Sports, British and Foreign*, 1843.

25. Portrait of John Samuel Wanley Sawbridge Erle-Drax, MP (1800–87) by Sir Francis Grant. (Sworders Fine Art Auctioneers)

26. Admiral Reginald Aylmer Plunkett-Ernle-Erle-Drax by George Charles Beresford, 1 May 1918. (Wikimedia Commons)

27. Jacob Rees-Mogg (right), then MP for North East Somerset, visits Boho Gelato's ice cream parlour, Weymouth with Richard Drax, 18 August 2020. (Finnbarr Webster/Getty Images)

28. Slavery Justice protest outside Charborough Estate, July 2021. (Stand Up to Racism, Dorset)

second husband was James Frampton of Moreton, father of James (born 1769) and Mary (born 1773). Two of her children married into the English aristocracy. Mary was her companion for many years but also spent time in London and was there for part of 1790, except when she and her mother went in early summer to visit her aunt Lady Vernon at her husband's estate in Glamorganshire at the mouth of the Neath River.[17] She noted:

> The peasantry were dirty and full of animals, and the numbers of poor came to be fed at the house, it was really difficult to keep free from them. The housemaids hired for the time all went about the house without shoes or stockings, and were not famous for honesty, at least pins, ribbons, &c., disappeared quickly if left about carelessly.[18]

ROYAL SOCIETY

The Frampton family were friendly with the Erle-Drax-Grosvenors and their manor at Moreton is just eight miles west of Charborough Park. On occasion, Mrs Sarah Frances and other Drax family members are mentioned in the journal. Within those years, there was a period Dorset was prominent on Society's calendar because of the patronage of the king and his family. George William Frederick succeeded to the throne in 1760 as George III on the death of his grandfather. On 8 September 1761 in the Chapel Royal, St James's Palace, the king married Princess Charlotte of Mecklenburg-Strelitz, whom he met for the first time on their wedding day. A fortnight later, on 22 September, George and Charlotte were crowned at Westminster Abbey. The tragedy in their lives was that from the age of 50, George had a recurrent, and eventually permanent,

---

17. James Frampton died in 1784 and it was his son James Frampton II who became a captain in the Militia and was tasked with his, the 2nd Company, in guarding a section of the Purbeck coast against the French. Later as a magistrate, as will be seen, he made the name Frampton notorious.

18. Harriot G. Mundy (ed.), *The Journal of Mary Frampton* (London: Elibron Classic, 1885 and 2005), p. 28.

physical and mental illness. In his most stricken periods, he would rave for weeks at a time. Although it has since been suggested that he had bipolar disorder or the blood disease porphyria, the cause of his illness remains unknown, if much discussed.

In April 1789, Mary Frampton went with some of her siblings to see the celebrations in London over the king's return to health. She wrote a letter to her sister, Mrs Shirley, on 24 April, from which these are edits: 'My Dear Sister – I must begin by telling you that the King was not the worse for his fatigue yesterday and that everything was conducted with the greatest order and regularity.' They had watched from the windows of a friendly upholsterer, Mr Silk, a lengthy procession to St Paul's for the celebration. Early on the Members of Parliament passed, including the leaders of the opposing parties: 'What pleased us much was the populace huzz'd Mr. Pitt, but hooted and hissed Mr Fox or at least the greatest number did so.'

Then came royalty.

> The prince himself followed in his own coach, drawn by six of the handsomest grey horses possible; and they were most elegantly ornamented, so that nothing could be finer than his equipage.
>
> Next followed the King's attendants, and after them the King and Queen in a coach made with glass all round; they were drawn by eight beautiful cream-coloured horses. While they were coming up to the door of St Paul's, the band played 'God save the King', and every hat was in the air, and the acclamations very great, but still louder on his coming out of the church.[19]

In June 1789, just three months after the most recent episode of mental illness, it was suggested the king should go somewhere on vacation to help his health. Dr Crane, author of 'Cursory Observations on Sea-Bathing', advocated the benefits of sea air, sea bathing and even seawater drinking as a cure for a wide variety of ailments and was quick to recommend his hometown of Weymouth as the best place for the king to convalesce.

---

19 Mundy, *Journal of Mary Frampton*, pp. 20–21.

SEA AIR

The king's brother, the Duke of Gloucester, owned a seafront house in Weymouth and agreed to lend this to George for his holiday. George, his wife, Queen Charlotte, and four of their six daughters arrived in Weymouth to, according to eyewitness accounts, a tremendous welcome from the locals. The words 'God Save the King' were ubiquitous as posters in windows and even on bathing assistants' waistbands. The local people were delighted that the king had recovered and were happy to see him so down to earth that he walked among them, and they let him know. The national anthem was played often. On one occasion, a band hid in a neighbouring bathing machine and struck up the anthem when the king went to bathe in the sea.

This was to be the first of 14 summer visits between 1789 and 1805 by the king and his family and lasted some weeks. It was later said that Weymouth was where he spent his happiest days and which, at the time, became the most fashionable resort in the land, even more so than Brighton where their dissolute and estranged son, the Prince of Wales, would summer. The king rose early and would often take a stroll along the promenade. His days were full of visits from politicians, aristocracy and military advisers. Britain was at war in many locations during his reign, including the American War of Independence, Spain, India and Napoleon's Revolutionary France. George and members of his entourage would go for day trips locally by horse or coach. The king liked to ride out to visit houses and farms and would stop to talk to the locals. According to one story, when out in his coach in Weymouth, King George encountered an absentee owner of a plantation whose coach and horses and accompanying outriders, some of whom may have been men of colour, were all far more resplendent than the king's. 'Sugar, sugar, eh!', exclaimed King George, 'All *that* sugar.'[20]

---

20. Whether this was Richard and Sarah Frances Grosvenor Erle-Drax out for some air is not recorded. It could have been one of number of local gentry who had plantations, such as Peter Beckford who owned a number of Jamaican plantations.

Among the constant companions were dignitaries, including Dorset landed gentry like Colonel Stephen Digby, a King's Equerry and friend. He owned Sherborne Castle and the Digby Estate.[21] Early in the royal holiday, Mr and Mrs Erle-Drax-Grosvenor were invited to visit the royal family at the resort. Charborough Park was just some 20 miles away. Over the years, they were to become part of the regular group of local landed gentry who attended him on his visits. They effectively became courtiers and eventually they had some duties at Court in London outside of the king's summer holidays. On 7 October 1791, the *Kentish Gazette* reported that the Erle-Drax-Grosvenors sent a present of rare fruits to the king and queen, which was gratefully accepted. There were also celebrations to participate in. Festivities took place when the king was in Weymouth when news of Nelson's 1798 victory at the Battle of the Nile arrived, and celebrations followed. On 8 September 1798, the Dorset Volunteers were amongst the troops reviewed by the king on the sands with Captain Richard Erle-Drax-Grosvenor at the head of his company.[22] A little later, there was a report of another review in which the infantry, the Dragoon Guards and the Weymouth Volunteers took part in a sham fight on Crook Hill at Chickerell, on the coast to the west of Weymouth, which was kept up for three hours.[23]

One of Mary Frampton's letters tells not only of her son James' wedding but of an amusing encounter with the king and his roaming entourage witnessed by Mrs Erle-Drax-Grosvenor. The wedding was between James Frampton and Lady Harriot Strangways of the Dorset family.[24] Mrs Phillis Frampton wrote to her sister-in-law, Mrs Heberden from Dorchester, on Thursday 12 September 1799:

---

21. The Digby Estate is still in the top ten largest Dorset estates.

22. *Gentleman's Magazine*, 7 November 1798, p. 80.

23. David Clammer, 'Dorset's Volunteer Infantry 1794–1805', *Journal of the Society for Army Historical Research*, vol. 89, no. 357 (Spring 2011), pp. 6–25.

24. The Strangways were headed by Lord Ilchester, who owned the Ilchester Estate, an enormous estate centred in Dorset but with land in other counties. It is still one of the three biggest estates in Dorset, along with the Charborough Estate, and is now headed by Charlotte Townend, who lives in Melbury House near the village of Evershot.

You will have seen by the newspapers that I have had a hurry of a different kind, and more embarrassing the visit of their Majesties, most unexpected, and totally without any preparation. We were sitting at work in my little room with Mrs Drax.[25] I happened to look out, and actually saw the King and Princess Sophia with their attendants, at my garden gate. I screamed out, threw down everything about me, and flew out to them. Mr Damer met me and told me the Queen and three other Princesses and their suite were following.[26]

He bid *me* attend to *them* and then kindly went in to Mary and told what was necessary to be done, helped to put the driving-room in order, and bespoke mutton-chops. By this time, they all arrived, and I ran through the house to meet them at the front door. The King called out, 'Well run, Mrs. Frampton'. Into the drawing-room they went, asked for Mary, talked very easily, and asked for her cuttings-out which of course they admired.[27] They then proposed walking and, we all went through my fields to the walks round great part of the town and returned the same way and they seemed much pleased.

I conducted them into my eating room, trembling lest the Collation should not be as it ought, but really was as well prepared as could be expected on so short a notice, cold partridges, cold meat of different sorts and removes of mutton chops and fruit – tea at the side-table. Mary made tea, Mr Damer carried it to them and I waited on their Majesties as they ate and Mary on the princesses.

The ladies they asked to sit down were, Lady Poulett, Lady Radnor, Lady Charles Somerset, Lady Matilda Wynyard and Lady Pitt. Miss Townsend stood with Mrs Drax.

After the repast the female part went well into all the bedrooms and approved and looked at everything everywhere. In short, they

---

25. Sarah Frances Erle-Drax-Grosvenor, not Mary Erle-Drax according to the notes.
26. The Damer family were elite Dorset landed gentry.
27. Cuttings-out were silhouette portraits.

were all good-humoured and easy. They stayed about two hours, and I hear from various hands that they were pleased with the day's amusement and thought all was so well conducted. This gives us comfort after our bustle.

The King goes away on Monday se'night to meet the Parliament but returns the following Thursday. Adieu, Love to all.

Yours ever,
Phillis Frampton.[28]

Copious daily reports of the king and family's social round appear in the newspapers of the time. *The Times* Court Circular at this time frequently identified the Drax-Grosvenors taking part in court activities and trips.

ROYAL WEYMOUTH

The Gentleman's Quarterly was especially attentive of the Weymouth visits. The accounts for 1799 and 1800 are typical. We find that our courtiers Mr and Mrs Drax-Grosvenor arrived in Weymouth on the evening of 25 August 1799, shortly after the royal entourage had settled into the Lodge. One of the big features that year was the 38-gun frigate *San Fiorenza*, which was now on Royal Navy duty in Weymouth to protect the king from any attack from the sea. It also provided sailing amusement for the family.[29] These reports reveal a social whirl, with firework displays and military sham battles and parades and in the evening many visits to the theatre a few yards down the road. The Theatre Royal in Weymouth was transformed by the king's attendance with leading actors and actresses like Sarah Siddons and the comedian Joe Grimaldi coming down from London and elsewhere to perform.

On 30 September, *GQ* reported:

---

28. Mundy, *Journal of Mary Frampton*, pp. 106–108.
29. The *San Fiorenzo* had been captured off Corsica and renamed after the port from which she had been taken.

His Majesty, the Princesses Augusta, Elizabeth, and Princess Charlotte, bathed. After breakfast, the King and Princess Sophia, accompanied by Lord Cathcart and General Garth, rode out on horseback on the Wareham Road. Her Majesty and the Princesses, with Countess Poulett, Lady C Durham and Mrs Drax-Grosvenor, took an airing in two coaches and four to Osmington. At night, the Royal Family saw 'As You Like it' and a sketch for 'The Orators' in which the famous actor Mr Quick appeared in the character of a lecturer.

On 3 October 1800, Mrs Mary Drax, the widow of Edward Erle-Drax, is with the Drax-Grosvenors at a select party thrown by the king. Mrs Mary Erle-Drax maintained correspondence with elite visitors for many years.[30] She corresponded with Queen Charlotte, the Duke of Cambridge, Princesses Mary, Amelia, Augusta, Elizabeth, the Duke of Kent, George, the Prince of Wales and many others.[31]

1804 was to be a significant year for the Drax-Grosvenors as they had a visit from the royals, as reported on 5 November in the *Salisbury & Winchester Journal*:

Their Majesties and the princesses left Weymouth at eight o'clock in the morning and at 11.30 they arrived at Charborough Park where they were received by Mr & Mrs Drax-Grosvenor with every possible mark of respect. Arrival and departure announced by Royal Salute of 21 guns. Stayed for 2 hours.

The next year, the king's health had so deteriorated that the annual visits to Weymouth ceased. The contacts made during those years continued. HRH Princess Elizabeth writes to Mary Frampton

---

30. 'Royal Journey to Weymouth', *The Gentleman's Magazine*: and historical chronicle, January 1736–December 1833; December 1800; *British Periodicals*, p. 1197.
31. The Drax family's private archive at Charborough has around 100 of these letters.

from Windsor Castle on 10 June 1807 and said, 'I hope to see dear Mrs Drax in a few days. Yours very sincerely.'

This is the period in which Jane Austen's novel *Mansfield Park* was set. Mansfield Park and Charborough could be interchangeable. Richard Erle-Drax-Grosvenor MP is of similar status to the fictional Sir Thomas Bertram MP who, too, is a slave plantation owner. His plantation is in Antigua, which he visits to make sure it run to a profit. Engaging in every other way, Sir Thomas is reticent about the slave trade when Fanny Price inquires.[32]

Dorset festivities continued and in April 1814, the *Chester Courant* reported:

> At Charborough Park, the seat of Erle Drax-Grosvenor on Monday last, in order to give as much publicity as possible to the glorious news (the downfall of Napoleon), the union flag was hoisted on the venerable tower, followed by a discharge of 21 cannon. The concourse of people was immense, who were all regaled with true English hospitality; it is needless to add that the loyal and worthy donors participated in the general joy which garlanded every face and the day concluded with the greatest mirth and conviviality.

The defeated Napoleon, however, escaped from exile, had one last throw, landed in the south of France in 1815, headed to Paris, and reassembled an army as he went, ultimately to take on the British and Prussians at Waterloo. After Waterloo, there was much concern about local landed gentry officers who might have been killed or wounded, as news came back from Belgium.[33]

From 1815 George III's mania was so severe that the Prince of Wales had to reign as Prince Regent, and the king died in 1820.

---

32. Jane Austen, *Mansfield Park* (London: Penguin Classics, 1985 [1814]).
33. Mundy, *The Journal of Mary Frampton*, p. 252.

14
Voices of the Enslaved

Perhaps the most famous of the African people who had been enslaved and later wrote their tragic stories was Olaudah Equiano. He was trafficked across the Atlantic in a slave ship as a teenager in the mid-1750s and later told of his arrival in Barbados:

> At last we came in sight of the island of Barbadoes, at which the whites on board gave a great shout and made many signs of joy to us. We did not know what to think of this; but as the vessel drew nearer, we plainly saw the harbour, and other ships of different kinds and sizes, and we soon anchored amongst them off Bridge Town. Many merchants and planters now came on board, though it was in the evening. They put us in separate parcels and examined us attentively. They also made us jump, and pointed to the land, signifying we were to go there. We thought by this we should be eaten by these ugly men, as they appeared to us; and, when soon after we were all put down under the deck again, there was much dread and trembling among us, and nothing but bitter cries to be heard all the night from these apprehensions, insomuch that at last the white people got some old slaves from the land to pacify us.

Upon landing they were conducted immediately to the merchant's yard, 'where we were all pent up together like so many sheep in a fold, without regard to sex or age'.

> We were not many days in the merchant's custody before we were sold after their usual manner, which is this: – On a signal given, (as the beat of a drum) the buyers rush at once into the yard where the slaves are confined and make choice of that parcel they like best. The noise and clamour with which this is attended, and the

217

eagerness visible in the countenances of the buyers, serve not a little to increase the apprehensions of the terrified Africans, who may well be supposed to consider them as the ministers of that destruction to which they think themselves devoted.

In this manner, without scruple, are relations and friends separated, most of them never to see each other again. I remember in the vessel in which I was brought over, in the men's apartment, there were several brothers, who, in the sale, were sold in different lots; and it was very moving on this occasion to see and hear their cries at parting. O, ye nominal Christians! might not an African ask you, learned you this from your God, who says unto you, Do unto all men as you would men should do unto you? Is it not enough that we are torn from our country and friends to toil for your luxury and lust of gain.

Equiano was young and so emaciated by his captivity that no one in Barbados wanted to buy him. The merchants decided to send him to New World colonies for sale and to fatten him with 'plenty of rice and fat pork' in the meantime. After a few weeks in Barbados, he was put on board a sloop bound for Virginia.[1] By the 1740s, British ships were carrying more African captives to plantations in the Americas and Caribbean than those of any other nation.

Equiano's memoir was published over 30 years after his arrival at Carlisle Bay, Barbados, in 1789. By that time, he was a leading figure in the British abolitionist movement. According to the historian Adam Hochschild, 'scholars have valued it as the most extensive account of an eighteenth-century slave's life and the difficult passage from slavery to freedom'. It was published just a few years after Edward Erle-Drax's 'Instructions' which functioned as a manual for running a plantation worked by enslaved Africans.

WEALTH EXTRACTION

Through the eighteenth century, Drax Hall plantation continued to grow sugar and distil rum and sell them on the European market

---

1. Olaudah Equiano, *The Interesting Narrative of the Life of Olaudah Equiano* (London: Privately published, 1794), pp. 56-70.

produced by a workforce of 250–300 enslaved people. Since the departure of Thomas Drax III (Thomas Shetterden Drax) from the island at the turn of the century, the family were absent land-lords, with possibly a few undocumented stays. In 1767, the Hon-ourable Abraham Cumberbatch was appointed as the attorney to the Drax Hall plantation by Thomas Erle.[2] According to records in the Barbados Department of Archives, Abraham Cumberbatch's powers of attorney to manage Drax Hall were renewed again in 1772.[3] Like many attorneys, Cumberbatch and his family lived in Barbados and had their own plantations and looked after those of absentee owners in return for fees. Attorneys were generally saving for their return to Britain, so profit poured back into the home nation. As Nick Hayes pointed out, it stimulated the British economy:

> All across the west coast of England, new estates were built, or old ones bought and remodelled, as a direct result of slavery. From the late 1600s to the early 1900s, it is estimated that one-sixth of Britain's country houses were bought by businessmen whose fortunes were sourced from colonial trade. The sugar barons made the most money, but it was also the moneylenders, the investors, the chain-makers and the shipbuilders that boomed.[4]

The Drax family had relied on attorneys like Cumberbatch to appoint white overseers to take charge of the day-to-day running of the plantation.[5] Working as an overseer of enslaved people was one

---

2. Abraham Cumberbatch was of a prominent West Indies colonial family who owned and managed slave plantations, of which the actor Benedict Cumberbatch is a descendant. BDA PoA Vol 39, p. 119. Abraham was the son of Abraham Cumberbatch (1727–1785) and the father of Abraham Parry Cumberbatch. The will of Hon. Abraham Cumberbatch of St Andrew Barbados was proved 23/11/1796. He left his wife Mary an annuity of £180 p.a. plus the £3000 settled on her under their marriage settlement and secured on Cleland and The Farm Plantations.
3. Cumberbatch was replaced in 1786 by George James and his associates.
4. Hayes, 'A Very English Theft'.
5. It is possible that family members visited Barbados and that Edward Erle-Drax was a resident for some time, but no confirmatory evidence has been found

way a British colonist who did not have family wealth could earn a good living in the West Indies. Olaudah Equiano condemned overseers for their cruelty:

> These overseers are indeed for the most part persons of the worst character of any denomination of men in the West Indies. Unfortunately, many humane gentlemen, by not residing on their estates, are obliged to leave the management of them in the hands of these human butchers, who cut and mangle the slaves in a shocking manner on the most trifling occasions and altogether treat them in every respect like brutes. They pay no regard to the situation of pregnant women, nor the least attention to the lodging of their field Negroes.[6]

There is no direct record of what life was like on Drax Hall plantation during the century, but there is no reason to assume that the conditions and treatment of enslaved people were better or worse than any other plantation.[7] There are not many voices at all from those twelve million captives who were brought from West Africa to the Americas and enslaved, or those estimated seven to eight million who were born enslaved, and those stories that were written down or printed are mainly from people who had been enslaved on American plantations, and even there, very few date to the eighteenth century.

With the West Indies, often the voices that have come down the years are British voices of those who were part of the government

---

in the public domain. It is possible that no family member went to Barbados until the 1920s.

6. Equiano, *The Interesting Narrative*, p. 134. Olaudah Equiano (c. 1745–31 March 1797) was enslaved until 1766, when, unusually, he was able to buy his freedom and became a writer and abolitionist.

7. The barbaric treatment of the enslaved people still reverberates down the generations. It is also worth considering the psychological damage to the overseers who were brought over from Britain (and Scotland) as young men and expected to inflict the most horrendous punishments on their workforce. What impact did this have on them and, if they returned home, to the people around them?

or military, worked on the plantations as owners, overseers, book-keepers or doctors, or were religious figures that administered to the spiritual welfare or were those who crewed the ships on the triangular trade. Some of those who wrote were not against slavery as such but were shocked at the way the slave trade and plantations were run. Some changed their mind due to what they saw and took against the inhumanity of slavery. Others supported slavery and proselytised as to how well slavery was conducted in the West Indies, if necessary, blaming allegations of cruelty on a few rogue planters.[8]

Some voices were never meant to be heard or seen by others and are candid. Perhaps the most infamous writer of them all was Thomas Thistlewood, who wrote for himself. Born in Lincolnshire in 1721, he was a second son of a minor member of the gentry. In 1746, Thomas, an educated man and voracious reader, joined a voyage with the East India Company that lasted until 1748. In 1750 and aged 29 years of age, he sailed from London to the West Indies to make his fortune. He found work at the western end of Jamaica, where he became an overseer of the Egypt sugar plantation owned by William Dorrill and then his son-in-law John Cope, where he was to be the overseer from 1751 to 1767.

Thistlewood was probably dissolute before he left England, as it was known he was a frequenter of prostitutes and a drinker. He is now known to history as the author of *The Diary of Thomas Thistlewood*.[9] The 14,000-page diary provides a detailed matter-of-fact record of his behaviour and a deep and unpleasant insight into plantation life and owner–slave relations over many years. It makes for extremely disturbing reading. Very quickly after the appointment, Thistlewood began raping the enslaved women supposedly in his care. His diary chronicles 3,852 acts of rape with 138 enslaved women during his 37 years in Jamaica, although Thistle-

---

8. An example is the writings of the Rev. H.E. Holder of Barbados who rails against the abolition do-gooders: Karen Williamson, *Contrary Voices* (Kingston, Jamaica: UWI Press, 2008), pp. 172–174.

9. Thistlewood's diaries are at the Beinecke Rare Book & Manuscript Library, Yale University, which purchased them in 2011. They are available online.

wood would claim it was consensual. The plantation owner John Cope was almost as cruel, and in 1756, Thistlewood recorded that when enslaved women Egypt, Susannah and Mazerine refused Cope's advances, Cope had them whipped and then raped two other enslaved women.

Thistlewood systematically raped enslaved girls and women; those that spurned his advances and ran away were caught, whipped, and put in chains, collars, or placed in field gangs. His self-recorded brutality towards the enslaved Africans, when they were perceived to have transgressed, was appalling. He seems to have taken delight in devising ever more disgusting punishments. In his 23 July 1756 entry, he described punishing an enslaved man: 'Gave him a moderate whipping, pickled him well, made Hector shit in his mouth, immediately put a gag in it whilst his mouth was full and made him wear it 4 or 5 hours.' Thistlewood's diary is an account of speedy personal descent into a moral abyss.

Thistlewood did well financially during his years in Jamaica. In 1767 he left the Egypt plantation and bought 160 acres of a farm called Breadnut Island Pen, where he raised livestock and grew vegetables and flowers. He also used it as a barracks for his enslaved people, whom he hired out to plantation owners. He wrote about purchasing enslaved people, noting that he paid £112 for two men and £200 for one boy and three girls. The two men were named Will and Dick. Will was about 25 years old and stood 5 feet 3-2/10 inches, and Dick was about 22 years and taller at 5 feet, 7-3/10 inches. The boy and girls were Coobah, aged about 15, Sukey, aged about 14, Maria, aged about 15 and Pompey aged about 16. One shudders to think about their lives.

Another account, this time from Barbados, initially written as letters to friends and family, was produced by a naval officer, Edward Thompson. He served on the West Indies station and returned in command of the 24-gun frigate *Hyeana* from 1779 to 1781. His lively letters detailing accounts of life on station were published in *Sailor's Letters* in 1766. He was outspoken in his criticism of white creoles,[10] especially the women. In Letter XXV from Barbados on 5 December 1756, he noted that the hospitality of the inhabitants is greater than on other islands 'but yet have that volatile spirit so peculiar to the Creole'.

The cruel tyranny exercised over the slave, is shocking to humanity: - a most horrid instance of which, was acted here the other day by a mistress to her female slave: the girl had committed some trivial domestick error, upon which, she [the mistress] commanded four of her servants to hold her down to the ground, while she absolutely exulted in smiles, and dropped hot sealing wax on the different parts of the back, till the poor creature expired in the most excruciating tortures.

Missing girl

Turton's, April 14, 1788

RUNAWAY, a black skin Negro girl, with slim legs, a round belly, small or no breasts, round faced, silly looking, and her hair growing almost to her eyebrows; squints a little; and limps much, and has a crooked great toe, all on the right side. Is supposed to be harboured by a Negro fellow called TOM on part of Drax Hall estate called the Hope, and loitering betwixt Gen. Haynes', the College and Foul Bay. Half a moidore reward to whoever will bring her to the subscriber on the above estate near Bridge-Town

HENRY FOWKE

— *Barbados Mercury*: Saturday, April 12, 1788

An example of a girl who had fled the Turton plantation in Barbados (*Barbados Mercury*, 1788)

---

10.   People of Europeans or West African descent who were born in the colonies.

> Was you accustomed to live with the planter's ladies, you would not be surprised at any cruelty, for they are taught in their very infancy, to flog with a whip the slave that offends them.

Where it was feasible the enslaved might run away. The local papers would have small ads offering rewards for those helping to recapture runaways.

THE SOMERSET JUDGMENT

George William Frederick, the Prince of Wales, was unusual in opposing slavery in the 1750s. The historian Andrew Roberts found a document written by the prince that Roberts said was 'denouncing all of the arguments for slavery and calling them an execration and ridiculous and "absurd"'. This was in an essay George III wrote as a teenager, arguing that slavery had no moral basis. Roberts added: 'George never bought or sold a slave in his life. He never invested in any of the companies that did such a thing.' But later George allowed the continuation of the slave trade and slavery and opposed the abolition movement behind the scenes, according to research by the historian Brooke Newman.[11] While there were always people who spoke out against slavery, the abolition movement only started to get underway by the mid-eighteenth century, and it did not get up much momentum until the 1780s. To encourage their fellow citizens to look into the face of the enslaved and see fellow human beings, British abolitionists distributed autobiographies of people who had experienced slavery, such as works by Ignatius Sancho, the Crafts, Olaudah Equiano and Mary Prince.

In 1772, a court case in London made the first small step towards abolition by a judgment from the Court of the King's Bench. This related to the right of an enslaved person on English soil not to be forcibly removed from the country and sent to the West Indies for sale. James Somerset was an enslaved African purchased by Charles Stewart, a customs officer then based in Boston, which was then a

---

11.   Isaac Chotiner, 'Why Andrew Roberts Wants Us to Reconsider King George III', *The New Yorker*, 9 November 2021.

town in the British crown colony in North America. Stewart made his slave Somerset return with him to England in 1769. Two years later, Somerset escaped, and he became a Christian. After Somerset was recaptured in November 1771, Stewart had him imprisoned on the ship *Ann and Mary* which was bound for Jamaica.

Stewart instructed the ship's captain that Somerset should be sold to a plantation for labour. Somerset's three abolitionist godparents from his baptism as a Christian in England were John Marlow, Thomas Walkin and Elizabeth Cade. They were appalled at Somerset's captivity and made an application before the King's Bench for a writ of *habeas corpus*. Captain Knowles produced Somerset before the Court of King's Bench, which had to determine whether his imprisonment was lawful.

Granville Sharp, a leading abolitionist who continually launched test cases against the legal justifications for slavery, supported Somerset. When the case was heard, five advocates appeared for Somerset, speaking at three hearings between February and May. Somerset's advocates argued that while colonial laws might permit slavery, neither the common law of England nor any statutory law made by Parliament recognised the existence of slavery, and slavery was therefore unlawful. The advocates also argued that English contract law did not allow for any person to enslave himself, nor could any contract be binding without the person's consent. The arguments focused on legal details rather than any humanitarian principles. When the two lawyers for Charles Stewart put their case, they argued that property was paramount and that it would be dangerous to free all the black people in England, who were said to number at the time approximately 15,000.

Lord Mansfield decided slavery had never been authorised by statute within England and Wales, and found it also to be unsupported within England by the common law:

It is so odious, that nothing can be suffered to support it, but positive law. Whatever inconveniences, therefore, may follow from the decision, I cannot say this case is allowed or approved by the law of England; and therefore, the black must be discharged.[12]

However, he did not comment on the position in the overseas territories of the British Empire. This test case resulted in the emancipation of enslaved people in England and Wales, who mainly were domestic servants.

ABOLITION

The story of abolition has been told many times in detail. The MP William Wilberforce's story is a hero's journey, but this book does not seek to repeat that biography. While researching this book, I realised not much had been written about the substantial organised counter-effort to the abolitionists known as 'The West India Interest'. These were the planters, their agents, slave traders and MPs who protected the interests of the plantation owners in the City of London, the ports and in Parliament. They were powerful and well-funded and had regional committees to preserve their privilege. Fortunately, there is now one excellent account.[13]

The West India Interest fought a sustained campaign to prevent abolition. To counter the personal accounts of the horrors of slavery published by the abolitionists to persuade the British public and opinion formers, the Interest maintained a propaganda war to portray plantation owners as running benign establishments. An early example was the influential booklet published in 1786 authored by Edward Erle-Drax and other owners. One of the preferred arguments used by the anti-abolitionists was that the conditions of the enslaved were better than many agricultural workers in Britain. This seemed an irony-free discourse. The conditions for agricultural workers in Britain (and those in other trades) were often appalling, not least in Drax's Dorset. There is an existential difference between being poor and exploited and being enslaved.

---

12. Stephen Usherwood, 'The Black Must Be Discharged – The Abolitionists' Debt to Lord Mansfield', *History Today*, vol. 31, no. 3 (1981).

13. Michael Taylor, *The Interest* (London: The Bodley Head, 2020).

The involvement of religious groups in the abolition movement saw a gradual change of attitude towards religion and slavery. By the turn of the nineteenth century, the persistent claim that enslaved people were sub-human and not capable of being Christians had been, for the most part, dismissed. In recognition of this potential congregation, the Church of England published a text *Select Parts of the Holy Bible for the use of the Negro Slaves in the British West-India Islands*. This has become known as the Slave Bible. It is notable for the sections that were left out from both the Old and New Testaments especially those referring to all men (people) being equal in the eyes of God.[14]

HUMAN BREEDING

As the cost of buying enslaved people rose, the plantation managers, ever pragmatic, had been careless of protecting pregnant enslaved women, making them work as before. Obtaining enslaved Africans was now more expensive and difficult. The owners' and overseers' attitude of neglect to pregnant enslaved women, as recorded by Olaudah Equiano, changed. The owners turned to encouraging slave women to provide children and be paid if the child lived. They saw it as a long-term investment.

As Beckles noted in his 2016 book, the plantation owners' economic thinking evolved as circumstances changed, and by the end of the eighteenth century, it had been refined to sophistication. They presented the discourse of labour in terms of gender, age and ethnicity. Productivity differentials and revenue projections were made for enslaved males and females, children and adults.[15]

They wrote as experienced authorities on slave administration and presented themselves as representative of progressive management thought. Also, they set out to show that successful slave

---

14.   I am grateful to Alan Smith, the First Estate Commissioner of the Church of England, for bringing this to my attention. There is one of the handful of surviving copies of the Slave Bible at Lambeth Palace.

15.   Beckles, *First Black Slave Society*, p. 197.

breeding was an effective political strategy for weakening the abolitionists' argument that enslaved women were, in fact, too brutalised to reproduce.[16]

Beckles' research showed that at Drax Hall and Mount Gay sugar plantations, enslaved women were paid 6s. 3d. for 'bringing out a child'. At birth, infants were valued between £8 and £10 3s. 6d.[17]

Some contemporary Drax Hall records are held at the Barbados Department of Archives. There is a batch from 1804–06 when John Barrow was appointed Attorney by Richard Erle-Drax-Grosvenor on 27 September 1804.[18] There is a two-page (partially damaged) letter from appointing John Barrow as his attorney.[19] Drax Hall was quite run down at the time and was undergoing renovation.

1804

[Number of enslaved people] 209 (Total)

An inventory of Drax Hall consisted of Inventory stores and utensils, 11th July 1803; a 'List of negroes', 22nd September 1804; and Condition of land, 22nd September 1804. A copy was made 6th October 1804.

The first part is an inventory of stores taken on the first day on which Forster Clarke (Attorney) entered on the management of the planation (11 July 1803). It covered the Boiling House, the Still House, the Curing House and In the Yard. Buildings include a Dwelling House ('quite out of repair'), Curing House, Still House, Rum House ('quite fallen to decay'), Horse Stable ('an indifferent shed'), Sick House ('indifferent and uncomfortable'), New Water Still ('built by Mr Clarke'). The 'List of the Negroes and their occu-

---

16. Ibid., p. 203.
17. Ibid., p. 307.
18. The BDA introduction to the Drax Hall folder said that the records had been lent to the BDA by Admiral Drax in 1969. Some of the records were retrieved by the family a year or so later.
19. It is possible that this was the same John Barrow (?–1832) who was owner of the Sunbury, Hampton and Upton plantations; www.ucl.ac.uk/lbs/person/view/2146643053.

pations on Drax Hall Plantation' was taken 22 September 1804, the day John Barrow 'took possession of the property'.[20]

Men: 56 (including 2 'absent many years')

Women: 69

Boys: 43 (including 12 'too young to work')

Girls: 41 (including 12 'too young to work')

The detailed listing was: Men; Boiler: 1; Driver: 2; Ranger: 1; Caster: 1; Carpenter: 2; Mason: 2; Cooper: 2; Smith: 1; House: 2; Groom: 1; Cook: 1; With the cattle: 2; Field: 30; Others; Including 2 'absent many years': 8; Total: 56

Women: Gang driver: 2; Sick nurse: 1; House keeper: 1; [Illegible]: 2; Washer: 1; Stock keeper: 1; [Other] 'cares little negroes'(?): 1; Raises labour? Cabou?: 21; Field: 19; Others: 20; Total: 69

Boys: 2nd gang: 11; 3rd gang: 19; Carpenter's boy: 1; Too young to work: 12; Total: 43

Girls: 2nd gang: 9; 3rd gang: 19; In the house: 1; Too young to work: 12; Total: 41

Total all: 209

Also listed were animals: 1 Bull; 56 Oxen; 45 Cows; 39 Calves; 27 Hogs; 40 Sheep; 8 Horses; 2 young colts.[21]

In the Drax family private archive are documents that are similar to those above. Admiral Drax's history notes that in 1805 Affraw delivered of a male child named Noah; Jemmey delivered of a male child named Jemmey Doll; Haggar delivered of a female child named Fibbah James and Kitty Gay delivered of a female child named Barbara. There were nine births that year. By the end of the year, it shows Slaves 205. Cattle 136. Horses 9. The manager paid out £3 2s 6d for giving birth. There is something particularly chilling about the documentation of enslaved women's names

---

20. For the letter from Richard Erle-Drax-Grosvenor, 27 September 1804, appointing John Barrow as his Attorney, see: BDA. Z9/11/6.

21. BDA. Z9/11/5.

(only ever a first name) followed by the gender of their child, when we know that each live birth represented a source of profit to the owners.[22]

Each mother would have been painfully aware they were giving birth to babies who, with their descendants, would forever be slaves. Other documents in the Barbados Department of Archives pick the same enslaved people as mentioned in the Drax private archive. In an 1804 return, Jemmy's name is there among many. In an 1820 return from agent Forster Clarke, it shows Affraw listed as a house servant aged 41. Bellah Spencer is listed a 1st gang labourer aged 53 and is likely related to Jomay Spencer who was listed as a ranger in the 1804 return; 56-year-old Queen is a sick nurse and died that year. A male called Quashey Anny is listed as a boiler, Johnny and Hector as Drivers, Sam Cooper as a carpenter. Daniel and Curtillo as coopers. Johnny Dixon listed as a ranger in 1820, aged 61, is dead by 1827. Quashey Spencer is a groom aged 56 and died in 1825. Peter, a house servant aged 46, died in 1823.

The official slave registers in Barbados lists many more for each year.

IN PARLIAMENT

The Whig politician and anti-slavery campaigner Charles James Fox, in the course of debate on the British slave trade in 1789, said 'that the question of the abolition of the slave trade, was a question between humanity on the one side, and interest on the other'.[23] William Wilberforce headed the Parliamentary campaign against the British slave trade for 20 years. The 1805 abolition bill failed in Parliament, and it was the eleventh failure in 15 years. The London Committee decided to renew pressure, and Thomas Clarkson went on a tour of the abolition committees nationwide to rally support. Such was the abolitionists' dramatic success in changing minds after years of campaigning; Wilberforce's bill to end Britain's part in slave trading was passed to a standing ovation in 1807 in the House. It

---

22. Ernle-Erle-Drax, *History of Charborough*, pp. 42–43.
23. *The Parliamentary History of England* (1816), XXVIII.

did not ban the ownership of enslaved people, and some 700,000 Africans remained enslaved in the British colonies, until slavery was banned outright – which would take over two more decades.

The 1807 Act was a hard-won battle to beat the far better-funded pro-slavery lobby. The Parliamentary historian H.M. Port stated that Drax Hall's absentee landlord Richard Erle-Drax-Grosvenor was MP was 'One of the die-hards who opposed the slave trade abolition bill.'[24] He has also been said to be a funder of the anti-abolition campaign. At the time, Parliamentary debates and votes were not well recorded. A Grosvenor did vote against abolition, but it could have been a relative with the same name who was also an MP. I could not find supporting evidence that Richard Erle-Drax-Grosvenor had funded the anti-abolition movement despite consulting leading authorities on the anti-abolitionists.[25] What is clear is that Richard was happy to continue with the Drax family plantation interests in Barbados. There is no evidence that he tried to liberalise the plantation regime or ever visited Barbados. Like the Erle-Draxes, Richard Grosvenor was also strongly anti-Catholic. His voting record seems thin. He seems to have mostly acted in the interests of his wider family, and class, supporting the Tories who were in a long period of government.

NO REBELLION

Despite the immense repression by the minority white population on their enslaved Africans, there were no armed rebellions or significant conspiracies recorded in Barbados between 1702 and 1816. Beckles noted that there has been no serious study of why no rebellions had taken place in that period, and he refers to the twen-

---

24. Port also noted that Richard Erle-Drax-Grosvenor's major preoccupation appears to have been attempting to secure a peerage. ERLE DRAX GROSVENOR, Richard (1762-1819), of Charborough Park, nr. Blandford Forum, Dorset and Swell Court, Som. | History of Parliament Online, last accessed 1 July 2024.
25. I wrote to H.M. Port to see if he could shed further light on the matter. However, he could not as he had written the biography in *History of Parliament* many years ago.

tieth-century Guyanese historian and civil rights activist Walter Rodney's observations:

> The beginning of such a study should take into account Walter Rodney's view that each day in the life of the enslaved was a day in which there was both struggle and accommodation and also that the political reading of shifts in the balance of power was a determining factor. Some Africans resisted more tenaciously and consistently than others, but there was no simple distinction between those who resisted and those who accommodated. Moments of struggle, Rodney notes, and moments of compromise appear within the same historical conjuncture, but ultimately resistance rather than accommodation asserted itself as the principal aspect of this contradiction. This was the case in the colony during the eighteenth century when a culture of non-violent resistance and relentless pursuit of socioeconomic betterment replaced the earlier anti-slavery militancy.[26]

PRESSURE MOUNTS

After the passing of the 1807 Slave Trade Abolition Act, discontent in the colonies slowly mounted. In 1809 the attorneys of the Codrington plantations informed their absentee landlord that the enslaved were growing restless and, while not in a rebellious mood, were being more aggressive in their demands. The appointment of new plantation staff, they said, could no longer be taken lightly, since the slaves' 'satisfaction with the manager is now of utmost importance'. In some instances, the enslaved demanded the removal of overseers; this was part of the politics of negotiation.[27]

In 1816 the enslaved in Barbados grew tired and angry, waiting to be made free, which they thought would be the natural progress from the 1807 Act. Enslaved people began planning the revolt after the Barbadian House of Assembly discussed and rejected the Imperial Registry Bill in November 1815, which called for the registration

---

26. Beckles, *First Black Slave Society*, p. 210.
27. Ibid., p. 217.

of colonial enslaved people. Believing this registration would make their lives more difficult, enslaved people secretly met in February to plan the uprising in April. 'Bussa's Rebellion' of 14–16 April 1816 was to be the largest slave revolt in Barbadian history. The rebellion takes its name from the African-born slave of the Bayley's plantation, Bussa, who is said to have led the uprising. Among Bussa's collaborators were Joseph Pitt Washington Franklin (a free man of colour), John and Nanny Grigg, senior domestic slaves, and Jackey on Simmons' Plantation, as well as other slaves, drivers and artisans. Jackey was a Creole driver who was an important figure.

Schomburgk, in his 1848 *History of Barbados*, stated that the earliest news of the outbreak reached Bridgetown on the Monday morning between one and two o'clock. The island was immediately placed under martial law.

> The command as general of the militia was conferred upon Colonel Codd, and the regular troops, in conjunction with the royal regiment of militia under Colonel Mayers, commenced their march between eight and nine o'clock on Monday morning towards the parish of St. Philip. The Christ-Church battalion of militia assembled on the first alarm at Fairy Valley, and the earliest opposition was made to the progress of the rebels by a detachment of that corps, which about noon met a large body of insurgents at Lowther's Yard. Several were armed with muskets, and they displayed the colours of the St. Philip's battalion which they had stolen.
>
> Bussa, King Wiltshire, Dick Bailey and Johnny led the slaves into battle at Bailey's Plantation on Tuesday, 16th April. He commanded some 400 rebels, men and women, most of whom were believed to be Creole, born in the islands. He was killed in battle, his forces continued the fight until they were defeated by superior firepower of the colonial militia.[28]

---

28.   Robert H. Schomburgk, *The History of Barbados* (London: Longman, Brown, Green and Longmans, 1848), pp. 395–396.

The governor of Barbados, Sir James Leith, reported that by September, five months after the rebellion ended, 144 people had been executed. Seventy people were later sentenced to death, while 170 were deported to neighbouring British colonies in the Caribbean. Alleged rebels were also subject to floggings during the entire 80 days of martial law.

Which plantations were attacked was indicative, as it is not unreasonable to assume that plantations in the area impacted by the rebellion, where the treatment was worst, were more likely to be ransacked. An inquiry into the rebellion was held, and an 1818 report was published.[29] It noted that a fifth of the island's canes were destroyed by fire, and some 60 of the island's plantations had been attacked and damaged. While Drax Hall plantation is not mentioned in the main body of the text, at the end is a list of damages suffered by the plantation, and Drax Hall is in the top ten with £4084. 9s. 5d. That Drax Hall suffered is in one way surprising as a contemporary map of Drax Hall shows militia housing on the outskirts of the plantation and according to the 1804 accounts the plantation had fortifications.[30] Neighbouring Mount plantation, now owned by the Earl of Harewood, was also severely damaged. Bussa's Rebellion was to be the first of several major nineteenth-century slave rebellions in the West Indies. Slowly attitudes to slavery were changing in Britain.

---

29. A copy can be found in the BDA.
30. After emancipation, the militia barracks became Drax Hall Tenantry, which is still a village.

15

After Napoleon

The Drax family reached the height of their social standing in the first years of the nineteenth century. They were intimate with George III and his family and the annual summer visits of the royal family and the social whirl that followed must have been the highlight to the year. For the rest of the year, the day-to-day life of Richard and Sarah Erle-Drax-Grosvenor can, to some extent, be reconstructed from the record of the newspapers' reports and other correspondence. Richard went to London on court and other duties; locally, he attended to the estate, improving the house, the park, the farmland and built cottages for the workforce. He kept in contact with the more significant local dignitaries. Richard socialised with men of similar status. He hunted. During the 'Bonie threat' he served in the militia. Richard Erle-Drax-Grosvenor's pockets were deep, as he and Sarah had an annual income of at least £20,000 a year, very substantial amount at the time and partly derived from the Drax Hall plantation in Barbados. It is also possible he owned the smaller of the two Staple Grove plantations in Christchurch parish.[1]

With his royal connections to impress, Richard extravagantly remodelled Charborough House, very much in the style and probably to the designs of the great architect John Nash. A mid-eighteenth-century painting of the house shows the gardens adjoined by agricultural land, while the late eighteenth-century estate plan shows a small park, the boundaries of which correspond to High Wood to the south-east, the parish boundary with Sturminster Marshall to the north, and the eastern boundaries of Furze Hill and Forty Acre Bottom to the west. The park was developed

---

1. UCL slavery database: according to a document in the Drax Hall and Drax Hope papers, Barbados Archives, 'An account of Negroes from Staple Grove 1818', the numbers in 1818 were: Living: 25, Increase: 6, Total: 31, Dead: 14.

during the second half of the eighteenth century and the diversion of the Wimborne to Dorchester road in 1811–12 meant it circumscribed rather than intersected the park. Richard also created a deer park which alone had an area of some 295 acres.

As with all local squires, there were family duties and church visits. Through the royal's annual visits, and what can be learnt from Mary Frampton's journal, there is some indication of what role the women played. There is the round of social visits, some just doing embroidery while chatting with friends of equal rank, hosting social events, overseeing the running of the house, spending time in London during the social season and doing good works.

The annual presence of the royal family continued to stimulate many events in the area around Weymouth and not a few were attended by the royals. The numerous balls were very popular. As Mary Shirley wrote in a letter from Dorchester to her great-aunt in October 1804, 'Dorsetshire is certainly the gayest county in England.' Thirteen-year-old Mary wrote to her aunt describing a ball held on 20 October and her dance partners.[2]

After 1805, with the king no longer attending Weymouth, and fewer visits by other members of royalty thereafter, the local landed gentry had to find other ways to amuse themselves in the summer. One of the other landed families that the Drax-Grosvenors were friendly with, were the Tregonwells.[3] Lewis D. Tregonwell lived at Cranbourne Lodge in Cranbourne Chase, which he had purchased from Thomas Erle-Drax and renovated. His militia troop had been tasked with protecting the Chase, a large area of farm and hunting landscapes.

Richard Grosvenor Erle-Drax had parliamentary duties as he had been returned to Parliament when his relative Robert Grosvenor, who had sat for Chester since 1790, succeeded as 2nd Earl Grosvenor in 1802, freeing up the seat in Parliament. As it was a family seat, Richard was subject to the powerful authority of Earl Grosvenor. He supported the administration of Lord Addington.

---

2. Mundy, *Journal of Mary Frampton*, pp. 118–121.

3. The Tregonwells had been linked by marriage to the Grosvenors and the Wyndhams; such was the close network of the landed gentry.

On William Pitt the Younger's return to power in 1804, the king, a visitor to Charborough during periods of residence at Weymouth, 'used every endeavour' to persuade Richard to support Pitt's new Tory ministry.[4] Although Richard was 'undoubtedly well disposed' and 'expressed the utmost willingness to comply', he and his brother, who had the other seat at Chester, each wished the other to make the first move, being 'fearful of offending Lord Grosvenor', who was 'strongly disinclined to Mr Pitt, on account of the Catholic question'. Pitt was prepared to give concessions to Catholics. Lord Grosvenor was not. George III put considerable pressure on Drax-Grosvenor to support Pitt, raising it during visits to Charborough:

> The King is much pleased at the increase of attendance in the House of Commons on the pending Defence Bill. Though the exertions he has made have not been crowned with the immediate success he expected, yet there is no doubt the effects will be found in a little time. Mr Drax Grosvenor is undoubtedly well disposed, and if the Earl of Chatham can get M.G Grosvenor to vote, his brother will not fail to come forward.[5]

After Pitt died in 1806, Lord Grosvenor went over to the Whigs, and changed his views on Catholic emancipation, but his relative Richard did not do the same. The Grosvenor interests' worst crisis came in the general election of that year. At the last minute, Earl Grosvenor forced Richard to stand down as MP without consulting Richard's supporters in Chester or the corporation, which were said to support Richard's position. Richard informed his constituents on 28 April 1807 that 'circumstances have arisen which prevent me from offering you my services', and it was later alleged that Lord Grosvenor discarded him because of his hostility to the Catholic Relief Bill.[6]

---

4. Although a Tory administration, there were not the clear party lines that exist today and some Whigs did join Pitt's administration or voted with it.

5. Arthur Aspinall (ed.), *The Later Correspondence of George III, January 1802 to December 1807* (Cambridge: Cambridge University Press, 1962).

6. ERLE DRAX GROSVENOR, Richard (1762-1819), of Charborough

BOURNE MOUTH

In 1810 the Drax's neighbours, Mr and Mrs Tregonwell, visited the area known as Bourne Mouth, a few miles to the south-east of their home. The inland area was gorse heathland and was very easy to get lost in. The beach, though, was a delight. They decided to buy some land and build a house there. The Tregonwells first occupied the house in April 1812. In 1814, Mr Tregonwell added to his Bourne Estate by purchasing more land until he held a considerable part of what is now central Bournemouth and right up to the beach. In some areas, the heath was replaced by planting conifers, starting Bournemouth's association with pine trees.

The journal of Mrs Arbuthnot described a visit made one August while she was staying at nearby Muddiford:

> I rode one day to a place called Bournemouth which are a collection of hills lately planted by a gentleman of the name of Tregunwell, who has built four or five beautiful cottages which he lets to persons who go for sea bathing. I was so charmed with the beauty of the situation that Mr. A. and I have half agreed to take one next summer for the sake of a little bathing.[7]

The first friends of the Tregonwell family to join the movement to use Bourne Mouth as a resort were the Drax-Grosvenors. As early as the year 1815, they took up a residence in a cottage on the south cliff.[8] The site is just ten miles from Charborough Park. Their closeness to the Tregonwells is shown by a manuscript written in 1815–16 by Sarah Frances containing caricatures of the Tregonwells and the Grosvenors and showing the lighter side of summer holiday life at Bourne. Mrs Grosvenor's sketches were for the enjoyment of the two families and their friends.

Park, nr. Blandford Forum, Dorset and Swell Court, Som. | History of Parliament Online, last accessed 1 July 2024.

7. *Journal of Mrs Arbuthnot, 1820–1832* (1950), vol. I., p. 333.

8. Cliff Cottage was in the location now covered by the Bournemouth International Centre (BIC).

An 1815 playlet is written by Sarah Frances and interspersed with her pen and ink cartoon sketches. One of her characters speaks of this 'lonely and rather desolate place' where the only neighbours were gypsies and smugglers. The playlet shows 'the Governor' Tregonwell as less than respectable. One drawing shows a small boat rowed by two men, one of whom carries a cask. Mr Tregonwell, with a bottle under his arm, is singing 'a Bournist's song'.[9]

The literary part of Mrs Grosvenor's manuscript is entitled 'A Peep into Futurity, or, Small talk at Bourne some 60 years hence, between the Dandies and the Elegantes of the day'. 'A Peep into Futurity' was intended as an amusing forecast of Bournemouth's growth and what its fashionable society might be like in the days of the founder's grandchildren. In the play, there are many references to 'the old gipsy, formerly the only inhabitant of Meg's Hill', and to Dr Grosvenor, of Meg's Hill, 'a seventh son, and grandson of Meg of occult sciences'. It is possible to infer that the romantic Mrs Grosvenor had identified herself with a real or imaginary gipsy, supposed to have frequented the south cliff in earlier days, and had perhaps named her house 'Gipsy Cottage'.[10] Alongside the Tregonwells, the Drax-Grosvenors, by dint of their wealth and leisure time, can be seen to have been the founders of the seaside resort of Bournemouth.[11]

---

9. David Young, *The Story of Bournemouth* (London: Robert Hale, 1957), pp. 44–49.

10. A 'Gypsey Cottage' did exist in precisely this locality, and this may well have been the house which, as 'Cliff Cottage', a thatched building of rustic appearance and the property of the Drax family, remained in existence until 1875.

11. Bournemouth developed a certain elegance from the very beginning. In 1846 a visitor was able to report on the existence of a 'handsome and spacious hotel, a range of commodious baths on the shore, and a series of elegant, detached villas of picturesque character'. Already it had become a fashionable resort. Until 1914–1918, Bournemouth was best known as a health spa, but in 1918 a change of image was called for, and Bournemouth was henceforward to be considered a resort. Symbolic of this image changing was the renaming of one of the town's main shoreline attractions 'Invalids Walk', in the Pleasure Gardens, which became 'Pine Walk' (Young, *The Story of Bournemouth*, pp. 53–54). My paternal grandparents, now long deceased, lived in Pine Road, Winton, Bournemouth, overlooking the recreation ground with an impressive row of pine trees: www.facebook.com/bournemouthlocalhistory/photos/a.847270145387993/16224873 01199603/?type=3, last accessed 1 July 2024.

CORN LAWS

However, life was grim for those who did not own land but worked around Charborough. The national context for the Drax-Grosvenors after victory at Waterloo in June 1815 is that there was a period of peace before the start of rapid industrialisation and the growth of the textile manufacturers and the railway. The decade after Waterloo was one of the most economically difficult in terms of the conditions of the poor, with great privation, shortages and considerable unrest.

For Parliament, the problem was bringing the wartime economy back to peacetime stability, with helping demobilisation of sailors and soldiers find jobs as there was high unemployment. Drax-Grosvenor was then part of a Parliamentary vote that was seen as a rampant piece of self-interest, as the majority of MPs were land-owners. The 1815 corn law – the Importation Act – was passed in Parliament, and its effect was to keep the price of corn artificially high against the market. The Act was designed to ensure a pro-tected home market in grain for the landholders in Britain and keep prices stable. Oxford Professor Lawrence Goldman said that Par-liament at the time was representative largely of the land-holding interest:

What landholders feared at the end of the Napoleonic Wars would be a sudden drop in price, particularly given the thought that cheap foreign corn from overseas would flood into British ports, reducing their remuneration. Their returns from rents from their tenants would drop. So they wanted to keep the price high.

Now in the minds of the rest of the community of almost every class, this looks like exploitation of their position. They control Parliament. They can pass laws that in a sense, line their own pockets.[12]

---

12.   BBC Radio 4, 'The Corn Laws', *In Our Time*, October 2013, www.bbc.co.uk/programmes/bo3dvbyk#:~:text=In%201815%20the%20British%20Government,by%20the%20Radical%20Richard%20Cobden, last accessed 13 July 2024.

Goldman noted that from the landholders' point of view, they had their rationale: 'They have a defence: they've paid very high taxes, land taxes during the Napoleonic wars to fund a British victory.'[13] Given Richard Drax-Grosvenor's background as a Tory and land-holder, it would have been surprising if he had not voted for the Act.

The Drax family continued to amass their wealth and had several prestigious properties in London: one in Upper Brooke Street would have been convenient for Parliament, another called Acton House, in Middlesex, most likely rented by them, and another at 17 Alpha Cottages, Regents Park. They also had a farmhouse and 176 acres near Wimbledon Common which they let out.

THE GRAND TOUR

Richard and Sarah Frances' son, Richard Edward, had been schooled at Westminster 1809–10; attended Christ Church, Oxford in 1815; and undertook a European tour 1818–19. With the war in Europe over, the British landed gentry were free to travel abroad once again. He appears in the travel journal of Mr Robert Moore, and they sign the register of the Hotel Krone in Schaffhausen, Switzerland, which reveals they stayed there on the 18 September 1818, presumably to see the famous Rhine Falls.[14]

The two wealthy British travellers journeyed through France, Switzerland and Italy throughout the second half of 1818. Moore detailed the pair's itinerary and gave an extensive account of sight-seeing, paying particular attention to the churches and cathedrals of France and to Italian art collections. Richard Edward often attended social functions and was introduced at court in Paris. Additionally, the writer frequently provided background information on the different locales he visited, and occasionally mentioned events from

---

13. Ibid.
14. Michael Heafford, 'British Travellers in Early Nineteenth Century Registers and Guest Books', *Studies in Travel Writing*, vol. 25, no. 3 (2021), 374–388. Moore is likely the Rev. Robert Moore (1778–1865) who was at Christ Church and a prebendary of Canterbury.

the recent Napoleonic wars, particularly during a visit to a French battlefield. Before their entry in the guest book of the Hotel Krone in Schaffhausen on 14 September, they were at the Rigi Kulm on 9 September as this was an 'essential' destination for British visitors to Switzerland in the nineteenth century.

On 4 October, they visited the Hospice of the Great St Bernard. Academic Michael Heafford suggested they did not cross the pass but descended again to the Rhone Valley and continued to Brig and across the Simplon to the Italian Lakes. Heafford noted that they seem to have been joined for some of their journey by Samuel Treherne Kekewich, a friend from Oxford.[15] They were on the summit of the Rigi together, at Schaffhausen at more or less the same time, entered Milan on the same day and left it for Turin only a day apart.[16] After the travellers reached Italy, they focused more on fine art, and the journal includes lists of the prominent art holdings in several palaces; it also notes visits to Da Vinci's *The Last Supper* in Milan and to the '*Mona Elisa*' in the 'Nicoli Palace'. From Laveno, they proceeded to Milan, which they entered on 15 October, leaving for Turin on the 27th. Robert Moore is recorded as leaving Florence for Rome on 10 December, but there is no record of Drax doing so. The final entry was made on 15 December 1818, just after the author and his companion arrived in Rome.[17]

On 8 February 1819, the recently re-elected Richard Drax-Grosvenor MP died at the age of 56. Despite his father's and his family's many attempts to get him a peerage it never happened. What to make of Richard Grosvenor? He played the part of a senior member of the landed gentry to a tee but without any great distinction. As an MP, he upheld the Grosvenor family interests but never, as far as can be ascertained, spoke in Parliament, but then that was

---

15. Samuel Trewhawke Kekewich, b. Bowden house near Totnes, Devon, 31 October 1796; educated at Eton; matriculated from Christ Church, Oxford, 27 October 1814; MP Exeter 1826–30; MP South Devon 1858 to death; sheriff of Devon 1834. d. Peamore near Exeter, 1 June 1873.

16. I thank Michael Heafford for his scholarly assistance by email on the travels of Mr Moore and Richard Edward Drax-Grosvenor, 25 July 2024.

17. Robert Moore's journal is in the collection of the University of Michigan's William L. Clements Library.

not uncommon. Somewhere there are portraits of him and his wife separately painted by John Hoppner around 1804.[18] As will be detailed later, these disappeared in odd circumstances and may now both be in the United States. However, there is a portrait of Richard's brother Thomas, by George Romney, painted in 1790, that may still hang in the Charborough House's green drawing room.[19]

For some years, Richard voted as Lord Grosvenor required, but it would seem the patriarch was liberal by comparison to his relative. Richard would not support Catholic emancipation, but then neither did a large section of the population, as was witnessed by the anti-Catholic riots of the period. He was clearly very socially able, and he and his wife were close to the royal family. It would appear his main activities were socialising and improving his estates.

THE LONDON TRAGEDIES

Good works and charity were part of the role for all members of the family, and even though Sarah Frances' husband had recently died, the lady of the big house was expected to open fetes and attend charitable events for the deserving poor. On 31 January 1820 *Salisbury & Winchester Journal* reported:

Mrs S. F. Erle Drax Grosvenor has with her wonted beneficence, bestowed her annual donations of food and clothing, with an

---

18. There is one known surviving portrait of Sarah Frances Drax. It is not the work of a master but shows a dark-haired woman in her twenties with a long face and slight smile. She is pictured sitting, wearing a bonnet tied with a scarf, where a dark curl protrudes, and a red cloak over a white blouse. On one side is a basket of fruit and her finger points at a passage in a book, but what the book is, is not apparent.

19. The portrait is inscribed 'Thomas Grosvenor, Esq. only brother of Richard Earl Grosvenor Anno 1790'. A companion portrait of Thomas's brother was ordered and paid for by Richard Erle-Drax-Grosvenor, and the receipt still exists: '3rd April 1804. Received of Edward Boodle, Esq. £42 for a portrait of the late Earl Grosvenor Esq. painted for Drax-Grosvenor Esq. – J. Hoppner.' E. Boodle was evidently Drax-Grosvenor's agent and made numerous payments for him, as his accounts dated 3 July 1798 include the following item: 'Paid Mr. Romney for a family picture by your order £105.'

increased quantity in proportion to the inclemency of the season, to the poor of her various parishes. Mr Erle Drax Grosvenor has also most liberally distributed near £200 in bread, beef and clothing among the poor of the same parishes.

After his father's death, Richard II was elected in his father's place as MP for New Romney.[20] He took ownership of Charborough and Drax Hall. In the 1820 Slave Register, John Mayers was shown as selling to Richard Edward Drax-Grosvenor 38 enslaved people. As this was recorded in the Slave Register it must have been an inter-plantation trade and not the purchase of smuggled captive Africans. As an MP, Richard Edward was nominally a supporter of the Lord Liverpool ministry. In his father's footsteps he voted against Catholic relief on 28 February 1821, keeping the family's anti-papist ethos alive, but I have been unable to discover any other trace of parliamentary activity.[21]

Further tragedy ensued when in 1821, Richard Edward manifested a mental illness so devastating that he was not lucid. Doctors could not come up with a diagnosis and said it was a matter for God.[22] His mother took care of the desperately unwell son. Perhaps the most tragic moment occurred when, on 15 June 1822, Mrs Drax-Grosvenor and her son, now 25, went out in their carriage for 'an airing', as the term was then. The *Annual Register* tells the story concisely:

A lady by the name of Drax-Grosvenor, who resided at Acton House, Middlesex and also at 17 Alpha Cottages, Regent's Park, was going with her son Mr Grosvenor, in her carriage, along the Hammersmith Road when a powerful fellow, named Taylor, formerly a labourer at Hammersmith, ran behind the carriage, and attempted to get up and ride. The groom, who was standing

20. The rotten borough of New Romney was dissolved by the Reform Act 1832.
21. ERLE DRAX GROSVENOR, Richard (1762-1819), of Charborough Park, nr. Blandford Forum, Dorset and Swell Court, Som. | History of Parliament Online, last accessed 1 July 2024.
22. The inquisition is recorded in TNA C211/7/D80.

behind the carriage, refused to let him get up, when the fellow seized the groom by the leg and pulled him to the ground. The groom, being injured by the fall, called for assistance; the coachman stopped the carriage and came to assist his fellow-servant, when Taylor attacked him, and beat him also. A mob was collected, and the lady in the carriage was greatly alarmed.

According to the report, a local tradesman called Mr Graham went with his assistant to apprehend Taylor; but the attacker was so powerful, that he knocked them about like children. Eventually, Mr Graham and his assistant did manage to take Taylor to a place where they could arrest him, having both taken a beating. Taylor was taken before J. Anderson, Esq. a magistrate at Hammersmith, and was examined. The Lady Drax attended to give evidence, and the attacker was ordered to be committed to prison, to take his trial for the offence.

But as he was about to be removed from the magistrate's room, he begged to speak a few words to the lady, when he made an affecting appeal to her not to prosecute him for the offence, on the score of humanity to his wife and children. The lady wished to extend mercy to the prisoner, but the magistrate could not suffer such an outrageous offence to go unpunished: and the man was ordered to be conveyed to gaol. The lady was so greatly affected at the appeal of the prisoner for mercy that she fell into the arms of one of her servants in a fit; she soon became convulsed, and by the time that medical aid could be obtained, she was a corpse. The body was laid out in the house of the worthy magistrate. The son of the lady was present, and he was in a state of grief almost beyond description of the awful event. The cause of death was registered as 'ossification of the heart'.

It is unknown whether Taylor was just drunk and out of control or whether there was more to the story.[23]

---

23. Taylor's sentence is not known.

DRAX OF DRAX HALL

This tragedy was to have another consequence. It seems that the experience sent her distraught son into some immediate mental trauma so severe that he was shortly afterwards declared a lunatic.[24] It is, in some ways, reminiscent of King George III's mental illness. It was so severe it was believed he would not recover. After his parents' deaths, he was in charge of the whole of Charborough and all its associated estates including Drax Hall in Barbados. As was the law at the time when a 'lunatic' had assets, the matter was referred to the Court of Chancery. His sister was older but was said to have no idea of business, so the court appointed his father's two brothers, General Thomas Grosvenor and Reverend Robert Grosvenor, to manage Richard Edward's affairs. According to the court record, the annual rental of the estates was worth some £22,000 per year, a vast sum. The court allowed £5000 per year for the upkeep of Richard Edward. Later legal documents show that: 'Affidavits by the attendant physician, the late tutor, and an intimate friend of the lunatic, stated that the establishment kept up for him was, in point of appearance, very handsome, and suitable to his rank and fortune, and that every attention was paid to his comfort and happiness.' There were periodic court reports of his life under the watchful eyes of the court and his guardians. For much of his time he stayed at the Regent's Park address. He stood down as an MP in 1826. On 13 August 1828, Richard died. He was unmarried. Cause of death was not stated, and there was no will.

Richard the lunatic left a very useful legacy. As Richard S. Dunn noted in *Sugar and Slaves*, the best way to grasp the character of plantation life in the seventeenth-century Caribbean is through the study of individual estate records, but few such documents have survived.[25] What Richard Edward left us, not that he was cognisant of the gift, are account books now in The National Archives in Kew. These cover the period 1822 to 1828 and were a requirement of the Court of Chancery that his guardians provided detailed accounts of the estate. So, there are two sets of large, elegant leath-

24. All documentation at the time uses the expression 'lunatic', and of course today we would not use the word for someone who had severe mental illness.
25. Dunn, *Sugar and Slaves*, p. 212.

246

AFTER NAPOLEON

er-bound account books all handwritten in a good hand. The first are the accounts for the Charborough Estate. They are full of fascinating detail, for example, the annual rent for each of the farms. The second set is more important, as they are the accounts of transactions of shipments of sugar from and supplies to the Drax Hall plantation and are again detailed. As for the history of Drax Hall, the only other surviving accounts in the public domain are in summary form and cover 1803, 1804, 1808 and 1811. These include monies spent purchasing enslaved people.[26]

The tragedies of the Drax-Grosvenors resulted in changes for the family that, in their way, would severely damage the family's reputation.

---

26. There may be more in the Drax private family archive to which I was not given access, but I cannot find any reference to them. Neither can I see any evidence that the account books in The National Archives have been referred to in the past.

16
Seeking Enclosure

English rhyme, circa 1764 (extract):

> The law locks up the man or woman
> Who steals the goose from off the common
> But leaves the greater villain loose
> Who steals the common from off the goose
> The law demands that we atone
> When we take things we do not own
> But what can plead that man's excuse
> Who steals a common from a goose.

(In The Tickler Magazine, 1 February 1821)

How did the Charborough Estate become so vast? As we have seen, one method was buying up land from neighbours using their rental income and sugar wealth. Another controversial method was enclosure, which the Erle-Drax family used extensively over the centuries. Traditionally, by the medieval period, a large area of each village or settlement was common land shared between the local people by communal and historical agreement. It was often waste or heathlands, sometimes an open field system and all a bit higgledy-piggledy. Before enclosure, typically, in many counties, there was a village system of open land which might be 100–300 acres in size, and these would be divided up into strips, which the villagers would farm, often for subsistence.[1]

Nominally, the land belonged to the lord of the manor. The village had rights of usage, which might be pasturing cattle, collecting turf and wood for fuel, collecting any fruit or berries or other kinds of subsistence food, and keeping fowl, but it was rights of usage and a

---

1. Some counties like Kent did not have much in the way of common land and had historically farmed by unified farms.

SEEKING ENCLOSURE

small piece of land and it could be a major part of villagers' income. Professor Rosemary Sweet has said the right to pasture was so that people with very small holdings of land, possibly only one or two acres, would have rights to common land. 'A cow could be a very important part of a family income, from producing milk and other by-products [and] could actually amount to at least the value of half a year's annual wages and so this could be a crucial supplement to families' incomes.'[2]

By the sixteenth century, with pressure to bring more land into production, landlords and their tenant farmers had begun working individually or together to take over common land. Effectively they privatised the commons using their access to the levers of power. It can be seen simply as theft, but the landlords and tenant farmers argued it was better utilisation of the land and often for more intensive farming. It was, of course, to their financial interest, and they argued that expanding commercial agriculture employed more local labourers. Where the lord of the manor had the freehold and agreement could be made between the tenants, it could be done informally.

Resentment over enclosures was a motivator for the English Civil War and a cause of localised unrest for centuries. The populace lacked any remedy for the consequences of continuous economic decline after about 1550. This meant grinding poverty and starvation, from which the peasantry had even fewer means of escape now that the rapacious middle class had been allowed to share in the profits of the post-dissolution land grab. Christopher Hill wrote that the early 17th century saw the first (limited) pro-enclosure act.

In 1621, in the depths of the depression, came the first general enclosure bill – opposed by some M.P.s who feared agrarian disturbances. In 1624 the statutes against enclosure were repealed.... the Long Parliament was a turning point. No government after

2.   BBC Radio 4, 'The Enclosures of the 18th Century', *In Our Time*, May 2008, www.bbc.co.uk/programmes/b00b1m9b.

249

1640 seriously tried either to prevent enclosures, or even to make money by fining enclosers.[3]

While there was organised resistance to enclosure, the Western Rising – mostly in Wiltshire – was less organised but lasted longer, from 1626 to 1632. Here the focus was 'disafforestation' – Charles I's privatisation of the extensive royal forests which covered vast swathes of the kingdom – and in which thousands of farmers and cottagers had long exercised common rights. The government appointed commissions to survey the land, proposed dividing it and negotiating compensation for tenants. The largest portions were leased to investors, mainly the king's friends and supporters, who in turn rented enclosed parcels to large farmers.[4]

After the Long Parliament was convened, there was a rising tide of protests and riots in the countryside. As the historian Brian Manning noted, 'This was directed chiefly against the enclosures of commons, wastes and fens, and the invasions of common rights by the king, members of the royal family, courtiers, bishops and great aristocrats.'[5] Between 1640 and 1644, there were anti-enclosure riots in more than half of England's counties, especially in the Midlands and North. Morrill noted: 'in some cases not only the fences, but the houses of the gentry were attacked'.[6] In July 1641, the House of Lords complained that 'violent breaking into Possessions and Inclosures, in riotous and tumultuous Manner, in several Parts of this Kingdom', was happening 'more frequently ... since this Parliament began than formerly'. They ordered local authorities to ensure 'that no Inclosure or Possession shall be violently, and in a tumultuous Manner, disturbed or taken away from any

---

3. Christopher Hill, *Reformation to Industrial Revolution* (London: Weidenfeld & Nicolson, 1968), p. 51.

4. Buchanan Sharp, *In Contempt of All Authority: Rural Artisans and Riot in the West of England, 1586–1660* (Berkeley, CA: University of California Press, 1980), pp. 84–85.

5. Brian Manning, *The English People and the English Revolution* (London: Bookmarks, 1991), p. 195.

6. John S. Morrill, *The Revolt of the Provinces: Conservatives and Radicals in the English Civil War, 1630–1650* (London: Longman, 1987), p. 34.

SEEKING ENCLOSURE

Man' ('General Order for Possessions, to secure them from Riots and Tumults'). This was rarely effective. One of the offices held by Sir Walter Erle the Puritan in 1643 was to suppress enclosure riots, presumably in Dorset, though nothing is known about Erle's activities in this post. Scattered enclosures took place in Dorset at the time, including at Bere Regis, the nearest village to Charborough.[7]

To give an idea of the benefits of the enclosure, there is an example from the Verney family in the 1650s. The Verneys of Buckinghamshire were distantly related to the Erles. Sir Ralph Verney decided to complete the enclosure of open fields and commons around their Claydon estate, an activity started by his father, Sir Edmund Verney, in the 1620s. Forty-two of the 53 farms on the estate were less than 20 acres. Sir Ralph took the view that these farms needed to be more viable in terms of contemporary agricultural practices. The standing arrangements meant they could not deliver anything but low rents, and in some cases, the tenants went bankrupt. Sir Ralph sought his tenants' agreement to enclose the commons and renegotiate their leases in Verney's favour, often entertaining them lavishly as he did so. As the historian of the Verney family noted:

> He then put fences, dug ditches and set hedges to establish larger pastures; and rents went up accordingly. It has been estimated that enclosure may have cost Sir Ralph around £600, but that raised the estate income by some £300 a year – quite a return on his investment.[8]

In the eighteenth century, enclosure began requiring a private or collective Act of Parliament to legitimise the claim. The 1773 Enclosure Act legitimised a land grab partly funded by West and East Indies fortunes and those owners returning from the colonies. They held a great deal of power in Parliament. Hayes commented: 'It is estimated that in 1765 there were forty MPs... with West Indian connections and, by 1784, twenty-nine MPs with direct

---

7. Goodwin, *Dorset in the Civil War*, p. 11.
8. Tinniswood, *The Verneys*, pp. 280–282.

East Indian connections.'[9] Also, an estimated six million acres of common land, a quarter of all cultivated acreage as well as grouse moors, was taken by the landed aristocrats, gentry and farmers in a period from the second quarter of the eighteenth century to the first quarter of the nineteenth century. The 1801 General Act of Enclosure made it much easier to evict squatters from village shared land and marginal freeholders and copyholders from their holdings. As David Olusoga observed, owning property was central to British culture. Your position in the 'natural order' was dependent on what property you owned and landed MPs made sure that protecting property was at the heart of English law.[10]

Professor Murray Pittock noted the people who did well from the enclosure were the new owners of the land because they had greater freedom to use the land and on a larger scale than ever before to develop it and to improve it. He said it marked the end of payment in kind terms; you could not use chickens for rent any more, it had to be cash. Being an MP and or a magistrate could help press through Enclosure Acts. Pittock noted: 'I think that one of the crucial things is that land ownership is intimately connected to parliamentary representation, and sometimes it's the same people who are involved.' Pittock made the point that becoming a Justice of the Peace was more dependent on owning land than having a significant income:

> Land is a way to authority, which is why it's prized. That's the crucial function of controlling society. The fact that the justice of the peace system is a landed system and right the way up from JPs to Knights of the Shire's to parliamentary legislation. The interests of the landowner are served by the law by making the law and by implementing it.[11]

The landowners could override the common law by using the power of their social standing in their own interests. The leading figures

---

9.   Hayes, *Book of Trespass*, p. 149.

10.   David Olusoga, *Britain's Forgotten Slave Owners*, BBC TV, 2015.

11.   BBC, 'The Enclosures of the 18th Century', *In Our Time*, May 2008, www.bbc.co.uk/programmes/b00b1m9b, accessed 29 August 2024.

SEEKING ENCLOSURE

of the Drax family have almost always been magistrates, more often than they were MPs. In 1817 the poet William Wordsworth looked wistfully backwards to feudalism and lamented the changes he saw around him. In a letter to Daniel Stuart, he complained:

> farmers used to formerly to be attached to their landlords, and labourers to their farmers who employed them. All that kind of feeling has vanished – in like manner, the connection between the trading and landed interests of county towns undergoes no modification whatever from personal feeling, whereas in my memory it was almost wholly governed by it.

These sentimental Wordsworth memories caught the sense of change.[12] Other poets had different perspectives on these changes. Three years later, the 'peasant poet' John Clare wrote the poem 'The Mores', critical of the impact of enclosure. Clare was capturing the impact of eighteenth-century enclosures.

ENCLOSURE IN DORSET

In Dorset the enclosures had a big impact on the communal life of the village. In neighbouring Sturminster Marshall, where the Trenchards were lords of the manor, Mr Ahuzzath Legg had told the Rev. Charles Mayo about life in the parish before enclosure. He recalled that when the common meadows were opened after the first hay crop, the tenants got together to organise the making of a huge syllabub, with each commoner contributing the milk of a certain number of cows, and the rector providing a bottle of wine. The whole thing was made in milking pails and drunk at a village festivity.

> This was a fitting communal festivity to cap all the collective efforts that went on, not just to farm the land within the village, but also simply to remember who was to do what, who had

---

12. John Lucas, *England and Englishness* (London: The Hogarth Press, 1990), p. 119.

responsibilities to whom, and who owned what. Yet, it should not blind us to the fact that Dorset society in the eighteenth and early nineteenth centuries was very deeply divided in terms of wealth, opportunities and possibilities in life.[13]

The owners of the Charborough Estate, enclosed from the seventeenth century, would continue to do so for 200 years. General Thomas Erle was involved in enclosures in Morden in 1695. Parliament helped the Erles finally eliminate medieval agriculture in Morden in 1781 with 'An Act for dividing and inclosing the several Commons, Common Heaths, and Waste Grounds in the Manor of Morden in the County of Dorset'. This was some 973 acres. The process could take a long time. At the village of East Stoke three miles west of Wareham, the Drax enclosure started in 1813 and finished in 1870.[14] The agricultural historian Barbara Kerr observed the Drax family showed considerable skill and independence in the management of their estates. Though, Kerr said, 'they were not entirely impervious to the enthusiasm of landed proprietors in the early 19th century: enlarging and planting the parkland, throwing farms together, enclosing and creating an environment favourable to field sports'.[15]

The Charborough Estate lands were then, as now, very varied, ranging from quality arable land towards the north, wetlands around the rivers, and woodlands, to heathland and marginal land. A set of manorial documents for this period relates to friction between two landlords over encroachments in a single heathland. The Court Baron of the Manor of Lytchett Matravers repeatedly

---

13. Henry French, 'Field, Fen and Family at Sturminster Marshall in the Eighteenth and Early Nineteenth Century' (2014), p. 6. Talk can be found at: www.academia.edu/9537001/Field_Fen_and_Family_at_Sturminster_Marshall_in_the_Eighteenth_and_Early_Nineteenth_Century.
14. Morden was, and is still, a beautiful piece of Dorset farmland set in a rolling landscape rising gently southwards from the River Winterborne and one of its tributaries.
15. Barbara Kerr, 'Land Usage in Morden with Special Reference to the Heathland', *Proceedings of the Dorset Natural History and Archaeological Society*, vol. 109 (1987), 32.

SEEKING ENCLOSURE

found 'That Thomas Erle Drax and Samuel Clark, his tenant in the Manor of Morden, have encroached and inclosed a great many acres of Common between White Moor and Berymoor and have builded largely upon it.' Every year between 1770 and 1786 the Court Baron found Drax and Clarke guilty of the same offence.[16] The manor was owned by the Trenchard family.

In one example of the encroaching Charborough Estate, by 1775, to the west side, a considerable part of the manor of Bere Regis had been enclosed. This map provides insight into the significant amount of land already enclosed and transformed into individual farms and 'closes'. While the three open fields in the valleys and lower slopes north of the village remained, they were gradually facing encroachment and enclosures. As the second map, this time in the north-east section of the first, shows, by 1846 even more of Bere Regis common land would be enclosed. It also shows the roads that needed to be built to service larger farms.[17]

These enclosed lands were leased out to new tenants. Historians of enclosure John Chapman and Sylvia Seeliger wrote that the process in Dorset was much influenced by the dominance of large estates:

> Families such as the Draxes of Charborough Park, the Welds of Lulworth and the Pitt Rivers held sway over great tracts of territory and all, or almost all of a good many parishes lay in the hands of a single owner, leaving the individuals concerned able to enclose almost at will. There was often little need to invoke the powers of Parliament since even if there were another minor owner, it may well have been possible either to reach an agreement to enclose or to ignore the common rights which nominally still existed.[18]

Professor Sweet noted that at the time there was probably more literature produced pronouncing the benefits to be gained from

---

16.   DRO D230/1 Court Book of the Manor of Lytchett Matravers 1770–1875.
17.   These maps were drawn by R.R. Sellman and can be found in his *Illustrations of Dorset History* (London: Methuen, 1960), p. 46.
18.   Chapman and Seeliger, *Enclosure, Environment and Landscape*, p. 53.

255

enclosure with some very effective publicists, 'and most notably Arthur Young, who is the most prominent agricultural writer from the 1760s onwards, who went around the country describing the progress of agricultural improvement'. Young, he noted, saw enclosure as a rational, enlightenment form of improvement, that justified the consolidation of units of land.[19]

Between 1750 and 1820, nearly 4000 Enclosure Acts in England were passed. Only a handful of open-field villages remained. This was not missed by the radical thinkers of the nineteenth century. Marx wrote, 'the expropriation of the mass of the people from the soil forms the basis of the capitalist mode of production'. His point was that workers who can produce all or most of their own subsistence are independent in ways that are alien to capitalism – they are under no economic compulsion to work for wages.[20] Enclosure added swathes of land to the Charborough Estate. The process lasted well into the nineteenth century. The tenants who agreed to take over common land would eventually sell out, their tenancies run out or go bankrupt and the land revert to the estate. That is how much land was accumulated over many centuries. Meanwhile, the Charborough Estate was now approaching 20,000 acres and a new 'improving' landlord was to be installed.

A WEDDING

On May Day 1827, Jane-Frances married. The *Hampshire Chronicle* reported the Anglican ceremony had taken place at St George's, Hanover Square, London, between John Samuel Wanley Sawbridge of Olantigh, Kent and Miss Jane Frances Drax-Grosvenor of Charborough Park, sister of Richard. The Drax family had a plush London home in St George's parish for 100 years, and it was a popular upmarket area for absentee plantation owners such as the Draxes and the Beckfords. Portraits of the married couple around

---

19. BBC Radio 4, 'The Enclosures of the 18th Century', *In Our Time*, May 2008, www.bbc.co.uk/programmes/b00b1m9b, last accessed 13 July 2024.

20. www.resilience.org/stories/2022-01-17/against-enclosure-the-commoners-fight-back/, last accessed 27 June 2024.

this time reveal John to be tall and thin, dark haired with a mutton chops beard, a sallow looking man without a strong jaw line. Jane is dark haired with a round attractive face, small lips and red cheeks as of the fashion of the time. In keeping with the family diktat, John S.W. Sawbridge took the name of Sawbridge Erle-Drax. He was to become perhaps the most controversial and flamboyant member of the Drax family.

John and Jane Frances had increasingly used Charborough House while the owner, her unwell brother, Richard Edward, was looked after in the family's home in Regent's Park, London and later, the lunatic asylum. To get a sense of John Drax, a man who dominated Charborough for nearly six decades, requires a resumé of his family background and wealth. His great-grandfather was Jacob Sawbridge MP. Born in 1665 and starting life with a very considerable fortune, Jacob Sawbridge was, as a City financier, a partner in the firm of Turner, Sawbridge, and Caswall, bankers. Jacob Sawbridge was a founder and director of the South Sea Company. It banked with his firm. To create more income, it took on the *asiento* granted in 1713 by a provision in the Treaty of Utrecht.[21] This contract entitled the company to send 4800 enslaved people to Spanish America annually for 30 years and to send one ship each year to engage in general trade. King George I became a governor of the company and profited from it.

To this point, Jacob Sawbridge was well regarded and elected as a Whig MP in 1715 for Cricklade, and he was doing so well that he bought a large mansion at Wye in Kent called Olantigh.[22] In 1720 the whole of London, and many more ordinary people throughout the country, became involved in the South Sea Bubble scandal. As previously noted, Henry Drax MP was given £1000 worth of shares. Shares rapidly rose to ten times their face value, specula-

---

21.   On 11 April 1713, France concluded treaties of peace at Utrecht with England, Holland, Prussia, Portugal and Savoy. By the treaty with England, France recognised the Protestant succession in England and undertook to give no further help to the Stuarts.

22.   Today notable for its surviving long brick wall, reminiscent of the 'Great Wall of Dorset'.

tion ran wild, and all sorts of companies, some bizarre, some fraudulent or just optimistic, were launched off the back of the mass
hysteria. Then the stocks crashed, and people all over the country
lost all their money. Butchers, candlestick makers and ladies' maids
who had bought their own carriages in the expectation of riches
became destitute almost overnight. As did the clergy and gentry,
losing their life savings; the whole country suffered a catastrophic
loss of money and property. Suicides became a daily occurrence.

The South Sea Company directors were arrested. When it
emerged that there had been frauds using the company, Sawbridge,
with the other directors in the Commons, were expelled from
the House, committed to the custody of the serjeant at arms, and
examined by the Parliamentary South Sea committee of inquiry.
He was questioned as to entries in the account books of his firm
purporting to show that £50,000 of the £574,000 South Sea stock
which was supposed to have been issued as bribes to Members
of Parliament. On the introduction of the bill to confiscate the
estates of the directors and other guilty parties for the relief of their
victims, Sawbridge petitioned the House for lenient treatment on
the grounds that whatever he had done 'that may have given offence
hath been through ignorance and inadvertency, without any private
or unlawful views or designs'. He was allowed to keep Olantigh and
£5000 out of a fortune of £77,000. However, the Commons considered him among the more culpable of the directors, all of whom
were banned from sitting in Parliament or holding public office.

The South Sea Company was allowed to continue trading to
recover and worked with the Royal African Company to purchase
34,000 enslaved people in West Africa over the following years. It
was the Erle-Drax family's share of the profits from this trading
that they went to court to decide who in the family would benefit.
Jacob Sawbridge died on 11 July 1748. Among his grandchildren
was Mrs Catherine Macaulay, the historian, more appreciated in
North America and France than at home. Catherine married into
the Macaulay family through George, a Scottish doctor. In her
famous six-volume *History of England from the Ascension of James
I*, she included what was intended as a vindication of her grand-

father Jacob. Her brother was John Sawbridge, the Whig MP for Hythe, who became the radical Lord Mayor of London and served as Sheriff of the City. They were both advocates of the Republicanism of Rome. John Sawbridge was also a close colleague of William Beckford, who twice held the post of Lord Mayor of London and was vastly wealthy partly because of his family plantations. William Beckford had acquired the Drax Hall plantation in Jamaica.[23]

On 12 May 1789, a debate was held in Parliament in which John Sawbridge opposed a motion to abolish the slave trade. He argued that it was an essential service, a kindness to remove Africans from their own country otherwise 'They would be butchered and executed at home.' He then continued that abolition would be 'a furious blow' to commerce. One of Sawbridge's allies, Nathaniel Newnham, put forward a petition on behalf of London merchants and shipowners in defence of the African slave trade, pointing out the 'fatal consequences' to the whole country if that trade halted.[24] It provides some idea of the cognitive dissonance that even liberals could show that John Sawbridge, on the one hand, opposed abolition and on the other he ardently championed the cause of Wilkes by promoting the Bill of Rights Society. Finally, of John Sawbridge Erle-Drax's ancestors John Sawbridge's son, Samuel, was to be expelled as an MP for Canterbury, accused of bribery, though he was allowed to return for a short period as MP in 1807. While he had land and property, he was saddled with mortgages. As a result of his debts, he went to live in Ghent in 1817 for a period to avoid his creditors.[25]

Samuel's son, John Samuel Wanley Sawbridge, was 27 (henceforth John Drax) when he married 39-year-old Jane Frances Drax-Grosvenor in 1827. It was said that her nickname was 'Crazy Jane', and there is a contemporary cartoon that suggests that she had been courted by Lord Paget, Marquis of Anglesey and Earl of Uxbridge.[26]

---

23. www.ucl.ac.uk/lbs/estate/view/2333.
24. Rodney Schofield, 'Release the Captives': The Sawbridge Response (Privately printed, 2020), p. 85.
25. Ibid., p. 138.
26. A contemporary letter says that the other woman in the cartoon was Jane Paget. Sources agree that the man was involved with Miss Calcraft, the letter claiming she had his baby, before transferring his affections to 'Jane', and that

It is not now known whether Jane Frances and John Sawbridge were a love match, a marriage of convenience, or a financial opportunity for him. Contemporary accounts suggest there was some affection between them. Jane Frances must have been impacted by the terrible tragedies in her family from 1819, and then with her brother Richard Edward dying in August 1828, a few months after her marriage. Jane inherited the estate's property and assets valued at the time as worth £135,000, producing a huge annual income of £23,000. Jane Frances had two daughters with John in a short time, Sarah Charlotte and Maria Caroline. In the early days, everything seemed to be in domestic harmony in Charborough House. In 1836, a painting by Miss Maria A. Chalon was shown at the Royal Academy annual exhibition of John and Jane's two young daughters. Three years later, Miss Chalon followed with a painting of John Drax, in full yeomanry officer's uniform.[27]

The reign of John Drax over Charborough was a long and increasingly despotic one.

---

he then went on to marry another woman. https://news.dorsetcouncil.gov.uk/dorset-history-centre-blog/2019/09/30/desertion-drinks-and-a-diarist/, last accessed 27 June 2024.

27. Chalon was Portrait Paintress to his Royal Highness, the Duke of York, and is considered one of the most talented and successful female British miniaturists of the early nineteenth century. These pictures may be those hung in the picture gallery, at least in Admiral Drax's time, of the two Miss Draxes in their nursery with a parrot. On the south-east wall was hung a picture of the two Miss Draxes with a dog and another of their father John Drax in a military uniform.

PART VI

The Wicked Squire

17

Captain Swing

The new squire of Charborough, John Samuel Wanley Sawbridge Erle-Drax (John Drax) already had considerable annual family income and had bought the manor of Longburton and Holnest near Sherborne in 1826. Aquiline in appearance, John Drax was given to extravagance, and the Charborough Estate was a ready source of cash.

These were turbulent times again in many parts of Europe. Revolution was in the air, and it swept across Britain as conditions for the working classes declined rapidly. This led to the emergence of trade unions, the Chartists and other organisations seeking political equality. Pressure grew for political reform, including for all men to have the vote, the end of rotten boroughs and the establishment of equal size constituencies. Some argued for 'reform or revolution', but the government resisted the demands. John Drax still held some radical views in his first years of marriage and favoured a Reform Act to extend the vote to more men, which was not a popular position with many other landowners of the county. Of all the ancestors of the modern Drax family, he was, at least in his younger years, the most liberal. Charborough and its squire John Drax were to make an extraordinary appearance in the Captain Swing protests in Dorset. Charborough's part has been virtually unreported in the history book accounts of Captain Swing.

CAPTAIN SWING

At the beginning of autumn 1830, relations between the Charborough Estate and its tenants seemed good by the standards of the day. Drax was noted for his 'bread and circuses' approach to keeping the locals happy. The *Bath Chronicle* of 23 September 1830 reported with the headline 'Charborough Park – a scene of gay festivity'.

Mr Drax had some time since signified to his tenants that he intended to give a silver cup to be run for by horses belonging to them. On Monday the race took place, an immense number of people were present. The ground selected with much judgement, a mile course was formed, and a convenient stand erected. The horses were handicapped. At the conclusion of the races, 200 tenants sat down to a sumptuous dinner given by the hospitable landlord. At 5 o'clock a merry dance commenced in the park which was kept up with much spirit until an early hour, it was further reported. Mr Drax has expressed his intention of making it an annual amusement.

The size of the guest list indicates how many farms were being rented on the estate. Given the events that followed, John Drax's initial reformism and generosity may have benefitted him greatly in these years. Agricultural workers, unlike tenants, were not enjoying his sumptuous dinners. Dorset had long been notorious for its low-wage economy and was always seen as one of the poorest-paying counties in the country. By 1830, a pay of six or seven shillings a week – less than subsistence – was not uncommon, whereas eight shillings or more was the rate in many other counties. Some Charborough Estate cottagers were said to do better, with wages of nine shillings a week, but any generosity was offset by the fact that for many, these went unpaid for 12 to 18 months.

Nothing had altered the social order in Dorset since the Glorious Revolution, unlike the north of England with industrialisation and East Anglia where agriculture was forging ahead with mechanisation. These devices allowed a reduction in the size of the workforce on farms. Many reports by charities and enlightened campaigners complained of the poor condition of the agricultural tied homes – hovels – in which Dorset labourers and their families rented from tenant farmers or landlords. Despite all these disadvantages, Dorset was not a natural seedbed for dissent. It had no significant towns and few major roads, and the railway would not reach into the county for another 30 years, so communication between the disaffected and trade unions and campaigning groups was hampered. Nevertheless, dissent did grow in some parts of the county.

Dorset agricultural historian Barbara Kerr noted of Bere Regis, a button-making village, that the corn laws protected the income of landlords and tenants at the cost of others.

> Bere, like other towns on the chalk downlands, was not a cheerful place in the mid-nineteenth century. Increases in the population made it difficult for the listless, undernourished inhabitants to find livelihoods in either the small-town trades, many of which were overcrowded, or on the large farms of the chalk download, where machinery was early introduced. It was the poverty of downland villages which, in the heat of the Corn Law debates, caused to be cited as the terrible shape of things to come for the whole country if Protections remained.[1]

In 1830 the economic depression created more rural unemployment and more pressure on creaking seams of the parish-based poor law system. In some areas, agitation turned to the destruction of the new machinery that was replacing manpower, and, in some cases, it turned to violence. Matters came to a head in November 1830 when bands of unemployed or poorly paid farm labourers attacked the houses of those they considered responsible for their situation, set fire to ricks, and destroyed threshing machines – an innovation which they considered to be one particular cause of their plight. The 'Captain Swing' agricultural riots in 1830 have been called 'The Last Labourers Revolt'. Captain Swing was not a person but a deliberately threatening name used as an umbrella for what was often seen as popular local uprisings seeking retribution on greedy landowners and employers.

Protests swept from the east across the country. The first recorded Swing disturbance in the region was at Maddington in Wiltshire

---

1. Kerr, *Bound to the Soil*, pp. 8–9.

on 8 November 1830 (which had been home to the Ernle family, and so the Drax family had estate land there). Then followed the destruction of a mill and ironworks at Fordingbridge on the Hampshire border and then a gathering of 400 labourers between Hindon and Semley, who stoned the landowner John Benett at Pyt House, though he escaped with his life.

The indigenous Swing mobilisation in Dorset started in the Bere Valley on 25 November. It appears to have been a pre-planned event as crowds of labourers gathered simultaneously at Bere Regis, Winterbourne Kingston and Tolpuddle, angry over their low wages. They refused to work until they were promised higher wages and increased parish support. A large crowd marched from Bere to Charborough House to protest to the area's largest landlord about their conditions. They were intercepted enroute by the landlord, John Drax, who promised to raise the labourers' wages to ten shillings per week and then led the crowd back to Bere Regis and treated them to beer at the public house.[2] Drax then stayed at the alehouse for the rest of the day and sent letters to all his tenant farmers to gather there so that they could publicly sign an agreement to raise their labourers' wages.

MAGISTRATE FRAMPTON

As a highly active magistrate and landowner, James Frampton of Moreton – Mary Frampton's brother, now 62 years old – was Dorset's most significant law and order figure. Frampton was always clear about the natural order and that people should know their place in the hierarchy – any dissent by the lower orders needed to be stamped upon by their betters. 'He was not, a popular man', said Dr Kevin Bawn, who added: 'In 1831 his manner towards the people was, described as "high and unbending" and he was a stickler, for deference, respect and the status quo.' Bawn continued, 'He would not be intimidated by mob violence, even though he was obliged to

---

2. Thomas Scriven, 'The Dorchester Labourers and Swing's Aftermath in Dorset, 1830–1838', *History Workshop Journal*, vol. 182 (2016), 6.

barricade his house "like an Irish mansion" and guard it with militia men.'[3]

Hearing of the first disturbances at Cranbourne Chase to the east, Frampton had ridden to the county town of Dorchester and sworn in some 200 special constables, mostly yeoman, burgesses and farmers. Drax's conduct particularly angered Frampton, and the magistrate rode to Bere Regis to confront him. Finding John Drax in the Bere Regis alehouse, Frampton tried to force Drax to raise some special constables and join him in putting down the local protests, but Drax refused. The following description is part of a letter from a Mr C.B. Wollaston, chairman of the appeal court (a relative of the Framptons) to Mr Okeden who presided at the criminal court:

Dorchester, Friday

I have now scarcely time to tell you that I arrived on Friday into this disturbed county and almost immediately set off for Moreton Hall, where Frampton was protecting his house against an intended attack from the inhabitants of Beer, of which he had had information - they having been exasperated against him personally, by his having gone there for the purpose of swearing in special constables and taking other means of protection - in opposition. I think they were encouraged by the defiant conduct of Mr. Drax, of which you will hear more.

Like Frampton, other local landowners[4] were extremely angry with John Drax for breaking ranks, one describing it as 'the most *defiant conduct* of Mr. Drax'.[5] James Frampton had a revealing confrontation with Drax, which Frampton later made a note of:

---

3. Kevin Bawn, 'Social Protest, Popular Disturbances and Public Order in Dorset, 1790–1838', PhD thesis, University of Reading, 1984, pp. 92–99.

4. Characterised by Baker as 'as heavily authoritarian and reactionary' in correspondence with author, 2 February 2022. See Leonard Baker, 'Spaces, Places, Custom and Protest in Rural Somerset and Dorset, c. 1780–1867', PhD thesis, University of Bristol, 2019.

5. Kerr, *Bound to the Soil*, p. 102.

we went to Mr Drax [in an alehouse in Bere Regis] to whom I was introduced & I hope I never shall see him again. - We told him our object & that we had spoken to the few persons we had met to desire them to come and be sworn. He said he had been to Shapwick this morning where Mr Portman had been & had promised the labourers ten shillings a week, for which he was angry as Mr Drax only meant to offer them nine shillings a week. We told him that we would never consent to make any promise to any persons who demanded an increase of Wages by a Mob. That they knew as Justices, we were always ready to listen to their complaints when they came quietly, but we would never grant anything to threats &c. He said he was not intimidated, never would be, & only granted this as their just due.

We tried to reason with him & to say that at least his granting this now would appear to them like having gained their point by this mode of assembling. He was all this time walking up & down the room talking like a madman & we were obliged to tell him our minds pretty strongly as to his misconduct & then called two respectable persons into the room & asked if they were ready to be sworn in. One of these spoke in favour of the labourers & thought they were right, &c, as their wages were too low. We said that was probably the case & as Justices we were ready at our meeting to listen to their complaints but never would when combined in a body this way. He seemed to decline being sworn & we asked the other man, & on his very naturally enquiring what particular duty would be required of him, Mr Drax said, 'To be knocked on the head to be sure'. On this the man of course declined, knowing his landlord's opinion, & we told Mr Drax that we would never suffer such language to be used to us, that the mischief would be incalculable, if he had said half as much in the street as he had been doing to us since we had been in the room & that as he was the means of preventing persons being sworn in to defend his & their property and, was determined to grant the Mob what they demanded, it was of no service to the County for us to remain there.[6]

---

6. DHC D124/242, Ilchester Papers, James Frampton, 25 November 1830. 'We' were Frampton and the Rev. George Pickard.

Whether it was Lord Portman of the Bryanston Estate or John Drax of Charborough who offered ten shillings a week first will probably never be known. Both were relatively popular with local people. The unilateral offers infuriated other neighbouring landowners as the agreed strategy for authorities in this region had been to break up Swing Riots by force and to deny all of their demands for increased wages.

Dr Bawn observed that this incident provides several insights, including Frampton's illiberal attitudes and Drax's arrogant independence.

It shows that something less than harmony prevailed, between the landowners, even in a small area; Drax's seat at Charborough was less than ten miles from Moreton, but the two men had never before met. It shows that there were difficulties in swearing in special constables, although it was almost unique for one of the propertied classes to be the cause of this. It shows that for all Frampton's criticisms Drax possessed a rapport with his tenants and labourers, even being prepared to 'meet them on their own territory, the alehouse at Bere', and being ready to raise their wages.[7]

NOVEMBER 1830

A letter, addressed to 'Mr Jas. Frampton, Moorton [*sic*] House' read as follows, in capital letters (with original spellings retained): 'AS YOU AND SEVERALL OTHER GENTLEMEN IN YOUR GREED SEEK THE RUIN OF HONEST MEN AND THE DEGRIDATION OF THERE FAMILYS BE SURE I WILL PAY YOU A VISIT WITH MY FRIENDS.' It was signed 'Captain Swing' and accompanied by drawings of a hanging figure, a skull and a flaming torch. Frampton was not to be discouraged by threats from 'Captain Swing'. He was determined to put down the protests using his own special constables and without Drax's support.

---

7.   Bawn, 'Social Protest', p. 93.

Frampton, writing to the Earl of Ilchester on the night of the 25th, stated his belief that the Bere Valley was now 'sound unless Tolpuddle being promised [higher wages] should make others discontented'.[8] Having visited Wareham and Dorchester on 26 and 27 November, he received word of a 'rising' at Winfrith on Monday 29th. The sources for the Winfrith incident are Frampton's own and his sister's.[9] Frampton prepared for a riot and assembled a force of 160 mounted and armed constables. James Frampton's sister recorded:

28th November – My brother, Mr. Frampton, was joined very early on that morning by a large body of farmers, &c., from his immediate neighbourhood, as well as some from a distance, all special constables, amounting to upwards of 150, armed only with a short staff, the pattern for which had been sent by order of Government to equip what was called the Constabulary force. The numbers increased as they rode on towards Winfrith, where the clergyman was unpopular, and his premises supposed to be in danger.

The mob, urged on from behind hedges, &c., by a number of women and children, advanced rather respectfully, and with their hats in their hands, to demand increase of wages, but would not listen to the request that they would disperse. The Riot Act was read. They still urged forwards and came close to Mr. Frampton's horse; he then collared one man, but in giving him in charge he slipped from his captors leaving his smock-frock in their hands. Another mob from Lulworth were said to be advancing, and as

---

8. Carl J. Griffin, 'The Culture of Combination: Solidarities and Collective Action before Tolpuddle', *Historical Journal*, vol. 58, no. 2 (2015), 443–480.

9. There are no surviving eyewitness accounts from within 'the mob' at any of the Dorset protests and virtually none from any participant except those given in evidence in court. One exception was rediscovered by Jo Draper for the *Proceedings of the Dorset Natural History and Archaeological Society* (vol. 124 [2002], 21–34) and was taken from the article that was printed in the *Dorset County Chronicle* on 10 December 1874: it records the memories of Mr Ward, who took part in protests at Woolland near Sherborne, of which he spoke. He refers to five men from his village who were transported for their part in the protests.

the first mob seemed to have dispersed, Mr. F. was going, almost alone, to speak to them, when he was cautioned to beware, as the others had- retreated only to advance again with more effect in the rear. The whole body of the constabulary then advanced with Mr. Frampton, and, after an ineffectual parley, charged them, when three men were taken, and were conveyed by my brother and his son Henry, and a part of the constabulary force, to Dorchester, and committed to gaol. I was at Moreton that day with Lady Harriot F.[10]

We know that two of the Loveless brothers, later of the Tolpuddle martyrs, were involved in the Swing protests. One was arrested but managed to escape.[11] The Captain Swing protests and attacks did not finish for some weeks. Bawn made the point: 'The proof of a pudding is in the eating': there were no Swing activities on Drax's Estate, and only two were recorded at Bere after the Frampton–Drax confrontation.[12] The *Dorset County Chronicle* reported that on 9 December there were fires set at Mr Alner's farm, near Bere Regis. However,

After the middle of December, there were very few tumultuous assemblies, but the incendiarism lingered on during the winter. At Mr Baker's farm at Bradford Abbas, near Sherborne, the corn stacks were fired, and there were also fires at Buckhorn Weston, and at Bere Regis. For the discovery of the Bere Regis fire, Mr Drax offered a reward of £100, besides the £500 offered by the Government.

RETRIBUTION

Special courts dealt with hundreds of labourers arrested during the disturbances. Many were sentenced to hang but most avoided exe-

---

10. Mundy, *Journal of Mary Frampton*, pp. 361–362.
11. 'Griffin, 'Culture of Combination', p. 462.
12. Bawn, 'Social Protest', p. 93.

cution, being transported to Australia instead. By the end of the month, Mary Frampton noted in her journal for 26 January:

> The last part of this month was passed tranquilly in Dorsetshire, if there were any discontents, they were only whispered, and no fires which could be traced as the act of incendiaries took place, and in general through-out the kingdom the state of the counties was less disturbed.
>
> Parliament opened on the 3rd February with intense anxiety of all ranks and parties as to the reform in Parliament promised by the Government, and with all Europe in a state of ferment. One of the motions made by Mr. Hunt on the first day of his appearance in the House of Commons, was for a petition to the King, to pardon all the unhappy men who had been convicted at the Special Assizes. Fortunately, however, as they were already on board the Transports, and the wind fair, the petition would be too late.[13]

With the threat passed, many tenant farmers gradually cut pay again and the poverty faced by rural communities became even deeper. Another magistrate, Rev. Henry Yeatman, who was a little more liberal than Frampton, wrote at the time that although 'several gentlemen in this county made promises to the lower orders' of an increase of wages 'from 4s and 6s to the height of 10s and 12s per week', this promise, 'now that the alarm and terror of the moment have subsided, has been broken in a manner the most treacherous and dishonourable'.[14]

Given that conditions did not improve, it is a wonder that there were no further protests. But the deterrents included the harsh punishments for those who took part in the Captain Swing protests. With magistrates like Frampton, Yeatman and like-minded others, protestors were very unlikely to get a sympathetic hearing at the Quarter Sessions. The question of whether John Drax reduced the

---

13. Mundy, *Journal of Mary Frampton*, p. 370.
14. Scriven, 'Dorchester Labourers', p. 7.

rent of his tenant farmers when he ordered them to pay higher wages is unanswered.

TOLPUDDLE

It was less than four years later that a group of men of Tolpuddle reacted in a much more peaceable way and yet achieved so much more in the long run, despite their severe punishment. By 1780, Tolpuddle consisted of numerous smaller farms, each employing a small number of labourers. In 1781, it was decided that there would be a village meeting each year where a delegation of labourers and the local farmers would agree to the entire parishes' wages. The local vicar, Dr Bernard Hodges, mediated these harvest meetings between 1784 and 1806, commenting that the labourers often demanded a 'fair wage, equal to their fellows in the neighbouring villages'.[15]

The Tolpuddle Martyrs were six agricultural labourers convicted of swearing a secret oath, prosecuted by James Frampton in 1834 and transported to Australia. The Tolpuddle men joined a union because in the years following Captain Swing wages fell back. Barbara Kerr's take on Captain Swing was that, after the Draxes displaced the Turbervilles, lesser gentry like the Ekins and Williams families were swept aside by efficient, progressive farmers like the Scutts.

Yet when in the winter of 1830 the ricks were burned at Bere the incendiaries, not the Scutts, were proscribed as revolutionaries. But these poverty-stricken labourers were endeavouring, no less than Metternich and the chancelleries of Europe, to hold back the forces of change so as to maintain in society the place which they believed was theirs by tradition and right.[16]

---

15. Parish Ephemera, DHC, PE-TOL/IN/3/1, ff. 18–25; 'Notes of Bernard Hodges Concerning the Vicarage of Tolpuddle with a Survey, 1784–1806', Tolpuddle Parish Ephemera, DHC, PE-TOL/IN/3/2, ff. 5-7.
16. Kerr, *Bound to the Soil*, p. 124.

The Martyrs' story has been much told and will not be repeated here except to note the close proximity of Charborough. While Tolpuddle is seen as a beacon of trade union protest, little attention has been paid to why there was no more social protest in Dorset, given the poor conditions of agricultural workers and their families. As Dr Bawn noted, most social protest history has been written by historians of the left in whose interest it is to find some sort of class conflict. 'Many of their findings are both valuable and incontrovertible; the "moral economy" of rioters, the practical knowledge of the law among ordinary labourers, the underground tradition of the 1790s, in northern England.' However, Dr Bawn observed that the difficulty is that any historian of social protest and, to some extent, popular disturbance, must have latent working-class solidarity as their starting point and expect to find endemic protest.

> The available data tend to support such work as has been done on certain regions, compared to the industrial areas, which spawned not only Luddites and Chartists but also revolutionaries. Dorset was untroubled, compared to the more agricultural counties of East Anglia Dorset was calmer. It will also be seen that the Swing disturbances left the county comparatively undisturbed.

Dr Bawn argued that the comparative absence of protest in Dorset was the result of local social and economic factors including the character and calibre of the gentry who dominated society.[17] This may explain why aside from Captain Swing and Tolpuddle, which were still geographically confined, Dorset agricultural workers were so hesitant to mass protest about their conditions as the odds were stacked in favour of the employers. Puritanism and Methodism would also have played a part. Lack of education for all but the gentry is another factor. But the risk of imprisonment was high, which in itself impacted on the individual's employability. Blacklisting union activists is not a recent phenomenon. The workforce

---

17.   Bawn, 'Social Protest', pp. 6–7.

could not just go elsewhere to work. The ordinary labourer could not just leave their village without the risk of being jailed for vagrancy.

The obvious conclusion would be that the Dorset landowners, often with unusually large estates, exerted tight control on the populace through extensive tenant farming, livings for the local vicars, employment, charity and accommodation. The control of the 'natural order' was aided by the landowners also being MPs, magistrates, sheriffs, military and militia commanders where the workforce was less rebellious than in other counties. During the 1830s, John Drax played a more subtle hand than Frampton. In facing a mass protest, he defused the situation, diverted costs to tenants, and then played a waiting game to allow wages to be reduced when further protest was unlikely. Frampton's authoritarian style has left him on the wrong side of history. But John Sawbridge Drax's name would, in the longer term, be an embarrassment to his family, too. If John Drax's demeanour seemed benign it was to gradually change over the course of his long tenure at Charborough. According to Barbara Kerr, 'The ground had been prepared for John Sawbridge's long career as an active, despotic and improving landlord.'[18]

The documentary record over many years suggests that John Drax was a disputatious and litigious individual. As early as 1830, the long-standing Charborough neighbours, the Trenchards, looked to arbitration after they claimed that the Charborough Estate had encroached on their boundaries at Tomson Farm. He and Sarah Frances fell out with his wife's Grosvenor uncles and took them to court in Grosvenor v. Drax about 'excessive' payments for the 'lunatic' Richard Grosvenor Erle-Drax's care. They also tried to seize land from General Grosvenor over land in Somerset and Suffolk whom he claimed was his wife's. At home, John Drax was to keep his bread and circuses rolling for some years but gradually became more obsessed with hunting and horse racing and all their associated feasting and drinking.

---

18. Kerr, *Bound to the Soil*, p. 128.

18
The Squire Goes A-Hunting

Squire John Drax was taken with some liberal causes in his younger days. The abiding issue of the May 1831 election was reform – the extension of enfranchisement to a wider group of men rather than just property owners.[1] Nationally, those who had acquired property and the power that came with it were not prepared to give up their dominant position. Early in the year, as the Captain Swing protests abated, various landowners and gentry in the counties were invited to raise a troop of yeomen to help preserve law and order. Despite being a reformer, he as a major landowner was expected to form a militia unit in case unrest returned. Drax's troop consisted of three officers and 50 troopers mostly from the Charborough Estate. Described as 'the ardent reformer of Wareham', he mustered, on 6 May 1831, his troop of local freeholders on horseback to ride to the hustings.

As the result of the large attendance at the nomination meeting for the Dorset vote, it was adjourned from the County Hall in Dorchester to nearby Poundbury. Fourteen thousand people descended upon the hustings in the ancient hill fort, mostly men 'eager for the fray'. While most were without a vote, they could influence the vote by the strength of their responses to the candidates. Pro-reform Lord Portman of Bryanston, proposed by J.J. Farquharson and Parry Okeden, declared that he stood alone as a reformer and attempted to call the crowd to order.[2] 'The Proper Humbug', Tory Sir Henry Bankes, of Kingston Lacey,[3] nominated

---

1. Just men, not women.

2. Edward Berkeley II, Lord Portman was married to Emma, the daughter of Henry Lascelles who was the largest British plantation owner and had received £26,000 in compensation after the abolition of slavery for releasing more than 1000 enslaved people.

3. Bankes had married Frances in 1784, who was daughter of William Woodley, who owned a plantation on St Kitts. She brought a £6000 dowry and plantations

by James Frampton of Moreton and William Hanham of High Hall, attempted to hold his ground against the weight of reform sentiment but was 'instantly assailed by the most appalling and discordant noises... the mob were determined that he should not be heard'.[4] This did not go unanswered by Bankes' supporters and so clashes ensued between 'Bankes' men', mostly from the isle of Portland, and groups of reformers from Poole and Wareham.

> About one hundred ruffians, who had entered the field armed with missiles and staves, attacked the freeholders, who were unarmed, and beat them in a most inhuman manner; at length the freeholders made a most determined rush, wrested the bludgeons from them, tore Mr Bankes' standard into shreds, and, with a cheer, drove these miscreants over the great extent of the field.[5]

Amongst those who resisted Bankes' bludgeon men were the mounted troopers of the Drax's Yeomanry Cavalry and 'who was himself on the hustings encouraging them and urging them forward by language and by signals'. Another pro-reform candidate, John Calcraft, complained at being left unheard and condemned the violence. Although Drax was censured for his part in the proceedings, it was popularly perceived that it was Bankes' hired thugs who were roundly blamed for the trouble.[6] *The Times* attacked Bankes' campaign, commented that 'we will do that credit to his sagacity to observe, that he very soon knew the county, as well as it knew him'. Dr Kevin Bawn said of Drax's response to the Captain Swing protests and the anti-reformists:

> This divide between Drax and his fellow landowners showed itself again during an Election Riot in 1831. When violence broke

---

to the family. Their son William Henry Bankes MP applied for compensation on abolition as a trustee.

4. *Dorset County Chronicle*, 12 May 1831.
5. *Sherborne Mercury*, 9 May 1831.
6. www.historyofparliamentonline.org/volume/1820-1832/constituencies/dorset, last accessed 14 June 2024.

out during the hustings in Dorchester, Drax used his 'company' of Yeomanry Cavalry to drive the Tory supporters and candidate from the field.[7]

The contest resumed on Tuesday 10 May 1831, but this time the occupants of the wagons from Bere and most towns and villages raised their hands and cheered Portman and Calcraft. Unable to speak without being harassed and with his supporters chased from the field, Bankes withdrew from the contest which allowed Dorset to elect two Whig candidates for the first time in its political history.[8]

1831 BY-ELECTION

The coronation of William IV and Queen Adelaide took place on 8 September 1831, and the bells of Bere and 'every parish church in Dorsetshire rang out merry and joyous peals'. Then, four days later, came 'the astounding news' that the MP for Dorset, John Calcraft of Rempstone (the illegitimate son of John Calcraft who had made his fortune as the paymaster of the forces), had slit his own throat 'in a fit of temporary insanity' and put an end to his life at his London residence. Calcraft had suffered bouts of depression since changing sides to support the Reform Bill and faced substantial bills for election expenses.

William Ponsonby of Canford House stood in his place in order to vote for the third reading of the Reform Bill but found himself facing a titled anti-reformer. It was a battle of the rival houses of Canford and St Giles, and the anti-reform candidate, the Honourable Anthony Ashley Cooper, later the 7th Earl of Shaftesbury (1801–1885). Elections in the nineteenth century were robust affairs because candidates with their tied people were expected to make an exhibition. Candidates would bribe supporters with free beer, and unsurprisingly these events were often marred with violence.

7. Bawn, 'Social Protest'.
8. www.historyofparliamentonline.org/volume/1820-1832/constituencies/dorset.

THE SQUIRE GOES A-HUNTING

John Drax was heavily involved, and in the heat of the election campaign, various pamphlets were posted showing he had not, as Ashley's election team were claiming, changed sides:

To the Freeholders of the County of Dorset

Brother freeholders

I have learnt with the greatest of surprise and indignation that the Agents of Lord Ashley and others have taken upon themselves to assert that I had changed my opinions on the subject of the Reform Measure and further that I had given my interest to His Lordship.

I therefore consider myself called upon this publicly to contract to, and in doing so, I cannot give a better proof, than in stating, that this day gave Vote for MR PONSONBY.

I cannot reconcile the idea of changing one's political opinions as one would an Old Coat.

Possessing large Landed Estates, I should be the last Man to advocate the 'Reform Measure' did I not know that it is greatly in favour of the Agricultural Interest; and that the plea of the Anti-Reformers that the 'Reform Bill is opposed that Interest' is not founded in fact.

I do hope and trust that all those who, on the occasion of the late Election gave their Votes in support of the REFORM CANDIDATES will continue true to the Cause.

Brother Freeholders

I remain with great respect

Your obedient humble Servant

J S W S Erle Drax

Charborough Park, 1st October 1831

Then, in reply, Ashley Cooper's supporters said:

LORD ASHLEY's Committee have authority to state, that in an interview which Lord Ashley had at Charborough Park, on Friday 30th Mr Drax stated to him that he would not exert himself in opposition to his Lordship, and that Lord Ashley or any other Person, was perfectly at liberty to Canvass his Tenantry.

The votes in this closely fought contest swayed between them for 15 days before settling at a majority for the declaration (Lord Ashley, 1,847; Mr Ponsonby, 1,811). Riots followed across eastern parts of the county, including Blandford and Poole, where the King William public house at Parkstone Cross was wrecked to shouts of 'Ponsonby for ever'.

THE 1832 ELECTION

In the 1832 election for Wareham, Drax was a pro-reform candidate against John Hales Calcraft (the legitimate son of John Calcraft the elder). *The Examiner* of December 1832 gave a graphic account:

Wareham 11th December. The Reformers have been defeated here by a majority of 35, after almost incredible exertion. The means by which the Tories have achieved their triumph are all their own. Perjury of the blackest hue, threats and intimidation of the most paltry kind have been employed for this once with success. We do not mean to charge Mr Calcraft with these things, but his friends have done it. The rotten borough or Corfe has been our ruin. Only one man of all its constituents (nearly 80) voted for Drax and reform. The smiles and frowns of the Bonds, Bankeses, Eldons etc induced to vote for Mr. Calcraft. Why did the Ministers tie the dead carcass to the living body? In Wareham (old Borough) Mr Drax had a majority of one, although Mr Calcraft owns 5/6th of the property of in the town and Mr Drax not one inch. This is a pretty strong symptom. Mr Drax has resolved to petition the House of Commons forthwith and a beautiful exhibition of truth, purity and patriotism will then be developed.[9]

---

9. 'Arguments for the Ballot', *The Examiner*, 23 December 1832, p. 1299; *British Periodicals*, p. 823.

Drax was to lose again at the 1835 election but would have better luck in later years.

HUNTING

Losing an election had one benefit for Drax because, of all his activities, what really excited him was hunting. He took the view that to be a great huntsman was the epitome of what the landed gentry should excel in. Charborough was great hunting country, and under his stewardship, a lot of effort went into extending it. We get a thumbnail sketch of him in one of the sporting magazines that flourished in the nineteenth century. On a hunting day in 1835:

> A little before twelve Mr. Drax made his appearance on his coverhack. He is tall (about six feet high) and thin, rides rather short, with a very graceful seat, and when he has a mind, can go along with the best of them, but generally takes a line of his own. In his appointments, he is one of the neatest men in England.[10]

Hunting in England was for the wealthy. As Professor Henry French noted in his paper about nearby Sturminster Marshall and successive Game Laws from 1671:

> So, hunting was restricted to people who possessed rights, privileges or titles that placed them among the ruling elite of the country.
>
> While there were lots of different forms of land tenure by the eighteenth century, and it was rare for a manorial lord to own outright all the land that comprised the manor, this right of access harked back to a time when lords *were* masters of all they surveyed, and it was guarded relatively jealously.[11]

---

10. Yorkshireman, 'The Rambler', *A New Sporting Magazine*, August 1835, pp. 9, 52; *British Periodicals*, p. 238 (BL).
11. French, 'Field, Fen and Family', p. 2.

DRAX OF DRAX HALL

To be able to hunt, you had to have legal access to swathes of land. Enclosure had worked for the landlords. The lord of the manor of Sturminster Marshall, John Trenchard, had the right to ride or walk over the land of everyone in the manor in pursuit of game and nobody had the power to stop him. Likewise, the whole landscape of east Dorset was modelled so that hunting could be enjoyed by John Drax and his friends and followers. The agricultural historian Barbara Kerr noted that if John Drax omitted engrossing from his calendar of landowners' duties, he gave particular attention to fashioning the countryside in the interests of foxhunting. Kerr reported that if tenants of newly enclosed downland, where numbers of furze covers were planted, grumbled about the 'scores of foxes' Drax was turning down, saddlers welcomed his enthusiasm for building the area around Bere into one of the most notable hunting districts in the county. 'In 1841 the Shaves, father and son, had the monopoly of saddle and harness making and in ten years they were only joined by one newcomer.' The Shaves became wealthy and went from owning two acres to 100 acres and stayed in the area until the 1960s.[12] Hunting was the pleasure of the royals, aristocracy and landed gentry and whichever others they deigned to allow.

The enclosures had removed the ability to take food sources like rabbits from the land without the permission of the landowners. All other hunting as practised by the lower classes and non-landed was called poaching, and at this period it was possible to be transported for taking rabbits on local land. Nevertheless, correctly engaging in hunting with its skills, etiquette and finery was a mark of the elite. In his history, Admiral Drax noted that John Drax was a peculiar man and on one occasion acquired some wild boars and released them at Charborough. He imitated the French and intended to hunt them. However, the boars attacked a park-keeper and gouged his horse, so he removed the tusked creatures from the estate.

Alongside his passion for hunting, John Drax liked a horse race, especially if his horse won. The Charborough Races held annually from 1832 for some years. Squire Drax would lay out a point-to-

---

12. Kerr, *Bound to the Soil*, p. 133.

THE SQUIRE GOES A-HUNTING

point course in the 1000-acre deer park as part of these races.[13] The *New Sporting Magazine* of 1840 gave a detailed account of the day:

> The park gates were at an early hour thrown open to the public, who taking advantage of a very fine morning, and encouraged by the pleasing collection of the last year's amusements, and the increasing popularity of Esquire Drax, now the high sheriff for the county of Dorset, had shortened the morning nap, and in large numbers poured in from all directions to evince their gratitude and high esteem, to enjoy the rustic pleasures of a country race, and partake of the well-known hospitalities of Charborough.
>
> Soon after one o'clock, the horses intended to run for the Yeomanry Cup were exhibited before the stand, four only in number; and there also appeared three only for the Hunters' Cup – one-mile heats – Crazy Jane took the lead each heat and kept it without difficulty, winning easy.

The report further reported that at two o'clock, some 140 of the elite spectators were invited to enter the mansion and partake of an elegant lunch laid out in the library. 'It is almost needless to say, that here was displayed that taste and truly hospitable and liberal feeling not to be surpassed, and but by very few equalled.' The reporter noted that every delicacy of the season was here provided in costly abundance; game, fruits and wines of the most delicate description being in such profusion, and of such quality, as to elicit universal approbation.

Drax was soon in a dispute with his influential neighbour, J.J. Farquharson of Blandford, over the rights to hunt across east Dorset, a dispute that would last years and would have been worthy of a Dickens novel. In 1848 the dispute was reported in the pages of *Acteon*, a sporting monthly magazine, and their correspondent clearly viewed the whole thing as a waste of everyone's time.[14]

---

13. Drax kept a herd of 180 deer for hunting.
14. Farquharson's Eastbury and Langton Estates in Dorset covered nearly 12,000 acres.

In speaking of the Charbro' country, it is by no means my intention or wish to enter any further into the merits of this unfortunate misunderstanding, but I really think that everyone who loves fox-hunting would rejoice to see the quarrel made up, and that sufficient country be given up to Mr. Drax to enable him to hunt with more regularity two and three days a week round that district which is now so seldom enlivened by the melodious music of a pack of hounds.

For the last few seasons Mr. Drax, whose health has not been the stoutest, has not been quite so regular an attendant upon his pack as he had hitherto been; still the turn-out is capital to this day, and distant indeed may the time be when the old yellow plus coats and black collars shall cease to adorn the huntsman and two whippers-in of the Charbro' hound.[15]

As the years went by, Drax suffered from ill health and ceased riding with hounds and the more vigorous forms of hunting. By the 1860s, all he was really able to do was shoot. As late as 1864 John Drax was still enclosing land near the park. Hutchins stated that digging in the enclosing fence posts, Drax's workers revealed a score or so of Anglo-Saxon burials.[16]

FRESH LEAVES AND PASTURES

One of the most detailed accounts of John Drax came in *Fresh Leaves and Pastures* by Jane Panton. She was born as Jane Ellen Frith in Regent's Park in 1847. Her father, William Powell Frith, was a successful painter, of the popular print 'Derby Day'. She married James Panton and lived near Wareham for many years. It is the goings-on around Wareham over time which featured in her memoir of 1909.

In *Fresh Leaves and Pastures*, Jane Panton tells of a shooting visit to the farm she was living at as a young woman in 1868. The squire is John Drax:

---

15. 'A Peep at the Provinces; or, the Crack Packs of England under Review', *Actaeon New Sporting Magazine*, March 1848; *British Periodicals*, p. 167.
16. Hutchins, *History of Dorset*.

THE SQUIRE GOES A-HUNTING

I shall never forget one day when the tenant of the 'North Farm' received the usual lordly intimation that his particular owner was coming to shoot and would require what he called luncheon prepared for him after the day's sport was over: that is to say, about half-past four. We knew of the proposed invasion only the afternoon of the day before, as if too much notice were given, the farmer might hide anything he did not wish the Squire to see. He might also in some mysterious manner import birds if he had surreptitiously killed those on his own land.

In consequence, when the imperative command to be ready for the Squire arrived, we were one and all pressed into the service. Plate was got out; old cut glass rubbed and polished until it shone again; the kitchen and dining-room were cleaned and furbished up... I verily believe that 'Little Auntie' and her two maids sat up all night to concoct that luncheon, for savoury smells pervaded the house all through the hours of darkness; and early as the household always was in the morning, the members thereof were up and about before 4 a.m. I could hear the stir and bustle, and solemnly cursed the Squire for causing my slumbers to be broken in on by the noise of clinking pails and stamping horses, while the labourers who were to act as beaters had to get through their day's work in the dark before the shooting began.

In those days I had never seen the Squire, and I was very anxious to do so, but I was told I was on no account to be visible, and that I must watch for him out of my window if I wished to look at him. The pretty farm servant was also sent home for the day and only the elderly cook and the aunt were hovering about when the party was due. It was one of the extraordinary habits of this special Squire that he turned night into day and day into night, and he only rose during the hours of light when sport was on hand.

He had already given up the hounds, but he still shot occasionally; and I was greatly surprised to find that he started to shoot between one and two, thus giving himself barely two hours sport, on that farm at any rate. Mr. R. waited about from 11 to 1.30, getting more angry as every hour went by; finally, we snatched

285

a meal standing round the kitchen table, and while doing so, a mounted messenger came up. 'The Squire and his friends were in the upper fields; please come at once and see that all was correct.' If the farmer had been the Squire's bond-slave he could not have been treated in a less courteous manner; but he could only clap on his hat, grasp his stick – he was not allowed to shoot, not he! – and, calling the men together, went off at once, when we proceeded to look to the so-called luncheon, which was more like an elaborate dinner than anything else.

It was quite dark when the sportsmen came to the house. I rushed up to my room, and, leaving the door open, heard all that was going on. The Squire fell over the doormat and uttered his usual volley of curses. One of his boon companions, already 'half seas over,' swaggered into the dining-room with his hat on, which presently he removed and gave to the farmer's wife, with strict injunctions to put it down by the fire and keep it warm, so that he should not take cold when he replaced it on his head. Yet a third was singing at the top of his voice; and all pushed and struggled into the dining-room, demanding to have their boots removed, without the smallest regard to their hostess' very good carpet and most immaculate chairs. Not one word of this shooting party is exaggerated.

I, moreover, heard the Squire remark that Mr. R. must be making a d---d good thing out of farming to be able to give him such a spread and such wine; and he departed with his charming following, whooping and shouting down the lane, leaving a couple of rabbits and a hare behind him, and doing that in a manner that made me long to throw them after him as he turned out of the Barton into the long dark lane. Yet Mr. R. had no lease of his farm – only a yearly tenancy: farms were then much sought after. Anything like independence of manner would have meant 'the sack', and Mr. R., who was by birth a Dissenter and a very strong Radical, formed one of the Squire's train at election time and voted blue, though his conscience was as pink as his cheeks when he had to go into the polling booth and record his vote for a man he not only hated, but despised. I recollect a sort of 'party'.

John Drax was certainly a complex personality with some profoundly unpleasant traits, entitlement being just one, and as the following chapter indicates, throughout his years at Charborough, he was a forceful and increasing malign presence.

19
Abolition and Compensation

In 1833 the Drax Hall plantation had 189 enslaved people working on what was, by Barbados plantation standards, one of the biggest on the island with nearly 1000 acres. For more than two centuries, Britain had been heavily involved in enslaving captive Africans and their descendants to work on plantations in the colonies. The trade in enslaved people from Africa and elsewhere was abolished in 1807, but the full abolition of slavery did not follow for another generation. Drax Hall had partially maintained an enslaved workforce by paying enslaved women to have children and by purchasing within Barbados. It is also likely that some African captives were smuggled into Barbados. It had continued to be run by attorneys and overseers. The author of *The Interest*, Michael Taylor, noted that the post-1807 second phase of the abolition campaign was long and as hard fought as the first. 'And when a renewed abolitionist campaign was mounted, making slave ownership the defining political and moral issue of the day, emancipation was fiercely resisted by the powerful "West India Interest"'.[1]

From Dorset emerged some of the people who were to be key figures of the abolition campaign supporting William Wilberforce MP. Wilberforce spent time in Dorset and visited campaigner Robert Wedderburn in Dorchester gaol in 1819. Wedderburn was the mixed-race son of James Wedderburn, a Scottish plantation owner, and his mother, who was enslaved. His mother had agreed to be sold if her son was freed. He was released and became a sailor and came to England. In a pamphlet, he asked whether an enslaved person had the right to kill their master. For his writings, he was jailed for sedition and blasphemy. Thomas Clarkson set up

---

1. Taylor, *The Interest*, cover.

an anti-slavery committee in Poole (five miles from Charborough) and spent time with anti-slavery campaigners in west Dorset.

One of the most significant abolitionists was to be Sir Thomas Fowell Buxton. He was the MP for Weymouth for 19 years and lived just outside of the town at Wyke Regis.[2] He helped to launch the British and Foreign Anti-Slavery Society (later the Anti-Slavery Society). In May 1823, Buxton introduced in the House of Commons a resolution condemning the state of slavery as 'repugnant to the principles of the British constitution and of the Christian religion' and called for its gradual abolition throughout the British colonies. He also pressured the government to send dispatches to the colonies telling plantation owners to improve the treatment of enslaved people.

In the wake of Buxton's 1823 parliamentary statement, the pro-slavery lobby realised they were losing the battle for the hearts and minds of the British public. The most powerful of the anti-abolition groups, The Society of West India Planters and Merchants, restructured itself, created a propaganda wing and became a more formally organised lobby.[3] In Parliament, the powerful West India interest, a group of around 80 MPs who had ties to Caribbean slavery, were joined by an additional group of some ten MPs who did not possess enslaved people themselves but still opposed any proposal to tamper with slave-owners' right to 'property'. The faction presented 'compensated emancipation', or the payment of money to slave-owners at abolition, to uphold property rights.

In the same year, Wilberforce published his 'Appeal to Religion, Justice, and Humanity of the Inhabitants of the British Empire on Behalf of the Negro Slaves in the West Indies', which claimed that the moral and spiritual condition of the enslaved people stemmed from their slavery and was not innate. Wilberforce argued the total emancipation of the enslaved was not only morally and ethically justified but also a matter of national duty before God. The

---

2. Weymouth features a statue of Buxton.

3. David Ryden, 'The Society of West India Planters and Merchants in the Age of Emancipation, c.1816–35', Economic History Society Annual Conference, 27–29 March 2015, p. 13.

campaign for abolition was making ground. It would, however, take another decade before the abolitionists won. At no point is there any evidence that the Drax family of the period did anything but support the continuing abuse of enslaved people. They were not dependent on the income, as much came from the English estates, but it was the financial icing on the family cake.

BARBADOS

Between 1825 and 1834, the Drax Hall plantation in Barbados produced an average of 163 metric tons of sugar and 4845 gallons of rum per year, which gave the family an annual net profit of £3591.[4] In today's terms, using the usual calculations, that would be a net profit of something in the region of £420,000 a year, though in effect it would be a great deal more. It was still proportionately less than it had been in the past.

As noted in Chapter 14, the voices of the enslaved were rarely heard, and it was not until 1831 that the first account of the life of a black enslaved woman from the West Indies was published in Britain, *The History of Mary Prince*. Mary Prince had been born enslaved in Bermuda, and her first-hand description of the brutality she had experienced greatly impacted the case for abolition. After passing through the hands of a succession of brutal owners, she eventually made her way to London as a servant. The autobiography was reprinted twice in its first year. Mary Prince became an important figure in the abolition movement.

Fowell Buxton's daughter, Priscilla, also became an important figure in the last wave of the abolition campaign against slavery. Early on, she was her father's special assistant in his campaigning for abolition. However, she increasingly became a force in her own right. In 1832, Priscilla Buxton (by now married and Priscilla Johnston) became the co-secretary of the London Female

---

4. Kathleen B. Butler, *The Economics of Emancipation: Jamica and Barbados, 1823–1843* (Chapel Hill, NC: The University of North Carolina Press, 1995), p. 56. See also TNA T71/557. Drax Hall Ledger, 1825–41, fols 30, 35, 82, 106, Z9/2/6.

Anti-Slavery Society. She was a lead organiser in a petition for the abolition of slavery, which was signed by 187,000 people. The petition took two people to carry it; it was the largest ever raised for abolition. The campaign was won that next year as public pressure and a deal with enslavers for compensation saw slavery banned.

In May 1833, John Hales Calcraft the Conservative MP for Wareham, presented to the House of Commons a petition from the inhabitants of the town praying for the abolition of colonial slavery.[5] Two months earlier, the correspondent Anti-Humbug had noted that 'The United Freeman's Society for the Old and New Borough of Wareham' had been inaugurated. Its objectives included securing a liberal and reforming candidate for the borough and to procure the abolition of slavery. The president was named as John Drax and his close colleague, John Brown, as vice president. Anti-Humbug did not think much of the society's membership and imagined meetings 'redolent with tobacco fume and at a table clammy with its swipy dregs'.[6]

ABOLITION

The Slavery Abolition Act of 1833 received royal assent in August 1833 and provided for the gradual abolition of slavery in most parts of the British Empire. At the time, no Drax family member was elected to Parliament, so they were not involved in the vote. Earl Grey's reforming Whig administration passed this Act. It expanded the jurisdiction of the Slave Trade Act of 1807. It made the purchase or ownership of enslaved people illegal within the British Empire, with the exception of 'the Territories in the Possession of the East India Company, Ceylon [now Sri Lanka], and Saint Helena'. At the time slavery was abolished, William IV was the reigning monarch, but he had always been ardently against abolition. Before becoming king, he held the title Duke of Clarence and spent time in the Caribbean, where he befriended plantation owners and boasted of con-

---

5. *Dorset County Chronicle*, 2 May 1833.
6. *Dorset County Chronicle*, 21 March 1833.

tracting a sexual disease. He made speeches in the Lords to defend slavery, arguing that it was vital to economic prosperity. He also argued that enslaved people were 'comparatively in a state of humble happiness'.[7] To achieve abolition the abolitionists had to bow to the idea that the enslaved were personal property. Throughout their campaigns the abolitionists emphasised that enslaved people were humans, not property. But to get slave owners to agree to emancipation, the deal was that they were compensated as though the enslaved were just chattels like land, property and livestock. The deeply embedded legal notion was that if you took another person's chattels you had to pay compensation.[8]

To abolish slavery Britain used the equivalent of 40 per cent of its annual national budget, which was £20 million to buy freedom for all enslaved people in the Empire at the expense of the British taxpayer.[9] Over 40,000 compensation awards were paid directly to 3000 families, but nothing was handed to the people who had been enslaved. To fund this, the British government took on a £15 million loan, agreed on 3 August 1835, with banker Nathan Mayer Rothschild and his brother-in-law, Moses Montefiore.[10] Some 800,000 enslaved people were manumitted across the plantations of the British Empire. According to the 1938 thesis on capitalism and slavery by Eric Williams – then an Oxford University scholar who would later become the first prime minister of Trinidad and Tobago – the abolition of slavery was fuelled not by Britain's newly discovered moral conscience but by its economic self-interest.[11] Certainly, many planters and plantations were carrying heavy debt burdens and the decline in sugar prices left little room for profit. These

---

7. David Conn, 'The British Kings and Queens Who Supported and Profited from Slavery', *The Guardian*, 6 April 2023.
8. This is a point made by David Olusoga in *Britain's Forgotten Slave Owners*, BBC TV, 2015.
9. What this is worth in modern terms is debatable. The usual figure is £1.3 billion, but in reality, it was a far greater part of the economy.
10. It is widely believed that the British government did not complete payments until 2015, but this is contested as it is to do with a technicality of government gilts and their repayment period.
11. Eric Williams, *Capitalism and Slavery* (London: Andre Deutsch, 1944).

planters were grateful to get back some money when compensation was offered for releasing their slaves.[12]

People who gave their primary address in Dorset made 53 claims for compensation for losing their enslaved people; 42 were successful. They include names such as Frampton, Brooke, Glover, Rev. William Butler, Frome, Barclay, Gordon and Drake. Their plantations were in Jamaica, Barbados, Nevis, British Guiana, St Vincent, Trinidad, Tobago and Antigua.[13]

The records list that John Drax claimed 'in the right of his wife' for enslaved persons at Drax Hall and was registered as claim number 3784 by his attorney Forster Clarke, who had been involved with the plantation since as early as 1803. The Drax family received £4293 in compensation for those 189 enslaved people. Having gone through the records of that period, Dr Butler was able to tell me that, unlike many of the planters, Drax Hall was not burdened with debt from merchants or the City of London.

APPRENTICES

In most cases, the enslaved people did not immediately get freed. When they did, they faced the problem of employment. Technically freed, the enslaved were compelled to work in unfreedom, without pay and under the constant threat of punishment as 'apprentices'. Then Barbados, as with other colonies, improvised a new way of working that was not too different from what went before, except that workers were now paid – a pittance. Some former slaves refused to work and just led a subsistence life. In many ways, the 'apprenticeship' years were more brutal than what had preceded them. When it came to punishing former slaves for perceived misdeeds, this moved from individual slave-owners to officers of the state. Publicly funded police, jailers and enforcers were hired in Britain and sent to the colonies. If apprentices were too slow in cutting cane, or other duties, or took time off, their white overseers could

---

12. Butler, *Economics of Emancipation*, p. xvi.

13. www.bridportmuseum.co.uk/wp-content/uploads/2017/05/Local-connections-with-slavery-vo.6.pdf, last accessed 1 July 2024.

have them punished by stipendiary magistrates. Punishments were meted out according to a formula, and often involving the tread-mill commonly used in the workhouses of England. Apprentices accused of laziness – what slave-owners called the 'negro disease' – were hung by their hands from a plank and forced to 'dance' the treadmill barefoot, often for hours. One apprentice, James Williams, in an account of his life published in 1837, recalled he was punished much more after 1834 than before.[14]

Post-emancipation Drax Hall plantation continued to send profits produced by its apprentices back to its absentee owners.

LESS BREAD AND MORE CIRCUSES

As a major Dorset landowner, John Drax was appointed high sheriff in 1840 on 'Buggins turn' and more pomp followed.[15] In honour of her majesty's judges when they came to Dorchester for the Assizes, he provided for their reception a fantastic display of pageantry in part paid for by the proceeds of slavery. There is a picture of the procession, and the general scene depicts the judges arriving at the court house in the High Street. Windows and roofs are crowded with spectators. The streets are lined with a number of pikemen dressed in a uniform similar to that of the Yeomen of the Guard. Behind them are the public cheering and waving their hats.

Through the 1840s, the agricultural depression continued, and many labourers were out of work. John Drax had increased Char-borough Park's size and got an Act of Parliament to allow him to divert the main Wimborne to Dorchester road by a lengthy dogleg. He decided to mark the boundary with what is now known as 'the Great Wall of Dorset'. Some said it was built to give the family privacy, while others have said it was built to give work to unem-

---

14.   See Kris Manjapra, 'When Will Britain Face Up to Its Crimes against Humanity?', *The Guardian*, 29 March 2018.

15.   The high sheriff of Dorset (as with other counties) was largely a status ap-pointment. The list of yearly appointees is a Who's Who gentry families and only becomes more merited orientated in the late twentieth century. The first woman was appointed in 1979. https://en.wikipedia.org/wiki/High_Sheriff_of_Dorset, accessed 14 July 2024.

ployed labourers for a considerable period. Some believe it was funded by the compensation he received on behalf of the family for freeing their 189 enslaved people.

The opening of the new road was reported by a local newspaper. The first coach, 'The Forester', performed the opening journey and when the coach arrived at the Charborough gate there was 'a plentiful supply of fine Charborough beer and other refreshments, liberally provided by Mr Drax'.[16]

PERAMBULATION.
MANOR of CHARBOROUGH, and part of the MANOR of EAST MORDEN.

NOTICE is hereby given, that a COURT of SURVEY and PERAMBULATION of JOHN SAMUEL WANLEY SAWBRIDGE ERLE DRAX, ESQ., and JANE FRANCIS his Wife, Lord and Lady of the said Manors, will be holden at the Cock and Bottle Inn, in the Manor of Morden, on MONDAY, the 13th of JULY next, at the hour of Ten o'clock in the Forenoon.

The Perambulation will commence near the World's End, and proceed in a north-easterly direction to Sturminster Field, and then along the eastern boundary to High Wood, and from thence along the south-east boundary to the eastern corner of Loppit's Barrow Wood, finishing at a Bound Stone placed in the said eastern corner of Loppit's Barrow Wood on the 20th day of May, 1839.

Dated this 30th day of June, 1840.

THOMAS SHETTLE, Steward.

Dorset County Chronicle, 2 July 1840.

Like many other compensated slave-owners, John Drax invested his money in transport infrastructure, in his case, mostly turnpikes. Unlike many other investing former slave-owners, his ventures provided little return.

Drax was finally elected to Parliament for the Wareham borough in the General Election of June 1841 as a Whig. His opponent was John Hales Calcraft, a Conservative.[17] In March 1842 a case was brought to court of The Queen v. Drax. Esq. MP. John Drax was accused of bribing Mr Thomas Hutchings, the landlord of Red Lion, with £15 to vote for him in the election in the previous year. Hutchings freely admitted being offered the bribe, but a series of

---

16. *Dorset County Chronicle*, 22 June 1843.
17. Both candidates would change parties at future elections. Calcraft eventually became a Liberal.

witnesses then said they could not remember or were not present at the key time. Mr Drax was found not guilty.[18]

In June 1846, *The Times* sent a reporter to Dorset who claimed that the landowners and farmers showed no sense of social responsibility towards their labourers:

> Apathy and indifference on the part of the landed proprietor, and the grasping and closefisted policy of the farmer, are the causes of the prevailing distress. The default of the one is apparent in his neglect to provide proper habitations in which the labourer may bring up his family in comfort and decency. In no county, notwithstanding the universal increase of population, is the want of new cottages so apparent, and the neglect of the landlord, in this point at least, so conspicuous. The latter, in withholding from the man who serves him a just and reasonable reward for his services, is acting neither wisely nor honourably. Both seem to have forgotten, or at least to have shut their eyes to the undoubted fact, that one of the surest methods of consulting the public advantage is to secure to the lower-class comfort and competence.[19]

In another report:

> I may here observe, that nowhere… have I met with so many cases of personal deformity, as well as… deafness, dumbness and idiocy, the causes of which… may be clearly traced to the want of proper and sufficient food, and the general mode of life which prevails amongst (the labouring classes).

That September, the *Illustrated London News* also sent a reporter and artist to Dorset to follow up *The Times* report. Its description of filth and the physical impairment of both men and their habitations led to the conclusion that 'in no county, notwithstanding the universal increase in population, is the want of new cottages so apparent, and the neglect of the landlord, in this point at least,

---

18. *Dorset County Chronicle*, 17 March 1842.
19. 'Condition of the Peasantry in Dorsetshire', *The Times*, 25 June 1846.

so conspicuous'. The article's illustrations included internal and external etchings of an agricultural worker's cottage in poor condition in the village of East Morden, near Bloxworth – a village which was part of the Charborough Estate. When the artist arrived in East Morden to make sketches he found that all the cottages were thatched and 'the roofs were not always impermeable to rain, while the walls were often so cracked that the wind could only be kept out by a stuffing of rags'.

The interior of a Morden labourer's cottage, 1846.
(*Illustrated London News*)

The cottages are built with mud walls, composed of road scrapings, chalk and straw; the foundation is of stone or brick, and on this the mud wall is built in regular layers, each of which is allowed to dry and harden before another is put over it.

Cottages were supported by props for keeping falling walls together, floors inside were made of mud and a 'heap of squalid half-clothed children rolling upon it' could be seen inside. Some of the cottages were described as almost in ruins while others were little better than hovels.

People would get to their bedroom by climbing up a ladder. Many windows had no glass and openings were stuffed with rags. In one room occupied by a family of eight, there were two tables, one chair and a 'rude bench' 4 feet long. The cradle was of rough boards clumsily nailed together.

The exterior of a Morden labourer's cottage, 1846.
(*Illustrated London News*)

ELECTED

John Drax became the Conservative (Tory) Member of Parliament for Wareham when he was finally elected in 1841. As previously detailed, Wareham was a rotten pocket borough with, at this time, just 342 electors, fought over by Drax and John Hales Calcraft. John Drax may have been a reformer, but he was also a protectionist in favour of the Corn Laws. The laws were supported by Conservative and Whig landowners but met opposition from industrialists and workers. The Anti-Corn Law League campaigned against these laws. Its leading figure was Richard Cobden, who, according to historian Asa Briggs, promised that repeal would settle four great problems simultaneously:

First, it would guarantee the prosperity of the manufacturer by affording him outlets for his products. Second, it would relieve the 'condition of England question' by cheapening the price of food and ensuring more regular employment. Third, it would make English agriculture more efficient by stimulating demand for its products in urban and industrial areas. Fourth, it would introduce through mutually advantageous international trade a new era of international fellowship and peace. The only barrier to these four beneficent solutions was the ignorant self-interest of the landlords, the 'bread-taxing oligarchy, unprincipled, unfeeling, rapacious and plundering'.[20]

The first Anti-Corn Law Association was set up in London in 1836; it was not until 1838 that the nationwide League, combining all such local associations, was founded, with Richard Cobden and John Bright among its leaders. Cobden was the chief strategist; Bright was its great orator. The League borrowed many of the tactics first developed by the slavery abolitionists while also attempting to replicate its mantle of moral reform. Its main target was the landlords, many of them MPs who benefitted from the Corn Laws they passed in Parliament.

As author Nick Hayes pointed out:

The Anti-Corn Law League saw slavery as a violent, extreme extrapolation of what was happening to the white workers of England. To them, the divide between black and white was a smokescreen to mask the fundamental issue: the exploitation of labour and land, the idea that certain sectors of society should have a greater share of the world than others.[21]

THE DRAX SISTERS

Three months before her mother died in December 1853, Sarah Charlotte Elizabeth Ernle-Erle-Drax – she was 24 years of age

---

20. Asa Briggs, *The Making of Modern England 1783–1867: The Age of Improvement* (New York: Harper and Row, 1959), p. 314.
21. Hayes, 'A Very English Theft'.

DRAX OF DRAX HALL

– had married Colonel Francis Augustus Plunkett Burton of the Coldstream Guards. Some three years older than her, he was the son of Admiral James Ryder Burton by his wife Anne Maria Plunkett, daughter of Randall Plunkett, 13th Baron of Dunsany. So started a convergence of the Plunkett and the Ernle-Erle-Drax family. In the year after her mother's death, the older sister Maria Caroline took out a civil case against John Drax, her sister Sarah Charolotte and her sister's husband. In Drax v. Drax, it seems that her sister, on marriage, was able to claim her inheritance from her mother, a chunk of the Charborough Estate that had been, up to that point, under her father's control. Her estate was located mostly around Bere Regis.[22]

All were living in Charborough House at the time and the legal documents listed the huge amount of land and properties owned by the estate, not only in Dorset, Devon, Yorkshire and Wiltshire, but other counties too. Clearly, the family had discussed who would get what and when bearing in mind what John Drax did not own personally would revert to the direct Erle-Drax bloodline on his death. They could not agree. Drax v. Drax is a 40-page appeal to the court by Caroline to appoint an 'indifferent' person to divide up the estate and wealth fairly. Caroline's plea retains a civil air, and she credits her father as having made improvements to the house and estate, including purchasing many suits of armour to fill the armoury he had built attached to the house. How the division went is not clear, but John Drax had access to Charborough Estate wealth for many more years.

Jane Panton, in her 1909 book, detailed Drax's wrongdoing and misadventures:

How well I recollect the 'wicked Squire' a man who might have come straight out of a penny dreadful, and whose existence would, I should think, be quite impossible in these days, for surely some journalist would have slain him with his pen and pilloried his doings in many a paragraph. He was an old man when I knew

22. The colonel represented Wareham in Parliament for a number of years and had died in 1867.

300

him forty years ago, but he looked as evil as any Mephistopheles could look, and his language was as revolting as his manners and customs.

He had inherited large estates from his wife, who soon died, leaving him with two daughters, to whom the property was to go should they marry. This would not, naturally, have suited his book at all, and they were kept in strict seclusion, but somehow the younger managed to make acquaintance with a neighbour's son; they eloped out of the library window and married. The Squire had to give up her share of the property, and he kept the elder sister closer and closer until she became a melancholy wreck and took to winding all the clocks, to mark the passing of the sorrowful hours, so that they should never be an instant different from each other. Then she never went out except to church, where she sat in the square pew that she would never allow to be cleared out of the chancel – she was lay rector – or improved in any way. Indeed, her interest in the church once took the embarrassing form of cleaning and repainting it in such a manner that it resembled a music-hall more than a grave place of worship, and all were thankful when the decorations faded and were replaced at her death by others more in keeping with the sacred building.

1865 ELECTION

Panton vividly recalled the rumbustious 1865 election at Wareham, featuring John Drax. As was her wont, the characters remain unnamed, but 'The squire from the north', now the Conservative candidate whom she also called the 'wicked squire', is clearly John Drax. He has fallen out of favour with the working people. John Hales Calcraft of Rempstone Hall is the rival 'squire from the south' as the candidate for the new Liberal Party,[23] which was replacing the Whigs as an electoral force. As an active supporter for Calcraft,

---

23. The Liberal Party was founded in 1859 as an alliance of Whigs, free trade-supporting Peelites and reformist Radicals.

she is positioned in the centre of the town at Liberal HQ at 'The red house' while awaiting the spectacle that follows:[24]

> Presently the candidates themselves hove in sight. The Squire from the north rode in at the head of his vassals. The labourers were accommodated in waggons decked with blue ribands, and the great horses were wreathed also in the Tory colours. The farmers as a rule rode splendid animals, for they were one and all ardent huntsmen, while yet more horses were bestridden by the Squire's neighbours and even the clergy did not disdain a place in his train.

> The Squire from the south had a vast following in his turn, but it, as a rule, consisted of a large and dangerous crowd of pitmen from the neighbouring clayworks, who were one and all spoiling for a fight.[25]

> The appearance of the candidates and their supporters on the hustings was the sign for the most appalling noise to be started. In vain the candidates, their proposers and seconders, endeavoured to make themselves heard; if there were a moment's cessation of the groans and cheers the two men mentioned before howled out a continuous chant of 'Our Squire for iver; throw 't'other in the river'. But as a rule, it was utterly impossible to hear a word of either speech.

> Finally, some of the clay-pit rout thrust dolls on long sticks into the face of the northern Squire, meaning to draw attention by these means to his well-known amatory adventures, while a couple of other dissentients cast loaves of bread in his face. His sayings about dear food and his dealings with his farmers were well known; and as one of his favourite remedies for the supposed

---

24. She was an admirer of Calcraft, who had been the MP for Wareham severally up to 1859. She said he was 'one of the most magnificent old men that I have ever seen'.

25. To the east of Wareham is an area of high-quality clay that was used to manufacture pots in prehistoric times and in the nineteenth century was dug and sent to 'The Potteries' in the north of England.

ABOLITION AND COMPENSATION

lack of prosperity among the landowners and farmers was a tax on wheat; and a return to Protection was his panacea for all ills, these sentiments had naturally made him more than usually unpopular, with the lower classes at any rate.[26]

Panton noted that the poor knew only too well what Protection was and were not going to support anyone who proposed its return by the Corn Laws.

> Not that the very poor had a vote; all the same, they could and did make a most tremendous noise, which increased every moment. Presently the crusty half of a loaf flew straight against the window of the Town Hall, which it smashed, and a most fearful row ensued. The farmers, armed with their heavy hunting-crops, rushed from the hustings and struck out right and left. The claypit men retaliated, but they were not in full force, and they were soon rapidly getting the worst of it. Indeed, the two big men were being thrust out of the town, when a batch of about thirty of their friends was seen rushing in over the bridge, waving huge palings which they had seized as they came along, and breathing fire and slaughter; and all bid fair to murder each other, when fortunately, the gigantic police inspector and his constables turned out.

> It was to be a damn close-run thing. The poll closed then at four o'clock, and at three we reluctantly discovered that every known vote was recorded save and except the doubtful seven, who had not been seen or heard of.

> Messengers both blue and pink were despatched hot-foot, and the blue man was beginning to look most disagreeably triumphant. Still the time went on, and the seven voters were still absent. The moments crept by. If they turned up and voted pink the Liberal was in by a bare majority of five; if blue, the state of the poll would still be in the northern Squire's favour. But just before the time a carriage came galloping into the market square, and out the seven tumbled; and as all to a man voted pink our candidate was in; and

---

26. Panton, *Fresh Leaves*, pp. 170–180.

DRAX OF DRAX HALL

the fearful noise that ensued will never be forgotten by anyone who ever heard it.

It turned out that the blue agent, having been driven to despair by the vacillation of the seven, had inveigled them out to an island in the estuary known as Horse Island, where horses were taken to be out at grass.

He knew that, deprived of this unknown quantity, the election was safe as far as his side was concerned, and after inspecting a horse or two that these men had for sale, he had made for the boat and left them on the island cursing. They were safe there until the tide turned at least, and by then the election would be over and won! Unfortunately, the noise the prisoners made was heard by some fishermen in the harbour; they came to their rescue, and the men were brought off in time to punish the agent by voting as they never intended to do, until he played them this dastardly trick. The declaration of the poll was followed by another free fight, until someone persuaded the Squire and his escort to depart.[27]

John Drax's relationship with his family, neighbours, workers and voters in Dorset was turning very sour.

---

27. Panton, *Fresh Leaves*, pp. 180–183.

20
John Drax, the Old Scoundrel

A fine portrait of John S.W. Sawbridge Erle-Drax, painted around 1850 by the Scottish artist and Royal Academician, Sir Francis Grant, presents the sitter as a benign and upright squire. However, in real life, wherever John Drax went, there was controversy. The older he got, the more irascible he became, and drink, his libido and then ill health seemingly played no small part in his moods. His dastardly misdeeds would fill a book alone, but some stand out and look worse 150 years later. Over the decades, the evidence suggests that John Drax's acts of generosity came at the expense, not from his poor investments, but from the Charborough Estate. They were aimed at the middle classes of east Dorset and those he sought to impress. They were not to the benefit of the wider family or agricultural workers. Drax eventually inherited Olantigh House from his father in 1851, but it was Charborough monies that funded his extravagances.

John Drax stood again at the 1868 election. Drax was very keen to remain an MP, not least as it enabled him to spend time in London with major figures of the day. He was a member of the Carlton and Windham clubs in St James. The membership of the men-only Carlton reveals his engagement with the Tories as the party moved towards becoming the modern Conservative Party. The winner was the Liberal candidate John Hales Calcraft. But shortly afterwards, Calcraft died, forcing a by-election. With leverage over his and his daughter's tenants he was elected to Parliament again and the next William Montagu Calcraft was not. The 1868 administration was Gladstone's first stint as Prime Minister. But Drax, according to the *Manchester Guardian*, was to become a part of the English language as a result of the new PM's sense of humour.

If any candidate were coming forward, or any particular step were contemplated in Dorset, the question of the wirepullers was always, 'Have you got Drax?' One sees the temptation to a catch-word, and Mr. Gladstone made it a favourite one. He heard it often in his Tory youth, and he would always say, 'How about Drax?' when he meant 'Are the local magnates favourable?' He used to laugh about the undue influence exercised by the Draxes of England. But all that is buried under hyphens now.[1]

Drax would also win at the General Election in 1874.

RENDER TO CAESAR

One example of John Drax's bloody-mindedness concerns a once-historic site in Wimbledon, south-west London, then owned by the Charborough Estate. Through the estate, John Drax controlled the Wimbledon hill fort known as Caesar's Camp, though, in fact, it had nothing to do with the Romans; it was a significant Neolithic monument. As the *Wimbledon Guardian* paper noted some 140 years later, what he did in 1875 is perhaps the worst case of vandalism Wimbledon has ever suffered outside wartime. 'The culprits were a builder called Dixon and a Member of Parliament, the landowner John Samuel Sawbridge-Erle-Drax. They destroyed the pre-historic Iron Age fort on Wimbledon Common dating back to 700 BC or earlier.'[2]

Before 1875 the fort had included circular ramparts nearly 20 feet high, topped with mature oak trees and surrounded by a 12-foot deep, 30-foot-wide ditch, enclosing some 12 acres of relatively flat land with a view of Epsom Downs. 'Drax, who became the owner of land stretching from Beverley Brook to Westside Common through his late wife's inheritance, leased some fields to a builder called Dixon who then built three large houses in Camp Road and moved on to the area of the fort itself.' Local antiquarians were

1. Our London correspondent, *The Manchester Guardian*, 26 May 1905.
2. www.wimbledonguardian.co.uk/news/9646547.heritage-wimbledons-worst-vandalism/, last accessed 27 June 2024.

appalled as he fenced off what had been an area for local recreation and history.

Campaigners eventually achieved Parliamentary protection for Wimbledon Common to prevent it from being built upon. Drax had had the opportunity to save the Iron Age fort for posterity by selling the land to the campaign group. He demanded an astounding £5000 per acre and that proved too much for the campaigners to raise. So Drax and Dixon simply levelled the fort. Bricks and scaffolding for more houses arrived on site, the trees were felled, the ramparts levelled, and the ditch filled. Although the Commons Conservators stopped any further action by securing a court order forbidding use for anything other than agricultural purposes, it was too late to save the fort, which was now unrecognisable.[3] Two years later, Drax was the subject of criticism in one case by *The Times* to which he replied in a dismissive and self-pitying tone, suggesting that the fort had nothing to do with the Romans and had no real historical value.

> I consider the Bill to be drawn in great injustice to owners, as being compulsory, having a clause of the Defence Act of 1860 inserted. In the case of railways, one is disposed to submit for the public good, but in this instance it is only to gratify certain parties at the expense of the public. If this so-called 'Caesar's Camp' were to be taken from me it would entail a very serious loss, as it is leased, the greater part for building purposes, and I should be shut out entirely from access to my estate.
>
> I am, Sir, your obedient servant,
>
> J. S. W. S. ERLE DRAX, Holnest-house, Sherborne.[4]

The Charborough Estate was at its largest during the latter part of John Sawbridge Drax's life, having land and property in many other counties. In 1876, *The Spectator*, using figures from the 1873 Return

---

3. A school hall and some roads in the Wimbledon area are named after the Draxes and there have been recent campaigns to have them renamed because of the association with slavery.

4. *The Times*, 20 March 1877.

DRAX OF DRAX HALL

of the Owners of Land, announced that one quarter of the land of England and Wales was owned by no more than 710 people in estates of 5000 acres or more. This 'Territorial Aristocracy', as *The Spectator* called them, held land often in several counties and might hold urban property and mineral rights as well as large agricultural estates.[5] Bateman's surveys, which followed between 1876 and 1883, show even more remarkably the fact that 64 per cent of the land of the county of Dorset was owned by 20 men and one woman in estates of 5000 acres or more. Twelve families owned 10,000 and more acres. All but two 5000-acre-plus landowners were resident in Dorset, possessing country seats; all but five had land elsewhere; three possessed London property. At the time of the 1873 return, the Dorset landowner was financially supported by the rents of his agricultural estates. He had made no substantial urban developments in the county from which to gather income, nor were there mineral deposits apart from stone which were worked. Oil deposits were known about but discounted because of their sulphur content.

SAWBRIDGE-ERLE-DRAX, JOHN SAMUEL WANLEY, of Holnest Park, Sherborne, &c.

Club. Windham, Carlton.	Dorset . . .	15,069	.	11,631
b. 1800, s. *jur. uxo.* 1828,	Kent . . .	3,173	.	3,292
m. 1827.	Lincolnshire .	1,610	.	2,449
Sat for Wareham.	Wilts. . . .	1,902	.	2,093
	Somerset . .	883	.	1,344
	York, N.R. .	623	.	1,034
Of this total, MISS DRAX is	Surrey . . .	327	.	1,322
retd. as owner of 8,953 acres.				
		23,587	.	23,165

From Bateman's 1883 survey. Column 1 is acres and column 2 is estimated annual return. According to Bateman, the Drax acres produced an estimated £23,165 pa.

The Drax estates came third in Dorset behind only the Pitt Rivers and Digby families. Panton pointed out that although the vast preponderance of agricultural land in Dorset was owned by landlords who built up their landholdings during the seventeenth and eight-

---

5. 'The Territorial Aristocracy of England', *The Spectator*, 4 March 1876.

eenth centuries, the actual work on the land and the improvement and innovation was done by tenant farmers. Looking back forty or more years to when she lived at 'North Farm' near Charborough and tenanted from the Drax family on an annual lease, she wrote:

> When I stayed there the bad times for farmers were just beginning to be very serious things. The power the landlords possessed was enormous. Every improvement the farmer made was for the benefit of the landlord; rabbits and hares cleared up his crops, he might neither shoot nor trap; and, indeed, all he might do was to sink his capital in the land, hoping vainly to retrieve it before his lease ran out or he was bidden to go. I used to ride all over the land with the farmer and hear what he had spent and what he had done with his fields; how he had drained such a piece of down land and put it down to corn, and how much it had cost him.

'Then,' continued Panton, 'the agent came along, noted the improvement, and had suggested that the place would be worth more rent at the end of the year, as all was looking so remarkably well.'[6]

POST-SLAVERY BARBADOS

Money was still coming in from the Barbados plantation to the Drax family. Drax Hall was run for the long-time absent landlords by manager, William Henry Smith. In 1840, the Barbados ruling body passed a Master and Servant Act which restricted the right to strike and other activity that might increase wages. The historian Henderson Carter noted that first Master and Servant Act of 1838 banning strike was met with strikes, just one day after legal emancipation.[7] These strikes were accompanied by a campaign of arson, burning sugar cane fields and the fuel used to power the sugar-processing machinery. The Colonial Office in London grasped that the

---

6. Panton, *Fresh Leaves*, p. 277.
7. Henderson Carter, *Labour Pains: Resistance and Protest in Barbados, 1838–1904* (Forgotten Histories of the Caribbean) (Kingston, Jamaica: Ian Randle Publishers, 2012), chapter 3.

situation was untenable and struck out the law. The next Act was less draconian, but still produced ten days of strike action, particularly strong in St George parish, the site of Drax Hall. These strikes were broken by the police and army, with hundreds of arrests. Strikes and civil disobedience were to be features of Barbados life for decades as planters tried to maintain their grip on the workforce.

The 1850s–1890s witnessed deepening injustice and escalating worker versus white elite conflict, the flashpoint of which was the Confederation Rebellion of 1876. On 17 April 1876, riots broke out on the island. Hundreds of African-Barbadian labourers plundered and set fire to the plantation estates. On 24 April 1876, the Colonial Office received five telegrams carrying the news of 'fearful riots' in Barbados. However, by that time the riots had been put down; Governor John Pope Hennessy had sent troops to make arrests and disperse the rebels. The riots had also broken out in the context of confederation. The Colonial Office was trying to implement confederation with the Windward Islands and the white Barbadian elite opposed it, while African-Barbadian labourers supported it. In the appendix to the subsequent Report on the Disturbances, William Henry Smith swore an affidavit that in late March a woman was convicted by police magistrates of stealing sugar cane from Drax Hall plantation and sent to prison. Shortly before, a boy had been convicted of a similar offence at Drax Hall and sentenced to six months in prison. Sugar cane was usually stolen because of hunger. In both cases the prisoners were released early to return to work on the plantation.

1880 ELECTION

John Drax had been re-elected as a Conservative for Wareham in February 1874. Jane Panton wrote of the 1880 election stating the last Wareham borough election before it was dissolved as a constituency was the most entertaining of the lot. 'I shall never forget that day as long as I live', she wrote as supporter of Montagu Guest of the Liberal Party, 'And we were early on the scene.'

JOHN DRAX, THE OLD SCOUNDREL

Large pink rosettes adorned all our adherents, but the blue ribands of the opponents outnumbered the pink by hundreds, and our hopes sank slowly into our boots. Though there were several free fights, the elections of that day and, indeed, of the present time, are nothing like as entertaining as they were before the ballot.[8]

The defeated Drax came out on the porch of the inn to make his farewell speech after the declaration of the poll, but when he was received with derisive yells and screams by the victorious party, 'he turned green with rage; paused for a minute to obtain silence, and then solemnly and completely cursed the town and the inhabitants thereof in the most appalling manner possible'. Then he called for his coach man and told him to put in his horses and drive him straight to the warmest locality known (ed – hell).

The man looked amazed, and faltered out that he did not know the way; but the Squire, with another loud oath, swore he would soon show him, and banged into the carriage, and the last thing seen of him was the fist he was indignantly shaking at every house and person he passed. He never stood again for the borough; education, the ballot, the advance of knowledge, all were against him; and the Conservatives knew that they must bring forward someone quite different, or the borough would remain a Liberal stronghold for the rest of its days.

'I will die with MP on my coffin', he used to swear, but when he died, the letters were not there, and the borough he had bullied and coerced for years had ceased to return a representative to Parliament and had been merged into one of the four quarters of the county.[9]

During his tenure in the House of Commons, Drax was known as the 'Silent MP'. It may be apocryphal, but he is said to have made only one known statement in the House, which reputedly was a request that the Speaker of the House have a window opened.[10] He rarely voted. After he moved to the right, being an MP can only be

---

8. Panton, *Fresh Leaves*, pp. 188–189.
9. Ibid., p. 58.
10. The History of Parliament cannot identify any time he spoke in the House.

NOT BRED AT CHARBOROUGH

Over the 60 years that John Drax reigned over the Charborough Estate some of his behaviour towards women would now verge on the illegal. Admiral Drax, in the mid-1950s, did his best to distance this embarrassing ancestor, describing him as the black sheep that every family has. The Admiral made some caveats; he observed that a large part of what we know about John Drax comes from stories and legends, and these, he said, no doubt had been exaggerated. Admiral Drax conceded that Jane Panton may have been correct, however; she had been critical of other Dorset people. The Admiral said the family referred to him as the old scoundrel because of his behaviour towards his two daughters and Charborough.[11]

As noted, Panton was successfully sued by Captain Marston of Rempstone Hall over a reference to a new inheritor of a Dorset landed-gentry family who had burnt important family documents. He felt it was clearly a defamatory and identifiable reference to him. I was able to correspond with Richard D. Ryder, the author of the 2005 book *The Calcrafts of Rempstone Hall*, of whom he is descendent. Captain Marston was a relative of the family, as son of Katherine Calcraft and the Rev. C.D. Marston. The captain was advised not to sue Panton by friends but nonetheless proceeded. In correspondence, Richard Ryder told me 'I get the impression that Panton's gossip was particularly accurate.'[12] Ryder has in his possession a copy of the legal file and a copy of the original book in which Marston and his lawyers, the Clarkes, made notes in the margins about Panton's various comments. Interestingly, many of the margin notes confirm Panton's accuracy, except when it came to a member

---

11. Ernle-Erle-Drax, *The History of Charborough*, p. 45.
12. Richard Ryder, correspondence with the author, December 2021.

JOHN DRAX, THE OLD SCOUNDREL

of the Calcraft family. When it comes to Panton's many comments about the 'wicked squire' they are in agreement with her portrayal, on the basis of personal experience.

The lawyer's[13] annotations merely identify the 'wicked squire' referred to on pages 56, 57 and 58 of Panton's book as: 'Depicted here is the late Mr Drax who lived at Charborough Park, Wareham and was the owner of a considerable landed property. The description of him is pretty correct. I knew him personally.' (Mr Clarke) EIC (Edward Clark? – Marston's agent) adds the words 'This perfectly true.' He adds opposite page 57: 'The description of Mr Drax and the anecdotes recorded about him on this, and the next page, are correct in detail.' Opposite the top of page 59, in a different hand (red ink), probably G.M. Marston's, concerning Drax's anger at the voters of Wareham when they did not elect him and he stormed off cursing them. 'Lady Caroline Calcraft has told Captain Marston this story many times.'

The domestic print run was destroyed in settlement of the libel action. Luckily, Panton's memoir was also published in the United States, and facsimiles can still be bought. Reading the book, I was struck by the authenticity and measure of Panton's voice. Often it is very detailed eyewitness accounts of a wide range of subjects encountered in a small town in the mid-1800s. It can be gossipy, but most of it is entirely innocuous, just a good sociological account of the people of this part of Dorset at the time. She is critical of a few and, towards the end, indicates that she preferred the way the town and country were in her youth to what had become. The writing style is a little old-fashioned, and her tendency not to name the people she is talking about can be irritating, but it is not hard to work out who they were; especially for those readers who lived through those times, it must have been blindingly obvious. She does not have a grudge against the landed gentry and praises the intellect and conduct of the then head of the Weld family at some length. Her bile is mainly directed at various points towards the wicked squire.

---

13. Meynell & Pemberton, London.

313

SEXUAL PREDATOR

In modern terms, Drax's behaviour towards his daughters looks suspiciously controlling. The family's version is that he disliked his two daughters for the reason that he was angry and disappointed at having no son. Panton's most serious allegation is that the wicked squire was a sexual predator of young women who lived in or by the estate. During the telling of the drunken visit in January 1868 by John Drax's shooting party for a demanded late lunch at North Farm, the young Panton is told to stay out of Drax's way. She also said in her first mention of the wicked squire's wrongdoings 'that the many lodges round the estate each held a fair and frail friend, and at the end as broken hearts'.

> About all these items I can say nothing personally, except about the denizens of the lodges; some of those at least owed their fall to the 'Wicked Squire', while I quite well recollect the hurry the village mothers were in to get their girls away from home and into decent service before the Squire realised they were pretty and grown up, lest they too should find themselves an object for his attention and be found a place under the housekeeper at the Hall.[14]

Another reference comes during Panton's account of the unruly election hustings in 1865, where the clay-pit men are trying to wind up the squire (John Drax) as he is speaking. 'Finally, some of the clay-pit rout thrust dolls on long sticks into the face of the northern Squire, meaning to draw attention by these means to his well-known amatory adventures.'[15]

All this could be considered gossip; however, I did find some startling supporting evidence. This is from the *Dorset County Express & Agricultural Gazette* in 1879 from the hearing of the extraordinary summons which has been issued against Mr J.S.W. Erle-Drax by a prostitute named Louisa Gray of 17 George Street, Marylebone,

14. Panton, *Fresh Leaves*, p. 58.
15. Ibid., p. 180.

JOHN DRAX, THE OLD SCOUNDREL

charging him with being the father of her illegitimate child, before the stipendiary, Mr Rutzen.[16] Mr Woodgate appeared on behalf of the plaintiff, and Mr Besley, barrister, defended. At a previous hearing, the complainant stated she was the daughter of a gamekeeper, formerly in the employ of Mr Drax and that so long ago as 1847 she was seduced by him. For some time afterwards, he made her an allowance of £100 a year. The connection was ultimately broken off, and she lived upon the town. 'However, of late it had been resumed and the result was that she had been delivered of a child of whom Mr Drax, who is 79 years, is the father.'

The defence was that this was simply a gross attempt at extortion and the woman was long past the age of childbearing. The complainant was again put in the witness box. Mr Woodgate handed her a card and she said it was a label attached to a brace of pheasants sent to her on 27 November 1878 at 37 Red Lion Square. The address was in Mr Drax's handwriting. She had received letters from him previous to that, one of them informing her that the hamper was about to come. The resumed intimacy between them was being carried on at that time.

In reply to Mr Besley's cross-examination, she said when she first went into Mr Drax's service she was between 16 and 17 years of age. She was not 18 at the time but she would not swear it was not on 26 May 1847. She was a still-room maid. Her birthday, her sister told her, was in December. She did not leave in July 1848: nor was she paid by a cheque on Drummond's on the 24 of that month, £34. 7s 6d for board wages and ordinary wages for one year and nine months up to that time. Mrs Fooks, the housekeeper, discharged her. In December 1847, she would have been 17.[17]

The cross-examination continued:

You have averred you have been allowed £100 a year by Mr Drax. At whose hands was that paid? – Mr Drax himself, she replied.

In what sums? - £20, £10, £7 and additional sums as pin money.

---

16. Tuesday 29 April 1879, pp. 2–3.
17. If Louisa Gray was seduced at the age of 16, this was some years before John Drax's wife Jane-Frances died on 29 December 1853.

Attend to this, woman! Do you mean that you had different sums or that you had a fixed sum? – Oh, he fixed the sum himself, and gave it to me.

He paid you himself. In what years? – It was 27 years ago, at least in 1851, when I came up to London.

Do you mean to say the first payment was in 1851? – Yes sir, and the first sum I received was £10.

When was the first? – When I was living in his service before I was discharged by the housekeeper.

Did it then cease until July 1851? No, I was to meet him, by appointment, at Great Collwood-gate at 9 o'clock, the night I was discharged.[18]

Mr Besley then took the witness through a list of her 54 convictions at Marlborough Street Police Court. In most cases, she admitted the conviction. Many were for drunk and disorderly conduct or assault.

Mr De Rutzen: You have the fact that this woman has been convicted over and over again and that she gets her living on the streets. How can you carry it any further than that?

Mr Besley: Because this woman's story is a tissue of falsehoods, and it is nothing but a conspiracy to extract money from an old man, and it is high time that these things should be exposed. Mr Drax would never have appeared otherwise.

She was then asked, 'Is it not the truth that Mr Drax never saw you until you had written to him for assistance to put you in business as a dressmaker, in the year 1878?'

She replied: 'I wrote and asked him if he would fulfil what he had promised me years ago.'

In reply to further questions, Louisa Gray said she was living at 17 George Street, and she could not swear it was not a brothel. Young women lived there, and they might go out and return with men. She did not interfere with other people's business.

---

18. Great Collwood was on the Charborough Estate.

JOHN DRAX, THE OLD SCOUNDREL

Alice Robens, a former prostitute and now a needle woman living at the same house, deposed she had seen the plaintiff suckling a child, and she was called up to attend the birth but was not present at the time. Ann Lawrence and Ann Williams declared they were at the confinement, the latter saying she saw the child come into the world.

Mr Besley explained that Drax was unfit to travel. The case was adjourned until the 30th. In reply to the magistrate Louisa Gray said she would be happy to be examined by the medical men in attendance. She was then taken into a private room and the hearing closed.

The woman was examined by three doctors, one of whom Dr Bond being the head of obstetrics and all the surgeons are satisfied that the woman *never had a child!*

It was thought that the worthless woman, after all her experiences, might have been in a position to make a charge of paternity against someone and had turned to a former employer as a person whose age and generosity pointed him out as the most likely victim.

It is unusual for witnesses to abet a fraud by broad swearing to an event that never happened. All the parties will be proceeded against for perjury and conspiracy.[19]

The Times covered the rescheduled hearing:

J. S. W. Erle-Drax, JP., of Olantigh Towers, near Ashford, Kent, appeared before Mr. De Rutzen in answer to the adjourned summons taken out by Louisa Gray, living at 17, George-Street, Lisson-Grove, requiring him to show cause why he should not contribute towards the support of her illegitimate child, of which she alleged him to be the father. Mr. Besley represented the defendant. Since the last hearing of the case, the complain-

---

19. *Dorset County Express & Agricultural Gazette*, Tuesday 29 April 1879, pp. 2–3.

DRAX OF DRAX HALL

ant's solicitor had withdrawn from acting for her, in consequence, as he said, of the disreputable way the evidence showed she had been living and from other matters which came to his knowledge. Miss Sarah Elizabeth Stride, Bernard-street, Russell-Square, now stated that the complainant came to her in January last and told her that she required help as she was likely to become a mother.

Eleanor Gould, living at 2, Winchester-Street, the sister of the complainant, said that the latter told her of her condition in November last and asked her to take her into her house.

She told her that she could not. Cross-examined, the witness said that she never was in the service of Mr. Drax. She had 10 or 11 brothers and sisters, but they were nearly all dead. Three of them were at one time living in Mr. Drax's service. The magistrate was surprised that the case, which was full of improbabilities from beginning to end, should have taken so long a hearing. He should therefore dismiss the summons.

Mr. Besley said that before leaving the Court he wished to emphatically deny certain assertions published in the newspapers. They could not disguise from themselves that this form of procedure caused great pain and anxiety to any man. Mr. Drax had suffered to some extent in consequence of these false statements. He emphatically denied that he had ever been on such terms with this woman as to make her an allowance or had at any time said that he would marry her on the death of his wife.

This all portrayed Louisa Gray, who was coming up to 50 years of age, as a ne'er-do-well, a recurrent drunk, prostitute and violent character and in this case a woman who had made an extortion attempt falsifying that she had had a child by the now elderly John Drax. The original newspaper headline summarises this position: 'A Vile Attempt at Extortion! Breakdown of the Case.'

Only now with greater knowledge of the abuse of women and its consequences, this story may be read very differently from what it did in 1879, as the fall of a very young woman at the hands of a powerful figure who seemed to be very controlling. It may well have been that it was an extortion attempt by a desperate woman who

JOHN DRAX, THE OLD SCOUNDREL

had no reputation, no longer married and probably finding it hard to make a living as a prostitute. If she was seduced (or raped) her life became chaotic and her life as a prostitute probably indicates that she did not have the references to carry on in service. Even in those days, it was well known for men of the landed gentry to take advantage of women servants and women of the lower classes. Those allegations were made against John Drax from multiple sources.

Even if he was successful in the Louisa Gray court case, John Drax's reign in Dorset was slowly coming to an end.

HARDY'S COUNTY

Dorset is most famous as home to the author Thomas Hardy (1840–1928), who made extensive use of places, people and stories of his native county, often thinly disguising locations with an altered name. *The Mayor of Casterbridge* (1886) is set in Dorchester, the county town. Charborough lies some 13 miles east of 'Casterbridge' as the crow flies, on the periphery of Hardy country. Charborough House and the nearby 120-foot folly tower are the models for 'Welland House' in the Thomas Hardy novel *Two on a Tower*, which was serialised in *Atlantic Monthly* in 1882. The story features Lady Viviette Constantine, the chatelaine of Welland House. She is bored and lonely as her hunting-obsessed husband, Sir Bount, has taken himself off to Africa to shoot lions.

In real life, this is about the period when John and Jane Frances Drax's eldest daughter Maria-Caroline was living her secluded life in Charborough. She made – or was pressured into making by her father, John Drax – a will which left all her part of the estate to her father for his life.[20] Had her father died before her, there would have been no further problems. However, she died first in August 1885. Admiral Drax complained that John Drax, after his elder daughter's death, systematically looted Charborough and borrowed £38,000

---

20. The arrangement was that, after his wife's death, John Drax owned Charborough for the length of his life. It would revert to his daughters if they got married or he died. Sarah did marry and inherited her part of the estate. Maria did not marry, and her inheritance should have gone to the sister on her death.

319

DRAX OF DRAX HALL

from the trustees of his marriage settlement. Drax had, many years before, bought an estate at Holnest, near Sherborne, where he took many of Charborough's most attractive treasures. He then schemed to pay off this mortgage by compelling his other daughter to pay his trustees £40,000 to buy back the land at the east end of the park he had acquired under his name. Drax requisitioned many of the family paintings hanging in the house and its gallery. He apparently took off to his other houses the family silver plate, including a Queen Anne silver dinner service, family portraits by various famous artists and even the gates of the lodges. He also looted the library and took a quantity of period furniture to Olantigh, his house in Kent. Later, a serious fire destroyed the books and furniture so that none of it could ever be recovered.[21] John Drax's delusions of grandeur found a final pinnacle with a monstrous gaudy mausoleum he had built at Holnest. He is said to have practised the funeral procession with himself in the coffin.

John Drax died two years after his unmarried daughter, very little lamented it would seem, and was buried in his overblown marble mausoleum at Holnest. A few years later, Charles Harper provided an insightful epitaph to John Drax after visiting Holnest Lodge, noting it was one of the seats of 'that eccentric person, the late J. S. W. Sawbridge Erle-Drax, of Charborough Park, long a member of Parliament for Wareham, and one of the last of the squires':

> The old-time squires were laws to themselves, and like no others. The product of generations of other many-acred squires of great port-drinking propensities and unbounded local influence, whom all the lickings administered at Eton did not suffice to bring to a proper sense of their intrinsic unimportance, apart from the accidental circumstance that they were the lords of their manors. 'Old Squire Drax,' as the rustics call him now that he is dead, might from his high-handed ways have formed an excellent model for a dramatist building up a melodrama of the old style.

---

21. Ernle-Erle-Drax, *History of Charborough*, pp. 45–46.

He was 'the Squire' to the very *n*th degree, with so extraordinary an idea of his own importance that here, on the lawn fronting Holnest Lodge, he caused to be erected in his own lifetime a memorial to himself.[22]

Harper concluded the burial arrangements were all 'exceedingly curious'. Dorset historian Barbara Kerr kept it simple and described Drax as an 'active, despotic and improving landlord'.[23] But of all of John Drax's many sins, upholding slavery does not seem to have been one, or at the very least, not to the extent of his predecessors. His wife came into the plantation after 1828, not long before abolition. John Drax was able to pick the compensation for freeing the slaves. He may have even been in favour of abolition. He did though, benefit from the income of the plantation in the post-slavery years where conditions for the former enslaved people and workers were still extremely poor.

---

22. Harper, *Hardy Country*, pp. 192–193.
23. Kerr, *Bound to the Soil*, p. 128.

PART VII

Four Barrels and a Smoking Gun

21
Commander Reginald Drax RN

From 1828 onwards, the Charborough Estate, Drax Hall Plantation and the outlying lands passed along the female line right through to 1916. John Drax took advantage of his rights bestowed by marriage for three and half decades after his wife's death, and he did not remarry. Two years after their marriage, Sarah and John Francis Plunkett-Burton had a daughter, Ernle Elizabeth Louisa Maria Grosvenor Burton, who would inherit the estate in time. In 1871, she had married her second husband, Lt John Lloyd Egginton, formerly of the 3rd Dragoon Guards from Cheltenham. She oversaw the vast estate and held an array of minor titles, such as the Lady of the Manor of Sibsey in Lincolnshire. Immediately after John Sawbridge Drax's death, Sarah Charlotte applied successfully to Queen Victoria to add Ernle to her and her husband's surname, so she became Mrs Egginton Ernle-Erle-Drax. It is notable that no one wanted the surname Sawbridge added, and it was dropped from the multiple-barrelled name for good.

The 1870s were also a period of deep agricultural depression marked by extreme poverty for many agricultural workers. They were marked by a fall, by half, in wheat and wool prices, followed by drops in other product prices. Britain shifted from a moderate food importer to a large importer, with almost total reliance on imported fodder and fertiliser.[1] Many tenants who had been farming for generations went bankrupt. With their deep pockets, the Drax family bought up many depressed farms. Typical was Philios Farm from having belonged in early times to the Filiol family. By the seventeenth century, it was owned by a family named Turner, who had become related by marriage to the Ekins family, who, in about

---

1. A. Offer, *The First World War: An Agrarian Interpretation* (Oxford: Clarendon Press, 1989), p. 81.

DRAX OF DRAX HALL

1690, inherited it. The Ekins family rebuilt the farm buildings in 1748, as that date appears in the west gable of the barn. It then remained in the hands of that family until at least the beginning of the nineteenth century, when after one or two changes of hand by sale, it was finally bought by John Drax and hence became part of the main estate. Looking through local newspaper reports, I was struck at the number of times hungry locals were prosecuted for taking turnips among other things from the Drax lands. In March 1892, Alfred Barney was sentenced at Wareham to 14 days' hard labour for picking snowdrops in Charborough Park belonging to Mrs Drax. A Mr F.C. Pearce, a solicitor, was incensed at the prosecution and wrote to a newspaper saying he was going to contact the Home Secretary over the case. 'The sentence is cruel, unjust, and utterly illegal, as unless, the flowers were cultivated, which I can prove is not the case, no conviction could be made, and no offence at law was committed.'[2]

SNOWDROPS IN CHARBOROUGH PARK.

Sir,—I am shocked to see that Alfred Barney was sentenced at Wareham to fourteen days' hard labour for picking snowdrops in Charborough Park belonging to Mrs. Drax.

I have known Charborough Park for at least thirty years ; the snowdrops have grown there without culture and in a state of wildness all that time, and probably for fifty years. No attempt whatever has been made to cultivate them. Until the present owner came into possession about five years ago, when the reign of King Log was changed to that of "King Stork," the village people were always free to gather these wild flowers, and also the wild daffodils, and the old Squire would not have dreamt of interfering.

The sentence is cruel, unjust, and utterly illegal, as, unless the flowers were cultivated, which I can prove is not the case, no conviction could be made, and no offence at law was committed. It is the mushroom case over again. I shall address the Home Secretary on the subject, being interested as a solicitor in seeing justice done ; but meantime this unfortunate country lad will have to go to gaol—his offence is a fondness for wild flowers—free to every one on God's earth.—I am, Sir, your obedient servant, F. C. Pearce.

31, Liverpool-street, E.C., March 21st.

Epworth Bells, *Crowle and Isle of Axholme Messenger*, 26 March 1892.

---

2. *Crowle and the Isle of Axholme Messenger*, 16 March 1892. The poet David Herring of Corfe Mullen showed me other cases of prosecuting for theft of snowdrops or daffodils that took place well into the 1930s.

In 1904, author Charles Harper commented on the poor condition of rented houses in Bere owned by the Charborough Estate:

Meanwhile, here are ruined cottages in the long street of Bere, whose condition has been brought about by just such causes, and whose continuation in that state is due, not to a redundancy of dwellings, but because the Lady of the Manor at Charborough, despising the insignificant rents here, will not trouble about, or go to the expense of, rebuilding. Hence the gaps in the long row, like teeth missing from a jaw.[3]

At about the same time, Sir Frederick Treves is on the 'Great Heath' researching for his book *Highways and Byways* in Dorset. Bere Regis, he surmised, has seen better days. It was, he noted:

once the residence of kings as well as a bustling market town. It is now merely a dull village adrift in a duller country. Its long street, of Quaker simplicity, has been at pains to strip itself bare of all that is bright or picturesque. Bere would seem to be enacting a penance for its past frivolities, to have become a village of sackcloth, and to have taken upon itself the vow of silence.[4]

The family's lack of concern in the welfare of the people of east Dorset was notable. Not only was there no interest in the estate, but there is also no evidence I can find that a member of the Drax family visited the Barbados Drax Hall plantation in the nineteenth century. Despite the family claiming that Sarah Charlotte did a good job with the Charborough Estate, it is likely that she and her daughter had let the estate decline, as evidenced by the state of their properties in Bere Regis and elsewhere. Sarah Charlotte died in 1905. In her will, she bizarrely requested that 'I direct that some preservative fluid shall be injected in the blood vessels of my body so as to prevent natural decay as far as possible, and that my body shall

---

3.   Harper, *Hardy Country*, p. 84.
4.   Sir Frederick Treves, *Highways and Byways in Dorset* (London: Macmillian, 1981 [1906]), p. 162.

be embalmed and placed in a coffin with a glass panel to be let into the lid. It is my desire that a circular mausoleum shall be built on the slope of the hill on the north-west side of the Cannon Clump in the Park at Charborough for the reception of the coffin.' In fact, she was buried in Charborough church. Her daughter Ernle had a stained-glass window put into the east window in her memory.

Keeping up the close links with the Plunkett family, her daughter Ernle had married her cousin John William Plunkett, 17th Baron of Dunsany, at St George's, Hanover Square, London. She was to be the mother of the 18th Lord Dunsany and Reginald Plunkett.[5] Dunsany is one of the oldest titles in the peerage of Ireland. They lived variously at the family seat of Dunsany Castle, County Meath, London and Kent. The 17th Baron was said to be a first-class and versatile sportsman, reputed to have been the best shot in England. He was fascinated by mechanics and science and developed his own X-Ray machine. After a brief illness, he died on 16 January 1899 at Dunsany Castle. His widow, from whom he was separated in his last years, was in residence at their Kent home of Dunstall Priory, Shoreham. Ernle was an absentee landlady spending her time in Kent as she suffered from ill health and did not find the Dorset climate conducive. Likewise, Drax Hall plantation was left in the hands of an attorney or rented out.

A NAVY MAN AT CHARBOROUGH

Reginald Aylmer Ranfurly Plunkett would prove to be a high-achieving member of the Drax lineage. He was born in Marylebone, Westminster on 28 August 1880 as Reginald Plunkett – he did not change his name to the full four-barrelled Drax surname until 1916. He was educated at Cheam School and was sent as a cadet to the Royal Navy training ship HMS *Britannia* from July 1894. Reginald was promoted to lieutenant in 1901 and served in the recently launched HMS *Rinaldo*, one of six Condor Class sloops, for a two-year tour on the China station. By 1909 his reputation

---

5. The elder brother would become the 18th Lord Dunsany, a celebrated Irish writer and author of more than 60 books.

was on the ascendant as a bright young officer who specialised in devising torpedo warfare tactics when they were still a new naval weapon.[6] In 1909, the Admiralty published the precocious Lieutenant Plunkett's book, *Modern Naval Tactics*.

When in 1912, the First Lord of the Admiralty, Winston Churchill, instituted the Admiralty War Staff, Reginald Plunkett was among the 15 officers selected to attend the new staff officer course. He was a founding member of the Naval Society, which from 1913 had issued the quarterly *Naval Review* to encourage new ideas on naval matters. Reginald Plunkett was one of the younger officers of the Grand Fleet known as the 'Young Turks' who increasingly criticised the defensive approach of the Admiralty. This was the age of the Dreadnoughts, battleships which promised a new era of naval power. With the threat of a European war growing, Reginald Plunkett reflected when writing to his ally Herbert Richmond (later also an admiral):

> I am getting in the habit of writing perhaps more freely than I ought to. I write in haste, sometimes with no knowledge of a situation beyond our own view of it, so if I write too much please make allowance for my Celtic temperament. I know you will use them, as I wrote them, only for the good of the Service – or rather the good of the Country, which comes before the Service.[7]

As the First World War began, he was appointed as Staff Officer to Sir David Beatty in the 1st Battlecruiser Squadron, an appointment he held until his promotion to captain in June 1916. Drax was 'a tall, good-looking sports-loving Irishman, who, like his chief, had unlimited courage and imagination', according to his soon to be brother-in-law, who served alongside him. Both were officers on HMS *Lion* and saw action at the naval battles of Heligoland Bight, Dogger Bank and Jutland. Drax's life was very nearly cut short at the Battle of Jutland. Drax was mentioned in Beatty's despatches after Jutland for his courage in observing the fall of shot. Drax would keep

---

6. *The Times*, Obituary, 1967, p. 12.
7. RIC 7/4, Drax to Richmond, 18 December 1914.

329

as a souvenir in Charborough House a piece of shrapnel that had landed on his foot during Jutland without harming him. HMS *Lion* had been hit a total of 14 times and took 99 dead and 51 wounded during the battle. She fired 326 rounds from her main guns and was credited with four hits on *Lützow* and one on *Derfflinger*.

1916 was a dramatic year for Reginald Drax, as in February, his mother, Lady Dunsany, died at the age of 60 at her home at Dunstall Priory, leaving Reginald the majority of her vast English estates in Dorset, Kent, Surrey, Wiltshire, Yorkshire and the West Indies. He assumed the additional surnames of Ernle-Erle-Drax on 4 October 1916 by royal licence. In April, Reginald now 36, married 23-year-old Kathleen Chalmers in Scotland. He was promoted to commander as the war drew to a close, and was awarded the Distinguished Service Order in 1918 for his command of the light cruiser HMS *Blanche* which undertook several dangerous missions mine-laying off the coast of the German Bight.

The Royal Navy was Sir Reginald Aylmer Ranfurly Plunkett-Ernle-Erle-Drax's life. Sir Reginald focused for many years on his career rather than the family estates. Recognised for his excellence in staff training, Drax was appointed the first director of the Naval Staff College, Greenwich, from 1919 to 1922. Reminiscing later, Drax recalled that he focused primarily on getting officers to think for themselves and to improve the Service. As he wrote:

> Without intelligent criticism you can have no progress; but in our Service, having sometimes criticism of the wrong sort, all criticism is looked on with suspicion. I know young officers who would tell you today that in their opinion certain things are wrong and ought to be put right, but they dare not say so officially because they believe their careers would be finished if they did so.[8]

Photographs of Drax in the early 1920s show him in his stiff RN officer's dress uniform as a tall, thin, but very fit-looking and handsome man with a ramrod straight back. He was said to be very

---

8. Robert L. Davison, 'Admiral Sir Reginald Drax and British Strategic Policy: Festina Lente', MA thesis, Wilfrid Laurier University, 1994, pp. 92–95.

attractive to women. The next posting was as president of the Naval Allied Control Commission in Germany from 1923 to 1924. This was a body that was designed to stop Germany from rearming itself after the war for anything except defence. Then, as a rear admiral, he commanded the 2nd Battle Squadron of the Home Fleet from 1929 to 1930. His wife, Kathleen, was something of a sportswoman and she took part in the Ladies Open Squash Championships that were held at the Queen's Club, West Kensington in London, in January 1931. In her match, she lost to the Scottish player Miss S. Knox 9–5 9–1 9–6.

Promoted to vice admiral on 24 September 1932, Reginald Drax held the post of Commander-in-Chief of the Americas and West Indies Squadron. The admiral and his wife were in attendance at the 1932 Olympic Games in Los Angeles and threw a glitzy party that was attended by US admirals Richard Leigh and Luke McNamee, several US Army colonels, the British and French consuls, California Governor James Rolph Jr and an assortment of European counts and princes.

According to actor David Niven, his career as an English heart-throb in Hollywood was accidentally launched by a visit to Vice Admiral Drax's flagship for a party. In his best-selling autobiography *The Moon's a Balloon*, Niven said that having left the British Army, he was on his uppers and bumming around America. He was staying for the weekend with an acquaintance called Lydia Macy in the millionaires' town of Montecito in California. On the first morning, he saw that HMS *Norfolk*, the Americas and West Indies squadron flagship, was moored at anchor in the bay. *Norfolk* was on a goodwill cruise along the coast of Mexico and California.[9] Lydia Macy told Niven they were invited to a cocktail party on the *Norfolk*

---

9. Built in 1928, HMS *Norfolk* was a County Class cruiser that also served in the Second World War. In September 1931, the crew of the *Norfolk* had been part of the Invergordon Mutiny over pay and treatment. Between 1932 and 1934, the cruiser was based at Ireland's Bay in Bermuda. Royal Navy ships based in Bermuda spent much of the year cruising around the Americas singularly or in small groups, stopping for goodwill visits while being available to respond to states of emergencies anywhere in the region. The entire squadron would exercise in Bermuda.

that evening. On board and much to his surprise, David Niven spied an old drinking partner, Anthony Pleydell-Bouverie, who was then the flag lieutenant to Admiral Drax. Niven got very drunk on pink gin, Lydia departed without him, and he overstayed and slept in a bunk, waking up with a stinking hangover.

Later Drax and Bouverie amused themselves at lunch by feeding Niven more pink gin and then pointing to the sight of the eighteenth-century British warship HMS *Bounty* out of the porthole – a replica built for the 1935 film – at full sail next to them. Prearranged, they put him, dishevelled but still wearing his dinner jacket, in the press barge at a PR junket for the launch of the film *Mutiny on the Bounty* with many of Hollywood's leading figures. Niven goes on to reveal it made him stand out and be recognised and become the only man 'to crash Hollywood in a battleship'. Drax's stint in Bermuda consisted of presiding over many such cruise cocktail parties for goodwill.[10] His wife and family members often spent time in Bermuda in those pre-air travel days, travelling by liner.

In 1934, Reginald Drax was knighted and that year Bermuda was visited by a curious Royal Navy expedition. A small crew of Royal Navy officers were sailing from Hong Kong to England in a newly built yacht called *Tai-Mo-Shan* (74 years later the yacht, still in pristine condition, appeared in the musical film *Mamma Mia*, captained by Pierce Brosnan). The 1934 voyage was a high-profile 14,500-mile trip expected to take seven to eight months. It had Admiralty approval as it was the kind of activity they liked adventurous officers to do during peacetime. The expedition was led by 26-year-old Lieutenant Robert Ryder, who had joined the Royal Navy in 1926. Along the way, the *Tai-Mo-Shan* stopped off at major ports in many countries as a goodwill gesture, and the crew became minor celebrities. When it came to the West Indies, they called into Bermuda as the home port for the American and West Indies Squadron. On arrival on 1 April, the yacht received a friendly and welcoming signal from Drax and made fast astern of HMS *Norfolk*, the squadron's flagship, now back at its base. The

---

10. David Niven, *The Moon's a Balloon* (London: Hamish Hamilton, 1972), pp. 162–165.

voyage had recently been difficult, and one of the crew had a stay in hospital. Faced with a three-week delay and behind schedule, they decided to make the best of it.

Taking the *Tai-Mo-Shan* for joy-trips for bathing and picnics for the squadron officers and wives was the order of the day. Ryder reported that they had taken the *Tai-Mo-Shan* for a short sail with a party of beauties, including Lady Drax and one of her daughters. The *Tai-Mo-Shan*'s captain seems to have enjoyed himself immensely, not least because, as he confessed to his parents in a letter, he had lost his heart to a girl who staying in the house. Ryder said that her husband was unfortunately a very senior officer, so he had to tread carefully when in her company.[11] Eventually, *Tai-Mo-Shan* left Bermuda to resume its voyage and arrived in Dartmouth, Devon, on 30 May, a day short of a year and 17,000 miles after setting off. The dashing figures of Drax and Ryder will reappear.[12]

After 150 years of absence, the Drax family took advantage of the Bermuda posting to visit the Drax Hall plantation in Barbados from time to time. I interviewed Fitzgerald Brereton in 2022 who had been born on the Drax Hall plantation some 100 years earlier. His father rented their home and some land from Drax Hall. Fitzgerald never worked on the plantation and became an electrician working elsewhere as his father would not allow his children to work on the plantation, and that caused tension with the plantation manager. Fitzgerald said efforts were made to rescind the lease to land the Brereton's rented on the plantation.

At 100, Fitzgerald's mind was still sharp, and he still preached at the church local to Drax Hall and drove around the island. He lived on the plantation until 1953 and then moved a few miles away to Ellerton, where he lived in a modest and well-kept bungalow. Speaking on the balcony of his Ellerton home, he said conditions on the plantation when he was young were hard. 'You could not aspire to better things. If you had a cow then it was expected to be used in part by the plantation, the same if you had a donkey. If

---

11. The implication is that she is Kathleen Drax.

12. Richard Hopton, *A Reluctant Hero* (Barnsley: Pen and Sword Press, 2011), p. 49.

you tried to improve yourself, you were said "to be getting above yourself".' I asked him whether he ever met Admiral Drax? 'I only saw a car come onto the estate, to the house, and someone would say "That's the Admiral". He would be on one of his visits. The Admiral did not live or stay on the plantation.' The house was the living accommodation for the manager and his family – who was always white. 'Did you ever go to the house?', I asked. 'No, the only black people that went there were the servants', he told me. He said there were often parties at the house where it was only white people from other plantations or Bridgetown. 'The apartheid in Barbados in those days was worse than South Africa', he told me. He recalled vividly the 1937 Bridgetown riots by poor Bajans. How much money the Drax family made from the plantation at this time is not clear. Sugar prices were not high and to protect their interests on the island, the Draxes relied heavily on the Pile family, who were (and still are) prominent in Barbados. During the Depression, Admiral Drax saw himself as a benign employer and wrote a note stating 'Charborough Ideals (at present unattainable)' in which he listed possible improvements. Some were eventually implemented included the Charborough Savings Bank which apparently never gave a return of less than 6 per cent and provided a half-yearly bonus to the men on the estate. It operated from 1923 to 1931.

In his 1956 account of his life, Admiral Drax thanked his wife as the consummate hostess, an unwritten requirement in the Royal Navy for the senior officer's wife to facilitate endless social events. Drax emphasised he had corresponded interwar with Churchill to push for more effective rearmament, sending him a copy of his article 'England's Last Chance' in October 1938, which he had to be careful to make sure Churchill understood that as Drax was a serving officer, it would not do if his senior officers got to hear of it.[13] Davison noted, 'Indeed, his only two criticisms of Churchill was the Prime Minister's insufficient attention to ensuring the British sea communications and the co-operation of all the services for a single objective.'

---

13.   DRAX 6/8, 'Drax & Churchill', 1966.

Drax was important in rejecting the doctrines of the First World War. The preoccupation with the concept of a Jutland-style battle, where the superior battle fleet would destroy its opponent no longer seemed relevant. Drax challenged that doctrine from early 1939, later writing:

> In the early years of the War, our Army, Navy, and Merchant Marine were suffering terrible losses because we were not receiving the close and constant support of the RAF, which was essential for our success. I do not blame the Prime Minister because he had, it seems, been persuaded by some of the airmen that they could win the War in a few months by bombing Germany if the Army and Navy could be told off and play by themselves...[14]

MISSION TO MOSCOW

Just before the Second World War started, Admiral Drax was chosen as the British representative of the Anglo-French military mission to Russia, which attempted to ally with the Soviets against German aggression. John Weitz wrote of this mission that it 'had no real power to negotiate... Drax was, politically speaking, a eunuch.'[15] Drax's French counterpart was General Aimé Doumenc, and the duo tried to discuss a possible alliance with the USSR with Soviet War Minister, Kliment Voroshilov. The British and French were outmanoeuvred by von Ribbentrop, the German Foreign Minister, who swiftly negotiated a Russo-German treaty of non-aggression. At the same time, Drax's group was engaged in vague staff talks in Leningrad. Drax was hobbled in that the British government did not provide him with transport to Moscow that would have got him there more quickly or any discretion to negotiate.

After the 1939 conferences, Admiral N.G. Kuznetsova commented acidly on British performance in this significant diplomatic battle. He noted a whole week passed before Neville Chamberlain announced to Parliament that the Cabinet appointed Sir

---

14. Davison, 'Admiral Drax', p. 119.
15. John Weitz, *Hitler's Diplomat: The Life and Times of Joachim von Ribbentrop* (New York: Ticknor & Fields, 1992), pp. 195, 204–206.

DRAX OF DRAX HALL

Reginald Drax head of the British mission. Kuznetsova said no one could be less suited for the job. 'Drax, ADC, was an old admiral in retirement who long lost all contact with Britain's Armed Forces.' Davison noted, 'Kuznetsov had a very definite axe to grind since he was compelled to show that the British did not desire an effective military agreement with the Soviet Union.'[16] Admiral Sinclair (head of MI6) wrote to Drax afterwards, 'It is an infernal shame... that they should send you to Moscow to try to clear up the mess that has been made out there by the politicians.'[17] Drax was clearly frustrated by the mission's failure.[18]

From 1939 to 1941 Drax was commander-in-chief at The Nore, whose role was to deal with naval operations and the bases at the estuary end of the Thames. He was involved in evacuating British troops from Dunkirk and preparing defensive measures for the anticipated German invasion. Drax's abilities were recognised within the Navy, since the First Sea Lord Admiral Sir Dudley Pound, known as a 'cunning old fox', brought him to the Admiralty to help keep Churchill's strategic follies down to a minimum, as in the Norway and bombing campaigns. It was said that Drax's intellectual bent and Pound's method of deflecting Churchill's unrealistic ideas, bureaucratically, merged very well. This had the added benefit of taking some pressure off the naval staff. Churchill also valued Drax's input in the decision-making process and thought it best to have the Admiral come into London once a week for consultation.[19]

Reginald Drax was friendly with Commander Ian Fleming RN who was in naval intelligence during the war. This relationship was going to have an impact on the Drax family that continues to this day. After the war, Ian Fleming became the author of the James Bond novels. In the book and film *Moonraker*, Fleming named the villain Hugo Drax.[20]

---

16. Davison, 'Admiral Drax', p. 65.
17. Donald C. Watt, *How War Came: The Immediate Origins of the Second World War 1938–1939* (New York: Pantheon Books, 1989), p. 459.
18. TNA: FO 371/29630.
19. Davison, 'Admiral Drax', p. 116.
20. The name Drax also appears as the villain in various gaming and graphic magazine stories.

336

RYDER AGAIN

In 1941 an acquaintance from the Bermuda posting appeared at Charborough. A man of action, Robert Ryder RN had made a big impression on Kathleen and her daughters when he took them sailing in the *Tai-Mo-Sham* during his stopover in Bermuda in 1934. In the early part of the war, Ryder had been assigned to captain the *Williamette Valley*, a Q-ship. This was a ship that looked like a merchant vessel but actually had hidden artillery pieces on board. The brainchild of Admiral Campbell, Q-ships were used successfully in the First World War against U-boats. U-boats tended to surface to use their guns rather than deploy precious torpedoes to sink lone merchant vessels. However, the captain of U-51 spotted *Williamette Valley* and over 40 minutes used three torpedoes. With the last explosion, the ship sank, Ryder was thrown out of the bridge into the water and found a piece of wooden flotsam to lie on. He was four days in the Atlantic south of Ireland, before he was picked up by a passing convoy. He had suffered severe sunburn on his face, hands and feet.

After a few days in hospital, he was invited to Charborough to recuperate, by then only walking with difficulty. He was there for a week and was delighted with the company, although Admiral Drax was away. Ryder and Kathleen Drax had struck up a friendship in Bermuda, but Ryder's attention was now drawn elsewhere.[21] As the week progressed, he became enamoured with the Drax daughter, Elizabeth, who was still a teenager. Now 33 years old, the dashing Ryder had been complaining to his parents in his letters that he had been feeling lonely and wanted to get to married. It soon became clear that Elizabeth was not interested.[22]

Admiral Drax was soon to return to Charborough but his war was far from over.

---

21. Hopton, *Reluctant Hero*, p. 112.
22. After his week at Charborough, Ryder returned to the war. A few months later he married Hilaire Green-Wilkinson. Ryder was later to command the famous St Nazaire raid. It was a high-cost raid, with many British casualties, but deemed partially successful. Ryder's exemplary courage earned him a Victoria Cross. After the war, he was elected a Conservative MP.

22
Admiral Drax RN, Twice Retired

Aged 61 years in 1941, Reginald Drax retired from the Royal Navy and returned to his estate in Dorset where he signed up as a private in the Charborough Home Guard.[1] Far from retiring from the debates around the conduct of the war, Drax intervened frequently. He was profoundly concerned about the strategic value of bombing Germany, which was consuming a large percentage of military resources. Frustrated, Drax published an article in the *Royal United Services Institution Journal* (RUSIJ) in November 1942. 'There is little help for Britain to win the war until our sea power, i.e., our power to control the sea communications of the world, has been greatly strengthened and made more or less unassailable.'[2]

In the spring of 1943, as the threat of German invasion receded, Private Reginald Drax of the Home Guard volunteered for duty as a commodore of convoys – the link between the merchant ships in a convoy and the naval escort, a task he was eminently skilled for. In The National Archives are the reports he was required to write on each of the convoys after they completed their voyages in the Atlantic. The records are all written in hand or typed by the Admiral. His repeated comments to senior officers were that the convoys were made vulnerable by ships that could not maintain a convoy speed of 10 knots. Just three examples were OS 65, which left Oban for Freetown on the West African coast and ports on 15 January 1944 with 53 ships. Before that, he had brought back convoy SC131 with 32 ships in May 1943 and HX251 with 88 ships in August 1943. In these convoys, the commodore was located in a merchant ship. With OS 65 it was the SS John Holt. His end-

---

1. It is hard to imagine Reginald Drax in an episode of TV favourite *Dad's Army*.
2. Davison, 'Admiral Drax', p. 125.

338

of-convoy report spoke well of the SS John Holt's leadership. 'Very good in all respects the captain and officers were very obliging.' They met Escort Group B3 at Oversay, and the report makes clear the threats. 'We met 2 or 3 U-Boats between Oban and Casablanca, but the escorts prevented them from attacking. Due to headwinds & heavy swell and poor steaming of no 55, the convoy was 24 hours late.'[3] Drax was critical of the fireman and stokers on the ships that straggled. Their job was to keep the coal fire up, creating the steam to power the ship.[4]

Admiral Drax's style of leadership came through from the personal account of George Tate who was the yeoman of signals to Admiral Drax. He clearly respected the Admiral as a senior officer. He told his wartime story to the BBC many years later.

I was a highly trained signals operator with a staff of six, having responsibility for communicating with the escort ships. The Admiral chose the ship that best served his purpose, which was the one with the best facilities on board, such as signal equipment, accommodation and radio staff.

On one trip in 1943, Tate received a signal advising of a possible attack, and he altered course by 45 degrees.

The Admiral was so annoyed that I had acted on my own initiative instead of awaiting orders that he sent me off the bridge. Later, however, he congratulated me on a swift manoeuvre that had reduced the severity of the losses and asked that I accept his apologies.

Later while on duty one night out in the Atlantic, Tate became aware of something moving just under the surface of the water. 'Training my signal lamp on the object I was horrified to see an

---

3. There is a book on this escort group, *The Echo of a Fighting Flower: The Story of HMS "Narcissus" and B3 Ocean Escort Group in WW2*, by Peter Coy.

4. TNA: ADM 199/314/ 1 Convoy OS 65; ADM 199/ 578/16 Convoy HX 251; ADM 199/580/15 Convoy SC 131; ADM 199/977/11 Convoy MKS80.

enemy submarine about to attack. I raised the alarm and action was taken to prevent our ship from being torpedoed. As a result, I was awarded the Distinguished Service Medal.'

It was very difficult for his wife Connie, Tate said, as she had joined the Women's Royal Naval Service (WRNS) while her brother had joined the RAF as a flight lieutenant in the Lancaster bombers Pathfinder Squadron and having her George on convoys.

> Connie was based in the Liver Buildings [an iconic building in the centre of the port of Liverpool used as a RN headquarters] – a very dangerous place to be. While I was on shore leave, Admiral Drax sent for my wife. He shook her hand and putting his arm round her shoulder he told her, 'Your husband is helping me to get through this war, I couldn't manage without him.'[5]

KEEPING THE HOME FIRES BURNING

In 1941, as the Draxes had returned to Charborough and, with the Admiral often away, Lady Kathleen organised its help with war work. They had evacuees or soldiers quartered in the house for much of the time. Three Drax daughters, Ernle, Doreen and Mary, served in the WRNS and Elizabeth in the Land Army.[6] As a 2nd Officer, WRNS, Doreen travelled a great deal across the world. Two of her tours included a secret trip, as cypher officer, with Sir Winston Churchill to the first Quebec conference (August 1943) to meet President Roosevelt, his advisor Harry Hopkins and their Chiefs of Staff, and a trip to Teheran in November 1943 for Sir Winston's conference with Roosevelt, Stalin and all the allied Chiefs of Staff. Their son Walter was at school when the war broke out, attending West Hill prep school in Titchfield, Fareham. The school was evac-

---

5. www.bbc.co.uk/history/ww2peopleswar/stories/82/a4136582.shtml, last accessed 26 June 2024.

6. Mary became Baroness Rothschild on her marriage to Baron Robert Rothschild, a Belgian diplomat who helped to draft the Treaty of Rome of 1957, the foundation of the European Economic Community (EEC). She was the former wife of Bobby Hollond.

ADMIRAL DRAX RN, TWICE RETIRED

uated to Atlantic House, Polzeath in Cornwall. Walter Drax joined HMS *Britannia* as a naval cadet in 1941. A few days before D-Day in June 1944, a US mechanised supply unit brought about 100 large army vehicles, mostly six-wheelers, and 700 men to Charborough and camped in the park. Admiral Drax remained a Commodore to the Convoys to the end of the war, bringing vital supplies to Britain. He never lost a ship from his convoys.

FINAL RETIREMENT

By then 65 years of age, Admiral Reginald Plunkett-Ernle-Erle-Drax retired again in 1945 after 51 years in the military, spanning two world wars. This time retirement was final. Back from the Atlantic, he worked alongside his wife Kathleen, improving the house, park and estate, developing his pet project, the Highwood Garden – their vision of natural beauty. Admiral Drax was obsessed with the creation of beauty at Charborough, following in the footsteps of his plantation-owning ancestors. Historically there seems to have been a need for those ancestors who had large incomes from slavery-based wealth to spend it on beautiful homes and fittings.[7]

Most of the estate's workforce had also returned from the war to resume their jobs in the daily and seasonal life of Charborough, as they and their predecessors had done for hundreds of years. Whether as a butler, forester, cook, house servant, carpenter, farmworker or gardener, the estate provided a good deal of employment for east Dorset residents. Like many of his family, Mr Phillip Cherrett had worked for the Drax family and had been there for 69 years. His son, Mr George Cherrett, a sawyer formerly in the Charborough Home Guard, was with them for over 37 years. The former Home Guard sergeant Ernie Hoare was, in his working life, the Charborough House chauffeur and mechanic for four decades. There was a great deal of loyalty to the family and their estate.

After inheriting the estate, Reginald had made efforts to buy back land and chattels lost by the Wicked Squire's looting, just as

---

7. Ernle-Erle-Drax, *History of Charborough*, p. viii.

his mother and grandmother had done. He also sought to acquire new land that rounded off gaps in the core estate. In 1921, he had acquired, along the eastern boundary, two or three fields from Mr Parke of the Henbury Estate. Then in 1932, he purchased from a neighbour, a Trenchard, the Windmill Barrow Farm and the Lytchett Highwood fields. This completed the Drax ownership of almost the whole area bounded by the three main roads. The park was now some 1500 acres and improvements were the order of the day. Lady Kathleen attended to the supervision of the modernisation and decoration of the interior of the house. Occasionally, the Admiral splashed out and, in 1930, bought a letter written by Lord Nelson, which he kept in the library.

By 1942, the vast Charborough Estate absorbed 30 farms,[8] the third largest family collection in Dorset, with only the Pitt-Rivers Estate (51) and Digby's Sherborne Estate (48) larger. Even the extensive Ilchester Estate only had 19 farms.[9] Families that had held these farms like the Rokes, Filiols, Skippets and Ekins had moved on. One of the farms absorbed into the estate was called Botany Bay Farm. At the nearby junction with the A31 main road is a red-painted four-sign fingerpost. From the late eighteenth century, shackled convicts who were to be transported to Australia were marched along this road on their way to Portsmouth from the various courts in the South-west including Dorchester. Legend has it that, as the jail guards were illiterate, this signpost was painted red as this told the guards that there was a nearby overnight stop in a farm barn. This farm became known as Botany Bay, as did the nearby pub.[10]

---

8.   After acquiring these family farms, they became tenanted farms. Today, few are still tenant farms. The farmhouses have mostly been separated from the farms and the farmyards are used for storage or rented out. Charborough Estate's arable farming is controlled from Miller's farmyard not far from the main house and is entered from the delightfully named Vermin Lane.

9.   Original source TNA MAF 80/545. W.A.E.C. Cultivations Subcommittee 1942.

10.   The signpost can be still seen on the A31 near Bloxworth, as can the pub. The farm is no longer a working part of the estate but is rented out to an agricultural machinery dealer.

DEATH AND TAXES

The Admiral told friends that running the estate from 1916 to 1956 was difficult, blaming creeping taxes and socialism. After the Second World War, there had been a landslide Labour victory, but, he complained, there was inflation and a constant fall in the value of sterling. His observation was that this all mattered less for the farmer or the manufacturer, for the farmer is heavily subsidised by the taxpayer and the manufacturer can steadily increase the price of what he sells. But he said that socialist legislation had pressured the landowner to increase expenditure for the upkeep of cottages and maintenance and improvement of farm buildings. Admiral Drax felt that under these difficult circumstances, the landowner should help the best farmers most, and the worst farmers least. Even the election of Sir Winston Churchill's Conservative government in 1951 and then the years of Labour in opposition did little to relieve Admiral Drax's concerns.

Many beleaguered estate-owners across the country handed their properties over to the National Trust or sold them off to the nouveau riche or even foreign purchasers. Like other landed-gentry families, the Draxes had been using private trusts effectively for centuries. In his time, the estate was extensively restructured so that the estate was passed on to the family and the benefit of family members for their lifetime. The family's wills showed this was an efficient protection against inheritance taxes, and given the value of the estate, relatively little tax was paid on death.[11] The Admiral railed against death duties as an intolerable strain. He complained it was merely a part of that modern levelling down process.[12]

Agriculture was changing. During Admiral Drax's time at Charborough, the amount of forestry significantly increased, and the estate had some 2000 acres of tree plantations, managed by a relationship with the Forestry Commission which produced revenue over the long term and had very favourable tax arrangements. The

---

11. After the death of a person in the UK, their will is placed in the public domain online.

12. Ernle-Erle-Drax, *History of Charborough*, p. 66.

first Commission land was leased from the Drax family in 1923, forming a large block north of Wareham. In 1953, two further plantations were created, one on each side of Boar Hill Drive, to commemorate the coronation of Queen Elizabeth II. The Admiral and his wife were among the guests invited to Westminster Abbey for the ceremony. Large commercial landowners had been able to avoid heavy taxation by being allowed to transfer their woodlands between two tax schedules, B and D, once during a lifetime.

In his history, Admiral Drax portrayed the landed gentry as central to society and its administration. He pointed to all the roles that the landed gentry tended to take on from MPs, JPs, military, militia, mayors, parish councils and, in some cases, as philanthropists. He pointed out the thousands of sons of the landed gentry who died in the First World War, as officers during the murderous trench warfare. Indeed, the landed gentry did contribute and were integrated into the hierarchy of society. If they were doing their duty to the community, they also benefitted by their powerful influence to make sure the system protected their family's place in it.

Researching the Plunkett-Ernle-Erle-Drax family (and this goes for many other landed-gentry families who were historically slave owners), one becomes conscious that there is a constant search for beauty both for inner gratification and also as a statement of personal culture. They make their own environment, whether by the riches of art and decoration in their homes and in the landscape around, without recognition of the public reflection on how the wealth that paid for it so often came from the sweat of those who lived in hovels. The Admiral's history is nostalgic about the past and particularly about the creation of beauty. There is an epic poem 'Charborough 1950' about the estate and its beauty, that contains the notion, as promulgated famously in 'Rule Britannia', that Britons will never be slaves. It is called 'The Darkest Hour' and has the lines:

> Men fought for England-England and high ideals,
> Truth and the beauty of their cherished land,
> Freedom from sore oppression and the weals
> Of Slavery and the taskmaster's brand.

In retirement, the Admiral still took an interest in military matters and wrote a long stream of papers published in military journals, copies of which are in his collection at Churchill College, Cambridge. One was notably entitled 'World War Three – The Pros and Cons'.[13] Aside from his estate duties, the Admiral was a bit of an innovator. He became fascinated by the potential of solar power and wrote a book about solar heating after he experimented with using solar to heat the house swimming pool. He advocated what we would now call rewilding – allowing wildflowers to grow in the woodlands with snowdrops, daffodils, violets, primroses and many other species. He was still managing a far-flung estate. In 1952, the estate still included Lincolnshire lands, and the tenants there presented a silver salver to the Admiral that year.

THE SILENT PLANTATION

Journeying from the north part of Charborough Estate to the south part requires crossing a road named Sugar Hill, a constant reminder of the source of much of the estate's wealth. In Admiral Drax's history, there is little mention of Barbados and the period of slavery. It is referred to very much in passing. More time is spent on a note about a herd of zebu, a species of cattle associated with Barbados kept at Charborough Park.[14] There is no indication that the family having once owned enslaved people was an issue in any way. Nor is there mention of how slavery had benefitted the family. The Admiral and his family were very active Anglicans, and in his papers is the script of a 'Ten to Eight' radio broadcast he delivered on the BBC referring to a private collection of quotations which have helped deepen his belief in God. This he expanded and printed as 'A few notes for Atheists and Agnostics'.

The Drax family kept the plantation running as absent landlords, but postwar a senior member of the family would try to visit once a year. It was no longer the money-spinner it had been in the seventeenth to nineteenth centuries. Nonetheless, sugar pro-

---

13. CCCA GBR/0014/DRAX 6.
14. Highland cattle, emus and peafowl were also kept.

duction in Barbados increased from an average of 50,444 tons per annum during the 1930s, to reach 74,593 tons in the 1940s and 191,000 tons (an all-time high) by the 1950s.[15] The family gave no indication why they continued to own Drax Hall. The Lascelles family, who had extensive plantation interests in the West Indies going back to 1648 and were perhaps the only other family who still owned their original plantations, finally sold out of Barbados after independence. Mount and Belle plantations were sold off by 1975.

A person who knew Drax Hall well in the Admiral's time, as a child, is Esther Phillips, now the poet laureate of Barbados and 70 when I interviewed her. 'I grew up in Greens – just across from Drax Hall. My grandfather kept cows in Drax Hall yard, and he would send me as a small child with a skillet to get milk. But it was terrifying to me as a small child because of the dogs that were kept there.' She has written poetry about her memories of Drax Hall. 'There is a sense of shame and a sense of guilt that I grew up, and for so many years, and did not know what this plantation house symbolised. I had no idea that when we were running and playing that we were actually running, playing and walking over the bones of our ancestors.'[16] She now knows there must be an unmarked cemetery near the house where enslaved people were buried. In 1966, Barbados was granted independence from the UK but remained part of the Commonwealth.

WALTER 'WOL' HENRY DRAX

Admiral Drax died in 1967 at the age of 87. His long life had saved the estate a good deal of tax as it had bridged the period of

---

15.   Ian McDonald, 'The Sugar Industry of the Caribbean Community (CARICOM): An Overview', report published by the Sugar Association of the Caribbean, 2004, p. 1.

16.   Tenantry communities like Greens surround the plantation. These were set up when the slave villages were demolished after manumission, and the freed enslaved people moved into common land around the plantations. As I saw for myself, the housing for most people is still very basic concrete houses. These are still poor areas. There are some more expensive properties in this beautiful countryside. In 2008, Walter Drax sold off a tranche of the plantation, about 200 acres, for development on some higher ground, which features higher quality homes.

maximum death duties. He had already made provision for most of his family through trusts.[17] His wife Kathleen outlived him by 13 years, dying in 1980, also at the age of 87. The Admiral's son Walter, known as 'Wol', had not emulated his father's distinguished career in the Navy but nonetheless had a varied service. Having joined as a cadet in the Second World War, he was too young to fight. In November 1945, he went to Tokyo in the battleship HMS *Anson* and then to Kure, and saw the remains of Hiroshima where the first atomic bomb had flattened the city. During the 1950s, as a naval officer, Walter Drax served on the frigate HMS *Burghead Bay* in the West Indies and in different roles on other navy ships. In 1957, Walter Drax, 27 years old, who contemporaries described as having the Drax good looks, trim physique and a strong personality, married the 26-year-old Honourable Pamela Weeks, daughter of Lord Weeks, chairman of Vickers Armstrong, engineers to the military. In advance of the wedding, her portrait was the feature in *Country Life* magazine.[18] They had five sons who were sent off to expensive prep and public boarding schools like Maidwell Hall, Harrow and Eton. Pamela proved to be cut from the same cloth as her predecessor Kathleen, the consummate wife of an officer and squire. The local Bere parish magazine noted her frequent engagement in local events, opening fetes, and doing good works around east Dorset.

In 1968 Walter retired from the Royal Navy at the rank of lieutenant commander to run the Charborough Estate following his father's death the previous year. As the sole male sibling, though the youngest child, the estate passed to him, and he centralised it around its core lands in Dorset, Yorkshire and Barbados. In 1970, Wol bought the 500-acre Copperthwaite allotment on the high moor above his Ellerton Estate in the Swaledale valley. It was grouse territory. Walter Drax was not to take to the national stage and concentrated on the estate and the county, taking on the traditional role of squire. Walter was a major supporter of the local Anglican

---

17.   His probate shows that his part of the estate was worth £105,102, and some £26,417 estate duty and interest was paid.

18.   15 February 1957.

church and apparently a strict father. A sporting man, he was a member of the South Dorset Hunt from 1965 to 1975. Walter's passion was golf, and he was a regular at the refined environs of the Isle of Purbeck Golf Club, above Studland with panoramic views of Poole Harbour. In 1976, he was elected an underwriting member of Lloyd's of London, which remains one of the few public indications that the Draxes had serious capital assets as well as land and property.[19] Mr Drax was appointed deputy lieutenant of the county and five years later became the high sheriff of Dorset like some of his ancestors – all in keeping with the natural order of the county as it had been for centuries. Those who knew his wife Pamela Drax spoke well of her. One told me, 'Pammy was a lovely woman, very kind. But Wol ruled the roost.' She was a patron of Julia's Hospice, a major Dorset hospice network. Despite all these posts, the Drax family tended to keep a low profile, and there was very little coverage in the news media.

THE DRAX COTTAGE SCANDAL

Over the decades the Drax family always presented themselves as benign landlords. Evidenced history tells a more nuanced story. Quite a few houses on the estate were occupied by staff as part of their remuneration package.[20] The more senior the staff member, the larger and better the house. Other properties were just tenanted. In 1956, like his predecessors, Admiral Drax had made the case that maintaining properties the estate rented out to a high standard was not economically viable. This was an argument that had run for many years and recalls Charles Harper's comment in 1905 about the poor state of their rented homes in Bere Regis. But, as with all

---

19.   Although his membership of Lloyd's is referred to in Walter's 2012 will as to be passed onto his eldest son. In 2021, Richard Drax said his father ceased membership some years before 2017. Lloyd's, incidentally, became one of the first institutions to pay some form of reparations for their involvement historically in the slave trade.

20.   All the front doors of Charborough Estate-owned houses are painted a particular shade of blue so that the Drax family can recognise what they own more easily.

things in the natural order, the landlord set the financial criteria. Admiral Drax had complained about the expense of maintaining the various cottages and houses around the estate. Many were more than 200 years old. Into the 1950s, old houses were not as prized for their character as they were to become and were often seen as a liability. The Admiral did not see these properties as assets though he said in 1956 he would like to see each employee's house fitted with and electric light, water, toilet and a bath, WC and modern drains. He also stated that they were building new cottages for farmers, farmworkers and estate employees.[21]

As 'Wol' Drax took over the estate, Rodney Legg, a local activist and writer, took up the cause of those Charborough tenants who felt their homes were being allowed to fall into severe disrepair. Legg had founded and published *Dorset: The County Magazine*.[22] Drax Estate cottage demolitions had been reported critically in *The Sun* newspaper as early as 1967. Seeing even more buildings neglected and demolished, Rodney Legg devoted six pages of the magazine to the story in 1972. He opened with the case of the Cakes. Wilfred Cake was born at the turn of the century, so he was 72 at the time. He and his wife Ivy lived in an eighteenth-century farmhouse near Morden Park Corner. The thatch had collapsed through their bedroom ceiling, and elder, ash, holly and grass grew from the roof above. Legg noted that a polythene sheet was lashed around to catch the water as it streamed down, and Ivy had sacrificed a side piece of her mahogany furniture to bolster the bulging ceiling. 'It's fairly dry inside – except when it rains', Mr Cake had remarked wryly. Wilfred had fought at Ypres and the Somme and was taken prisoner by the Germans after shrapnel smashed his ankles in the trenches of the Hindenburg Line.

---

21. Ernle-Erle-Drax, *History of Charborough*, pp. 61–62.

22. Patrick Wright, *The Village that Died for England: The Strange Story of Tyneham* (London: Faber & Faber, 2002). The lords of manor for Tyneham were the Bonds, long-time friends of the Draxes. Legg was also a prominent figure in the long campaign to get nearby Tyneham, 'The village that died for England', back from the Ministry of Defence after it was retained as a military training area after the Second World War.

Legg wrote that the Cakes had known the hard life for most of the century. Their names had been on the application list for a council house for the preceding ten years. The farmhouse was Charborough Estate property where they were given a bathroom with help of a government grant. The Cakes told Legg in 1972 that they had been visited about two years earlier by the Drax agent, who said the house was not worth repairing. 'They won't do anything,' Mr Cake explained. 'They told me they won't repair it and I have to get out. We have got nowhere else to go.'

> They did a bit of thatch once, about seven years ago, and my son paid for it, I think. I work for them when they ask and I don't get anything for it, but I live in the house. I've got the cottage and I don't pay rent. So I do odd jobs for nothing.

Legg then documented other properties that had been demolished. Some of the cottages had still been in good condition after the war but allowed to fall into disrepair. Legg stated at the time:

> Unfortunately, the Drax family have a long history of acting differently from the way most of us behave. Others would have sold these country cottages at vast profit and established the equivalent of a stockbroker belt for Bournemouth's richer businessmen and solicitors. Instead, in the past two decades the Draxes have happily destroyed a part of the national stock of houses and this is as much our business as theirs.

Legg had had an hour-long conversation with Walter Drax which was mostly off the record. According to Legg, Drax did say 'What we are trying to do is preserve the best. Each cottage has to be decided on its merits and these are some of the factors which we take into account in deciding a cottage's future – its conditions, its site.' In the end, they agreed on a statement for Legg to print: 'After discussion with the editor, Mr Drax was convinced that no amount of discussion would suffice to persuade him to accept the other side of the picture which has not been represented in this article. It is gutter journalism.'[23]

The Guardian picked up on Rodney Legg's 'Drax Cottage Scandal', as he headlined the investigation in the magazine, which their reporter said:

Involved the demolition of over thirty 200-year-old quaint cottages, for apparently unfathomable reasons. Very briefly for it is a tale of much colour and even more detail back in the sixties, Admiral Sir Reginald Aylmer Ranfurley Plunkett-Ernle-Er-le-Drax, now deceased, began a scorched earth policy to deal with the problem of decaying cottages.

Legg claimed that when the Admiral died, the policy was continued by Walter Drax. The *Guardian* report continued:

It's not just cottages either, that Lt Cdr Drax likes to demolish. Any old, interesting building will do. For instance, in July 1970, an eighteenth-century barn stood on Drax territory, a barn noted by the Royal Commission on Historical Monuments. On August 1, 1970, a Dorset County Council official was due to visit then at 3pm to decide whether it should qualify for on-the-spot listing. But by eight in the morning, a host of demolishers descended on the barn and by the end of the day it was buried, brick by brick in a deep hole. The Wareham and Purbeck Rural District Council have placed around 25 closing or demolition orders on Drax cottages on the grounds that they were beyond repair at reasonable expense.

The *Guardian* reporter said they had tried to talk to Walter Drax but was told the family had decided they would 'not produce a counterblast and just leave it alone. There is very much another side to the story. We're proud of our housing record in Morden.' It is not known whether any further buildings were demolished or what the

---

23.   Rodney Legg, 'The Drax Cottage Scandal', *The Dorset County Magazine*, edition 28 (winter 1972), pp. 19–28.

final total is. The Cakes house may have survived, as it is still listed as an estate property. By 2016, the Drax family still owned at least 125 properties in Dorset. Since then, they have sold off a handful, usually those that were not in Charborough Park. Many of their Bere Regis properties were sold off long ago. Those old cottages, houses, mills and barns that survived are now worth, of course, a premium.

In the early 1990s, a doctoral student from Birkbeck College looked into the widely held view that the estates of the landed gentry had largely gone and specifically examined what had happened in Dorset. In her excellent thesis, for which she was awarded her PhD in 1995, geographer Janet Waymark noted:

Landed estates present an important part of the cultural and economic landscape in Dorset today. Of the twelve families owning 10,000 acres or more in Bateman's Survey of 1883, ten remain, most retaining 5,000 acres or more, and they have been joined by others post-Bateman.

In Dorset, Waymark noted, the 'leaders of the agricultural interest' largely remained in the saddle. And furthermore, ambitions to maintain or develop their great estates took on a new dimension with state aid after the Second World War.[24] She demonstrated that a surprisingly large amount of Dorset, far from being sold off, had remained in the hands of the long-standing landed gentry, most impressively, the Drax family. In 2025, the National Trust is now the biggest landowner, Crichel Down Estate is now owned by an American billionaire and the Bryanston Estate was sold by the Crown Estate to Lord Rothermere, owner of the *Daily Mail*, but little else has changed. Order has prevailed.

---

24. Janet Waymark, 'Landed Estates in Dorset since 1870: their Survival and Influence', PhD thesis, Geography Department, Birkbeck College, University of London, 1995.

23

Richard Drax, 14 Years an MP

The Plunkett-Ernle-Erle-Drax family of Charborough would have continued to live in relative obscurity into the twenty-first century had it not been for the oldest of Wol's sons, Richard, becoming a public figure, firstly, as a journalist – later working for the BBC as a reporter – then as a Member of the British Parliament, but more recently because of his controversial response over the family's legacy of slavery.

Born in 1958, he was sent to an expensive prep boarding school and then to one of Britain's top public schools, Harrow. As the oldest son, Richard inherited the estate on his parents' deaths, and he became head of the family.[1] As the incumbent of the Charborough House and head of the Charborough Estate, Richard Grosvenor Plunkett-Ernle-Erle-Drax is the eighteenth in succession from John Erle of Ashburton, twentieth in the direct male line from Christopher, First Baron Dunsany (created 1439) and twenty-fifth in lineal descent from King Henry III, 1206–1272, a Plantagenet king.[2]

After Harrow, he spent time as a 'jackaroo' on an Australian sheep farm. On his return, rather than go to university, he went to Sandhurst officer training school and joined the Coldstream Guards. He served in a number of countries including Germany, Cyprus, Kenya, Brunei, Hong Kong and the United States, and under-

---

1.   His father died in 2017 and his mother in 2019.
2.   Richard has four younger brothers. Jeremy is the next and directly owns land and property in Dorset. He is a property developer and made it into the *Sunday Times Rich List* around 2009 when he also donated £25,000 to the Conservative Party. After Eton and military service, the third son became a teacher in a public school in the north-east of England. The fourth son, also Eton-educated and a former soldier, is a friend of Prince William and is a tech businessman. The youngest is a recovery psychotherapist.

353

took three tours in Northern Ireland during 'the Troubles'. Richard unsuccessfully tried to get into the Special Air Service (SAS) and towards the end of Richard's seven-year military service, he was promoted to captain.

In 1985 Richard Grosvenor Plunkett-Ernle-Erle-Drax, 27, married the 19-year-old Zara, the sister of the then British royal nanny Tiggy Legge-Bourke at the Guards Chapel, Wellington Barracks. Tiggy had achieved celebrity status for looking after Princes William and Harry. Zara brought royal connections, and King Charles's sister, Princess Anne, attended the Draxes' wedding with her daughter, Princess Zara, as a bridesmaid. Richard and Zara Drax had two boys and two girls. Their eldest daughter was a good friend of Prince Harry during childhood. Richard's wife was also a friend of the then Prince Charles, and in one newspaper report, a photograph showed her accompanying him at Ascot in the early 1990s. On leaving the army, Richard studied land management at the Royal Agricultural College, near Cirencester, the modern-day precursor for the eldest male of the landed gentry, who would be taking over the family estate. However, his father Wol remained firmly in charge. At the late age of 31, Richard decided he wanted to be a reporter and joined the *Yorkshire Evening Press* newspaper where he was, for a time, an education correspondent and then ran the Malton area office. While seeking to break into broadcasting, Richard freelanced at Tyne Tees TV. He then joined BBC Radio Solent and went to the regional TV news programme *BBC South Today*, where he spent nine years. He became one of the station's onscreen reporters, working across the south of England and occasionally abroad. Several of his colleagues told me he was best at 'action man' reports. One eyewitness recalled him striding across smouldering Purbeck heathlands with his camera crew struggling to keep up, as he reported on another major summer grass fire in Dorset.

Zara and Richard divorced in 1997, after which he married his flame from his teenage years, Eliza Dugdale, whose father, Commander James Dugdale RN, had been an aide to the Duke of Windsor in Bermuda during the Second World War. The reignited flame burnt out quickly and divorce followed. Later, he married Elsebet, an interior designer from Norway. She is a horsewoman, a keen bridge player, supports charities and is an engaging hostess to the shooting weekends that the couple like to throw for friends and influential figures from London.

POLITICS

In the mid-2000s, Richard Drax apparently surprised himself by deciding he wanted to go into politics, following in the footsteps of so many of his ancestors. The Wareham constituency had been eliminated long ago, in 1885, and absorbed into the Mid Dorset and North Poole constituency.[3] In 2006 he was selected as the Conservative parliamentary candidate for South Dorset to oppose Labour MP Jim Knight. To get elected, Knight had broken a very long run of Conservative MPs in the seat.[4] The Conservative Party selection event for South Dorset was intense, apparently with 30 applicants. But the local landowner won out, citing a very conservative manifesto that appealed to his local party. Some of his BBC colleagues were surprised at this move and told me that they did not think he was politically minded, and had just taken it that his political views were very old-fashioned.

The writer of a profile of Richard Drax for *Dorset Life* in 2013 observed that when most men have a mid-life crisis, they get a motorbike or take up a new hobby. Drax already had expensive top-of-the-range BMW motorbikes and a range of pursuits typical of the landed gentleman. Rather than being in a midlife crisis, he told the writer, his was a crisis over the direction of the United Kingdom. Richard Drax admitted he was becoming a bit of a Victor Meldrew – shouting at the TV and throwing newspapers in

3. Charborough Park is mostly in this constituency.
4. Dorset has been a very conservative county with five Conservative MPs up to the July 2024 General Election, where four were removed, replaced by Liberal Democrats or Labour.

the bin. He took the view that everything he loved in this country was under attack. He felt he should try and do something.[5]

Now a Tory candidate, Richard Drax resigned from the BBC and took on more responsibilities on the family estate as his parents were now well past retirement age. As the 2010 election approached, he went on the stump around the constituency in the pursuit of votes, finding himself engaged in such delights as playing table tennis with pensioners in their weekly club meeting in Swanage. His manifesto was centred around leaving the European Union and reducing immigration, and it resonated with many South Dorset voters. He was elected with a majority of 7443. He described himself as an avowed patriot and Royalist, and one of his favourite hymns is 'I Vow To Thee My Country', which he finds very emotional. Richard Drax has been a lifelong admirer of British tradition. His political hero is Margaret Thatcher.[6] It is said that the Prime Minister David Cameron advised his new MP to drop his four-barrelled surname and be known simply as Richard Drax.

Sasha Swire, author of the mischievous *Diary of a MP's Wife*, wrote of her and her husband – who was then a Tory MP in Devon – spending a shooting weekend at Charborough, and said Richard Drax was a handsome man, but his right-wing views were 'off the scale'. She then lists his voting record in the House of Commons and noted he voted against a 2016 amendment that required private landlords to make their homes 'fit for human habitation'. She concluded he was an unreconstructed, old-style landed Tory and 'probably the only one left'.[7] His Parliamentary record showed Drax generally voted against climate change mitigation, equality and rights legislation, same-sex marriage and gay rights. He opposed tax rises for high earners, windfall taxes and a bankers' levy. He used the phrase 'we must get our country back'. In the 2019 election, the

---

5. Paul Burbidge, 'Not Your Usual MP', *Dorset Life*, January 2013. *Dorset Life* magazine and its website have sadly ceased publication.
6. British Prime Minister, May 1979–November 1990.
7. Swire, *Diary of an MP's Wife*, pp. 497–499.

majority of South Dorset voters liked what the Conservatives had to offer and Richard Drax increased his majority to 17,153.

IMMIGRATION AND BREXIT

All this coalesced in his key election promises – restricting immigration and his belief that leaving the EU would enhance the British nation. He was above all a proponent of Brexit. On the day before the 2016 vote, his website said he had no doubt the country would be freer, safer, more prosperous and in control of its destiny if it left the EU. He claimed what was sold as a trading agreement was now an unwieldy bureaucracy, run from the centre, with ever closer union. As an MP he had been a long-standing member of the Conservative Party's European Research Group (ERG), which will be remembered as the ardent lobby for the Brexit experiment. Richard Drax gradually raised his profile in the Commons, speaking more often in debates, talking to journalists and sitting on the Defence Select Committee. He was never offered a ministerial post and told friends he would not want to be a minister as he wanted to be free to speak his mind.

Richard Drax's 'small state, large estate' politics appeared rooted in a concatenation of High Church Anglicanism, a survival-of-the-fittest ethos, and libertarianism. The religious influence was passed down by his parents and grandparents. There is also a strong streak of pragmatism. The Charborough Estate farming, forestry and property empire has had subsidies and tax breaks for many years. Richard Drax's dislike of the EU did not stop the estate accepting millions of pounds of EU Common Agricultural Policy (CAP) subsidies. My 2020 estimate of the overall value of Charborough, based on the local land and property market, valued the estate at least £150 million.[8] By dint of his birth, during his time as an MP Richard Drax became acknowledged as the wealthiest land-owning Member of the House of Commons. In contrast, his constituency contains some of the least socially mobile people in the country.

---

8. The estimate has not been challenged and the total worth is now likely greater as a result of the relaxing of planning laws.

Most things have stayed the same for the large Dorset estates over the decades, with the largest estates covering one-sixth of the county and concentrated in the east of the county.[9] The biggest family-owned estate in Dorset is now the Draxes of Charborough. Their agricultural land is far more valuable for its tax benefits than the profits from what grows on it. After he took over as the head of the Charborough Estate, he has sought to improve its revenue stream. Following in his grandfather's footsteps, he is alive to renewables' economic potential, particularly that of solar power. On a number of occasions in the 2000s, the estate sought to increase its income through large solar panel or building projects but was seen off by dogged opposition by campaign groups, including the Campaign to Protect Rural England (CPRE).[10] More recently, a solar energy company rents fields on the southern border of the estate.

BARBADOS

It is the unique ownership of Drax Hall 'Sugar Plantation One', the once slave-worked plantation in Barbados that has made this Richard Drax internationally known. At the time of our first *Observer* story in December 2020, in response to our pre-publication questions he acknowledged that he was the executor of his parents' estates and controlled the Drax Hall plantation. He then formalised his coming ownership of the Drax Hall (Plantation One) in his declaration for the Register of Members' Interests, saying 'Currently administering a business property in Barbados, title to be transferred to me in due course.'[11]

---

9. https://whoownsengland.org/2020/01/04/the-ten-landowners-who-own-one-sixth-of-dorset/, last accessed 27 June 2024.
10. The estate does rent out land to a commercial solar farm at Wool in Purbeck.
11. On completion of his parents' probate in February 2022, Richard Drax changed his declaration in the Register of Members' Interests to include owning 'a business property in Barbados'. A few other changes had been made and can seen at: https://publications.parliament.uk/pa/cm/cmregmem/220503/220503.pdf, last accessed 8 July 2024.

In recent years Richard Drax's politics became the target of criticism and protest by a range of UK campaign groups. Stand Up to Racism Dorset extensively campaigned for the Drax family to pay reparations and demonstrated outside the iron gates of Charborough and in Weymouth. Extinction Rebellion also held demonstrations outside the park over his climate change votes. Local animal rights protestors protested at his support of the South Dorset Hunt and poverty campaigners pointed to his wealth and compared it with the plight of his then constituents in Weymouth and Portland. Judging by his blog and photo-ops in the local media, he would undoubtedly claim he has worked hard to improve the local economy, employment and social mobility. After 14 years as an MP, Richard Drax lost his seat in South Dorset in the Great Tory Disaster that was the 2024 General Election.[12] Unlike many unseated MPs, he did not have to find a new job, but like so many of his ancestors, right back to Walter Erle the musician in 1560, at the end of public service he returned to running the Charborough Estate full time.

Charborough remains resolutely located in the farming, hunting, shooting, fishing and riding tradition of the large British estate, a world of Land Rovers, Purdey shotguns and Barbour jackets. There have been a few members of the family with liberal views over the years, but they had never been important enough to make changes to the narrative. The family have come to epitomise the British Squirearchy.

It is not known at the time of writing what Richard Drax intends to do long term with the Drax Hall plantation. In May 2024, the Drax Hall plantation harvested the sugar cane crop as it had done for nearly 400 years, producing some 700 tonnes for refining. The plantation has been managed for 40 years by the same Barbadian. There is no need for the 300 workers of the eighteenth century as

---

12. He was undone by the sudden rise of the right-wing Reform Party, which took many votes away from him, allowing the Labour candidate to win. Richard Drax came second and was replaced by Labour MP Lloyd Hatton, who came from a working-class background and was from within the South Dorset constituency, having grown up in Weymouth.

these days the cutting and transportation are done with specialist mechanical equipment.[13] When the crop is completed, there is still the annual festival of Grand Kadooment that marks 'crop over' that takes place in the summer in Bridgetown.[14] Journalist Jonathan Smith talked to several retirees who had been agricultural workers of colour on the Drax Hall plantation and spoke of how hard the work was and that it was not well-paid.[15]

Richard Drax's critics often claim that the family made their money from Drax Hall's sugar and slavery. It is not correct, as I have noted in earlier chapters. But is true they made a lot of money from the Drax Hall plantation over centuries. My analysis is that for several centuries it was providing up to a quarter of the vast Charborough Estate's income, somewhere in the range of £3000–£5000 a year. As noted, between 1825 and 1834, the Drax Hall estate in Barbados produced an average of 163 metric tons of sugar and 4845 gallons of rum per year, which gave the family a net profit of £3591 a year. It is likely at this time the wider Charborough Estate in Britain was producing about £15,000 to £20,000 a year. Drax Hall's

---

13. Tracking down those in Barbados and the diaspora who have historical connections to Drax Hall plantation workers has not been easy. Many families whose ancestors were enslaved in the colonies have surnames related to their owners, overseers or the plantations they were held on. That is why many people of colour from the West Indies have surnames that are clearly British in origin. Their African names were lost in captivity and replaced by surnames that were, in effect, identification tags. Few descendants of those who worked at Drax Hall plantations in Barbados and Jamaica seem to have had the surname Drax. I met one woman of colour whose family includes the surname Drax and who believed there had been an interracial 'outside marriage' in the family many years ago. She did not want to be identified and that is respected.

14. In 1990, I was lucky enough to go to the festival, to meet up with at the festival legendary Soca singers Gabby and Grynner and watch the Masquerade Bands parade. I then went to meet with musician Eddy Grant at the Bayley's plantation house, where he lived and had a recording studio. At that time the former leader of the 1960s group The Equals and then solo star with many hits, Eddy Grant was the most famous musician on the island. Today, Rihanna is the global superstar who was brought up and often returns to Barbados.

15. Paul Lashmar, Jonathan Smith and Alan Selby, 'Wealthy Tory MP Raking in Cash from Sugar Plantation Where Thousands Died During Slave Trade', *Sunday Mirror*, 12 December 2020.

extra revenue would have made a great difference to the family's financial resilience. In 2025, Drax Hall land is valuable. Barbados has a housing crisis and it being a small island, land which can be developed commands a very high price per acre, even compared to UK rural land. Fifty acres of Drax Hall fields are worth more than £3 million on the open market.

REPARATIONS

For *The Observer* and *Sunday Mirror* articles in 2020 when Jonathan Smith and I raised the question of slavery and his ancestors with Richard Drax, he replied: 'It is deeply, deeply regrettable, but no one can be held responsible today for what happened many hundreds of years ago.'[16]

Sir Hilary Beckles responded: 'It is no answer for Richard Drax to say it has nothing to do with him when he is the owner and the inheritor. They should pay reparations.' Sir Hilary added that historically, in previous centuries: 'The Drax family has done more harm and violence to the black people of Barbados than any other family. The Draxes built and designed and structured slavery. Richard Drax has to acknowledge the criminal enrichment that he is the recipient of.'[17] The Barbadian Prime Minister Mia Mottley has stated her nation seeks reparations from UK and EU. At the time in 2020 when the statue of Admiral Lord Nelson was taken down in Bridgetown because of Nelson's links to slavery, Prime Minister Mottley said: 'We were forced to build a nation without the wealth which was extracted from us plantation by plantation... We ought to have achieved more [after independence]. But it is largely because we did not have anything in the kitty to start with when we became independent nations.'

The eminent Jamaican international jurist Judge Patrick Robinson, noted, when launching the 115-page Brattle Report in June 2023: 'Reparations have been paid for other wrongs and obviously far more quickly, far more speedily than reparations for what I

---

16. Ibid., p. 1.
17. Ibid.

consider the greatest atrocity and crime in the history of mankind: transatlantic chattel slavery.'[18] The economic consultancy The Brattle Group was asked to draw up a report estimating the scale of reparations that should be paid for the chattel trade between 1510 to 1870, covering 31 countries that engaged in transatlantic slavery. This would include compensation for loss of life and liberty, uncompensated labour, personal injury, mental pain and anguish and gender-based violence. The Brattle Report is an important waymark in making the case for reparations, as it is described as the most comprehensive financial analysis of transatlantic slavery. It estimates that the 31 enslaving countries procured 801.58 million life years of free labour on which they were able to prosper.

Some British families who have a history of plantation ownership have sought to reconcile with those left with the legacy of slavery in the former colonies. The Trevelyan family made a significant gesture. In the eighteenth and nineteenth centuries, six members of the Trevelyan family owned about 1000 enslaved people on six plantations in three island parishes in Grenada. Laura Trevelyan, then a New York-based BBC News anchor and journalist, had travelled to Grenada to explore her family's past and make a film. She was deeply troubled by what she found, stating, 'If anyone had "white privilege", it was surely me, a descendant of Caribbean slave owners', she said. 'My own social and professional standing nearly 200 years after the abolition of slavery had to be related to my slave-owning ancestors, who used the profits from sugar sales to accumulate wealth and climb up the social ladder.' The family decided to do something few other descendants of plantation owners had yet done and to apologise.

Laura Trevelyan, John Dower and other Trevelyans travelled to Grenada in February 2023 with a letter signed by 107 members of the family apologising for their ancestors' role in slavery. This was presented at a ceremony in conjunction with the local and the umbrella regional Caribbean Reparations Commission (CRC). 'To

18.   Paul Lashmar, 'Tory MP's Historic Family Links to Slavery Raise Questions about Britain's Position on Reparations', *The Conversation*, 1 September 2023.

the people of Grenada, we the undersigned write to apologise for the actions of our ancestors in holding your ancestors in slavery', the letter stated: 'Its damaging effects continue to this present day. We repudiate our ancestor's involvement in it. We apologise to the surviving descendants of the enslaved on these estates, for the continuing impact on their daily lives, their health, and their well-being', the family said in the statement.

Laura Trevelyan personally donated $100,000 to the reparations committee for a fund to study the economic impact of slavery. The local commission described the apology and planned financial contribution as a 'clarion call to other families, institutions, governments in Europe to acknowledge their wrongs, apologise and commit to repairing the harms done by their ancestors'.[19] Other families have apologised for their role in Caribbean slavery, including Alex Renton, the author of a history of his family's ownership of enslaved Africans. His family has also contributed to social causes in the Caribbean. The Lascelles family of Harewood House were one of the biggest owners of plantations and enslaved people. They too have also apologised. King Charles III has announced an investigation into the royal family's role in slavery.[20]

Historian Professor Howard W. French, has commented:

The concept of transgenerational guilt – meaning historical guilt assumed by the descendants of people who committed atrocities in the past – is contentious. Where slavery is involved, the British public itself is sharply divided on racial lines, with white people broadly opposing reparations, and people of African descent even more broadly supporting them.

There are few stories better suited than that of the Draxes to support the arguments of those who today demand payment for

---

19. Paul Lashmar and Jonathan Smith, "'My Forefathers Did Something Horribly Wrong": British Slave Owners' Family to Apologise and Pay Reparations', *The Observer*, 4 February 2023, p. 1.

20. www.independent.co.uk/life-style/royal-family/king-charles-slavery-royal-family-b2315742.html, last accessed 1 July 2024.

the wrongs of history bound up in the transatlantic slave business, plantation agriculture and empire.

Professor French believes Drax should hand the plantation over to the Bajan people:

> No one knows how today's claims against the Drax family will play out. I have a favourite solution.
>
> The hilltop estate that produced so much wealth for the family and so much suffering and horror for the Africans brought there should be turned into a museum that spotlights the long downplayed African origins of the modern age.[21]

After memories of slavery being suppressed for generations, many people in Barbados now want to commemorate their ancestors. The once lost burial ground of the Newton plantation is now a monument at and visiting it is a sobering experience, a gentle grass slope encircled by trees where hundreds of enslaved people were buried. The Barbadian government is funding a memorial museum of slavery. A statue of Bussa, who is said to have led the unsuccessful 1816 rebellion, dominates a key roundabout near Bridgetown. Sir Hilary Beckles, the Barbados poet laureate Esther Phillips, Barbados MP Trevor Prescod and many other Bajans have been emphatic in saying that they want to see the Drax Hall plantation given to the island as a memorial to slavery.

---

21. French, 'Chasing Slavery's Ghosts'.

PART VIII

Nemesis

24

In Conclusion

The year 2027 is the 400th anniversary of James Drax's arrival in Barbados. He was dynamic, entrepreneurial, innovative and knighted twice. It could be argued that Sir James, through being the first to cultivate sugar in the colonies, was a catalyst for the expansion of the British Empire and creating the conditions for the Industrial Revolution. Regardless of his many strengths, he was no adherent to the rule of law and was an enabler of repression. Repression of enslaved Africans was continued by his family long after his death. As with so much history, economics trumped ethics, if the benefits were to be personal. Primarily, his wealth came off the back of captives from Africa. The contrast could not be clearer. Having 'lived like a Prince', Sir James Drax was buried in a church-yard in the City of London, with full pomp and ceremony. Many of his descendants are buried in London or Barbados.[1] For 200 years, their enslaved and impoverished workers, many of whom will have died early due to the harsh conditions and brutality, were buried in unmarked graves in an unlocated burial ground on Drax Hall plantation.

Attitudes to slavery in the Empire have changed in Britain over the last 50 years. The nation's narrative had been that Britain had been the first country to abolish the slave trade (1807) and then early to abolish slavery (1833). Much was made of the Royal Navy's West Africa Squadron's post-1807 mission to intercept ships trafficking enslaved people between Africa and the Americas. This became the dominant response to Britain's role in slavery, posed as something to be proud of, rather than a redemption for past sins. By

---

1. Sir James' older brother left and did not return to Barbados. William Drax died on 17 December 1669 in London. There is a memorial floorplate in the Parish Church of St Helen, Bishopsgate.

the twentieth century Britain's involvement with slavery had been normalised and sanitised. In his family history, Admiral Drax passingly refers to slavery in terms of a novelty in the family records but without wider reflection. His only observation, without embarrassment, was that average prices at this time appeared to be £75 for a slave, £30 for a horse and £15 for a bull.[2] In 1956 such a lack of introspection was unremarkable.

What was consigned to British history now has developed a tail, a legacy and that tail has a sting in it. Today, Britain has a sizeable population of people who, or whose parents, or even whose grandparents or earlier, came to Britain from the Empire, and whose ancestors were African or of other legacies and were enslaved on plantations. Many former British colonies are now independent with some becoming republics. Now questions are asked as to whether Britain has been honest about its history. When I was at school, there was no mention of the captive West Africans shipped by the British and other nations to the Americas to be enslaved; the number we now know may have been 12 million captives, many of whom died premature deaths and many who were effectively killed by their captors. This crime against humanity has more recently been compared to the Holocaust.[3] At the same time, the extent of the wealth that accrued to the Empire from plantations that had enslaved people has become clearer.[4]

The growth of the British Empire, from Ireland to the Americas to Asia and Africa, was predicated on the enclosure of colonised land, free or low-cost labour and wealth extraction. Popular British

---

2. Ernle-Erle-Drax, *History of Charborough*, pp. 42–43

3. Professor Sir Hilary Beckles addresses the UN General Assembly, https://caribbeannewsglobal.com/professor-sir-hilary-beckles-addresses-the-un-general-assembly/, 26 March 2024, last accessed 7 July 2024.

4. The Brattle Report estimates these harms were inflicted on 19 million enslaved people of African heritage over the span of four centuries. These 19 million include those Africans kidnapped and transported to the Americas and Caribbean and those born into slavery. It does not include those who were taken to the East rather than to the West. One of the favourite counterclaims of cultural warriors today is that Britons were made slaves as well, particularly in North Africa. The number of people including Britons enslaved by the Barbary Pirates pales into insignificance compared to Transatlantic slavery.

IN CONCLUSION

history is framed in particular ways, with the British TV fixation on the romantic exploits of buccaneering pirates, *Downton Abbey*-style glittering balls, and *Brideshead Revisited.* It is as though there is a public aching for the perceived glory and certainties of the past. A younger generation are more interested in a reckoning, symbolised by the toppling of Edward Colston's bronze statue into Bristol harbour. Although a self-defining aspect of being British is that you were not a slave, it was not a privilege that was extended to others until 1833. It was exceptionalism. Colonists, politicians, religious leaders and even philosophers like John Locke and polymaths like Sir Hans Sloane created various justifications for slavery. The one that embedded itself was the notion that people of darker skin colour were sub-human, which not only provided an excuse, but created a racist ideology that has been sustained. The idea of a natural or divine order added a lower rung – a classification by skin colour.

The idea that still perpetuates in some quarters is that, in the past, slavery was acceptable, and it was a different time. For some, even back then, it was never acceptable. In 1718–1720, the Quakers Benjamin and Sarah Lay went to Barbados where they were appalled to see the conditions under which slaves were kept. The Lays refused the standard excuse, to refer to Africans as 'savage' or 'barbarian'. They used those descriptions for slave-traders and owners of European descent. Benjamin used Biblical passages to resist the racial division of the world, emphasising Acts 17:26: God 'made of one blood all nations of men for to dwell on all the face of the earth'. There are few moral absolutes, but the evil of slavery is one. The Lays recognised that; but historically the Drax ancestors did not. There is not a mention in the public domain and public archives I can find that any Drax until the twenty-first century showed any public remorse about the slavery practised by their ancestors.[5]

There are threads of the history of the Plunkett-Ernle-Erle-Drax family that seem to pull together over the generations. Access to

---

5.   Lashmar et al., 'Wealthy Tory MP Raking in Cash from Sugar Plantation Where Thousands Died During Slave Trade'. If any reader knows of an earlier apology, please contact me.

the levers of power and thus wealth, which Walter the Musician achieved and was followed by the generations of MPs, courtiers, magistrates and sheriffs, balancing their sense of public duty with the need to expand the estate. From the early days they recognised that attending public schools gave access to the vital networks to promote the family's interests. The dislike of taxation that Walter the Puritan manifested carried on down into the twentieth century. The undoubtedly brave General Thomas Erle brought a martial tradition to the family. Sir James Drax brought an entrepreneurial energy that was a triumph of economic success over morals. For generations after Walter the Musician, who likely started life as a Catholic but converted to Protestantism, there was anti-papism especially in the eighteenth century.

Admiral Drax said in 1956 that in the past many of the landed gentry had wealth but that was matched by onerous responsibilities. He pointed out that the landed-gentry officers suffered a huge number of casualties during the First World War. The landed gentry, he noted, provided benefits to those within their domain and, for instance, created much employment. Much of what the Admiral says is true but it also true that, in Dorset, as in the rest of Britain, some families have retained huge wealth over the centuries while most ordinary people have little.

As I would hope this book shows, wealth extraction through enslaved Africans is only part, if by far the worst part, of the story. As landed gentry, the Drax family ancestors had been in a position to expand their wealth, as well as to provide public service (the two can and often do work at the same time). Their documented story started with Walter the Musician, who was able to profit from the dissolution of the monasteries. The English Civil War gave Walter the Puritan MP financial opportunities to profit from running Parliament's war logistics. They were able to make land grabs through enclosure from the seventeenth century, well into the nineteenth century, that increased their holdings. That they held the land gave them control over tenants, renters and agriculture workers, and it also provided them with capital resources to buy out tenants when there was an agricultural downturn. They supported

IN CONCLUSION

the Corn Laws that kept up the price of bread to their advantage. Landowners have many benefits that are not available to the rest of the tax-paying population, for example, until 2025 the Agricultural Relief on Inheritance Tax, as voted for by Parliament.

Despite Admiral Drax's mid-twentieth-century claims that the nobility and landed gentry were now vestigial, today they are in full health and wealth in many parts of the UK. In *Who Owns England?*, Guy Shrubsole showed that half of England is owned by less than 1 per cent of its population, around 25,000 people. Around a third, he estimated, is still owned by the aristocracy and the gentry. The wonderfully over-named Plunkett-Ernle-Erle-Drax family continue as before, secure in their great wealth and sense of their place in history, Dorset and the United Kingdom. The Draxes are not one of the great aristocratic families, but they have had status due to their connections, including with the royal family. The 'natural order' continues, but like the landscape of Charborough, it is not natural but very much man-made and bent to the will of those with power and resources. As this book has shown, the inhabitants of Charborough House have been present at many major events in British history, sometimes for better and sometimes for worse, but the heads of the family have always been able to exert influence much greater than the ordinary citizen. They are a living monument to inequality. And yes, as Richard Drax said in 2010, it can be a class war issue. But inequality was increased, not reduced, by the governments he supported. Inequality, though little mentioned by politicians, is *the* cancer of modern world.

A BATTLE FOR BRITAIN

There is much to be proud of in British history, especially in its concepts of rights such as parliamentary sovereignty, representative government, judicial independence, *habeas corpus*, freedom of speech, rule of law and the end of torture. There runs through the better British character a strong sense of decency, and that is why we had always been at the forefront of the development of democracy, painful and slow as that progress often was. The majority of

371

British people have never been drawn to the authoritarian mindset, and perhaps that is why we did not have our Stalin, Hitler, Mao or Putin. By the end of the Second World War, we did have an overwhelming belief in our own superiority.

Seventy years on, Britain is now a multicultural society where many citizens' heritage lies is in the former colonies. Despite the Common Sense Group of Conservative MPs 'Battle for Britain', slowly a warts-and-all but inclusive narrative emerges of what black, brown and other minorities' ancestors experienced, that does not minimise slavery, racism, class, misogyny, religious persecution, forced migration and exploitation.

The days of the British-led Commonwealth and the British royals as heads of state are coming to an end. One of the most absolute rejections of the colonist legacy of the British Empire came when Barbados removed the British royal family as head of state in November 2021. In the twenty-first century, it would seem the former colonies' relationship with the United Kingdom has levelled, with the hosts less inclined to pay homage to the former colonial masters. Prince Charles, as he was then, had diplomatically attended the ceremony where Barbadians had celebrated their five decades of independence. The celebration also featured the replacement of the British monarch as the head of state with a Barbadian, Sonia Mason, as president. The Prime Minister of Barbados, Mia Mottley KC, is seen as a progressive and dynamic force on the global stage who has been elevated by merit, not birth. She speaks of racism, the climate crisis, developed countries' obligations and reparations for centuries of slavery and wealth extraction: all subjects that Britain has dragged its heels on, despite the fine words.

Jamaica and St Kitts & Nevis may remove the British monarchy as heads of their states. There are now many experts and commentators who contend that chattel slavery was the catalyst for white supremacy and racism, born of a need to justify the unjustifiable. I can recall growing up in Britain from the 1950s and the extensive casual racism that existed everywhere alongside the violent forms. You only have to see how it casually emits even at the highest levels of State. Take former Prime Minister Boris Johnson's references to

IN CONCLUSION

'watermelon smiles' and 'flag-waving piccaninnies' in a *Telegraph* column about a trip by Tony Blair to West Africa. In a *Spectator* article, he wrote: 'The problem is not that we were once in charge [of Africa], but that we are not in charge any more... If left to their own devices, the natives would rely on nothing but the instant carbohydrate gratification of the plantain.'[6]

That racism needs to be recognised and owned. As a child, I was taught the British were superior to any other nation. Somehow, we deluded ourselves and, in decline, blamed everyone else, particularly our nearest neighbours for our failings. Those least inclined to understand Black Lives Matter as having a good cause, accuse anti-racism protestors of intolerance. But some progress is made in inclusion and self-reflection in wider society.

Writing this book has been challenging. I have had to review my own opinions. It has taken me too until my seventh decade to fully grasp how fooled I was by the previous silence around this part of our history. During my research, conversations with Barbadians have been particularly important and none more than Esther Phillips, the poet laureate of Barbados. She has been on a journey with her poetry. Her early works do not make mention of slavery, but her newer works certainly do. She feels that like many in Barbados, she ignored slavery, but her journey has taken her back to her ancestors. She told me it was not until recently she realised that the landscape of Barbados, which she had once viewed as nothing but beautiful, held dreadful secrets. 'I still struggle with my failure back then to understand what either the sugar plantations or the great houses represented in terms of trans-Atlantic slavery.' She further said: 'I cannot trust the Keatsian concept of truth and beauty as I must have done then. The truth of what lies beneath my landscape is very, very ugly. Trans-Atlantic slavery was brutal, an atrocity, a crime against humanity. The DNA of my ancestors is in me. So are their voices. And I will speak for them as they speak to me,' Esther told me.

---

6.   See www.theguardian.com/commentisfree/2023/jun/19/boris-johnson-black-britons-warned, last accessed 1 July 2024. Johnson did eventually apologise for these phrases.

Silence is very important to Esther, a recognition that her ancestors learnt to be silent to survive and she says, even now many Barbadians would prefer to move on rather than deal with what was once silent and ashamed. As I have said, I tried to find the voices of those enslaved at Drax Hall or even in Barbados. Esther Phillips says that she now feels it her duty to speak for her ancestors who worked at Drax Hall and other plantations. It is emotional. Perhaps one of her most powerful poems is where she speaks for the mother of Adofoh, a boy born into chattel slavery and how the mother realises she cannot be soft to her son. She has to toughen his ankles to be able to wear shackles and his back so he can take the lashes of the whip. Esther captures in this poem the sheer perversion of slavery and how it upturns the natural state of nurture.

My Ancestors Gifted Me Their Silence
When Silence is Not

Ssshhhh… Let her walk free, unhindered, into the new world.
She must not see the crimson dawn and think of –

Let her see only purple flowers growing in the cut rock;
not hear the back-breaking –

She must remember only the smell of ripe plums and guavas
rising from the gully; never the stink of –

Let her gaze at the lacy leaves in the cluster of bamboo trees
and not see that the branches were cut, stripped and used for –
The thick pole with holes cut into the crossbars was where they –
The dark spot left by jamoon berries was once the stain of –

Shhhhhh… She's walking west of the big house
next to what she knows only as the "Yard."
We were barely her age when massa summoned us
to his quarters. We were not the same when we came back…

The children born to us were never ours to love
as we wanted. Massa could sell them whenever he chose to!
Better some had never seen the morning light;

IN CONCLUSION

better they'd been buried along with their navel-strings
under this same earth!

But this girl… walking… She is one our *Abrewa* saw
when we gathered late in the evenings
speaking over a pot of water so no one else could hear us.
It was then the old wise woman whispered her vision that… one
day –

Sshhh… Let the girl child think it's only birds, crickets,
grasshoppers, the wind slipping through the khus-khus
that she hears. Never the sounds of our – Sssshhhhhhh!

O my Ancestors, so late for me to unwrap,
layer by layer, this gift of your silence!
But today I place my birth caul over my eyes
so I may see

> and I weep
> for the bones I find here
> the solitary cowrie shell
> a broken comb,
> shreds of the osnaburg that roughened
> your once-smooth ebony skin
> gave no ease to your torn flesh

I shed these tears for my oblivion:
false buffer of empire that shrouded my hearing, veiled my sight,
turned me, bastard child, away from my true Mother.

Now I unwrap the love
you forced into silence, like a hedge to protect me
until the time would come for safer passage.

What can I give you in return in these late years,
this late awakening?
The pledge of my voice, my words; the rest of this walking.

© Esther Phillips

Reading the detail of the brutality of what was done to slaves for hundreds of years is profoundly disturbing. For instance, Thomas Thistlewood's diary is a voyage into deep depravity. I was reminded of Equiano Olaudah's words:

> These overseers are indeed for the most part persons of the worst character of any denomination of men in the West Indies. Unfortunately, many humane gentlemen, by not residing on their estates, are obliged to leave the management of them in the hands of these human butchers, who cut and mangle the slaves in a shocking manner on the most trifling occasions and altogether treat them in every respect like brutes.[7]

I did wonder what emotional damage was done to the overseers who employed such brutality. The story of the woman slave-owner who kills her slave for a minor transgression by slowly pouring hot wax over her back, sticks in the mind. Esther Phillips' says, 'It is not possible to destroy the soul of someone else and not be destroyed yourself.'

Terrible punishments were also employed against the poor and workers in Britain but rarely as brutal or extensive and what happened to enslaved people in the colonies. For some reason the one small story that has stayed with me is the sentence of 14 days' hard labour that was imposed on Alfred Barney in 1892 for picking uncultivated snowdrops in Charborough Park. Not least, as the owner was not even living there. It is petty and typical but exemplifies the extremes the landed and their overseers made to protect their property. It is one of many similar court cases. Even in the 1930s people were being prosecuted for taking snowdrops or daffodils from Charborough Park. It does poignantly undermine the notion that the owners of landed estates are just custodians for the wider public.

Do I think reparations should be paid? The question of reparations can only be fully answered by those whose ancestors were enslaved.

---

7. Equiano, *The Interesting Narrative*, p. 134.

IN CONCLUSION

Sir Hilary Beckles, who leads for reparations for CARICOM, said during a visit to Jamaica:

> The legacies of slavery continue to derail, undermine and haunt our best efforts at sustainable economic development and the psychological and cultural rehabilitation of our people from the ravishes of the crimes against humanity committed by your British State and its citizens in the form of chattel slavery and native genocide.[8]

What I think is unimportant by comparison. What I do think is that reparations are at least as much about recognition and redemption as money, and that must happen. The problem for those from whom reparations are asked, is that it takes the power and agency away from them and puts it the hands of those who once had no power. If Britain is ever going to re-establish its moral leadership role in the world again as an outward-looking, democratic and progressive nation, it needs to come to terms with its past.[9] Pretending that hundreds of years of enforcing slavery in the colonies is all in the distant past and has no consequences or debts in the present is foolish. Britons have come to believe their own propaganda.

As I have mentioned before, as a schoolboy in England in the 1950s and 1960s, I was educated that the British abolition of slavery showed how great Britain was, rather than discussing the horrors of the previous centuries of British-authored chattel slavery. The historian and author of some of the most challenging books on slavery, Eric Williams, joked in the 1960s that 'the British historians wrote almost as if Britain had introduced Negro slavery solely for the satisfaction of abolishing it'.[10] Slavery was an abomination with long-

---

8. Hilary Beckles, 'Reparation Issue Will Cause Greatest Political Movement if British PM Fails to Resolve, Beckles Warns', *Jamaica Gleaner*, 15 September 2015, https://jamaica-gleaner.com/article/news/20150927/reparation-issue-will-cause-greatest-political-movement-if-british-pm-fails, last accessed 5 July 2024.
9. In the author's view, Britain's role as a world policeman has been so incompetently implemented as to be criminally negligent, with reputational disasters none more than the invasion of Iraq in 2003.
10. Eric Williams, *British Historians and the West Indies* (New York: Holmes & Meier, 1964), p. 233.

term consequences. Religion, philosophy and politics are sullied by their justifications for what was essentially immoral economic motives. Greed can always find its defenders who can twist the moral imperative to allow for wealth extraction.

I can only wonder how I would have survived in a plantation. The basic human urge for freedom would have been suppressed as submission and deference were learnt by the lash of the whip. Those who could not conform to this punishment often died the most terrible deaths. We will never know of the experiences of the family of Moncky Nocco who were given preferences by Henry Drax in his 'Instructions' of 1669 and who must have survived by hard work and an understanding of what their Drax owners and overseers required by way of hierarchy and deference. Or the enslaved women Affraw who delivered a child Noah on 6 February 1805, or Haggar who delivered a female child named Fibbah James on 25 May of that year.[11] Their silence should be recognised by our own silent reflection on their lives and the thousands of other enslaved people who are likely buried unmarked somewhere on the Drax Hall plantation.

Leading CARICOM figures described the Drax Hall plantation as a 'killing field' and a 'crime scene' from the many enslaved Africans who died there in terrible conditions between 1640 and 1836. Beckles estimated that as many 30,000 slaves died on the Drax plantations in Barbados and Jamaica over 200 years. The precise location of those burial grounds, except for the Newton plantation, remains a mystery. Maps and local reference documents failed to specify slave burial grounds and we know that the enslaved held special affection for those burial grounds and wanted them close to their homes and the village. Today, respect for the ancestors by marking their burials has become symbolic for descendants in Barbados, as elsewhere. One gesture that would go a long way would be identify the burial ground for enslaved people at Drax Hall and mark it with a memorial.

---

11.   Both passingly referred to in the Admiral's *History*, p. 42.

IN CONCLUSION

BY JINGO

I suggest those who objected to the fervour of Black Lives Matter, and the question of Britain's culpability over slavery, sense that David Olusoga and others like him are pulling on a twisted strand that will unravel a particular embroidery of history, ruining an illusion of just how benign Britain was, and what is the 'natural order' as deigned by God, our betters, and prescribed by long-dead historians of jingo. Slavery was the most blatant and inhumane form of exploitation and wealth extraction in the British Empire. As David Olusoga has emphasised, slavery was not an annexe; it was a foundation on which Britain's City skyscrapers were built. It reveals the links between exploitation, military might and control of the levers of power. And the West Indies were the sandpit of capitalism.

There needs to be a grown-up accurate, ethical history if the UK is not to continue on its path to being a small inward and backwards-looking island. The British refuse to address as a nation the inequalities that leave much of the world exploited, poor and in an environmental disaster while reducing the international aid budget. What the current and next generations choose to do to reconcile the legacy of the British Empire and its consequences will be symbolic of what direction Britain will take in the future and how it will be viewed in the world.

Above all, the Drax family is unique as the only family that owned 'Sugar Plantation One', Drax Hall, that was created as Barbados was settled and was worked by enslaved Africans for 200 years and remained owned in the twenty-first century by the senior member of the family, who in the most recent incumbent was also a British Conservative MP. As an MP, Richard Drax was hardline on immigration to the UK while sitting on a fortune that was in part created by the enforced migrations of Africans. He spoke much about the former and little about the latter.

As the debate over slavery heated up, Richard Drax has led the policy of reticence on the legacy of slavery and the wealth it created for his family and for many, it is tone deaf. Richard Drax's handful of 'slavery was wrong' comments when confronted by reporters on the subject have not sufficed. When interviewed by journalists he is known to stipulate that he will not discuss slavery or personal matters. It was only when *The Observer* and *Sunday Mirror* published the fact that he was inheriting 'Sugar Plantation One' in the British Empire where he his ancestors had held slaves for 200 years did, he register and confirm his interest. He also retains tight control over family archives that would be better sitting in a public archive so that his family's role in history can be better understood.

By his few limited comments on the subject, Richard Drax has stood firm against any kind of reparation for his ancestors' involvement in slavery and has raised his public profile far more than being a BBC Reporter or an MP. During the time I was researching and writing this book, Richard Drax became *the* negative symbolic figure in the slavery reparations debate. Pressure grew on him, and he flew to Barbados to meet with the PM Mia Mottley to discuss the issue. The Barbados government well understood that he symbolised, as an MP and a descendent of a founder plantation owner, his wealth and reluctance to provide recognition was everything that was wrong with the way Britain treated Barbados and the colonies. In the private meeting between Drax and Mia Mottley and then with other reparation advisers to the Bajan government, he was offered two options, one a package of reparations including all or a substantial part of Drax Hall. If he refused, Mia Mottley said they would go to law.[12] By the time of writing this book, he had made no public announcement about his intentions.

The Drax family have produced many fascinating characters, who have been present in key moments of British and Caribbean history. But the one who stands out most starkly over the centuries, as the instigator of chattel slavery, is James Drax. What does this say to a multicultural Britain? Richard Drax may not have a racist bone in his body and is described by those who know him as a charming man. But, unless he has a Damascene conversion on the controversy, Richard Drax will be most remembered as a man who was too deeply rooted in the past and left his family on the

---

12. Paul Lashmar and Jonathan Smith, 'Barbados Plans to Make Tory MP Pay Reparations for Family's Slave Past', *The Observer*, 27 November 2022.

IN CONCLUSION

wrong side of history. An agreement with the people of Barbados would help rescue this situation. Handing over all or part of the Drax Hall plantation with supporting funds might be a gesture that would improve the Drax family's reputation not only in Barbados but across quite a bit of the world. Despite Richard Drax's claim that slavery was a long time ago and he could not be held responsible, the legacy of slavery continues to impact on many, not least on those who refuse to recognise the winners and losers of Britain's role over several hundred years. This story is not finished for the Plunkett-Ernle-Erle-Drax family.

Archives

Early in my research, I found that Richard Drax's grandfather, Admiral Drax, had deposited two sets of family archives, those of General Thomas Erle and his own personal archive to the Churchill College Archive at the University of Cambridge, where they can be consulted, and so I did.

I read *A History of Charborough 1066–1956,* a 117-page book by the Admiral, privately printed for friends and family. Copies of the Admiral's book are held in two archives. I also bought a copy from a bookseller. It is a romantic and sanitised view of the family history in which Barbados and slavery are only lightly touched upon.

Through the Admiral's writings, I became aware that there was also a family archive at Charborough. By this time, as I was learning so much new about British (and Dorset) history, I had decided to write a history of the family. I had spent seven years as the Honorary Editor of the *Proceedings of the Dorset Natural History and Archaeological Society* (DNHAS), the academic annual of the Dorset County Museum, so I was not new to Dorset history. But so much I was learning was new, at least to me. In its 140 years, the *Proceedings* had hardly ever published a paper that referred to the Drax family or Charborough.

I was not seeking or expecting to write an authorised history, and given the newspaper articles of which I had been co-author, I did not think this likely. Quite a few of the Dorset landed gentry have deposited their family archives at the Dorset History Centre, like the Weld family of Lulworth, but not the Draxes. I did want to see the family archive, so in January 2022, I wrote and emailed Richard Drax asking for access. Over the years some scholars have been granted access. I received no reply. I knew that in the summer of 2020 the Dorset County Archivist Sam Johnston, based at the Dorset History Centre, had written to Richard Drax asking him whether he would consider depositing the Charborough archive or at least giving access to the material to scholars. Richard Drax was to the point in his reply: 'We are a very private family, and I'm afraid we do not share historical material.' Clearly, something had changed since his grandfather had made substantial efforts to put some archives into the public domain.

After identifying key documents, I requested copyright permission from CCCA detailing and contextualising the material I wished to quote. The head archivist Andrew Riley advised me that the family retained copyright for the deposited material. He kindly wrote to Richard Drax requesting copyright permission on my behalf. Eight months later Richard Drax spoke to Andrew Riley to state he would not be giving permission. It is of course Richard Drax's prerogative, but it grates that a then MP would restrict academic freedom and freedom of expression over the use and discussion of archival material. I would understand more had the material not been in the public domain and was private, but it was held in one of the UK's leading public and scholarly archives.

There was also some material in the Department or Archives in Bridgetown, Barbados, released from Drax Hall Plantation by the admiral around 1969 that had some interesting material too. I was able to access these materials during my visit to Barbados in 2022. Unfortunately, a storage room at BDA was hit by lightning in 2024 and many archives burnt. I do not know whether this included Drax Hall acquisitions.

However, there is much material about the family in various repositories like The National Archives at Kew, and, if anything, it has been hard to edit the available material into just one book.

The UCL slavery database estimates the numbers of slaves the British shipped on the transatlantic trade.

	Great Britain		
1551–75	1685	1726-50	554,042
1576–1600	237	1751–75	832,047
1626–50	33,695	1776–1800	748,612
1651–75	122,367	1801–25	283,959
1676–1700	272,200	Total	3,259,441
1701–25	410,597		

Family Trees

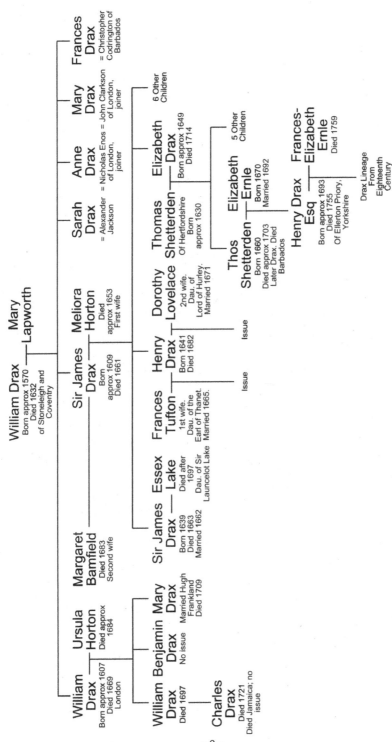

Drax Lineage to Eighteenth Century

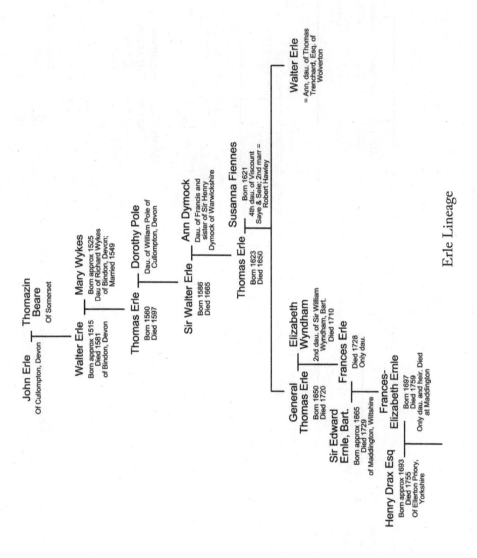

FAMILY TREES

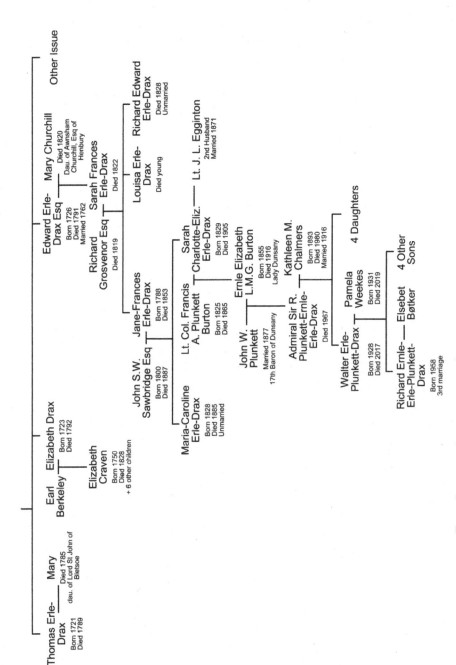

Drax Lineage from Eighteenth Century

Ten Major Dorset Landowners 1883–2020

Year 1883			Year 1990		
Estate(s)	*Landowner*	*Area*	*Estate(s)*	*Landowner*	*Area*
Charborough	John Sawbridge Erle-Drax and Miss Drax	15,069 In Dorset of total of 23,587	Charborough	Admiral Drax.	15,000 acres
Kingston Lacy	W Bankes	19,228	Kingston Lacy	National Trust	16,000 approx
Lulworth Castle	R Weld	15,478	Lulworth Castle	Weld family	15,000
Ilchester Estates	Lord Ilchester	15,981	Ilchester Estates	Hon. Charlotte Townshend (nee Fox-Strangways)	11,000
Various including Tynedham	Tyneham owned by the Bonds		Bovington Camp, Blandford Camp, Lulworth Range	Ministry of Defence (MOD)	11,304 acres
Crichel Down Estate	Lord Alington (Sturt family)	14,756		Marten family	7,800
Rushmore Estate	General Augustus Henry Lane-Fox Pitt Rivers	24,942	Rushmore	Fox-Pitt-Rivers family	10,000?
Shaftesbury (Wimborne St Giles) Estate	Earl of Shaftesbury	17,317		Earl of Shaftesbury	9,000
Bryanston Estate	Viscount Portman	7795 acres of Portman's 33500 acres.		Bought by the Crown in 1950 from the Portman family	
Sherborne Castle	Wingfield Digby family	21,230	Sherborne Castle	Wingfield Digby family,	21,230
Cranborne Estate	Cecil family	7,000 acres in Dorset of 20,000		Cecil family	

Year 2020		
Estate(s)	*Landowner*	*Area*
Charborough Estate	Richard Drax and family	13,870 acres (actual 15,000+)
Various – largest is Kingston Lacy	National Trust	21,772 acres
Lulworth Castle	Weld family	12,000 acres
Ilchester Estates (Abbotsbury & Membury Estates)	Hon. Charlotte Townshend	11,327 acres
Bovington Camp, Blandford Camp, Lulworth Range	Ministry of Defence (MOD)	11,304 acres
Crichel Down Estate	Crichel Dorset Holdings / Richard Chilton (US billionaire)	7,932 acres
Rushmore Estate	Pitt-Rivers family	7,500 acres
Shaftesbury (Wimborne St Giles) Estate	Earl of Shaftesbury	5,700 acres
Bryanston Estate	Viscount Rothermere (Daily Mail proprietor)	4,700 acres
Sherborne Castle and Estate	Wingfield Digby family	15,000 (Waymark 2001)
Cranborne Estate	Marquess of Salisbury, Robert Gascoyne Cecil	7,796 acres

Acknowledgements

Thanks especially to: Jonathan Smith for working with me on the original and continuing Drax-related stories for the *Observer* and *Sunday Mirror*. Thanks to the then *Observer* editor, Paul Webster, and news editor Steve Bloomfield for their support.

Thanks to: local historian Phillip Browne and Mary Hart from Dorchester for spending time in the local archives on my behalf. Also, archivist Sam Johnston of the Dorset History Centre, Bill Evans, Professor David Leigh, Adrian Gatton, Jon Lee Anderson and Nicholas Sandon for reading through the draft. My wife, Anna for tough early copy editing. Neil Sentance for professional copy editing, David Olusoga for his encouragement.

In Barbados: Fitzgerald Brereton, Trevor Marshall, Kevin Farmer, Professor Pedro Welch, Frederick E. Alleyne

For advice, information and permissions: Dr Leonard Baker, Dr Kevin Bawn, Dr David Brown, David Burnett, Professor John Chapman, Richard Danbury, Professor Henry French, George Greenwood (*The Times*), Roger Guttridge, Nick Hayes (*The Book of Trespass*), poet David Herring, Adaobi Tricia Nwaubani, Richard Ryder, Alex Renton, David Ryden (University of Houston Downtown), Professor Angelique Richardson, Guy Shrubsole, Alan Smith, First Church Estates Commissioner, The Church Commissioners for England, Dr Michael Taylor, Andrew Riley of the Churchill College Archives Cambridge. Chris Drakes of the Drax, Dracas(s) & Drakes history website who went to great lengths to help me. There are many others who want to remain unnamed.

My colleagues at the Department of Journalism at City, St George's University of London, an outstanding team of journalism educators and especially to Professor Mel Bunce and Dr Glenda Cooper.

ACKNOWLEDGEMENTS

Matthew Parker undertook groundbreaking research for his book *The Sugar Barons* on the Draxes in Barbados, which I have inevitably drawn upon.

I would like to thank Rodney Schofield of Kent for letting me have the last copy of his privately printed book on the Sawbridges, *Release to the Captives*.

I am very grateful to the Poet Laureate of Barbados, Esther Phillips, whose poetic insights helped me understand a deep Barbadian perspective.

Barbados Department of Archives, Barbados Museum Archives, Churchill College Archives, Cambridge, Dorset History Centre, Dorchester, The National Archives, the Institute of Historical Research and UCL Library, City, St George's University of London Library.

To the Covid Arms conspirators who patiently listened to my latest research findings.

Index

ill refers to an illustration; *n* to a note

Abbot's Court Farm 192-3
abolitionist movement 224-6, 230-1,
   288-93
  see also anti-abolition movement
Acteon (magazine) 283-4
Adventurers 99*n*, 101-4, 115, 127
  see also Merchant Adventurers
agricultural workers
  living conditions of 264-5, 296-7,
    297*ill*, 298*ill*
  poverty of 226, 325-7
Alleyne, Captain Reynold 115
American War of Independence
  (1776) 201
Americas, colonisation of 18, 81-4
Amity (ship) 83
Ann and Mary (ship) 225
anti-abolition movement 226, 259,
  289
anti-Catholic sentiments 84-5
  London riots (1778) 206-7
Anti-Corn Law Association 299
Anti-Corn Law League 298
Anti-Humbug (correspondent) 291
Applewaite, Thomas 36
Arawak people 19, 21, 24, 44*n*
Arbuthnot, Harriet *The Journal of Mrs
  Arbuthnot* 238
Arminius, Jacobus and Arminianism
  87-8
Arundell, Robert 122-3
Ashbee, Andrew 70
Atkins, Jonathan 148, 150
Atlantic Monthly 319
Austen, Jane *Mansfield Park* 216

Ayscue, Admiral George 120-1, 132

Bacon, Gareth 10
Baldwin, James 1
Bamfield, Margaret *see* Drax,
  Margaret
Bankes, Frances 276*n*
Bankes, Sir Henry 276-7
Bankes, Sir John 97
Bankes, Sir Ralph 108-9
Barbados xvii*map*
  colonial settlement in 17-23, 116
  deportation of criminals and POWs
    to 37-8, 41, 124-5, 127
  emigration of white people from
    142-3
  hurricane (1780) 201
  population of (1644) 48, 52
  rainstorm (1656) 130-1
  strikes in 309-10
  white population of 52
  withdraws from Commonwealth
    (2021) 372
  women settlers in 37
Barbados Department of Archives
  219, 228, 230
Barbados Land Tax Authority 7
Barney, Alfred, sentenced to hard
  labour for picking snowdrops 326,
  376
Barrow, John 228, 228*n*
Bateman's Survey 308, 352
Bath Chronicle 264
Battle of Almanza (1707) 176
Battle of Aughrim (1691) 169-71

INDEX

Battle of Jutland (1916) 329–30

Battle of Landen (1693) 171–2

Battle of Sedgemoor (1685) 163

Battle of Steenkerk (1685) 171

Battle of the Boyne (1690) xiv, 169*n*, 169–70

Battle of the Nile (1798) 212

Battle of Waterloo (1815) 216
  aftermath of 240

Bawn, Kevin 266–7, 269, 271, 274, 277–8

Beatty, Sir David 329

Beckford, Peter 193

Beckford, William 259

Beckles, Sir Hilary 8, 37, 116, 126, 227–8, 231–2, 361, 364, 377–8

Bedford, Earl of 95

Beech, Sir Thomas 196

Behn, Aphra *Oroonoko, or the Royal Slave* 151

Belgrave, Lord 205

Bell, Philip 115, 116, 118

Bennett, Michael 131, 152

Bentley, Martin 127–8

Bere Regis, Dorset 64, 184–5, 184*n*, 251, 255, 265–7, 300, 327, 348, 352

Berkeley, Augustus, Earl of Berkeley 194

Berkeley, Edmund, Lord Putnam II 276*n*, 276–7

Berkeley, Edward II 276, 276*n*

Berkeley, Elizabeth 194–5

Berkeley, Sir Henry 96

Biet, Father Anton 27, 40*n*, 40–2, 129
  observations on slavery 49, 151

Bill of Rights Society 259

Bingham, John 90

Black Death 64–5

Black Lives Matter 1–2, 10, 373, 379

Blackburn, Robin 47

Blagrave, Daniel 139

Blake, General Robert 120

Blome, Richard 51–2

Book of Common Prayer 91

Booke of Certayne of the Queyns Ordynary as yet to no Place Appoynted 67

Botany Bay Farm 342

Bourne Mouth (later Bournemouth) 238, 239*n*

Braddick, Michael J. 56

Brattle Report (2023) 361–2, 368*n*

Breadnut Island Pen farm 222

Brereton, Fitzgerald 333–4

Bridenbaugh, Carl and Roberta 41–2, 134

Brideshead Revisited (tv programme) 369

Bridgetown 23, 129
  riots (1937) 334

Briggs, Asa 298–9

Bright, John 299

British and Foreign Anti-Slavery Society (later Anti-Slavery Society) 289

British Empire 368–9
  post-war immigration to UK 368
  teaching in schools about 368–70

Brotherly Assistance Loan 101–2

Brown, David 46, 100–1, 103–4, 106

Browne, John 87, 95, 291

Bryanston Estate 352

Burton, Admiral James Ryder 300

Burton, Colonel Francis Augustus Plunkett 300

Burton, Ernle Elizabeth Louise Maria Grosvenor, Lady Dunsany 325

Bussa's Rebellion (1816) 233–4, 364

Butler, James, Duke of Ormond 104, 104*n*

Buxton, Priscilla 290–1

Buxton, Sir Thomas 289

Byam, Major William 117, 120–1

393

Byam, Samuel 208
Cabot, John and Sebastien 20*n*
Cade, Elizabeth 225
Caesar's Camp, Wimbledon 306–7
Cake, William 349–50, 352
Calcraft, John Hales 280, 291, 295, 298, 301–2, 305
Calcraft, Sir John 190, 193, 193*n*, 277
  suicide of 278
Calcraft, William Montagu 305
Cameron, David 356
Campbell, Admiral 337
Campaign to Protect Rural England (CPRE) 358
Cape Ann Colony 83–4
Captain Swing riots (1830) 265–75, 270*n*, 277–8
Cardiff Hall, Jamaica 139
Cardinals' Cap (London tavern) 131
Caribbean Community Reparations Committee (CARICOM) 8, 8*n*, 377–8
Caribbean Reparations Commission (CRC) 362–3
Carlisle Bay 23, 37, 120
Carlton Club 305
Caroline, Queen 186
Carter, Henderson 309
Carteret, George 186
Catholic Relief Act (1778) 206
Catholic Relief Bill (1791) 237
Cavendish, William, Duke of Newcastle 105, 105*n*
Chafin, Thomas 163
Chalmers, Kathleen *see* Plunkett-Ernle-Erle-Drax, Kathleen
Chalon, Maria A. 260, 260*n*
Chamberlain, Neville 335
Champante, John 142
Chapman, John 255
'Charborough 1950' (poem) 344

Charborough Estate xviii*map*, 63–4, 248–9, 307–8, 342, 342*n*, 357–8
  acquisition by Walter the Musician 72
  demolition of rented properties in 348–51
  enclosures of 178, 248–56, 254–5
  improvements to 341–2, 342*n*
  profits from 360–1
Charborough House xiii, 59–63, 158, 187, 203, 235–6
  burning by Royalists of 105, 108–9
Charborough Park 60*n*, 60–1, 216, 235–6
  hunting in 282
Charborough Races 264, 283–4
Charborough Savings Bank 334
Charles I, King 22–3, 84–6, 90, 250
  imposition of ship money by 86–7
  marriage to Henrietta Maria 84
  trial and execution of 107
Charles II, King xiv, 116, 131–2, 160–1
Charles III, King 363, 372
Charlotte, Queen 209, 211
Chartists 263
Cherrett, George and Phillip 341
Chester Courant 216
Christian Frederick Charles Alexander, Margrave of Ansbach 197–8
Christianity: and slavery 227
Church of England: attitudes to slavery of 227
Churchill, George 206
Churchill, John 162*n*, 163, 165, 167
Churchill, Mary *see* Erle-Drax, Mary
Churchill, Winston 329, 334, 336, 340
  Marlborough: his Life and Times 176–7
Clare, John 'The Mores' (poem) 253
Clarke, Edward 82
Clarke, Forster 230, 293
Clarkson, Thomas 203, 230, 288–9

INDEX

Cliffe, J.T. *Puritan Gentry* 78, 85–6
Cobden, Richard 298–9
Codd, Colonel 233
Codrington, Christopher 28, 150–1, 150*n*
Codrington family 232
Colleton, James Edward 180*n*
coffee production 185
Colleton, Madam Elizabeth 180*n*
Colleton family 116–7, 150
Colonial Office 309–10
Colston, Edward: toppling of statue of 1–2, 1*n*, 369
Colt, Sir Henry 25–7, 39
Columbus, Christopher 138*n*
Combes, Thomas 46
Committee for Irish Affairs 101
Committee for Powder Match and Bullet 103
common land 248–9, 252–4
Common Sense Group 9, 10, 372
Confederation Rebellion (1876) 310
Cooke, Captain Samuel 128
Cooper, Sir Anthony Ashley 34, 88–9, 159–60, 278–80
Cope, John 221–2
Copperthwaite Moor 5, 347
Corfe Castle siege 96–8, 108
Corn Laws 240, 265, 298–9, 303, 370–1
Coromantee people 148*n*
cotton production 30, 201
Courteen Association 116
Courteen, Sir William and Philip 19–20, 23
Courteen family 44
Courtis, Edward 120
Covenanters 91
Covid-19 pandemic 3, 7
Craft, Ellen and William 24
Crafterio (satirical writer) 190
Cranbourne Lodge 192

Crane, Dr 'Cursory Observations on Sea-Bathing' 210
Craven, Lady Elizabeth 194, 195–8
 Abdoul et Nourjad 197
 Folle du Jour (play) 197
 Journey Through Crimea to Constantinople 197
 The Miniature Picture (play) 196
Craven, William 195–8
Crichel Down Estate 352
Cromwell, Oliver xiv, 101, 103–4, 107, 124, 131
Cromwell, Richard 107, 131–2
Cromwell, Thomas 71
culture wars 9–10
Cumberbatch, Abraham 219, 219*n*

Daily Mirror xv
Damer, Joseph, 1st Lord Milton 205–6, 213
Davis, David 3
Davison, Robert L. 334, 336
Denis, Captain Robert 120
Devereux, Robert, Earl of Essex 94
Devereux, Sir Walter 83
Dickinson, Henry 175
Digby, Colonel Stephen 212
Digby, George 91–2
Digby, John Earl of Bristol 167–8
Diggers 104
Dodington, George Bubb 186
Dolling, Joseph 159, 173
Domesday Book 63
Dorchester 78–9, 81
 fire (1613) 79
Dorchester Company 82–4
Dormer, Robert, Earl of Carnarvon 98
Dorrill, William 221
Dorset xviii*map*
 enclosures in 253–6
 impact of Civil War on 94–9
 land ownership in 308
 MPs for 355*n*
 poverty in 264–5, 296–7

Dorset: The County Magazine 349
Dorset County Chronicle 271
Dorset County Express and Agricultural Gazette 314
Dorset Echo 1, 2
Dorset Life 355
Dorset Militia 165, 167–8
Dorset Volunteer Rangers 205–6, 212
Doumenc, General Aimé 335
Dower, John 362–3
Downton Abbey (tv programme) 369
Draper v Drax 183*n*
Drax, Anne 123
Drax, Charles 139, 139*n*
Drax, Dorothy 143
Drax, Elizabeth *see* Berkeley, Elizabeth
Drax, Elizabeth (daughter of Elizabeth) see Craven, Lady Elizabeth
Drax, Elizabeth 'Betsy' 179–88
Drax, Frances 27, 137
Drax, Henry 133, 137, 140, 143–8, 150–3, 203
  death of 143, 153
  elected MP for Wareham 188–90
  'Instructions on the Management of a Seventeenth Century Barbadian Sugar Plantation' (c.1679) 144–7, 144*n*
Drax, Henry II 154, 178–80, 182–90, 192, 194, 201–3, 257
  elected MP for Wareham 188–90
Drax, James II 129, 130, 133, 137
Drax, Sir James of Hackney 133
Drax, Jane Frances 256–7, 259
Drax, John (naval logistician) 18
Drax, John (brother of Sir James) 123, 141–3, 143*n*
Drax, John (19th century head of Charborough Estate *see* Sawbridge Erle-Drax, John
Drax, Margaret 130, 136–7, 150
Drax, Mary 190–1, 340*n*

Drax, Meloria 129
Drax, Richard (b.1958) xiii, xv, 201, 216, 340–1, 353–64, 353*n*
  attitude to family's role in slavery xv, 361, 379–80
  as Conservative MP 2–3, 7–8, 355–6, 359
  marriage to Eliza Dugdale 354–5
  marriage to Elsebet 355
  marriage to Zara Legge-Bourke 354
  ownership of Drax Hall Plantation 358–61, 380
  refusal to pay reparations for slavery 361–2, 380
  views on Brexit 3*n*, 356–7
  views on immigration 2, 2*n*, 356, 379
  voting record 356–7
Drax, Sir Edward 17
Drax, Sir James xiv, 6, 17, 29–30, 46, 51, 116, 129–34, 367, 370
  lifestyle of 36–7, 38–40
  personal qualities 134–7
Drax, Thomas III 219
Drax, Walter 347–8
Drax, William 17
Drax, William II 27–8, 137, 139
Drax family 17–18
  as landlords 348–9
  visit to Barbados 333–4
  wealth of 3–6, 4*n*, 7–8
Drax Hall, Dorset 62
Drax Hall Plantation 6, 139, 180–1, 201–2, 218–20, 234, 358–60
  inventory 228–9
  profits from 290, 360–1
Drax Hall Plantation House xiii, 7, 28
Drax Hope Plantation 28, 143
Duckett, Mary and Major W. 185
Dunn, Richard 39–40, 138, 151–2
  Sugar and Slaves 246
Dunsany family 328

INDEX

Duras, Louis de, Earl of Feversham 163
Dutch slave trade 45
Dutch West India Company 127

East India Company 103*n*, 103-4, 172, 221
Eastbury House 186
Edward VI, King 69-70
Egginton, Lt John Lloyd 325
Ekins family 325-6
Elizabeth 1, Queen 45, 74
Ellerton Estate 179, 182, 333-4
Enclosure Act (1773) 251
enclosures 109, 178, 248-56, 282,
  riots against 250-1
English Civil War 94-102, 106-8, 249, 370
  impact on slave trade 115-9
English East India Company (EEIC) 103-4, 103*n*, 115-6, 133, 172
Englishman's Journal 187
Enos, Nicholas 122-3
Enscombe Estate 190*n*
enslaved people 44-5, 367
  attitudes to 46, 54, 203
  artisan class 142-3
  children of 52
  claim for legal right not to be removed from England to the West Indies 224-5
  comparative cheapness of 49-50
  employment difficulties after freedom 293-4
  as entertainment 50-1
  inventories of 228-9
  life expectancy of 49-50, 53
  living conditions of 52, 55, 145-6, 220, 220*n*
  mortality rates of 128-9, 146, 378
  names of 360*n*
  punishing of 55, 149, 220, 222-5, 293-4, 376

purchase prices of 222, 368
rebellions by 148-9, 232-4
registration of 233
enslaved women 49, 202, 288, 290, 378
  rape of 221-2
  used for breeding 202, 227-30, 288
Equiano, Olaudah 217-8, 220, 220*n*, 224, 227, 376
Erle, Christopher 75, 76, 78-9, 82, 89-90
Erle, Frances *see* Ernle, Frances
Erle, Susanna 90, 110
Erle, Thomas I 75-9, 89
Erle, Thomas II 8, 89, 105
  marriage to Susanna Fiennes 90, 110
Erle, Thomas III, General xiv, 111, 15860, 158*n*, 178-9, 181, 254, 370
  military career of 169-79
  MP for Wareham 159-60, 174
  role in Monmouth Rebellion 161-5
Erle, Sir Walter, the Musician xiii, 65-79, 370
  acquires Charborough 72-3
  elected MP for Poole 79-80
  ennobled 80
  'Maister Erle's Pavane' 65-6
  marriage to Mary Wyke 72
Erle, Walter II, the Puritan xiii, 75-9, 84-8, 104-6, 108-11, 370
  imprisoned for refusing to pay ship money 86-7
  marriage to Ann Dymock 80
  role in Civil War 94-8
  travels to Low Countries 88-9
Erle-Drax, Edward 201-2
  Instructions for the Management of a Plantation in Barbadoes and for the Treatment of Negroes 202-3, 226, 378

397

Erle-Drax, John xiv–xv, 141–2, 263–6, 276–8
  and Caesar's Camp 306–7
  and Captain Swing riots 265–9, 272–5
  character 281–4, 305–19
  civil case brought by Maria Caroline 300–1, 305
  death of 320–1
  defrauds daughters 319–20
  love of hunting 281–7
  Wareham by-election (1831) 277–80, 281–4
  Wareham election (1832) 280–1
  Wareham election (1841) 295–6, 298–9
  Wareham election (1868) 305
Erle-Drax, Mary 203–4, 215
Erle-Drax, Sarah Frances *see* Erle-Drax-Grosvenor, Sarah Frances
Erle-Drax, Susannah: attack by Taylor and death of 244–5
Erle-Drax, Thomas 188, 190–2
  robbed by highwayman 188, 190–2
Erle-Drax family: merger with Grosvenor family 204–5, 300
Erle-Drax-Grosvenor, Richard 204–5, 205n, 206, 231
  death of 242–3
  social connections of 235
Erle-Drax-Grosvenor II, Richard Edward II 204
  attacked by Taylor 244–5
  elected MP for New Romney 244
  mental illness of 246–7, 287
  travels in Europe by 241–2
Erle-Drax-Grosvenor, Sarah Frances 204, 208, 209, 235, 243n
  charitable works by 243–4
  A Peep into Futurity (play) 239
Ernle, Elizabeth 'Betsy' *see* Drax, Elizabeth 'Betsy'
Ernle, Sir Edward 177–9

Ernle, Frances 174, 177
Ernle-Erle-Drax, Maria Caroline 300, 319
Ernle-Erle-Drax, Sarah Charlotte 299–300, 325, 327–8
European Research Group (ERG) 2–3, 357
European Union: and CAP subsidies 5, 357
Examiner, The 280
Exchange of London (ship) 28
Exclusion Bill (1679) 160, 165
Extinction Rebellion 10, 359

Farquarson, J.J. 276, 83
Fawkes, Guy 78
Fellowship (ship) 82, 83
Ferris, John P. 73
Fiennes, Celia *The Journeys of Celia Fiennes* 157–9
Fiennes, Susanna, *see* Erle, Susanna
Fiennes, Willliam, 1st Viscount Saye and Sele 89, 104, 105
Fincham, Captain John 24
Flecknoe, Richard 'On the Riches o' th' Barbadoes' 44
Fleming, Ian *Moonraker* 13, 336
Floyd, George 2
Forestry Commission 343–4
Foster, Captain Nicholas 119
Foundling Hospital, London 192
Fountaine, Mrs Sarah 153
Fowler, Corinne 10
Fox, Charles James 230
Frampton, James of Moreton 206, 209n, 212, 277
  and the Captain Swing riots 266–7
Frampton, Lady Harriet 212–4
Frampton, Mary 208, 210, 212, 236, 272
Frampton, Phillis 208–9, 212–4
France, fear of invasion by 206–8
Franklin, Joseph Pitt Washington 233

INDEX

Frederick, Prince of Wales 186–7, 189
Frederick Henry, Prince of Orange 88
Freke, Lt Colonel Robert 173
French, Henry 281
French, Howard 48–50, 363–4
Friel, Ian 128
Frith, Willliam Powell 284
Futter, Captain James 37, 39

Galway, Lord 176
Gascoigne, Stephen 151
Gasper, Julia 194–5, 198
General Act of Enclosure (1801) 252
General Advertiser, The 189
General Joint Stock for East India 172
Gentleman's Quarterly 214–5
George I, King 257
George II, King 183, 186
George III 197, 206, 209–10, 224, 235
 health of 209–10, 216, 246
 visits to Weymouth 210–2, 214–6
Gibbes, Philip 202*n*
Gibbon, Edward *The History of the Decline and Fall of the Roman Empire* 192
Ginkell, General 170
Gladstone, William 305–6
Glorious Revolution (1688) xiv, 264
Goldman, Lawrence 240–1
Goodland, William 128
Goodwin, Tim 93, 94–5
Gookin, Vincent 131
Gorges, Ferdinando 141, 141*n*
Grant, Sir Francis 305
Gray, Louisa: brings summons against Drax 314–9
Great Wall of Dorset xiii, 1, 294–5
Grenada 362–3
Grenville, Lord 191
Grey, Lord 291
Grigg, John and Nanny 233
Grimaldi, Joseph 214

Groenewegen, Amos van 21
Grosvenor, General Thomas 205, 246
Grosvenor, Reverend Robert 246
Grosvenor family: merger with Erle-Drax family 204–5, 300
Guardian 351–2
Guest, Montagu 310
Guinea Company 123
Guines, Count of 195
Gunpowder Plot (1605) 78

Hallet, John 150
Hampton Court 66, 70
Handler, Jerome 46, 53–4, 124–5
Hanham, William 277
Hardy, Thomas
 The Mayor of Casterbridge 319
 Tess of the D'Urbervilles 184
 Two on a Tower 60–1, 319
Harper, Charles E. 320–1, 327, 348
 Hardy Country 60–1
Hawley, Francis 171
Harwood, Richard 144–6, 144*n*
Hatton, Lloyd 359*n*
Hawkins, Sir John 45
Hawkins, William 45
Hawley, Captain Henry 23–4, 51, 51*n*, 173
Hay, James, Earl of Carlisle 18, 22–3
 assignment of Barbados to 115–6
Hayes, Nick 219–20, 251–2, 299
 The Book of Trespass 61
Hayes, Sir John 9–10, 43
Heafford, Michael 242
Helms, M.W. 73
Hennessy, Joh Pope 310
Henrietta Maria, Queen 84
Henry VIII xiv, 67, 68
 and break from Rome 65
Higman, B.W. 35–6
Hill, Christopher 109, 249–50
Hill, Roger 92

399

Hilliard, William 21, 24, 30, 33, 37, 46, 117
History of Charborough 1066-1956 11
History of Parliament, The 159–60
HMS Anson 347
HMS Blanche (ship) 330
HMS Bounty 332
HMS Britannia 328, 341
HMS Burghead Bay 347
HMS Hope 128
HMS Lion 329–30
HMS Norfolk 331n, 331–3
HMS Rinaldo 328
Hoare, Ernie 341
Hobbes, Thomas *Behemoth* 100
Hochschild, Adam 218
Hodges, Dr Bernard 273
Holdip, James 21, 27, 30–2, 36
Holles, Denzil 95, 101, 104–5
Holnest Mausoleum 320
Hooper, Robert 127n, 127–8
Hopkins, Harry 340
Hopper, John 243
Hopton, Sir Ralsph 96
horse-racing 282–3
Horton, Meliora *see* Drax, Meloria
Howard, Bartholomew 122–3
Howard, Catherine (wife of Henry VIII) 67–8
Howard, James, Earl of Suffolk 86
Hudson, Colin 6
Hudson Bay Company 137, 150
Hughes, Ann 106–7
Humphry, Ozias 196
Hundreds, land administration 63n
hunting 281–7
Hutchings, Thomas 295–6
Hutchins, John 170, 185
  The History of Dorset 63–4, 284
Hyde, Sir Edward 98, 100
Hygeana (ship) 222

Ilchester Estate Lord 212n, 342

Illustrated London News 296
'Immortal Seven' letter to William III 166
Immyns, John 71
Imperial Registry Bill (1815) 232–3
Importation Act (1815) 240–1
indentured servants 20n, 24n, 24–5, 43, 48, 55, 124–6
  expiration of contracts 141
  Irish servants 125
Irish campaign (1689-92) 169–71
Irish Rebellion (1641) 101

Jamaica 137–40, 372
Jamaica Coffee House, London 140
James I, King 18, 22, 80, 84
  relations with Spain 80–1
James II, King 161–8
James, Duke of York 159, 161
James Scott, Duke of Monmouth 161–4
Jeffreys, George, Judge 163
John, King 64
Johnson, Boris 3, 372–3
Jones, Inigo 59

Kekewich, Samuel Treherne 242, 242n
Kendall, Thomas 133
Kentish Gazette 212
Keppel, Richard 197
Kerr, Barbara 64, 254, 265, 273, 275, 282, 321
Knight, James 'Jim' 355
Knollys, Dorothy 42
Knowles, Captain 225
Knox, Captain Robert 172
Kuznetsova, Admiral N.G. 335–6

Ladd, John 122
land ownership 91, 252–3, 371
landed gentry 73, 109, 344, 370
Lascelles, Henry 276n
Lascelles family 346, 363

INDEX

Last Labourers' Revolt 265–73
Laud, Archbishop William 91
Lawrence, Sir Edward 81
Lawrence, Oliver 93
Lay, Benjamin and Sarah 369
Leddoze, George 96
Legacies of British Slavery (online database) xv
Legg, Ahuzzath 253
Legg, Rodney 349–51
Leith, Sir James 234
Letters from a Peeress of England to her Eldest Son 198
Levellers 104
Ligon, Richard 32–5, 38, 116–7, 125
  lifestyle of 38–9
  observations on slavery 34–5, 37–9, 50–3, 55, 136
Limerick, siege of 169–70
Little, Patrick 98, 110
Lloyd's of London 348, 348n
Locke, John 160, 369
London Evening Post 188
London Female Anti-Slavery Society 290–1
London Gazette 188
Louis III, King of France 54
Louis XIV, King of France 168–9
Loveless, Dorothy *see* Drax, Dorothy
Loveless Brothers 271
Luttrell, Narcissus 167
Lyttleton, George 186

Macaulay, Catherine *History of England from the Ascention of James I* 258–9
Macy, Lydia 331–2
Mamma Mia! (film) 332
Manchester Guardian 305
Mann, Sir Horace 189
Manning, Brian 250
Mansfield, Lord 225–6
Marie Bonaventure (ship) 46

Marlow, John 225
Maroons 137–8
Massachusetts Bay Company 84
Marston, Captain G.M. 312–4
Marx, Karl: on enclosures 256
Mary Tudor, Queen 70, 74
Mary, wife of William III 166, 168
Mason, Sonia 372
Mason, Reverend Willliam 196
Massie, Joseph 191
Master and Servant Act (1840) 309
Mayes, Colonel John 233, 244
Mayflower (ship) 81–2
Mayo, Reverend Charles 253
Merchant Adventurers 99–100, 99n, 127
  see also Adventurers
Mercurius Rusticus (newspaper) 97 97n
Middleton, Peter 133, 167
Middleton, Captain Thomas 115
Mintz, Sydney *Sweetness and Power* 135
Modyford, Colonel Thomas 53, 117, 120, 123–4, 132, 138–9
Molesworth, Colonel Guy 117
Moncky Nocco (enslaved man) 48–9, 147, 378
Monmouth Rebellion (1685) 161–4, 162n
Montefiore, Moses 292
Moonraker (film) 336
Moore, Robert 241
Morden, Dorset 178, 254, 297–8
Morning Chronicle 195
Morrill, John 250
Mottley, Mia 52, 361, 372, 380
Mount Gay Plantation 228
Mount Plantation 36, 234
Mundy, Elizabeth 208
Mutiny on the Bounty (film) 332

Nanton, Sir Robert 86

401

DRAX OF DRAX HALL

Napoleon 1, Emperor of the French 207–8, 216
Nash, John 59, 235
National Trust 10, 343, 352
Naval Allied Control Commission, Germany 331
Naval Review 329
Naval Society 329
Navigation Acts 47, 121, 123, 132, 135
Nelson, Admiral Lord Horatio 342
  removal of Bridgdetown statue of 361
New Model Army 99, 103, 104–5
New Sporting Magazine 283
Newcastle Propositions (1646) 105n
Newman, Brooke 224
Newnham, Nathaniel 259
Newton Plantation 364, 378
Nipho, Jerome 163
Niven, David *The Moon's a Balloon* 331–2
Noell, Martin 131, 133–4
Noell family 50, 115, 127
Nugent, Robert 190–1, 195

Observer, The 7, 8–9, 358, 361, 380
Odiarne, Beatrice 43
Oistin, Edward 36, 36n
Okeden, Parry 276
Olantigh House 257–8, 305
Oldmixon, John 42
Olive, The (ship) 19–20
Olusoga, David 252, 379
Olympic Games (1932) 331
overseers 35, 219–20
  psychological impact of overseeing enslaved people on 220n, 376
Oxford University 76–7

Paget, James 71
Panton, Jane Ellen 207–8, 302n
  Fresh Leaves and Pastures 284–7, 300–3, 310–2
  sued by Captain Marston 312–4

Parker, Matthew 6, 24–5, 122, 129, 132
Parr, Catherine (wife of Henry VIII) 68–9
Pelham, Henry 190–1
Pelham, Thomas 82
Pennington, D.H. 89
Pennoyer, William 103, 103n, 115
Penson, Lilian 142
Peter (ship) 21
Peterhouse Henrician (musical mss) 66
Pevsner, Sir Nikolaus *The Buildings of England* 59–60
Philios Farm 325–6
Phillips, Esther 346, 364, 374–5 (poem)
Pile family 334
pineapples 25–6
Pinney, Azariah 163–4
Pinto, David 67, 72
Pitt, George 173
Pitt, John 189, 190
Pitt, William, the Elder 186
Pitt, William, the Younger 205, 237
Pitt-Rivers family 308, 342
Pittock, Murray 252
plantation owners: lifestyle of 38–41
plantation wives 41–3
Pleydell-Bouverie, Anthony 332
Plunkett, Randall, 13th Baron of Dunsany 300
Plunkett-Burton, Sarah and John Francis 325
Plunkett-Ernle-Erle-Drax, Admiral Reginald Aylmer Ranfurly 60–1, 312, 334, 368, 370
  on Anglo-French mission to Soviet Union 335–6
  death of 346–7
  Modern Naval Tactics 328–9
  naval career of 328–31, 335–6
  post-war life of 341–5

402

INDEX

Plunkett-Ernle-Erle-Drax, Kathleen 330-1, 337-40, 347
Plunkett-Ernle-Erle-Drax, Richard *see* Drax, Richard
Plunkett-Ernle-Erle-Drax, Walter Henry 6-7
Plunkett-Ernle-Erle-Drax family xiv, 11-12
Plunkett family, merger with Ernle-Erle-Drax family 300
Ponsonby, William 278, 280
Poole, Dorset 5, 187n
Port, H.M. 231
Port Royal, Jamaica 137
Portman, Colonel Sir William 167
Portugal, and slave trade 44, 127
Poulett, Lord John 96
Pound, Admiral Sir Dudley 336
Povey, Thomas 131
Powell, Captain Henry 17, 20-1, 23, 31
Powell, Captain John 19-20
Prescod, Trevor 364
Pride, Colonel Thomas 107
Prince, Mary 224
 The History of Mary Prince 290
Puritan ministers 85-6
Puritans 76n, 76, 78-81, 84, 92
 persecution of 81-2
Pym, John 92

racism 372-3
Raince, Monsieur (overseer) 49
Raleigh, Sir Walter 80
Rees-Mogg, Jacob 3
Reform Bill (1832) 278
 anti-Reform Bill 278-9
Reform Party 359n
Renton, Alex 363
reparations 361-4, 376-7
Reynolds, Sir Joshua 195
Ribbentrop, Joachim von 335

Rich, Robert, Earl of Warwick 99-100
Richmond, Herbert 329
Ridgeriders 'What Celia Sees' (song) 158n
Roberts, Andrew 224
Robinson, Patrick 361
Rochefort, Charles de 40
Rockingham, Lord 191n
Rodney, Walter 232
Romney, George 243
Roosevelt, Franklin D. 340
Rose, The (ship) 160
Rothschild, Nathan Mayer 292
Rothschild, Lord Robert 340n
Rothschild, Mary 340
Rotz, John 19
Royal African Company 150, 258
royal forests, privatisation of 250
Royal Navy. West Africa Squadron 12n, 367
Royal United Services Institution Journal (RUSIJ) 338
Roydon, Sir Marmaduke 23
rum 34
Rupert, Prince, Duke of Gloucester 99
Russell, William, Earl of Bedford 95
Ryder, Richard *The Calcrafts of Rempstone Hall* 312
Ryder, Robert 333, 337, 337n
Ryves, Bruno 97n

's-Hertogenbosch siege (1629) 88
Sackville, Edward, Earl of Dorset 89n
Said, Edward *Orientalism* 54n
St Ann's, Jamaica 138, 138n
St John, Henry 175
St John, John, Baron St John 190-1
St John, Mary *see* Drax, Mary
St Kitts and Nevis 18, 25, 46, 372
St Nazaire raid 337n
Saladoid-Barrancoid people 19

403

Salisbury and Winchester Journal 215, 243

saltpetre 102–3

Samuel (ship) 122–3, 128

San Fiorenza (ship) 214

Sancho, Ignatius 224

Sancroft, Archbishop William 168

Sandon, Nicholas 66–7, 70, 72, 74

Sarsfield, Patrick 168

Savage, Richard, Earl Rivers 175–6

Sawbridge, Jacob 257–9

Sawbridge, Samuel 259

Schofield, Rodney *Release the Captives: The Sawbridge Response* 259

Schomburgk, Robert *History of Barbados* 233

Scott, Christopher L. 162, 162*n*, 164

Scott, John 32

Scottish wars 91–3, 101

Searle, Daniel 123

Seeliger, Sylvia 255

Select Parts of the Holy Bible for the Use of Negro Slaves in the British West India Islands (Church of England) 227

Settlers Beach 20, 20*n*

Seymour, Edward, Earl of Hertford 68

Seymour, Edward 1ˢᵗ Duke of Somerset 69

Seymour, Jane (wife of Henry VIII) 68

Seymour, Thomas, 1ˢᵗ Baron Seymour 69–70, 72

Sharp, Granville 225

Shaves family 282

Sherborne Castle siege 95

Sheridan, Richard 31

Shetterden, Thomas 153–4

ship money 86–7

Shirley, Mary 236

Shrubsole, Guy 4
  Who Owns England? 371

Siddons, Sarah 214

Silvester, Constant 115

Sinclair, Admiral 336

Slave Code
  (1636) 51*n*, 51–2
  (1661) 53–5, 143

Slave Register (1820) 244

Slave Trade Abolition Act (1807) 231–2, 291

Slave Voyages Database 128

Slavery Abolition Act (1807) 291

Slavery Abolition Bill (1805) 259

slavery and slave trade 45, 47
  abolition of (1807) xv, 230–1
  changing attitudes to 367–9
  chattel slavery 6, 51–3, 136, 292, 362, 372, 377
  compensation for owners xv, 292–3
  costs of abolition 292–3
  status not recognised in English law 225
  triangular trade in 45, 123, 127–8
  see also enslaved people

Sloane, Sir Hans 149, 149*n*, 369

Smith, David Chan 38

Smith, Jonathan 7, 360–1

Smith, William Henry 309–10

Society of West India Planters and Merchants 289

Some Memoirs of the First Settlement of the Island of Barbados 51*n*

Somerset, James: wins legal right not to be removed from England to the West Indies 224–5

South Sea Bubble 182–3, 257–8

Spain, and slave trade 127

Spectator, The 307–8, 373

Speightstown, Barbados 148–9

Stalin, Joseph 340

Stamp Act (1765) 191, 191*n*

Stand Up to Racism 359

Staple Grove Plantations 235

Stawell, Sir John 96

INDEX

Stede, Edward 151
Stewart, Charles 224–5
Stone, Laurence 81, 90–1
Strangways, Lady Harriet *see*
    Frampton, Lady Harriet
Strangways, Robert 173
Strangways, Sir John 90
Strangways, Thomas 161, 167
Strangways family 212*n*
Strawberry Hill House 196
Strode, Sir Richard 83, 84
Strode, William 87
Strowde, Thomas 71
Stuart, Daneil 253
sugar production 31–7, 152
    exports to London of 152–3
    industrialisation of 47
    monopoly granted to English
        traders 121
    price-fixing of 191–2
Sun, The 349
Sunday Mirror 7–8, 361, 380
Sweet, Rosemary 249, 255–6
Swire, Sasha *Diary of an MP's Wife*
    356
Sydenham, William 90

Tai-Mo-Shan (yacht) 332–3, 337
Tate, George 339–40
Tawney, R.H. 109
Taylor, Michael *The Interest* 288
Thirty Years War (1618–48) 79
Thistlewood, Thomas *The Diary of*
    Thomas Thistlewood 221, 376
Thomas Honor (ship) 151
Thompson, Edward *Sailor's Letters*
    222–4
Thompson, Peter 147–8
Thomson, Edward 120
Thomson, Maurice 45–6, 83, 103*n*,
    103, 115–6, 123, 133
Thomson, Sir William 133
Thornhill, Sir James 59–60, 178

Thornhurst, Thomas 93
Times, The 203, 277, 296, 307, 317
tobacco production 26–7
Tolpuddle Martyrs 273–4
Tonquin Merchant (ship) 172
trade unions 263, 274
Treaty of Oxford (1643) 96
Treaty of Rome (1957) 340*n*
Treaty of Utrecht (1713) 257, 257*n*
Tregonwell family 236, 236*n*, 238–9
Trenchard, Henry 173
Trenchard, Sir George 81
Trenchard, Sir John 90, 97, 282
Trenchard, Sir Thomas 87, 95
Trenchard family 253, 255, 275
Trevelyan, Laura 362–3
Treves, Sir Frederick *Highways and*
    Byways 327
Truss, Liz 3
Tudor court, music in 70–1
Tufton, Frances *see* Drax, Frances
Tufton, Sir William 23–4
Turberville, John 105, 184–5
Turberville, Mary *see* Duckett, Mary
Turberville, Sir Payne de 184
Turberville family 184–5

Underdown, David 78–9

Vane, Lady Frances 194
Vassall, Samuel 115, 115*n*
Venables expedition 40, 40*n*
Venner, Lt Colonel Samuel 162
Vere, Baron Horace 88, 88*n*, 98
Verney, Sir Ralph 251
Vernon, Henry 197
Villiers, George, Duke of Bucking-
    ham 89
Virginia Company 82, 84
Voroshilov, Kliment 335

Wade, Nathaniel 162
Walkin, Thomas 225

Walpole, Horace 186, 189–90, 194–8
Walrond, Humphrey 117–8, 120
War of the Spanish Succession 176
Wareham, Dorset 190, 193
  by-election (1832) 280–1
  election (1841) 295–6, 298–9
  election (1865) 301–4, 314
  Great Fire (1762) 193
Waymark, Janet 352
Weber, Max: and the Protestant ethic 77
Wedderburn, James 288
Wedderburn, Robert 288–9
Weinstock, Maureen 83
Weitz, John 335
Wentworth, Thomas, Earl of Strafford 91–2
West, Colonel William 108
West India Interest 226, 288–9
Western Rising 250
Weston brothers (indentured servants) 25
Weymouth: visits by George III 210–2, 214–6
Whistler, Henry 40–1
White, Reverend John 78–9, 81, 82, 84, 99, 99*n*
White Lion (ship) 100*n*
white supremacist attitudes 55–6
Whiteway, William 80–1, 82, 84, 86
Wilberforce, William 203, 226, 230–1, 288
  'Appeal to Religion, Justice and Humanity of the Inhabitants of the British Empire on Behalf of Negro Slaves in the West Indies' 289–90
Wilkes, John 259
William 1, the Conqueror 63

William III, Willliam of Orange 161, 165–8
William IV, King 278, 291–2
William and John (ship) 17, 20, 44, 45
William Henry, Duke of Gloucester 211
William Herbert, Earl of Pembroke 20, 20*n*
Williamette Valley (ship) 337
Williams, Eric 292, 377
Williams, James 297
Willoughby, Christopher 133
Willoughby, Sir Francis 119, 132
Wilmot, John, Earl of Rochester 174
Wimbledon 306–7
Wimbledon Guardian 306
Winthrop, Henry 44
Winthrop, John III 83–4
Wollaston, C.B. 267
Wollstonecraft, Mary 196*n*, 197
Wolsey, Cardinal Thomas 66
Wolverstone, Charles 23
women in Erle-Drax family 208–9, 236
Wood, James 123
Wordsworth, William 253
World War I 335
World War II 335
Wyke, Alice 72
Wyke, Mary, marriage to Walter the Musician 72
Wyke, Richard of Bindon 72
Wyndham, Elizabeth 158

Yeardley, George 100*n*
Yeatman, Reverend Henry 272
Yeomanry Cavalry 277–8
Yorkshire Evening Press 354
Young, Arthur 256

The Pluto Press Newsletter

Hello friend of Pluto!

Want to stay on top of the best radical books we publish?

Then sign up to be the first to hear about our new books, as well as special events, podcasts and videos.

You'll also get 50% off your first order with us when you sign up.

Come and join us!

Go to bit.ly/PlutoNewsletter